A SUPPLEMENTARY HAND-LIST

OF THE

MUḤAMMADAN MANUSCRIPTS

IN THE LIBRARIES

OF THE

UNIVERSITY AND COLLEGES

OF CAMBRIDGE

A SUPPLEMENTARY HAND-LIST

OF THE

MUḤAMMADAN MANUSCRIPTS

INCLUDING ALL THOSE WRITTEN
IN THE ARABIC CHARACTER

PRESERVED IN THE LIBRARIES
OF THE
UNIVERSITY AND COLLEGES
OF CAMBRIDGE

BY

EDWARD G. BROWNE, M.A., M.B., F.B.A., F.R.C.P.,

SIR THOMAS ADAMS'S PROFESSOR OF ARABIC AND FELLOW OF PEMBROKE COLLEGE
IN THE UNIVERSITY OF CAMBRIDGE

CAMBRIDGE:
AT THE UNIVERSITY PRESS
1922

CAMBRIDGE UNIVERSITY PRESS
Cambridge, New York, Melbourne, Madrid, Cape Town,
Singapore, São Paulo, Delhi, Mexico City

Cambridge University Press
The Edinburgh Building, Cambridge CB2 8RU, UK

Published in the United States of America by Cambridge University Press, New York

www.cambridge.org
Information on this title: www.cambridge.org/9781107624030

First published 1922
First paperback edition 2013

A catalogue record for this publication is available from the British Library

ISBN 978-1-107-62403-0 Paperback

TABLE OF CONTENTS

PREFACE

SINCE, twenty-two years ago, I published the *Hand-list* of which this volume is the continuation and supplement, some eight hundred manuscripts in the Arabic character have been acquired, mostly by purchase, by the Cambridge University Library. The various College Libraries contain an almost equal number, of which, with the exception of King's, Trinity, and in part St John's, no list or catalogue has hitherto been published. Of these manuscripts, 1577 in all, the nature and contents are briefly described in the following pages.

In this *Supplement* I have followed, with trivial variations, the method of arrangement and description adopted in the original *Hand-list*, published in 1900, and fully explained in the Preface to that work, to which, in order to avoid vain repetition, I refer the reader. In my system of transliteration I have adopted two slight modifications in representing ظ by *ẓ* instead of *dh*, and the long vowels by *á*, *í* and *ú* instead of the more cumbrous and artificial *ā*, *ī* and *ū*, which are appropriate rather to the *Gradus ad Parnassum* than to any living language.

The MSS. here described are for the most part in Arabic, Persian, Turkish and Urdú or Hindustáni, with a few in Pushto or Afghání, Panjábí and Eastern Turkí, etc. The Malay MSS., of which there are a considerable number (including some threescore, numbered **Add. 3755** to **Add. 3816**, presented by Mr R. J. Wilkinson in November, 1900), have fared worse than they deserve, being mentioned only under their class-marks (pp. 274–5 *infra*) without title or description. As there is at present no one in this University who is conversant with the Malay language, I endeavoured to obtain the help of some competent scholar from outside, but, unhappily, in vain; so that they still await the attention of some student possessing the necessary qualifications and leisure for dealing with them.

Few of the MSS. described in the following pages are of outstanding interest. The Library of King's College contains one of the only two known MSS. of Gardízí's *Zaynu'l-Akhbár* (**No. 213** of the Pote Collection, p. 121 *infra*) and Náṣir-i-Khusraw's *Zádu'l-Musáfirín* (**No. 216,** p. 119 *infra*), besides MSS. of the rare *Ṣafwatu'ṣ-Ṣafá* (**No. 87,** p. 137 *infra*), *Siyásat-náma* (**No. 219,** p. 128 *infra*), and *Sháh-náma-i-Sháh Isma'íl* (**No. 238,** p. 129 *infra*). The Fitzwilliam Museum (McClean Collection, **No. 198,** p. 211 *infra*) possesses a fine old MS. of Mu'ín-i-Yazdí's history of the Muẓaffarí dynasty, the *Mawáhib-i-Iláhí*, copied in 778/1377, eleven years before the author's death. Amongst the acquisitions of the University Library especial attention may be drawn to the following works on Heresies and Controversy: Wahhábís, **Or. 26**[2] (**No. 823,** p. 135) and **Or. 738** (**No. 652,** p. 106); Shaykhís, **Or. 16** (**No. 771,** pp. 126–7); Ḥurúfís and Bektáshís, **Or. 41** (**No. 1366,** p. 224), **Or. 45** (**No. 759,** p. 124), **Or. 532** (**No. 1429,** p. 238), **Or. 544** (**No. 1430,** p. 239), and three MSS. of the *'Ishq-náma* of Firishta-záda, **Or. 44, Or. 531** and **Or. 702** (**Nos. 860–2,** p. 141); Bábís, **Add. 3704** and **Add. 3705** (**Nos. 1431–2,** p. 239), **Or. 843** and **Or. 943** (**Nos. 1433–4,** pp. 239–240); a general refutation of heretics entitled *Ṣawá'iq-i-Muḥriqa* ("Consuming thunder-bolts"), **Or. 660** (**No. 838,** p. 137).

The number of MSS. remarkable for their antiquity is also inconsiderable. The thirteenth Christian (seventh Muḥammadan) century is ostensibly represented only by six, of which the date of one, unrecorded in the colophon, is conjectural (**Or. 910,** p. 207), while another (**Or. 595,** pp. 251–2), though dated 618/1221, is evidently much more modern. The remaining four are **Or. 53–4** (p. 222), dated 640/1242–3; **Or. 49** (p. 235), dated 662/1263–4; **Fitzwilliam 193**[1] (p. 165), dated 681/1282–3; and **Or. 712** (pp. 235–6), dated 685/1286–7. The fourteenth Christian (eighth Muḥammadan) century is represented by ten MSS., two of which (**Add. 3637,** top of p. 151, and **Or. 926,** p. 242) are undated and placed only by the character and appearance of their writing. The other eight are **Corpus 123** (p. 178), where the words following "seven hundred" are obliterated; **Or. 579** (p. 128), dated 712/1312–3; **Or. 709** (p. 75), dated 753/1352; **Or. 540** (p. 128), dated 759/1358; **Or. 681** (p. 235), dated 775/1373–4; **Or. 841** (p. 24), dated 782/1380–1; **Or. 782** (p. 249), dated 784/1382–3; and **Or. 478** (p. 142), dated 789/1387. The fifteenth Christian (ninth Muḥammadan) century is represented by about thirty MSS. which it is hardly worth enumerating.

The Catalogues and other books to which references are most often made, with the abbreviations by which they are in some cases denoted, are as follows.

British Museum Catalogues by the late Dr Ch. Rieu. **B.M.A.C.** is the old Arabic Catalogue (1846–1871) written in Latin; **B.M.A.S.** the Arabic Supplement (1894); **B.M.P.C.** the old Persian Catalogue in three volumes (1879–1883); **B.M.P.S.** the Persian Supplement (1895); **B.M.T.C.** the Turkish Catalogue (1888). Mr A. G. Ellis's *Catalogue of Arabic printed books in the British Museum* is also occasionally cited. Mr E. Edwards's recently published *Catalogue of the Persian printed [and lithographed] books in the British Museum* has not been cited, though advance sheets were placed at my disposal by the kindness of the author and Dr Barnett.

Berlin Catalogues. The Arabic Catalogue, in ten volumes, is by W. Ahlwardt (1887–1899); the Persian (1888) and Turkish (1889), in one volume each, by W. Pertsch.

Cambridge Catalogues. My Catalogue of Persian MSS. (1896) and Hand-list of Muḥammadan MSS. (1900) are cited as **P.C.** (or **Cambridge Pers. Cat.**) and **Hand-list** respectively. The list of the MSS. in the Pote Collection in the Library of King's College published in the *J.R.A.S.* for 1867 by the late Professor E. H. Palmer, and the Catalogue of the Oriental MSS. in the Library of Trinity College by the same scholar (1870) are denoted as **King's Cat.** and **Trin. Cat.** respectively. Other special catalogues compiled by myself and published in the *J.R.A.S.* are my *Catalogue of 27 Bábí MSS.* (1892), *Some Notes on the Literature and Doctrines of the Ḥurúfí Sect* (1898, pp. 61–94), *Further Notes on the Literature of the Ḥurúfís* (1907, pp. 1–49), and the *Persian MSS. of the late Sir Albert Houtum-Schindler* (1917).

The late Dr H. Ethé's two great catalogues of the Persian MSS. in the India Office in London (1903) and the Bodleian Library in Oxford (1889) are cited as **I. O. Pers. Cat.** and **Bodl. Pers. Cat.** respectively.

Other Catalogues less often cited are Sprenger's *Oude Catalogue*, Flügel's *Vienna Catalogue* (3 vols.), and E. Blochet's *Catalogue de la Collection de Manuscrits formée par M. Ch. Schefer* and *Catalogue des Manuscrits persans de la Bibliothèque Nationale.* Brockelmann's admirable *Geschichte der Arabischen Litteratur* (2 vols., Weimar, 1898 and Berlin, 1902) has been constantly beside me and has proved invaluable. Use has also been made of Baron Victor Rosen's *Collections Scientifiques*, of Elliot's *History of India*, of E. J. W. Gibb's *History of Ottoman Poetry* (6 vols., 1900–1909), and of Wüstenfeld's *Geschichtschreiber der Araber* (Göttingen, 1882). Of Oriental sources, Ḥájji Khalífa is cited in Flügel's edition, and Ibn Khallikán in the Baron McGuckin de Slane's English translation.

In the cataloguing of the Persian manuscripts in King's College Library I received valuable help from the late Mr Ballard of Clare, who in 1900–1901 examined and described all that portion of the Pote Collection. His work showed great promise for one who had so recently begun the study of Persian, and his premature death soon after he left Cambridge cut short a career from which I had expected much. Mr S. Hillelson, now Director of the Gordon College at Khartoum, also rendered me great assistance in cataloguing the Corpus Oriental MSS., while to Mr Herbert Loewe of Queens' (afterwards of St Catharine's) I am also much indebted for help in examining the contents of several other College libraries. This help was the more precious because of the comparative inaccessibility of the libraries in some of the smaller Colleges. To Mr A. Rogers of the University Library I am also indebted for much valuable help in reading the proofs and checking the class-marks and sizes of the MSS.

During the final reading of the sheets for the Index I discovered a disconcerting number of Errata, of which a list follows, and I hope that all who use this book will begin by making the corrections in the text there indicated. It is with the most unqualified satisfaction that I write the concluding words of a book which I fear will yield little more entertainment in the reading than it did in the writing, but which, defective as I know it to be, has occupied a good deal of my time during the last twenty-two years, and will, I venture to hope, be of use to my fellow-students.

EDWARD G. BROWNE.

CAMBRIDGE.
June 10, 1922.

ERRATA

Page 39, **No. 229.** For "708/1308–9" read "807/1405."
,, 40, **No. 233,** and p. 78, **No. 457** should be combined in one entry.
,, 44, **Nos. 252, 253.** For موموم read موسوم.
,, 49. **Christ's, Dd . 3 . 2** should be numbered **283*.**
,, 56, **No. 324.** For *Tuqwiyat* read *Taqwiyat.*
,, 88, 8 lines from bottom. For *Majním* read *Majnún.*
,, 94, **Nos. 566–571.** For "**Corpus 129**" read "**Corpus 124,**" twice.
,, 101. Omit article **621,** which duplicates **613.**
,, 105, **Nos. 649, 650. Add. 4510 (G)** has a duplicate class-mark **Or. 297.**
,, 109, **No. 670.** For "Andalasí" read "Andalúsí."
,, 111, l. 6. For "Muḥammad" read "Muḥammadan."
,, 112, **No. 691.** For لا بن read لأبن.
,, 113, **No. 696.** For "**Christ's, 13 . 4 . 22**" read "**Christ's, Dd . 4 . 12*.**"
,, 125, 3rd line from end. For "W. M. Lowe" read "W. H. Lowe."
,, 126, **No. 770.** For *Falúsifa* read *Falásifa.*
,, 128, **No. 784.** For "**Trinity, 5 . 13**" read "**Trinity, R . 13.**"
,, 131, l. 2. For "Sa'du'lláh" read "Sa'du'd-Dín"; and in l. 3 "-taftázání" should begin with a capital letter.
,, 136, **Nos. 829, 830.** To these should be added **Or. 972** on p. 325.
,, 137, 4 lines from end. Insert "Albert" after "Sir."
,, 139, **No. 849.** For "**Christ's, Dd . 4 . 6**" read "**Christ's, Dd . 5 . 6.**"
,, 147, **No. 893.** "*Waḥshí*" should be in Roman, not italic type.
,, 151, **No. 911.** For "**Add. 3639**" read "**Add. 3637.**"
,, 164, **No. 1002.** For النّخو read النّحو.
,, 169, last line. For "sixth" substitute "twelfth," or for "Christian" "Muḥammadan."
,, 176, **No. 1062.** The name appears to be "Hibgame," not "Hibgane." Cf. p. 308 and the Index, p. 333.
,, 187, l. 3. For *Aujuman* read *Anjuman.*
,, 189, l. 5. For "**Corpus, No. 151**[1]" read "**— 150**[1]."
,, 193, **No. 1174.** For "Bey" read "Beg."
,, 212, **No. 1287.** For "**Trinity, R . 13 . 8**" read "**— R . 13 . 18.**"
,, 213, **Nos. 1295, 1296.** To this article should perhaps be added **Corpus, 98**[3]. Cf. p. 84, last four lines.
,, 219, **No. 1332.** Read "who was born in 467/1074, and died in 538/1143."
,, 262, l. 3. For "Ghaffúr" read "Ghafúr."
,, 283, l. 23. For "Sandars Collection" read "Sandars Bequest."

PART I

TITLED MANUSCRIPTS ARRANGED IN ALPHABETICAL ORDER OF TITLES

I. TITLED MANUSCRIPTS ARRANGED IN ALPHABETICAL ORDER

1 (p) آتشکدهٔ لطف‌علی بیگ **Or. 60 (12)**

The *Átash-kada*, a well-known Biography of Persian poets, composed about 1174/1760–1 by Luṭf-'Alí Beg Ádhar. See *B.M.P.C.*, p. 375. Ff. 268 of 30·5 × 13·8 c. and 22 lines; small neat Persian *ta'líq*; rubrications; dated 1273/1856–7. Bought of Naaman, May 3, 1901.

2 (a) آثار البلاد للقزوینی **King's, No. 11**

The *Átháru'l-Bilád* of Zakariyyá b. Muḥammad b. Maḥmúd al-Qazwíní. Ff. 364, good large *naskh*, with rubrications, n.d. See Palmer's *King's Cat.*, p. 19; Wüstenfeld's edition; Brockelmann, i, 481.

3 (a) الآداب الباقية **King's, No. 38**

A volume containing two treatises, of which the first, by Zaynu'l-'Ábidín, appears to be a commentary on the second composed by 'Abdu'l-Báqí and entitled *al-Ádábu'l-Báqiya*. Both treat of the Science of Controversy (*'Ilmu'l-Jidál*).

The date 1095/1684 occurs at the end of Part II. See Palmer's *King's Cat.*, pp. 19 and 27.

4 (a) الآداب الحنفيّة و غيرها **Or. 36 (8)**

A volume of 121 ff. of 21 × 15 c. and 15 ll. written in a small and neat *naskh*, and dated 1241/1825–6 containing: (1) *Al-Ádábu'l-Ḥanafiyya*, text and commentary (ff. 1–7); (2) Text of the same alone (f. 8); (3) Note on *ar-Risálatu'l-'Aḍudiyya* with gloss of Abu'l-Fatḥ on No. 1 (ff. 9–47); (4) Another gloss of Abu'l-Fatḥ (ff. 48–67); (5) A gloss by one Dá'úd on a Commentary on the *Shamsiyya*.

Bought of Naaman, Nov. 5, 1901.

5 (p) آداب عالمگیری **King's, No. 45**

The *Ádáb-i-'Álamgírí* of Shaykh Abu'l-Fatḥ, entitled Qábil Khán Munshi'l-Mamálik, who died in 1073/1662–3. Collected by Ṣádiq-i-Muṭṭalibí in 1115/1703–4. See *B.M.P.C.*, p. 399[b], and Palmer's *King's Cat.*, p. 4.

6 (a) آداب المتعلّمين **King's, No. 24**

A small, very badly written tract bearing this title. Copied by Mír Ḥusayn, and dated Rajab 21, without mention of year.

7 (p) آداب المسافرين **Or. 511 (9)**

The *Ádábu'l-Musáfirín*, containing notices of Ṣúfí saints, by Áqá Taqí of Khúy.

Ff. 282 of 22 × 17 c. and 15 ll.; poor Persian *ta'líq*; dated 1256/1840–1; bought of Hannan and Watson, August 20, 1904.

8 (t) آداب المنازل **Or. 704 (12)**

The *Ádábu'l-Manázil*. For a similar, but apparently not identical, work see Pertsch's *Berlin Turkish Cat.*, No. 153.

Pp. 525 of 32 × 18 c. and 19 ll.; good, large *naskh*, pointed, with rubrications; bought of Géjou, Dec. 1906.

9 (a) الابراهيميّة فى شرح الألفيّة فى الفرائض **Add. 3617 (11)**

Al-Ibráhímiyya, a commentary on a rhymed treatise on religious obligations entitled *al-Alfiyya*, based, apparently, on the *Minháju't-Ṭálibín* of an-Nawawí.

Ff. 122 of 27 × 18 c. and 19 lines; large, clear *naskh*; verses and titles in red; dated Rabí' ii, 863 (Feb. 1459); bought of Géjou, Feb. 14, 1900.

10 (p) ابواب الجنان **King's, No. 40**

The *Abwábu'l-Jinán* of Mírzá Muḥammad Rafí' of Qazwín (d. 1105/1693–4). See Palmer's *King's Cat.*, p. 3; *B.M.P.S.*, p. 152; *P.C.*, No. xxiv; *Camb. Hand-list*, No. 1, etc. Clear *ta'líq*, first and last leaves supplied, undated. Seems to contain the first only of the three books.

11 (t) اثمار الحدائق **Or. 701 (8)**

The *Athmáru'l-Ḥadá'iq*, a list of the Ottoman Sultans to 1255/1839–40, with dates of accession, death, etc., duration of reigns, and brief summaries of notable events, compiled in 1262/1846 by Shem'í. This portion occupies ff. 1–6, and is followed by a list of Grand Vezírs (جدول صدور عظام) from 728/1327–8 to 1258/1842–3.

Ff. 26 of 20·8 × 13·2 c.; dated 1266/1849–50; bought of Géjou, Dec. 1909.

12, 13 (a) احكام النجوم **King's, Nos. 193, 203**

Two copies of a treatise on Judicial Astrology (*Aḥkámu'n-Nujúm*) by Yaḥyá b. Muḥammad b. Abí Shukr al-Maghribí al-Andalusí.

See Palmer's *King's Cat.*, pp. 19 and 22. **No. 193** begins abruptly with a table of contents, it is written in a clear *naskh* with rubrications. **No. 203** concludes with a Persian treatise of 17 ff. on the calendar. Neither is dated.

14 (a) احكام النجوم **King's, No. 30**

A treatise, without proper title, on Astrology, by Abu'l-Ḥasan b. Abí Ḥaṣíb of Kúfa.

See Palmer's *King's Cat.*, p. 19. Poor but legible *nasta'líq*, dated Jumáda ii, 1047/Oct.–Nov. 1637.

15 (p) احكام النجوم **Trinity, R. 13. 9**

A treatise on Astrology, by Ikhtiyáru'd-Dín Muḥammad. Ff. 75; good *naskh*.

16 (p) احوال بیبی جُلیانا **King's, No. 20**

The Adventures of Bíbí Juliana, composed in 1187/1773–4 by Gaston Bruit for Mar. Gentil, who died in A.D. 1799.

See Palmer's *King's Cat.*, p. 3; *B.M.P.C.*, p. 822; and Palmer's French translation of this book.

17 (p) احوال راجههای جیپور **King's, No. 4**

An account of the Rájás of Jaypúr and their genealogies (*nasab-náma*).

See Palmer's *King's Cat.*, p. 3.

18 (t) احوال قيامت **Queens', No. 12**

A Turkish account of the Resurrection, beginning:

بلگل كم الله تعالى جبرائيل ميكائيل دن صكره يرتدى آلخ

Dated 1022/1613–14. Compare *Camb. Hand-list*, p. 3.

19 (a) احياء علوم الدّين للغزالى **King's, No. 23**

An abridgement of al-Ghazzálí's great *Iḥyá'u 'Ulúmi'd-Dín* entitled *al-Mukhtaṣṣ*. From the concluding words, which are as follows, it appears to be only a portion of the work:—

كتاب شرح عجائب القلب و هو الكتاب الأوّل من ربع المهلكات من كتاب احياء العلوم،

20 (a) احياء الميت فى فضايل اهل البيت **Add. 3722[2] (8)**

Iḥyá'u'l-Mayt fí faḍá'ili ahli'l-Bayt ("the Revivifying of the dead, on the virtues of the Holy Family"), by Jalálu'd-Dín as-Suyúṭí (d. 911/1505). See Brockelmann, ii, 149.

Ff. 42–57 of the MS. are described under the title كتاب الصّادح و الباغم; small, neat *naskh*; rubrications. Bought of Naaman, Nov. 23, 1900.

21, 22 (p) اخبار الاخيار فى آثار [اسرار] الابرار **Corpus, No. 126**
King's, No. 18

Two copies of a work by 'Abdu'l-Ḥaqq b. Sayfu'd-Dín at-Turk ad-Dihlawí al-Bukhárí, entitled *Akhbáru'l-Akhyár fí Asrár* [or *Áthár*]*i'l-Abrár*, a biography of Saints.

See *B.M.P.C.*, p. 355, and Palmer's *King's Cat.*, p. 3. The [K]ing's **MS.** is dated 1109/1697–8, the **Corpus MS.** 1243/[18]27–8. The latter comprises about 400 ff. of 25 × 16 c. [wri]tten in fair *nasta'líq*.

اخبار جهانگيرى **King's, No. 6**

Akhbár-i-Jahángírí by Muḥammad Ṣádiq of Dihlí. [Palm]er's *King's Cat.*, p. 3.

24, 25 (a) اخبار الدُّوَل و آثار الأُوَل **Or. 654 (12)** **Or. 759 (8)**

The history of Abu'l-'Abbás Aḥmad b. Sinán al-Qaramání entitled *Akhbáru'd-Duwal wa Átháru'l-Uwal.* The Author was born in 939/1532–3 and died in 1019/1610–11. See *B.M.A.S.*, p. 295 (No. 491); *B.M.A.C.*, pp. 147 and 428; Wüstenfeld's *Geschichtschr. d. Araber*, p. 257 (No. 550); Brockelmann, ii, 301; *Camb. Hand-list*, p. 3.

Or. 654 comprises ff. 119 of 30·3 × 18·5 c. and 26 ll.; clear, small, modern *naskh*, with rubrications; defective at end, breaking off in the middle of ch. xliii on Tímúr; bought of Géjou, Feb. 12, 1906. **Or. 759** comprises ff. 102 of 21 × 14·5 c. and 25 ll.; small, poor *naskh*; defective at beginning; dated 1099/1687–8; bought of Géjou, May 13, 1907.

26–29 (p) اختيارات بديعى **Add. 3614² (10)** **Add. 3644 (8)** **Or. 877 (11)** **King's, No. 25**

Four complete or partial copies of the *Ikhtiyárát-i-Badí'í*, a well-known work on Materia Medica by 'Alí b. Ḥusayn al-Anṣárí, known as Ḥájjí Zaynu'l-'Aṭṭár. The book was so named in honour of the Princess Badí'u'l-Jamál, to whom it was dedicated. See *B.M.P.C.*, p. 469; Ethé's *I.O.P.C.*; col. 1252 *et seqq.*; Ḥájji Khalífa, i, p. 197; *P.C.*, p. 212, etc.

Add. 3614 contains, on ff. 141^b–172^a, the Second Discourse of this work, on compound medicaments (for description of MS., see *infra, s.v.* كفايهٔ مجاهديّه). **Add. 3644** comprises ff. 452 of 19 × 11·2 c. and 20 ll.; poor, scratchy *ta'líq*; rubrications; bought of Sethian, May 9, 1900. **Or. 877,** dated 1169/1755–6, comprises ff. 329 of 28·2 × 17 c. and 19 ll.; coarse but clear Indian *ta'líq*; bought of G. David, Feb. 28, 1912. The **King's MS.** is dated 1169/1755–6: see Palmer's *King's Cat.*, p. 4.

30 (p) اخلاق پادشاهى **King's, No. 7**

Shaykh Bahá'u'd-Dín 'Ámilí's *Akhláq-i-Pádisháhí.* See Ethé's *Bodl. Pers. Cat.*, col. 1469, and Palmer's *King's Cat.*, p. 4. The work was composed in 1055/1645–6. This copy is not dated.

31, 32 (t) اخلاق علائی **Or. 490 (8)**
Or. 767 (7)

Qináli-zádé's *Akhláq-i-'Alá'í*, composed in 971/1563–4, as indicated by the words فرّخ سال in the following chronogram:

سالی که بود حساب او فرّخ سال ، آغاز شد این رساله فرّخ فال ،

Or. 490 comprises ff. 290 of 16·2 × 11·3 c. and 19 ll., and was bought of Géjou on Aug. 18, 1904. **Or. 767** comprises ff. 187 of 19 × 12·5 c. and 19 ll., is written in a good *ta'líq* with rubrications, and was bought of Géjou on Feb. 20, 1908.

33–36 (p) اخلاق مُحْسِنی **Or. 515 (9)**
Corpus, No. 12²
King's, No. 15
Queens', No. 7

The well-known ethical treatise entitled *Akhláq-i-Muḥsiní*, by Ḥusayn Wá'iẓ-i-Káshifí. See *Camb. Hand-list*, pp. 4–5.

Or. 515, dated 951/1544–5, comprises ff. 149 of 22·2 × 14·7 c. and 17 ll.; good *ta'líq*; rubrications and gilt margins; bought of Hannan, Watson & Co., Aug. 20, 1904. The **Corpus MS.** is written in various hands, *ta'líq* and *shikasta*. For the **King's MS.** see Palmer's *King's Cat.*, p. 4. The **Queens' MS.** is a very pretty copy, written in a minute hand.

37–41 (p) اخلاق ناصری **Or. 269 (9)**
Or. 270 (9)
Christ's, Dd. 4. 2
King's, No. 19
Queens', No. 5

The *Akhláq-i-Náṣirí* of Naṣíru'd-Dín-i-Ṭúsí.

The two University Library MSS. form part of the Cowell Bequest. **Or. 269** comprises ff. 114 of 24 × 16·4 c. and 17 ll.; dated 1086/1675–6; fair *nasta'líq* with rubrications. **Or. 270** comprises ff. 250 of 22·4 × 13·4 c. and 15 ll.; *ta'líq*; rubrications; dated the fifth year of Farrukh-Siyar. The **Christ's MS.,** which ends with a *fál-náma* of 15 × 15 squares, is written in a poor but legible *ta'líq*, comprises ff. 160 of 27·8 × 17·6 c. and 25 ll., and bears the seal of Archibald Swinton on the fly-leaf. For the **King's MS.** see Palmer's *King's Cat.*, p. 4. The **Queens' MS.** was copied in 1020/1611–12 by Shaykh 'Alí of Láhiján.

42 (a) ارجوزة ابن سينا **King's, No. 232**

A rhymed treatise on Medicine (*Arjúza fi'ṭ-Ṭibb*) ascribed to Shaykh Abú 'Alí ibn Síná, or Avicenna, beginning:

الطبّ حفظ صحّةٍ و برءُ مرض ' من سببٍ فى بدنٍ منذ عرض '

and accompanied by the commentary of the Qáḍí Abu'l-Walíd Muḥammad b. Aḥmad b. Rushd. See Ḥájji Khalífa, i, 246 (No. 463), who gives the dates of decease of the author and commentator as 428/1036 and 595/1198 respectively; *B.M.A.S.*, No. 801, p. 544; and Brockelmann, i, 457, Nos. 81, 82.

Written in a large, clumsy hand and undated.

43 (a) ارشاد الأذهان الى احكام الايمان **Or. 447[1] (10)**

Portions of a work on Shí'ite Jurisprudence entitled *Irshádu'l-Adhhán ila Aḥkámi'l-Ímán*, by al-Ḥasan b. Yúsuf al-Ḥillí, who died in 726/1325–6. His biography is contained in the *Qiṣaṣu'l-'Ulamá* (lith. Ṭihrán, A.H. 1304), pp. 269–275, where 75 of his works (amongst which this is No. 45) are enumerated. See also Brockelmann, ii, 164.

Ff. 49 (*lacuna*) + 6 (*lac.*) + 4 (*lac.*) + 8 (*lac.*) + 6 (*lac.*), in all ff. 73 (with five *lacunae*) of 23·4 × 16·5 c. and 20 ll. Bought of Messrs Hannan, Watson & Co., August 29, 1903.

44 (p) ارشاد السّالكين **King's, No. 1**

The *Irshádu's-Sálikín* of Yúsuf b. Shaykh Muḥammad Najmu'd-Dín Gurdízí, a work on Ṣúfíism. See Palmer's *King's Cat.*, p. 4. Scribe, Núr Muḥammad b. Ghulám Ḥusayn.

45 (p) **Add. 3739 (12)**

اساس الايمان در مناقب علىّ بن أبى طالب

Asásu'l-Ímán, concerning the lives and attributes of the Twelve Imáms, in twelve sections, by Wálih, preceded by a full table of contents by Muḥammad Báqir b. 'Alí al-Qá'iní.

Ff. 269 of 31 × 20·5 c. and 21 ll.; clear *ta'líq*; bought of Sethian, Nov. 28, 1900; written in 1128/1716.

46 (a) [كتاب] الاسباب و العلامات **Or. 200 (8)**

A work on Medicine entitled *Kitábu'l-Asbáb wa'l-'Alámát* ("the Book of Causes and Symptoms") composed for Ulúgh Beg by Burhánu'd-Dín Nafír b. 'Awaḍ b. Ḥakím al-Mutaṭabbib in explanation of a text by Shaykh Najíbu'd-Dín Muḥammad b. 'Alí b. 'Umar as-Samarqandí. See Ḥájji Khalífa, No. 594. Ff. 300 of 20·7 × 12 c. and 29 ll.; small, neat *nasta'líq*; rubrications. Bought of Géjou, Oct. 23, 1902. Dated Ramaḍán 4, 916/Dec. 5, 1510.

47 (p) اسرار الأولياء **King's, No. 35**

Asráru'l-Awliyá ("Secrets of the Saints"), being the teachings of Farídu'd-Dín "Ganj-i-Shakkar" (died 664/1265–6), collected by Badru'd-Dín Isḥáq. See *B.M.P.C.*, p. 973, and Palmer's *King's Cat.*, p. 4. No date.

48 (t) اسرار حقايق و رموز دقايق **Or. 223 (7)**

Asrár-i-Ḥaqá'iq wa Rumúz-i-Daqá'iq ("Mysteries of Verities and Riddles of Subtleties"), by Shaykh 'Alí b. Mukhliṣ b. Ilyás, better known as 'Áshiq Pasha, who died in 733/1332. See Gibb's *Hist. of Ottoman Poetry*, vol. i, pp. 176–200.

Ff. 120 of 17·2 × 12·3 c. and 15 ll.; neat *riq'a*; rubrications; dated 1252/1836–7. Bought of Naaman, Nov. 12, 1911.

49 (h) اسرار محبّت **Corpus, No. 66⁹**

Asrár-i-Maḥabbat ("Mysteries of Love"), by Maḥabbat Khán, a collection of Urdú verse. Ff. 15 of 25 × 15·5 c.; *ním-shikasta.*

50 (p) اسرارنامه **Or. 685⁶ (10)**

Selections from the *Asrár-náma* ("Book of Mysteries") of Shaykh Farídu'd-Dín 'Aṭṭár.

Bought of Géjou, May 10, 1906; undated.

51 (a) اسفار ملّا صدرای شیرازی **Or. 734 (14), Or. 735 (10) Or. 736 (10), Or. 737 (13)**

A complete copy of the *Asfár*, or philosophical treatises, of Mullá Ṣadrá of Shíráz, in four volumes of different sizes. **Or. 734** (vol. i) comprises ff. 229 of 34·5 × 21 c. and 29 ll.;

good modern *naskh*; rubrications; dated 1273/1856–7. **Or. 735** (vol. ii) comprises ff. 194 of 27 × 17·7 c. and 25 ll.; good *naskh*; rubrications; dated 1230/1814–15. **Or. 736** (vol. iii) comprises ff. 209 of 26 × 16·3 c. and 24 ll.; fair *naskh*; rubrications; dated 1272/1855–6. **Or. 737** (vol. iv) comprises ff. 220 of 34 × 21 c. and 29 ll.; small *naskh*; rubrications; dated 1273/1856–7. Bought of Géjou, March 27, 1907.

52 (a) [كتاب] الاسعاف فى احكام الاوقاف **Or. 481 (7)**

A work on Jurisprudence entitled *Kitábu'l-Is'áf fí Aḥkámi'l-Awqáf*, by Ibráhím b. Músá al-Ḥanafí of Ṭarábulus (Tripoli).

Ff. 74 of 18·2 × 13·5 c. and 21 ll.; small *naskh*; rubrications; dated 971/1563–4; bought of Géjou, Aug. 18, 1904.

53 (p) اسكندرنامه **Add. 3692 (13)**

A prose version of the *Iskandar-náma*, or Romance of Alexander the Great, in Persian. With rude illustrations.

54–56 (a), 57 (p) [كتاب] اشارات ابن سينا **Or. 746 (10)**, **Add. 3611 (10)**, **Or. 205 (10)**, **King's, No. 231**

Four different works, three in Arabic and one in Persian, on the *Ishárát* of Avicenna (Shaykh Abú 'Alí b. Síná). **Or. 746** (10) contains the commentary of Fakhru'd-Dín Muḥammad b. Ḍiyá'u'd-Dín 'Umar ar-Rází, and comprises ff. 65 of 24·7 × 16·3 c. and 23 ll.; legible modern *naskh* with rubrications; undated; bought of Géjou, March 27, 1907. **Add. 3611** (10) contains a super-commentary on the *Ishárát* by Quṭbu'd-Dín ar-Rází, entitled *Kitábu'l-Muḥákamát*. It comprises ff. 200 of 24 × 12·7 c. and 26 ll., is written in a minute *nasta'líq*, with rubrications, dated 1071/1660–1, and was bought of Géjou in 1899. **Or. 205** (10) contains another commentary on the *Ishárát* entitled *al-Mabáḥithu'ṭ-Ṭabí'iyya*, and is described under that title. **No. 231** of King's College contains another commentary in Persian by the celebrated Naṣíru'd-Dín-i-Ṭúsí. This is written in a compact and clumsy but legible *ta'líq* on pages of 22 × 12 c., and is undated.

58 (a) [كتاب] الاشارات فى علم العبارات **Add. 3618 (12)**

The *Kitábu'l-Ishárát fí 'ilmi'l-'Ibárát* of Shaykh Khalíl b. Sháhín az-Záhirí. The work is divided into 80 chapters, of which a complete Index is prefixed (ff. 1b–2b).

Ff. 146 of 32·8 × 21 c. and 31 ll.; dated 1248/1832–3; bought of Géjou, Feb. 14, 1900.

59 (a) اشارات القرآن **Add. 3631**

A concordance of the *Qur'án* entitled *Ishárátu'l-Qur'án*, composed by Ḥájji Muḥammad Ṣáliḥ al-Qayṣarí, known as Ḥajji Ṭarún, in 1258/1842.

Copied in 1259/1843 by Sayyid Núḥ b. Aḥmad al-Ḥamídí. Ff. 40 of 17 × 10·8 c. and 15 ll.; small, good Turkish *naskh* with rubrications.

60 (a) [كتاب] الأشباه و النّظائر **King's, No. 227**

Kitábu'l-Ashbáh wa 'n-Naẓá'ir, a manual of Ḥanafí Jurisprudence by Zaynu'l-'Ábidín b. Ibráhím b. Nujaym al-Miṣrí. See *Camb. Hand-list*, No. 886, p. 162.

A bulky volume written in a large, clear Indian *naskh*. Each page measures 22·4 × 15·5 c.

61 (a) [كتاب] اشراسيم الهنديّة **Or. 25 (10)**

A book on Astrology and Natural Magic entitled *Kitábu Ishrásími'l-Hindiyya.*

Ff. 55 of 24 × 16·7 c. and 15 ll.; coarse, clear *naskh*; rubrications; dated 1285/1868–9; bought of J. J. Naaman, Feb. 5, 1901.

62 (a) [كتاب] الإشراف فى اختلاف الأربع الأشراف **Add. 3645**

The *Kitábu'l-Ishráf fí 'Khtiláfi'l-arba'i'l-Ashráf*, a juristical work on the differences between the four Orthodox Schools in matters of law, by the Wazír 'Awnu'd-Dín Abu'l-Muẓaffar Yaḥyá b. Muḥammad b. Hubayra ash-Shaybání.

Ff. 260 of 20·3 × 14·5 c. and 19 ll. to the page, written in good *naskh* with rubrications, no date. Bought of Sethian, May 9, 1900.

63 (a) اشراق التواريخ **Trinity, R.13.41**[1]

Ishráqu't-Tawáríkh, a historical work by Mawláná Qará Ya'qúb b. 'Aṭá b. Idrís al-Qaramání.

See Palmer's *Trin. Cat.*, pp. 88–90.

64 (a) اشرف الوسائل الى فهم الشّمائل **King's, No. 41**

Ashrafu'l-Wasá'il ila fahmi'sh-Shamá'il, ascribed to Ibn Ḥajar.

Transcribed before 995/1587. See Palmer's *King's Cat.*, p. 19.

65 (t) اشعار بهيّة فى الفاظ تركيّة **Add. 3715** (6)

A Turkish Anthology, the poets cited being arranged alphabetically.

Pp. 70 of 15 × 9·3 c. and 19 ll., written in a small, scratchy *nasta'líq* with rubrications, and dated 1047/1637–8. Bought of Naaman, Nov. 23, 1900.

66 (a) اطباق الذّهب **King's, No. 46**[1]

Aṭbáqu'dh-Dhahab, by Sharafu'd-Dín Abu'l-Maḥásin 'Abdu'l-Mú'min[1] b. Hibatu'lláh b. Muḥammad, commonly known as Shufurwah of Iṣfahán. The work comprises a hundred *Maqálas* or "Discourses." It is dated 1141/1728–9.

See Palmer's *King's Cat.*, p. 49; *Camb. Hand-list*, p. 7; and Brockelmann, i, 292, xvii.

67 (a) اطواق الذّهب **King's, No. 46**[2]

The *Aṭwáqu'dh-Dhahab*, or "Collars of Gold," of the celebrated philologist az-Zamakhsharí (d. 538/1143). See Brockelmann, i, 292, xvii.

68 (a) اعتقاد الامانة المسيحيّة **Trinity, R.13.14**

An Arabic translation of the Christian confession of faith, or Catechism, in which the Arabic stands opposite the Latin text, the former having interlinear glosses in Dutch. With this

[1] *Sic* for *-Mun'im*.

is bound in the same volume the edition of *al-Káfiya* printed at Rome in 1592. The Arabic is written in a very bad European hand.

See Palmer's *Trin. Cat.*, p. 26.

69 (p) اعجاز خسروى **King's, No. 12**

The *I'jáz-i-Khusrawí*, an epistolary manual composed by the celebrated poet Amír Khusraw of Dihlí in 719/1319. Not dated.

See Palmer's *King's Cat.*, p. 4; *B.M.P.C.*, 527.

70 (a) اعلام الأخيار **King's, No. 39**

A large collection of biographies, entitled by Palmer (I know not on what authority) *A'lámu'l-* (or *I'lámu'l-*) *Akhyár*, by the Qáḍí Maḥmúd b. Sulaymán al-Kafawí (*circ.* 920/1514).

Ff. 586, not dated. See Palmer's *King's Cat.*, p. 20, and Brockelmann, ii, 83.

71 (a) إعلام السّادة الأماجد بفضل بناء المساجد **Or. 583 (7)**

A work on the merit of building mosques, entitled *I'lámu's-Sádati'l-amájid bi-faḍli biná'i'l-masájid*, by Shaykh Shamsu'd-Dín Abú 'Abdi'lláh Muḥammad b. Khalíl al-Ḥusayní (*circ.* 870/1465). See Brockelmann, ii, 77.

Ff. 26 of 18·1 × 13·5 c. and 17 ll.; defective at end; good *naskh* with rubrications. Bought of Géjou, July 14, 1909.

72 (t) الإعلام بأعلام بلد الله الحرام **Or. 672 (12)**

A history of Mecca entitled *al-I'lám bi-A'lámi Baladi'lláhi 'l-Ḥarám*, originally written in Arabic in 988/1580 by Quṭbu'd-Dín Muḥammad b. Aḥmad, and translated into Turkish by the poet 'Abdu'l-Báqí (d. 1008/1599–1600). See Ḥájji Khalífa, No. 949; Brockelmann, ii, 382; and *Camb. Hand-list*, p. 8.

Ff. 112 of 30 × 10·5 c. and 27 ll.; poor *nasta'líq* with rubrications; dated 1098/1686–7. Bought of Géjou, Feb. 17, 1906.

73 (a) إعلام النّاس فيما وقع للبرامكة مع خلفاء بنى العبّاس **Or. 23 (9)**

A historical romance about the Barmecides (*Álu Barmak*) and their relations with the 'Abbásid Caliphs, entitled *I'lámu'n-*

Nás fí-má waqa'a li'l-Barámikati ma'a Khulafá'i Bani'l-'Abbás, by Muḥammad Diyáb al-Itlídí (*circ.* 1100/1688). See Brockelmann, ii, 303; *Camb. Hand-list*, p. 8.

Ff. 155 of 23 × 16·5 and 22 ll.; good modern *naskh* with rubrications. Bought of Naaman, Feb. 5, 1901.

74 (a) الافق المبين **King's, No. 34**

Al-Ufuqu'l-Mubín, a manual of Shí'ite theology and metaphysics, by Mír Báqir Dámád (*circ.* 1070/1659).

Written for the most part in fair *naskh*, with supplies at the beginning in other and less legible hands, not dated. See Palmer's *King's Cat.*, p. 20.

75, 76 (p) اقبالنامه **Christ's, Dd.3.17**
Corpus, No. 207

Two copies of the third volume of the *Iqbál-náma* of Mu'tamad Khán (d. 1049/1639) containing the history of Jahángír. The **Christ's MS.**, dated 10 Sha'bán, 1219/Nov. 14, 1804, contains 163 ff. of 22·4 × 12·8 c. The **Corpus MS.** comprises 77 ff. of 30 × 20 c., and was copied in a careless *nasta'líq* hand in 1231/1816. See *B.M.P.C.*, p. 255.

77 (p) اقبالنامه **King's, No. 33**

Two volumes of the same work, the first containing the history of Jahángír's ancestors, especially Akbar (abridged from the *Akbar-náma*), the second the history of Jahángír. Vol. i is dated 1063/1653, and vol. ii 1086/1675–6.

78 (a) اقليدس **Trinity, R.13.39**

Euclid's Geometry in Arabic (كتاب تحرير اصول اقليدس). See Palmer's *Trin. Cat.*, pp. 86–7.

79 (t) الاقوال المسلّمة فى غزوات مسلمة، **Or. 469[5] (8)**

A tract of 29 leaves on the religious wars of the Muslims.

Ff. 222^a–251^a of 21·1 × 11·7 c. and 23 ll., written in fair *nasta'líq* with rubrications, and dated 1160/1747. Bought of Géjou, Jan. 29, 1904.

80–82 (p) اكبرنامه **Christ's, Dd. 5. 5; Corpus, No. 206; King's, No. 31**

The *Akbar-náma,* or History of the Emperor Akbar, by Abu'l-Faḍl-i-'Allámí (b. 958/1551, d. 1011/1602–3). See *B.M.P.C.*, pp. 247–251 and references there given.

The **Christ's MS.** is written in a good Indian *ta'líq* on 331 ff. of 33·8 × 21·6 c. and 23 ll., and is undated, but bears the impress of a seal dated 1164/1751. The **Corpus MS.** appears to be an abridgement of the *Akbar-náma,* like which it covers the first 46 years of Akbar's reign, "from which year onwards, by reason of the decease of Shaykh Abu'l-Faḍl, the *Akbar-náma*, in which five years remained to be written, is incomplete." There is no introduction or colophon. The writing is a cursive *nasta'líq*, and the leaves measure 24 × 16 c. The **King's MS.,** consisting of all three vols. bearing the same number (31), was transcribed in 1007/1598–9, four years before the Author's death. See Palmer's *King's Cat.*, p. 4.

83 (a) اكرّ ثاودوسيوس **Trinity, R. 13. 52**

A treatise by Theodosius on the use of some kind of Astrolabe or Celestial Globe, translated into Arabic by Qusṭá b. Lúqá (d. 220/835). See Brockelmann, i, p. 204, *d*, *f*, and *g*, where three treatises with similar though different titles are mentioned.

See Palmer's *Trin. Cat.*, p. 139.

84 (t) اكسير دولت **Or. 469^{4} (8)**

A Turkish treatise on Politics, Ethics and Statecraft, entitled *Iksír-i-Devlet.*

Ff. 162^{b}–221^{b} of 21·1 × 11·7 c. and 23 ll., written in fair *nasta'líq* with rubrications, apparently copied in 1160/1747. Bought of Géjou, Jan. 29, 1904.

85 (p) الف ليله و ليله **Corpus, No. 176**

The first volume of a Persian version of the *Alf Layla* or "Thousand and One Nights," following the original pretty closely and coming down to the Story of Núru'd-Dín 'Alí.

Written in a good modern *nasta'líq* hand (n.d.) on leaves of 31 × 19 c.

86, 87 (p) الفاظ ادويه **Corpus, No. 15**
King's, No. 29

A Persian treatise on Pharmacology and Materia Medica, written by Núru'd-Dín Muḥammad b. 'Abdu'lláh, physician to 'Aynu'l-Mulk of Shíráz, in 1038/1628–9, and dedicated to Sháh Jahán.' It has been edited by F. Gladwin, Calcutta, 1806. See also Ethé's *Bodl. Cat.*, No. 1603.

For the **King's MS.** see Palmer's *King's Cat.*, p. 4. The **Corpus MS.** comprises ff. 134 of 21 × 11 c., is written in *nasta'líq* on leaves of 21 × 11 c., and is dated 1222/1807–8 or 1229/1814.

88, 89 (a) الالفيّة (الخُلاصة) **Add. 3647 (9)**
Add. 3726 (9)

The celebrated rhymed Grammar known as the *Alfiyya* of Jamálu'd-Dín Muḥammad b. 'Abdu'lláh b. Málik (d. 672/1273), with the Commentary of his son Badru'd-Dín, and the Gloss on that Commentary of Shaykh Zaynu'd-Dín Abú Yaḥyá Zakariyyá al-Anṣárí. See Brockelmann, i, p. 298, *B.M.A.C.*, p. 237, DIX, etc.

Add. 3726 is the older MS., being dated Rabí' ii, 895 (Feb.–March, 1490). It comprises ff. 171 of 21·1 × 15·2 c. and 23 ll., is written in legible *naskh* with rubrications, and was bought of Naaman on Nov. 23, 1900. **Add. 3647** comprises 146 ff. of 20·9 × 15·4 c. and 27 ll., written in fair *naskh* with rubrications at Baghdád in Jumáda i, 1175 (Dec. 1761) by 'Abdu'r-Raḥmán b. Ḥájji Bakr, and was bought of Sethian on May 9, 1900.

90 (a) الأمراض الجُزئيّة **Or. 446 (11)**

A medical treatise on local ailments by Nafís b. 'Awaḍ b. Ḥakím al-Kirmání. See *B.M.A.C.*, p. 224; Brockelmann, i, 457, 82, b, and ii, 213. The author died in 850/1446–7, and was physician to Ulugh Beg.

Ff. 268 of 27·7 × 15 c. and 29 ll.; written in poor and cramped *naskh* on bad brown paper with rubrications; undated. Bought of Hannan, Watson & Co., August 29, 1903.

91 (a), 92, 93 (p) (*Gospels*) انجيل — **Or. 643[1] (8); Emmanuel, 3.2.1; Jesus, No. 1**

Or. 643[1] contains fragments of an Arabic translation of the Gospels, arranged for reading in Church. This MS. comprises ff. 9 of 20 × 14 c. and 17 ll., written in a coarse, bad *naskh* hand with rubrications. It was bought from the Convent of "Amba-Beshòwi at the Natron Lakes" in Nov. 1840, and was presented to the Library, with a leaf of Coptic, on Jan. 31, 1882. The **Emmanuel MS.** is a Persian translation of the Gospels, written on one side of each leaf only (as though intended for printing), and presented to the College in 1681 by Richard Kidder. The **Jesus MS.** contains a Persian translation of the Gospel of St Matthew, except the last two verses, and is written in a good Indian *ta'líq* hand.

94–101 (p) انشای ابو الفضل (مکاتبات علّامی) — **Add. 3640 (11); Christ's, Dd. 3.14; Corpus, Nos. 46, 62, 110, 136, 167; King's, No. 3**

Eight manuscripts of the whole or portions of the well-known *Inshá*, or Epistolary Models, of Abu'l-Faḍl-i-'Allámí, prime minister of the great Emperor Akbar. This book is also known as *Mukátabát-i-'Allámí*. See *B.M.P.C.*, p. 396.

Add. 3640 comprises ff. 163 of 27·3 × 15·9 c. and 15 ll., is written in a large, clear *ta'líq* with rubrications, and is undated. It was bought on April 23, 1900. The **Christ's MS.** is written in a good *ta'líq*, but is incomplete at the end. It is undated and contains 136 ff. of 22·7 × 16·3 c. and 14 ll. Of the **Corpus MSS., No. 46,** dated 1265/1849, contains Book iii only, and is written in *nasta'líq* on pages of 29·5 × 16 c. **No. 62,** also apparently incomplete, is undated, and is written in careless *nasta'líq* on pages of 25 × 17 c. **No. 110,** also undated, is a small thick volume, written in fair *nasta'líq* on pages of 17 × 11 c., containing Books ii and iii only. **No. 136,** also undated, contains Book ii only, and is written in a *ním-shikasta* hand on ff. 93 of 24 × 16 c. **No. 167,** also undated, contains Book i only, and is written in *shikasta* on pages of

27 × 18 c. The **King's MS.** comprises pp. 253 and was copied in 1109/1697–8. See Palmer's *King's Cat.*, p. 5.

102 (p) انشای بدایع **Corpus, No. 9**

A collection of letters of Indian origin entitled on the fly-leaf as above *Inshá-yi-Badáyi'*.

Copied at Sháhjahánpúr in A.D. 1827 in a careless *nasta'líq* on pages of 24 × 16 c.

103 (p) انشای بیانی **King's, No. 27[2]**

Inshá-yi-Bayání, an Epistolary Manual by 'Abdu'lláh b. Muḥammad Marwáríd, poetically named *Bayání*, who succeeded the eminent and famous Mír 'Alí Shír Nawá'í in the service of Sulṭán Ḥusayn Mírzá (906–922/1500–1516).

See Palmer's *King's Cat.*, p. 5. The MS. is dated 1055/1645.

104–106 (p) انشای بیدل **Corpus, No. 51[1]; Corpus, No. 57[1]; King's, No. 44**

Inshá-yi-Bídil, an Epistolary Manual by 'Abdu'l-Qáḍir, poetically named *Bídil* (d. 1133/1721 *aet.* 79). See *B.M.P.C.*, p. 811[a].

Of the **Corpus MSS. No. 51[1]** was copied at Serempore in 1206/1791–2, and is written in *nasta'líq* on pages of 30 × 18·5 c. **No. 57[1]**, undated, is written in *shikasta* on pages of 22·5 × 13 c. The **King's MS. No. 44** was copied in 1164/1751. See Palmer's *King's Cat.*, p. 5.

107 (p) انشای جامعه **Corpus, No. 227[1]**

Letters of kings, princes and other notable persons compiled from various sources. The compilation appears to have been made in 1134/1721–2.

Written in *ním-shikasta* on pages of 20 × 14 c.

108, 109 (p) انشای جامی **King's, Nos. 27[3], 28**

Epistolary models of the great poet and mystic Mullá Núru'd-Dín 'Abdu'r-Raḥmán Jámí. See Flügel's *Vienna Cat.*, p. 286; Ethé's *I. O. Cat.* 1387; and Palmer's *King's Cat.*, p. 5. **No. 27[3]** is incomplete.

110 (p) انشای خلیفه (= جامع القوانین) **Corpus, No. 84²**

The *Inshá-yi-Khalífa* or *Jámi'u'l-Qawánín* of Khalífa Sháh Muḥammad.

Pp. 73 of 26 × 16 c., written in careless *nasta'líq*.

111 (p) انشای دلکشا **Corpus, No. 39¹**

The *Inshá-yi-Dilgushá* of Sayyid Nithár 'Alí b. Sayyid A'ẓam 'Alí.

Ff. 62; *ním-shikasta*; dated 1239/1823–4.

112 (p) انشای طاهر وحید **Corpus, No. 31²**

The *Inshá*, or Epistolary Models, of Ṭáhir Waḥíd, who was secretary to Sháh 'Abbás the Ṣafawí. See Ethé's *Bodl. Cat.*, No. 1387, and *Ind. Off. Pers. Cat.*, No. 1653.

113 (p) انشای ملّا طغرا **King's, No. 22**

The *Inshá-yi-Mullá Ṭughrá*. See *B. M. P. C.*, p. 743ᵇ, xvii; Ethé's *Bodl. Cat.*, No. 1389. There is a Cawnpore edition of Ṭughrá's tracts and letters.

See Palmer's *King's Cat.*, p. 5. This MS. is dated 1181/1767–8.

114 (p) انشای عبد الحیّ **King's, No. 32**

The *Inshá* of 'Abdu'l-Ḥayy.

See Palmer's *King's Cat.*, p. 5. Dated 941/1534–5.

115, 116 (p) انشای فائق **Corpus, No. 192²** **Corpus, No. 164**

The *Inshá* of Muḥammad Fá'iq.

No. 164 is a lithograph (though placed amongst the manuscripts) of 35 pp. of 27 × 17 c., undated. **No. 192²** comprises ff. 36.

117 (p) انشای فیض بخش **Corpus, No. 192³**

The *Inshá* of Fayḍ-bakhsh.

118–120 (p) انشای مادهورام {Corpus, No. 95 / Corpus, No. 127 / King's, No. 36}

The *Inshá* of Mádhúrám, a collection of official correspondence compiled in 1140/1727–8. See *Camb. Pers. Cat.*, No. clxxxix, p. 281.

Of the **Corpus MSS. No. 95** comprises ff. 100 of 21×13 c., and is written in *nasta‘líq*, while **No. 127** is written in a similar hand, its pages measuring 26 × 17 c. The former is dated 1218/1803–4 and the latter 1252/1836–7. For the **King's MS.,** which is dated 1196/1782, see Palmer's *King's Cat.*, p. 5.

121 (t) انشای مرغوب **Or. 743 (8)**

A Turkish Epistolary Manual entitled *Inshá-yi-Marghúb*.

Ff. 96 of 21·6 × 14·5 c. and 21 ll., written obliquely across the page in good modern Turkish *riq‘a*, and dated 1241/1825–6. Bought of Géjou, March 27, 1907. See *Camb. Handlist*, p. 17.

122 (p) انشای مسعودی **Corpus, No. 54**[2]

The *Inshá-yi-Mas‘údí*, a collection of letters written for the most part early in the thirteenth century of the *hijra* (last quarter of the eighteenth century of the Christian era).

The leaves measure 15 × 10·5 c., and the writing is a *ním-shikasta*. The MS. is dated 1240/1824–5.

123 (p) انشای میرم سیاه قزوینی **King's, No. 27**[1]

The *Inshá*, or Epistolary Manual, of Míram Siyáh of Qazwín, poetically surnamed *Pír*, containing letters to various notable contemporaries, including Bábur, Humáyún, Sháh Isma‘íl, Ḥusayn Wá‘iẓ-i-Káshifí, etc. The author died after 957/1550. See Ethé's *Ind. Off. Cat.*, No. 2061, and Palmer's *King's Cat.*, p. 5.

This MS. is dated 1055/1645.

124 (p) انشا **Add. 3734**[2] **(9)**

An anonymous and untitled Epistolary Manual.

For description of the MS. see under سراج منیر. This portion occupies ff. 44^b–54. Bought of Sethian, Nov. 28, 1900.

125–127 (p) انشای هرکرن **Christ's, Dd. 3. 15 / Corpus, No. 72 / Corpus, No. 84[1]**

Inshá-yi-Harkarn, a well-known Epistolary Manual by Harkarn.

The **Christ's MS.** is entitled as above in an English label attached to the MS., but the author's name is given in the text as Shihábu'd-Dín Aḥmad. Cf. **Nos. 225** and **226** *infra*. It begins:

جنود نا معدود حمد ملازم حضرت مالك الملك الخ

Of the **Corpus MSS., No. 72** is written in *nasta'líq* and comprises pp. 100 of 21 × 13 c., **No. 84**[1] comprises pp. 22 × 16 c., and is written in a careless *nasta'líq*.

128 (p) انشای ایزد بخش رسا **Corpus, No. 17[2]**

An Epistolary Manual by Ízad-bakhsh Rasá.

Ff. 45 written in *ním-shikasta*, dated 1249/1833–4.

129 (p) انوار الاله فی شرح اسماء الله الحُسْنَى **Add. 3686 (8)**

Anwáru'l-Iláh fí Sharḥi Asmá'i'lláhi'l-Ḥusná ("Lights of God in explanation of the Most Beautiful Names of God"). It appears to treat of acrostics (*mu'ammá*), and to be the work of a pupil of Mawláná Mír Ḥusayn Mu'ammá'í.

Ff. 60 of 20·8 × 12·2 c. and 17 ll.; good *nasta'líq* with rubrications; late fifteenth or early sixteenth century. Bought of Naaman in September, 1900.

130 (a) انوار التنزيل و اسرار التأويل **King's, No. 70**

The well-known Commentary on the *Qur'án* of Náṣiru'd-Dín al-Bayḍáwí entitled *Anwáru't-Tanzíl wa Asráru't-Ta'wíl*. In the margins is written the more ancient and still more celebrated Commentary of az-Zamakhsharí entitled *al-Kashsháf*.

The MS. is beautifully written in a fine *naskh* hand with rubrications between golden borders. It was copied at Damascus in 980/1572–3. See Palmer's *King's Cat.*, pp. 20 and 27.

131–135 (p) انوار سُهیلی Or. 900 (8); Corpus, No. 131–2; Corpus, No. 134; King's, No. 21; Queens', No. 2

Five copies of the well-known *Anwár-i-Suhaylí* of Ḥusayn Wá'iẓ-i-Káshifí (d. 910/1504–5).

Or. 900, described as "an abridgement of, or very different recension to, the printed text," comprises 179 ff. of 19·7 × 11·5 c. and 14 ll. in text, with 26 ll. in the margin. It is written in a good *ta'líq*, with rubrications and floral ornaments, is undated, and is described in the colophon as "the story of Kalíla and Dimna." The two **Corpus MSS.** are both poor specimens, written in cursive *nasta'líq* or *ním-shikasta*. **No. 131–2** has been much injured by damp. Its pages measure 23 × 12 c. and it is dated 1214/1799–1800. **No. 134** is acephalous and has *lacunae* elsewhere. Its pages measure 35 × 21 c. and it is dated 1238/1822–3. The **King's MS. No. 21** is also badly written; it is dated 1147/1734–5. The **Queens' MS. No. 2** is the oldest and best: it is dated 972/1564–5, and is written in a minute, neat *ta'líq*.

136 (t) انیس العارفین (ترجمه‌سی) Or. 925 (7)

A Turkish translation by Ja'far Chelebi, known as *Tájí-záda*, of the *Anísu'l-'Árifín* ("Gnostic's Companion") of the Persian poet Qásimu'l-Anwár, who died in 837/1433–4. See *B.M.P.C.*, pp. 636–7. The MS., belonging to the Lynch Bequest, comprises 52 ff. of 19 × 11·6 c. and 19 ll., is written in a fair *ta'líq* with rubrications, and was transcribed before 1061/1651.

137 (p) انیس الموحّدین Or. 510[1] (11)

A work on Shí'ite Theology entitled *Anísu'l-Muwaḥḥidín*, by Mullá Muḥammad Mahdí Niráqí, containing a Preface and five chapters "on the Five Principles" (فی الأُصول الخمسة).

Comprises ff. 44 of 27·7 × 18·5 c. and 17 ll., written in good, clear Persian *naskh* with rubrications, by Muḥammad Háshim al-Ḥusayní, known as Mírzá Bábá, in 1219/1805. Bought of Messrs Hannan and Watson on August 20, 1904.

138 (a) اوضح المسالك الى معرفة البلدان و الممالك **Or. 918 (8)**

Awḍaḥu'l-Masálik ila ma'rifati'l-Buldán wa'l-Mamálik, a geographical work by Muḥammad b. 'Alí Sipáhí-záda (d. 997/1587). See Brockelmann, ii, pp. 46 and 453. The MS., which forms part of the Lynch Bequest, was copied by Mullá Ṣáliḥ ad-Dúrí in 1197/1782, and comprises 141 ff. of 22·5 × 15·8 c. and 21 ll.

139 (a) الايساغوجى للأبهرى **Or. 418 (8)**

The *Ísághújí* (Εἰσαγωγή), with Commentary of Athíru'd-Dín al-Abharí (d. 663/1264). See Brockelmann, i, 464; *Camb. Hand-list*, p. 18.

Ff. 30 of 21·3 × 14·8 c. and 11 ll.; fair *naskh*; rubrications; dated 1179/1765–6. Bought of Géjou, Aug. 29, 1903.

140 (a) الايساغوجى **Jesus, No. 15**

The *Ísághújí* of al-Khúrí Buṭrus b. Buṭrus b. Isḥaq aṭ-Ṭúlání, Maronite Archbishop of Aleppo, who flourished about A.D. 1703. See *B.M.A.S.*, No. 44.

Presented to the College by Samuel Lyde (d. A.D. 1860).

141 (a) الايضاح فى الفروع **Trinity, R. 13.48**

Al-Íḍáḥ fi'l-Furú', a work on the applications of Jurisprudence, by Abú 'Alí Ḥasan b. al-Qásim aṭ-Ṭabarí.

Ff. 344. See Palmer's *Trin. Cat.*, pp. 129–130.

142 (a) ايضاح الايضاح فى شرح الايضاح **Or. 841 (6)**

A Commentary on the *Íḍáḥ* entitled *Íḍáḥu'l-Íḍáḥ*. See Brockelmann, i, p. 295.

Ff. 260 of 17 × 11·3 c. and 19 ll.; fair old *naskh*; text overlined with red; dated 782/1380–1. Bought of J. J. Naaman, Feb. 8, 1911.

143 (a) ايضاح الدّلالات فى سماع الآلات **Or. 210 (9)**

Íḍáḥu'd-dalálát fí simá'i'l-álát, a treatise on the lawfulness of listening to music, by Shaykh 'Abdu'l-Ghaní an-Nábulúsí (d. 1143/1731). See Brockelmann, ii, 347, No. 33.

Ff. 44 of 21·7 × 16·3 c. and 19 ll.; small neat *naskh*, dated 1088/1677–8. Bought of J. J. Naaman, Oct. 12, 1902.

144 (p) آئين اكبرى **King's, No. 5**

The *Á'ín-i-Akbarí* of Abu'l-Faḍl Mubárak-i-'Allámí (d. 1011/1602–3), author of the *Akbar-náma* (see above, Nos. **80–82**) of which this is really the third volume. See *B.M.P.C.*, p. 251.

Not dated. See Palmer's *King's Cat.*, p. 5.

145 (p) آئينهٔ بخت **King's, No. 42**

Á'ína-i-Bakht ("the Mirror of Fortune"), a historical and biographical work composed, apparently, in 1068/1657–8, and divided into forty sections entitled *Mu'áyana* (معاينه). Ff. 120.

See Palmer's *King's Cat.*, p. 5.

146 (p) آئينهٔ حق نما **Queens', No. 1**

Á'ína-i-Ḥaqq-numá ("the Truth-revealing Mirror"), a well-known apology for the Christian Religion by François Xavier. See *B.M.P.C.*, p. 4.

147 (p) آئينهٔ سكندرى **Corpus, No. 187**

Á'ína-i-Sikandarí ("the Mirror of Alexander"), a *mathnawí* poem by Amír Khusraw of Dihlí in imitation of the *Sikandar-náma* of Niẓámí of Ganja.

Dated 1274/1857–8. Ff. 173 of 22 × 17 c., written in *shikasta*.

148 (p) آئينهٔ شاهى **King's, No. 37**

Á'ína-i-Sháhí ("the Royal Mirror"), a Persian translation of the Arabic *Ḍiyá'u'l-Qalb* ("Light of the Heart") of the same author, Muḥammad b. Murtaḍá, known as Muḥsin, composed about 1066/1655–6, for Sháh 'Abbás II the Ṣafawí.

See Palmer's *King's Cat.*, p. 5.

149 (p) باز نامه **Corpus, No. 13**

A treatise on falconry, entitled *Báz-náma*, by Sayyid 'Arab-i-Najafí, a native of Balkh who migrated to India and entered the service of the Emperor Akbar.

Written in *nasta'líq* on pages of 23 × 13 c., which are considerably wormed; undated.

150 (h) باغ و بهار **Or. 881 (16)**

A Hindustání story-book entitled in the colophon (dated 1244/1828–9) *Bágh u Bahár* and *Chahár Darwísh*, bought of G. David on July 3, 1912. Pp. 263 of 36·8 × 21 c. and 15 ll., written in a large, clear, coarse, Indian *ta'líq*, for an Englishman named Hume or Home.

151 (a) بحار الأنوار **Or. 436[5] (8)**

An abridgement of the seventh volume of the great work on Shí'a traditions entitled *Biḥáru'l-Anwár*. This volume deals with the Imamate.

Ff. 65^b–87^b, of 20·3 × 12·3 c., written in good *naskh* with rubrications; incomplete at end. Bought of Hannan, Watson & Co., Aug. 29, 1903.

152 (a) بحث المطالب **Or. 463 (9)**

Baḥthu'l-Maṭálib, a work on Arabic grammar by Jibríl b. Farḥát (d. A.D. 1732).

This MS. was transcribed by Buṭrusu'l-Bustání (d. A.D. 1884) in A.D. 1841, is annotated by Dr Cornelius Van Dyck, the learned American missionary in Syria, and was presented to the Library by his son Dr Edward Van Dyck. It contains ff. 132 of 22·5 × 17 c. and 19 ll., and is written in clear *naskh* with rubrications.

153 (p) بحر الأنساب **Corpus, No. 205[1]**

A historical and genealogical work containing notices of prophets, contemporaries of the Prophet Muḥammad, the Imáms, etc., by Muḥammad Ja'far Ḥusayn.

Written in *shikasta* on paper measuring 25 × 15 c.

154 (a) بحر الجواهر **King's, No. 51**

Baḥru'l-Jawáhir, a work on Medicine and Materia Medica, by Muḥammad b. Yúsuf of Herát, the physician.

See Palmer's *King's Cat.*, p. 20. Written in bad *ta'líq* with rubrications.

بحر الغرائب

Baḥru'l-Ghará'ib. See under *Lughat-i-Ḥalímí.*

155 (a) بحر المذاهب **Or. 866**

An account of different sects entitled *Baḥru'l-Madháhib,* by 'Abdu'l-Wahháb al-Qudwá'í al-Qannawjí Mun'im Khán, composed about 1125/1713. See Brockelmann, ii, pp. 417–8.

From Professor Robertson Smith's library. Written in fair *ta'líq* with rubrications on pages of 22·6 × 14·5 c. and 17 ll., undated.

156 (a) بحور العين (فى الفقه الحنفى) **Or. 21[1] (9)**

A work on Ḥanafite Law entitled *Baḥúru'l-'Ayn,* by 'Alí Efendi, Muftí of Tripoli.

Ff. 1–72 of 22·2 × 15·3 c., dated 1208/1793–4. Bought of J. J. Naaman, Feb. 2, 1901.

157 (t) بدء الامالى قصيده‌سنك ترجمه‌سى **Or. 208[3] (8)**

A Turkish translation of the Arabic *qaṣída* known as *Bad'u'l-Amálí* by Siráju'd-Dín 'Alí b. 'Uthmán al-Úshí al-Farghání, who wrote it in 566/1163. See Brockelmann, i, 429.

The MS., of which this portion occupies ff. 32ᵇ–37ᵇ, is described below (p. 29) under *al-Burda.* Bought of J. J. Naaman, Oct. 12, 1902.

158 (p) بدايع العقول **King's, No. 61**

Badáyi'u'l-'Uqúl, a Persian version of the Sanskrit *Vetála-pañchavim gatika,* or 25 Tales of a Demon told to King Vikramaditya. This version, stated by Count Serge d'Oldenburg to be unique, was composed in the reign of Awrangzíb in 1082/1671–2.

See Palmer's *King's Cat.,* p. 25. The MS. was transcribed in 1198/1783–4.

159 (a) البدر المُنير فى اسرار الاكسير **Add. 3701 (8)**

A treatise on Alchemy entitled *al-Badru'l-Munír fí Asrári'l-Iksír,* by Aydimir b. 'Alí b. Aydimir al-Jaldakí.

Ff. 72 of 21 × 15 c. and 16 ll., written in poor scrawly modern *nasta'líq*, undated. Bought of J. J. Naaman, Nov. 7, 1900.

160 (a) بُرْءُ ٱلسَّاعة **Add. 3696 (10)**

Bur'u's-Sá'at, a medical treatise on instantaneous cures, followed by another on the Diet of the Sick (*Kitábu Aghdhiyati'l-Marḍá*) by the great physician Abú Bakr Muḥammad b. Zakariyyá ar-Rází. See Brockelmann, i, 234, No. 9.

Dated 1113/1701–2. Bought of Sethian, Nov. 5, 1900. Ff. 132 of 25·5 × 14·5 c. and 21 ll.; written in a poor, modern cursive *ta'líq* with rubrications.

161 (a) بديعيّة فى مدح النّبىّ **Or. 585 (8)**

An ornate rhetorical poem in praise of the Prophet, written in imitation of another similar poem by Taqiyyu'd-Dín Abú Bakr b. Ḥujja al-Ḥamawí (d. 837/1434), and beginning:

من العقيق و من تذكار ذى سلمِ، براعة العين فى استهلالها بدمِ،

Al-Ḥamawí's poem is itself an imitation of the *Burda* of al-Búṣírí (see immediately below). See Brockelmann, ii, 16.

Ff. 51 of 28 × 12·5 and 11 ll.; excellent *naskh* within gold and blue borders, not dated. Bought of Géjou, July 14, 1905.

162–169 (a, p, t) بُرْدة البوصيرى **Or. 207 (8)**, **Add. 3712 (12)**, **Or. 208[1] (8)**, **Or. 26[1] (8)**, **Trinity, R. 13. 25**, **Christ's, Dd. 3. 21[2]**, **Corpus, 75[1]**, **Emmanuel, 3. 2. 7**

The celebrated *Burda*, or "Mantle-poem," of al-Búṣírí (d. 694–1294) in praise of the Prophet; two *takhmís* (quintet) poems based on the same; a defence of the same; and three Commentaries on the same in Arabic, Persian and Turkish. See Brockelmann, i, 264–7. The proper title of the poem is *Al-Kawákibu'd-durriyya fí madḥi Khayri'l-bariyya.*

Or. 207 contains the *Burda* (ff. 15^b–38^a of 19·1 × 13·1 c. and 9 lines) preceded by Arabic prayers and doxology and some instructions in Turkish (ff. 1^b–10^a), and another Arabic poem (ff. 11^b–15^a) beginning:

لك الحمد يا ذا الجود و المجد و العُلى ،

تَبَارَكْتَ تُعْطى مَنْ تشآء و تمنع ،

Written in fine large *naskh* in black and gold between red and gilt lines, undated. Bought of Naaman, Oct. 12, 1602.

Add. 3712 contains a *takhmís*, or quintet, or "fivesome," based on the *Burda*, and composed by Shaykh Sharafu'd-Dín Muḥammad b. Ḥammád. [It seems to be identical with the *takhmís* of Násiru'd-Dín Muḥammad b. al-Fayyúmí: see *B.M.A.S.*, No. 1080, p. 680.] Ff. 29 of 30·3 × 21·3; 3 hemistichs of the original text of the *Burda* are followed by 9 of the additional hemistichs. Bought of Naaman, Nov. 23, 1900; not dated.

Or. 208[1] contains (ff. 1^b–8^b out of ff. 78) another *takhmís* of the *Burda* by Abú 'Abdu'lláh Muḥammad b. Sa'íd ad-Dallásí al-Búṣírí. Written in good *naskh* on pages of 21·3 × 15 c. and 15 ll. Bought of Naaman, Oct. 12, 1902; undated.

Or. 26[1] contains a refutation by Shaykh Dá'úd b. Sulaymán al-Baghdádí al-Khálidí an-Naqshbandí of an attack on the *Burda* and its author by a certain Wahhábí writer, composed in 1269/1852–3. Ff. 4^b–74^a of 19·3 × 14·5 c. and 12 ll.; clear *naskh*; rubrications; undated. Bought of Naaman, Feb. 5, 1904.

Trinity, R. 13. 25 contains the Arabic commentary on the *Burda* of Shamsu'd-Dín Abú 'Abdi'lláh Muḥammad b. Aḥmad b. Marzúq at-Tilimsání (d. 781/1379) entitled *Ṭíbu'l-Ḥabíb fí Sharḥi qaṣídati'l-Ḥabíb*. See Brockelmann, i, 265, l. 11. Ff. 350.

Christ's, Dd. 3. 21[2] contains a Persian translation of and commentary on the *Burda*, preceded by an Arabic devotional tract and followed by a few other short Arabic tracts, one of which is dated 1134/1721–2. Ff. 21 × 12·8 c. and 11 ll.; good *naskh*.

Corpus, No. 75[1] contains a Turkish commentary on and paraphrase of the *Burda*, comprising also the Arabic text, and preceded by a prose preface. Ff. 43 of 20 × 14 c., written in Turkish *nasta'líq*.

Emmanuel, No. 3.2.7, contains five parts, of which the first is the *Burda*, the second the same with Persian metrical paraphrase, the third an Arabic fragment, the fourth prayers and the fifth poems.

170 (h) برق لامع **Corpus, No. 138**

Barq-i-lámi' ("the Gleaming Lightning"), an anonymous *mathnawí* poem in Urdú containing a controversy between a Shí'a and a Sunní, written from the extreme Shí'a point of view. The date of composition is given in the chronogram لعنت بر ابو بکر = 983/1575–6.

Ff. 52 of 33 × 22 c., written in good clear *nasta'líq*.

171 (p) برزونامه **King's, No. 56**

A *mathnawí* poem in the style of the *Sháh-náma* entitled *Barzú-náma*, but not agreeing with the poem described under this title in *B.M.P.S.*, No. 195. It deals with the adventures of Rustam and Suhráb, and is ascribed in the colophon to Mawláná Shamsu'd-Dín Muḥammad Kawíj.

Dated 829/1425–6, in error, apparently, for 1019/1610–11. See Palmer's *King's Cat.*, p. 5.

172 (a) البرهان فى الصرف العربى **Or. 864 (8)**

An acephalous work on Arabic grammar entitled *al-Burhán*, or more probably an abridgement thereof, since it concludes as follows:

انقضى و تمّ تلخيص المقالة الثانية من كتاب البرهان '

Written in a coarse but legible *naskh* on 434 ff. of 20 × 12 c. and 14 ll.; first leaf missing; dated Sháhjahán-ábád, 1135/1722–3. Robertson Smith Bequest. The volume is described on the back as containing the Logic of Aristotle.

173 (p) برهان مآثر **King's, No. 64**

The *Burhán-i-Ma'áthir* of 'Alí b. 'Azízu'lláh aṭ-Ṭabáṭabá'í, a history of the Bahmaní and Niẓámsháhí dynasties from

742–1004 (1341–1595) composed about the latter date. See *B.M.P.C.*, p. 314ᵇ; Palmer's *King's Cat.*, p. 6.

Ff. 427.

174 (a) بستان العارفين **King's, No. 59**

The *Bustánu'l-'Árifín* of Abu'l-Layth Naṣr b. Muḥammad b. Ibráhím b. al-Khaṭṭáb as-Samarqandí (d. 383/993). See Brockelmann, i, 195–6; Palmer's *King's Cat.*, p. 20; and *Camb. Hand-list*, p. 21.

Ff. 83; clear *naskh* with rubrications.

175 (t) بشارت‌نامهٔ رفیعی **Or. 569 (9)**

A Turkish Ḥurúfí poem by Rafí'í known as *Bashárat-náma*. See *B.M.T.C.*, and E. J. W. Gibb's *History of Ottoman Poetry*, vol. i, pp. 344–5 and 369–76.

Ff. 75 of 24 × 16·8 c. and 15 ll., large, clear Turkish *riq'a* with rubrications; dated 1268/1851–2. Bought of Géjou, July 14, 1905.

176 (a) بُغْيَة المرتاد لتصحيح الضّاد **Or. 19 (7)**

Bughyatu'l-Murtád li-taṣḥíḥi'ḍ-Ḍád, by Shaykh Abu'l-Ḥasan 'Alí b. Ghánim al-Qudsí, d. 1004/1595. See Brockelmann, ii, 312.

Ff. 21 of 17·7 × 13 c. and 15 ll.; good, clear *naskh* with rubrications; undated. Bought of Naaman, Feb. 5, 1901.

177, 178 (p) بلبل‌نامه **Or. 257³ (8)**
Or. 274¹ (8)

Two copies of the *Bulbul-náma* of Shaykh Farídu'd-Dín 'Aṭṭár, both from the Cowell Bequest. The first comprises ff. 22 of 20·3 × 15 c. and 11 ll., and was copied in a large, clear Indian *nasta'líq* in 1273/1857. The second, copied in the same year, occupies ff. 1ᵇ–21ᵃ of 21·5 × 16 c. and 11 ll., is written in a clear Indian *ta'líq* with rubrications, and is followed by the *Mihr u Mushtarí* of 'Aṣṣár of Tabríz, and two Sanskrit works, the *Srútabodha* of Kálidása and the *Dhúrtasamáyana Nátak*.

179 (a) بلوغ المنا فی تراجم اهل الغنا ' **Or. 745 (8)**

Bulúghu'l-Muná fí tarájimi ahli'l-Ghiná, by Muḥammad Efendi b. Aḥmad b. Maḥmúd b. Muḥammad al-Ganjí b. Abí 'Aṣrún (*circ.* 1150/1737). See Brockelmann, ii, 448.

Ff. 92 of 21 × 16·4 c. and 15 ll., fair modern *naskh*, not dated. Bought of Géjou, March 27, 1909.

180–187 (p) بوستان سعدی **Or. 289 (9)**, **Or. 290 (10)**, **Or. 685⁵ (9)**, **Or. 942 (8)**, **Corpus, No. 119**, **Corpus, No. 153**, **Emmanuel, 3.2.5**, **Trinity, R.8.25**

The celebrated poem of Sa'dí of Shíráz entitled the *Bústán*.

Or. 289 comprises ff. 148 of 24 × 15·5 and 12 ll., written in good *ta'líq* on tinted paper within gilt and coloured borders, and dated 1010/1602. This MS. and the following are from the Cowell Bequest.

Or. 290 comprises ff. 150 of 26·4 × 17·1 c. and 15 ll., and is written in a poor Indian *ta'líq* and undated.

Or. 685[5] contains on ff. 120^b–128^a short selections from the *Bústán*, undated. Bought of Géjou, May 10, 1906.

Or. 942, presented to the Library in Feb. 1916 by Mr G. le Strange, who bought it from the late M. Stanislas Guyard, comprises 134 ff. of 19·7 × 12·3 and 15 ll., and is written in a fair *ta'líq* with rubrications and interlinear glosses, and is undated.

Corpus, No. 119, contains an anonymous and fragmentary commentary on the *Bústán*, written in 1232/1816–7 in a scrawly *nasta'líq* on pages of 19 × 12 c.

Corpus, No. 153, contains the *Bústán* and the *Gulistán* of Sa'dí, both incomplete, undated and carelessly written on pages of 23 × 15 c.

Emmanuel, 3.2.5, contains the *Bústán*, dated 1026/1617. It was presented to the College by Thomas Leigh.

Trinity, R.8.25 (bound up with **R.8.28**), contains the *Bústán*, imperfect at beginning and end, undated, and written in *ta'líq* on 116 ff. of Indian paper.

188 (p) بوستان خیال **Christ's, Dd. 3. 19**

An Anthology of Persian poetry entitled *Bústån-i-Khayál* ("the Garden of Phantasy") compiled by Bektásh-qulí Abdál-i-Rúmí. The date of compilation is given by the chronogram بیکتاش قلی ابدالم (=951/1544–5). Ff. 73 of 21×11·5 c. and 13 ll.; undated; good *ta'líq* with rubrications.

189 (p) بهادر شاه نامه **King's, No. 47**

The *Bahádur Sháh Náma*, or History of Bahádur Sháh, by Mírzá Muḥammad Dánishmand Khán, being the official record of the first two years of the reign of Sháh 'Álam Bahádur Sháh. See *B. M. P. C.*, p. 272*a*. The MS. is undated. See Palmer's *King's Cat.*, p. 6.

190–192 (p) بهار دانش **Christ's, Dd. 4. 15** / **Corpus, No. 8** / **King's, No. 48**

The *Bahár-i-Dánish*, a well-known collection of stories by Shaykh 'Ináyatu'lláh (d. 1088/1677–8), with a Preface by Muḥammad Ṣáliḥ, the Author's pupil. The work was completed in 1061/1651. The **Christ's MS.** is written in a legible Indian *ta'líq* and contains 326 ff. of 28·5 × 19·5 c. and 17 ll.

193 (p) بهارستان **Or. 696 (8)**

The *Baháristán* of Jámí.

Ff. 137 of 20·5 × 13 c. and 11 ll.; good *ta'líq*; rubrications; undated. Bought of Géjou, December 1906.

194, 195 (p) بهار سخن **Corpus, No. 86** / **King's, No. 49**

The *Bahár-i-Sukhun*, a collection of letters and other prose compositions by Muḥammad Ṣáliḥ of Lahore. See *B. M. P. C.*, p. 398a.

The **Corpus MS.** contains ff. 434 of 18×11 c., the first leaf missing, and many leaves badly stained. It is written in *nasta'líq*, and dated 1104/1692–3. The **King's MS.** is dated 1139/1726–7.

196–200 (p, h) بهاگوت **Corpus, No. 27; King's, No. 52; King's, No. 54; King's, No. 57; King's, No. 62**

Translations into Persian and Hindí of the celebrated Sanskrit poem the *Bhágavad-Gítá*.

Corpus 27, containing a verse translation "into a language described as Brij-Baka," comprises about 270 ff. of 23 × 13 c. Written in *nasta'líq* and undated. **King's 52** contains a Hindí verse translation of the *Bhágavad* of Dayá Rám, written about the end of the eighteenth century of the Christian era in a very bad Indian *ta'líq* with rubrications. **King's 54** contains a Persian versified translation of the *Bhágavad* of Ṭoṛalmal, followed by a few quatrains and other poems, comprising ff. 217 and copied in 1132/1719–20. **King's 57** contains the *Bhágavad Bhúpatí* in Hindí verse, comprises ff. 320, and is dated 1178/1764–5. **King's 62,** in two volumes, contains a Persian prose translation of the *Bhágavad-Gítá* (vol. i containing the first nine chapters), copied in 1193/1779. For the four King's MSS., see Palmer's *King's Cat.*, pp. 25–26.

201 (t, a, p) بهجة اللّغة **Or. 533 (10)**

A Turkish-Arabic-Persian dictionary entitled *Bahjatu'l-Lughat* by Muḥammad As'ad, comprising ff. 317 of 26·7 × 16 c. and 13 ll., written in clear *naskh* with rubrications, and undated. It is one of 11 MSS. bought of Géjou on Nov. 1, 1904.

202 (p) بهجة المباهج **King's, No. 58**

An account of the lives and miracles of the Twelve Imáms by Abú Sa'íd Ḥasan b. Ḥusayn of Sabzawár, a Shí'ite, entitled *Bahjatu'l-Mabáhij*. It comprises 42 sections, is founded on the *Mabáhiju'l-Mubhij* of Muḥammad b. Ḥusayn b. Ḥasan al-Kundurí, while it is in turn one of the sources of the *Zínatu'l-Majális*. See *B. M. P. C.*, p. 758b, and Palmer's *King's Cat.*, p. 6. The MS. is dated 1199/1784–5.

203 (a) ‹بهجة المحافل . . فى أخبار النبىّ الكامل› **Add. 3667 (8)**

Bahjatu'l-Maḥáfili'l-mutaḍamminatu li-akhbári'n-Nabiy-yi'l-Kámil, a work on the biography of the Prophet by Shaykh Yaḥyá b. Abí Bakr al-'Ámirí (d. 893/1488). See Ḥájji Khalífa, No. 1965, and Brockelmann, ii, 72.

Ff. 216 of 21·5 × 15·4 c. and 23 ll., written in clear, coarse *naskh* with rubrications in 1158/1745. Bought of Sethian, July 17, 1900.

204 (a) البهجة المرضيّة فى شرح الألفيّة **Or. 186 (7)**

A commentary on the *Alfiyya* of Ibn Málik, by Jalálu'd-Dín as-Suyúṭí, entitled *al-Bahjatu'l-Marḍiyya fí Sharḥi'l-Alfiyya*. See Brockelmann, ii, 155, No. 246.

Ff. 97 of 17·1 × 10·8 c. and 20 ll.; small legible *naskh* with rubrications dated 789/1387. Bought of Géjou, July 3, 1902.

205 (a) ‹بيان السُّنّة و الجماعة› **Trinity, R. 13. 19**

A treatise on Ḥanafí law entitled *Bayánu's-Sunna wa'l-Jamá'a*, by Abú Ja'far Aḥmad b. Muḥammad aṭ-Ṭaháwí (d. 321/933). See Brockelmann, ii, 173–4. This is followed by eight or nine other short tracts. The MS. was transcribed in A.D. 1566, and contains ff. 77, written in *naskh*.

206 (p) بيان فارسى **Or. 34 (8)**

The Persian *Bayán*, the chief work of Mírzá 'Alí Muḥammad the Báb (shot at Tabríz in A.D. 1850), to whom the Bábí and Bahá'í sects owe their origin. See Baron V. Rosen's *Collections Scientifiques de l'Institut des Langues Orientales de Saint-Pétersbourg*, vol. iii, *Manuscrits persans*, pp. 1–32; *Catalogue and Description of* 27 *Bábí Manuscripts* by E. G. Browne in the *J. R. A. S.* for 1892, pp. 450–1 and 698–9.

Ff. 166 of 19·8 × 14·5 c. and 19 ll.; good *naskh*, with rubrications, undated. Bought of Naaman, Feb. 5, 1901.

207 (p) بيتال پچيسى **Corpus, No. 69**

A Persian version of the Hindí *Baitál Pachísí*, or "Tales of a Demon."

Written in an ugly *nasta'líq* hand at Lucknow in 1262/1846 on leaves of 25 × 17 c.

208 (p) بیچ گَنِت **King's, No. 50**

A Persian translation of Lailáwatí's *Bích Ganit,* a Sanskrit work on Arithmetic.

A small, untidy volume, undated. See Palmer's *King's Cat.*, p. 25.

209 (p) بیسرنامه **Or. 651² (8)**

The *Bí-sar-náma* of Shaykh Farídu'd-Dín 'Aṭṭár.

Ff. 85^b–91^b of 19·3 × 11 c. and 15 ll.; clear *ta'líq*; rubrications; dated 1201/1786–7. Bought through Quaritch at the O'Kinealy sale on Jan. 15, 1906.

210 (p) بیکت چنتامن **King's, No. 66**

A Persian version of the *Bekat-i-Chantámaní,* undated. See Palmer's *King's Cat.*, p. 25.

211, 212 (h) پدماوت **Corpus, No. 146**
King's, No. 55

The *Padmávat,* a favourite Indian legend. The **Corpus MS.** contains an Urdú verse translation by Ghulám 'Alí Mashhadí and Ḍiyá'u'd-Dín, written in *nasta'líq* on pages of 25 × 17 c., undated, but quite modern, and defective at the end. The **King's MS.** contains a version of the same original in the Brij Bháshá dialect, and is also undated. See Palmer's *King's Cat.*, p. 26.

213 (h) پربوده ناٹك **King's, No. 53**

The *Prabodh Náṭak,* a Hindí work, followed on p. 112 by another Hindí work in verse.

Ff. 130, written in bad Indian *ta'líq* in the 18th year of Muḥammad Sháh. Palmer (*King's Cat.*, pp. 20 and 26) describes this MS. as containing also a work entitled *Badáyi'u'l-Khalq* of which I find no trace.

214 (p) پنج رقعات **Corpus, No. 12[4]**

The *Panj Ruqa'át* of Ẓuhúrí, first part.

Ff. 18, written in cursive *nasta'líq*, and dated 1242/1827.

215–217 (p) پندنامهٔ عطّار **Or. 692 (7) / Or. 923 (9) / Christ's, Dd. 3. 23**

The *Pand-náma*, or "Book of Counsels," of Shaykh Farídu'd-Dín 'Aṭṭár.

Or. 692 contains also a Turkish commentary on the poem by 'Abdu'r-Raḥmán Efendi, who lived in the time of Sulṭán Muḥammad IV (A.D. 1648–1687). It comprises 121 ff. of 19·1 × 13 c. and 19 ll., is written in a fair Turkish *naskh* with rubrications, is undated, and was bought of Géjou in December, 1907. **Or. 923** comprises 80 ff. of 20 × 14·5 c. and 15 ll. in the first part and seven in the second. The former (ff. 1–30) contains an acephalous *Pand-náma*, probably 'Aṭṭár's; the latter (ff. 31–80) a collection of Persian letters, devoid of diacritical points, and very difficult to read. **Christ's, Dd. 3. 23** contains a large selection of Turkish and some Persian poetry, including the *Pand-náma*, and is dated 975/1567–8. Ff. 182.

218 (p) پندنامهٔ سعدی **Corpus, No. 17[4]**

The *Pand-náma*, or "*Karímá*," of Sa'dí of Shíráz.

Ff. 11, written in *ním-shikasta* in 1248/1832–3.

219 (t) پندنامهٔ گلشنی **Or. 175 (8)**

The Turkish *Pand-náma* (or *Pend-námé*) of Gulshaní (Gulshení).

Ff. 32 of 19·4 × 12 c. and 17 ll.; small, neat Turkish *ruq'a* with rubrications, undated, but modern. Bought of Géjou on January 1, 1902.

220 (h) پندنامه (?) **Corpus, No. 99**

An Urdú poem by Ḥájji Walí, entitled, apparently, *Pand-náma*, but the title is very illegible.

Ff. 17 of 18 × 11 c., written in a scrawly *nasta'líq*.

221 (h) پوتهی بهاوتی و غیره **King's, No. 60**

Four poems in .Hindí or Urdú, of which the titles and authors' names are given as follows:

(۱) پوتهی بهاوتی (دکهن) (۲) پوتهی چتراول (فاضل علی)
(۳) سب سیا (بهازی) (٤) فاضل علی پرکاش (سگهدیو)

Written in Indian *ta'líq* with rubrications. See Palmer's *King's Cat.*, p. 26.

222 (? h) پوستك بهاكا **Corpus, No. 133**

A poem bearing the above title in some Indian language other than Urdú but written in the Arabic character, on pages of 24 × 18 c. in good *nasta'líq*, undated.

223 (t) تاج التواريخ **Or. 472 (10)**

Táju't-tawáríkh ("the Crown of History"), a well-known history of the Ottoman Empire from A.H. 670–926 (= A.D. 1271–1520), by Sa'du'd-Dín Ḥasan Khán, known as "*Khoja Efendí.*" See *B. M. T. C.*, pp. 51–3.

Ff. 394 of 24 × 15·5 c. and 22 ll., excellent *naskh* with rubrications, dated 1024/1615. Bought of Géjou, Jan. 29, 1904.

224 (p) تاج المآثر **King's, No. 68**

Táju'l-Ma'áthir, a history of the Emperors of Dihlí from A.H. 587–614 (= A.D. 1191–1217), by Ḥasan Niẓámí. See *B. M. P. C.*, p. 239, and Palmer's *King's Cat.*, p. 6.

225, 226 (p) تأريخ آشام **Christ's, Dd. 3. 7**
Christ's, Dd. 3. 15

Two MSS. of a history of Assam, apparently during the years A.H. 1068–1073 (A.D. 1658–1663), in which last year it was concluded, and of the disastrous campaign of Mír Jumla. Its proper title is *Fatḥiyya 'Ibratiyya.* See *B. M. P. C.*, p. 266. The author is Ibn Muḥammad Walí Aḥmad, surnamed Shihábu'd-Dín Ṭálish. **Dd. 3. 7** contains 121 ff. of 23·6 × 16·4, and was copied at Murshidábád. **Dd. 3. 15** contains 99 ff. of 22·5 × 14·5 c. and 15 ll. Cf. **No. 125** *supra.*

227 (t) تأريخ آل عثمان **Or. 661 (9)**

Ta'ríkh-i-Ál-i-'Othmán, a history of the Ottoman Sultans, by Muḥammad (called *Kyüchük*, "Little") Nishánji (d. 979/1571–2). See *B. M. T. C.*, p. 25.

Ff. 105 of 21·5 × 13·5 c. and 18 ll. Copied in 1000/1591–2, in Turkish *nasta'líq* with rubrications. Bought of Géjou, Feb. 12, 1906.

228 (p) تاريخ احمد شاه دُرّانى **Corpus, No. 180**

A history of Aḥmad Sháh Durrání, by 'Abdu'l-Karím 'Alawí, written in cursive *nasta'líq* on pages of 25 × 16 c., and dated 1281/1864–5. The latter part of the work is written on the margins of the first half.

229 (p) تاريخ الفى **King's, No. 112**

The *Ta'ríkh-i-Alfí*, in two volumes, containing respectively ff. 590 and 752, of which the first is written very well, the second very badly. The history (which should come down to 1000/1592) is incomplete, ending with the death of Tímúr in 708/1308–9.

See Palmer's *King's Cat.*, p. 6.

230 (a) تأريخ بغداد (مختار ذيل—للسّمعانى) **Trinity, R.13.66**

The second volume of an abridgement of as-Sam'ání's continuation of Ibnu'l-Khaṭíb's *Ta'ríkh Baghdád*, or History of Baghdad. See Brockelmann, i, 329–330, and Palmer's *Trin. Cat.*, pp. 152–3. As-Sam'ání died in 562/1167.

The volume contains ff. 202.

231 (p) تأريخ جونپور **Or. 263 (9)**

A history of Jawnpúr by Khayru'd-Dín Muḥammad of Iláh-ábád (Allahabad), presented to the late Professor E. B. Cowell at Jawnpúr on Feb. 22, 1861, by H. C. Acten (?).

Written in poor but clear Indian *ta'líq* with rubrications on pages of 23·2 × 15·4 c. and 9 ll. Cowell Bequest.

232 (p) تأريخ الحكماء **King's, No. 97**

A Persian version of the *Ta'ríkhu'l-Ḥukamá*, or "History of the Philosophers," of Shamsu'd-Dín Muḥammad ash-Shahrazúrí (vii cent. of the *hijra*), presumably the work properly entitled *Rawḍatu'l-Afráḥ wa Nuzhatu'l-Arwáh*. See Brockelmann, i, 468–9.

Ff. 56, undated, written in a bad Indian *shikasta*. See Palmer's *King's Cat.*, p. 6.

233 (a) تأريخ الخميس فى احوال نفس نفيس، **King's, No. 78**

Ta'ríkhu'l-Khamís fí aḥwáli nafs[in] *nafís*, a biography of the Prophet and of his successors down to 982/1574, by Ḥusayn b. Muḥammad b. al-Ḥasan of Diyár Bakr. See Brockelmann, i, 381. This volume comprises a Preface, 3 *Ṭalí'as*, 3 *Rukns*, and 11 *Mawṭins*.

The MS. is dated 1064/1653–4. See Palmer's *King's Cat.*, p. 27.

234 (p) تأريخ دلگشا **King's, No. 71**

Ta'ríkh-i-Dilgushá, a history of Shahjahán and his predecessors, by 'Ináyatu'lláh (d. 1088/1677–8).

See Palmer's *King's Cat.*, p. 7. The MS. is undated.

235 (p) تأريخ دلكشاى شمشير خانى **Corpus, No. 108**

A well-known prose epitome of the *Sháh-náma* of Firdawsí, with extracts from that poem, giving an account of the legendary Kings of Persia, known as *Ta'ríkh-i-Dilgushá-yi-Shamshír-Khání*, by Tawakkul son of Túlak Beg. See *B. M. P. C.*, p. 539[b].

Written in scrawly *nasta'líq* on pages of 21 × 12 c. The last 8 ff. contain a *qaṣída* beginning:

ای دل ار خواهی که ره یابی سوی دار آلجنان،
در مدیح مصطفی و مرتضی بگشا زبان،

236–238 (p) تأريخ رشيدى **Or. 293, 294, 295; Or. 961 (12); Christ's, Dd. 4. 7**

The *Ta'ríkh-i-Rashídí* of Mírzá Ḥaydar Dughlát, son of Muḥammad Ḥusayn Gúrkání, the cousin of Bábur, who founded the so-called Moghul Dynasty in India. See Sir E. Denison Ross's translation of this work entitled a *History of the Moghuls of Central Asia*, by N. Elias and E. D. Ross, London, 1898.

Or. 293–295, copied by Bahá'u'd-Dín in 1272/1855–6 from an original transcribed in Cashmere in 952/1545–6, for the late Professor E. B. Cowell, consists of three volumes comprising ff. 191, 378, and 107 respectively. The leaves, which measure 33 × 23·8 c. and contain about 18 lines each, are written on one side only. Cowell Bequest. **Or. 961,** bought of Sir E. Denison Ross on Nov. 28, 1917, undated, and copied by a scribe of Yárkand named Muḥammad Músá b. Ḥáfiẓ Rúzí b. Mír Qúzí, comprises 146 ff. of 29·8 × 22·3 c. and 23 ll. By an error of the binder, ff. 133–141 are bound after f. 146. The **Christ's MS.,** wrongly described in a note on the title-page as *Tawáríkh-i-Humáyún*, comprises 393 ff. of 25·3 × 16 c. and 15 ll., is clearly written in *ta'líq*, and was presented to the College by John Hutton.

239 (p) تاریخ شهادت فرّخ سیر **King's, No. 94**

History of the death of Farrukh-Siyar and the accession of Muḥammad Sháh by Muḥammad Bakhsh "Áshúb" (d. 1199/1784–5), compiled in 1196/1782, at the request of Jonathan Scott, whom the author met in Colonel Pollier's house at Lucknow. The history ends with the year 1158/1745. See *B. M. P. C.*, p. 944.

Two volumes, written in very bad Indian *shikasta*. See Palmer's *King's Cat.*, p. 7.

240 (p) تأریخ شیر شاه **King's, No. 80**

The history of Shír Sháh, properly entitled *Tuḥfa-i-Akbar-Sháhí* (it was written by order of the Emperor Akbar in 987/1579), by 'Abbás b. Shaykh 'Alí Shirwání. See *B. M. P. C.*, p. 242.

The MS. is dated 1097/1686.

241 (a) **Or. 523 (8)**

تأريخ العارفين و ما ولى فى مصر و الشام من...السلاطين

Ta'ríkhu'l-'Árifín, a history of the Caliphs, Kings and Sultans who reigned in Egypt and Syria, by Shaykh Mar'í b. Yúsuf b. Abí Bakr...al-Karamí al-Maqdisí al-Ḥanbalí (d. 1033/1624). See Brockelmann, ii, 369, No. 18, where for the first two words of the title as given above are substituted the words *Nuzhatu'n-Náẓirín* (نزهة النّاظرين).

Ff. 49 of 21 × 15·6 c. and 27 ll.; very poor *naskh* with rubrications; dated 1161/1748. Bought of Luzac, Aug. 27, 1904.

242 (p) تأريخ العالى فى سلك اللآلى **King's, No. 73**

Ta'ríkhu'l-'Álí fí silki'l-La'álí, a history of the "Mogul" Emperors of Dihlí beginning with the accession of Sháh 'Álam Bahádur Sháh I in 1119/1707–8.

The MS. is dated 1199/1785. See Palmer's *King's Cat.*, p. 7.

تأريخ فرشته

See *infra*, *s.v.* گلشنِ ابراهيمى

243, 244 (p) تأريخ قطبشاهى **Christ's, Dd.4.10**
King's, No. 89

Two MSS. of the *Ta'ríkh-i-Quṭbsháhí*, a history of the Quṭbsháhís of Golconda from the establishment of their power until 1025/1616. See *B. M. P. C.*, pp. 320–321.

The **Christ's MS.** comprises 222 ff. of 24·8 × 15 c. and 15 ll. The **King's MS.** is dated 1199/1784–5. See Palmer's *King's Cat.*, p. 7.

245 (p) تأريخ كشمير **King's, No. 81**

A history of Cashmere (*Ta'ríkh-i-Kishmír*) by Ḥaydar Malik b. Ḥasan Malik b. Malik Muḥammad Nájí, from the earliest times to its conquest by the Emperor Akbar. See *B. M. P. C.*, p. 297^b. It is followed by an account of Cashmere entitled *Ta'ríf-i-Kishmír* by Mullá Ṭughrá.

The MS. is dated 1197/1783. See Palmer's *King's Cat.*, p. 8.

246–248 (p) تأريخ گزيده **Or. 944 (9)**
Or. 967 (13)
King's, No. 114

The well-known manual of general history entitled *Ta'ríkh-i-Guzída* ("the Select History") by Ḥamdu'lláh Mustawfí of Qazwín. See *B. M. P. C.*, pp. 80–82, and the facsimile edition and translation in the "E. J. W. Gibb Memorial Series," vols. xiv, 1 and xiv, 2.

Or. 944 consists of 2 vols. in one case. The first is a MS. of 385 pp. of 22·9 × 14·8 c. and 23 ll. copied at Tabríz in 1225/1810, obtained from M. Richard by Mr G. le Strange at Shíráz in Aug. 1879, and presented to the Library by the latter in Feb. 1916. It is written in a good modern Persian *ta'líq* with rubrications and many marginal glosses and variants in le Strange's and other hands. The second volume contains additions to the above in a note-book containing lxxxvi written pages of 19·7 × 15·9 c. and 12 ll. **Or. 967** is the rough draft of an English translation made by Mr G. le Strange (who presented it to the Library in April, 1918) from M. Richard's MS. (**Or. 944**) mentioned above at Shíráz between August 18, 1879 and Feb. 28, 1880. For the translation Mr le Strange also made use of an old undated MS. belonging to Mírzá Ja'far Khán of Shíráz. The MS., written, save for the concluding pages, on blue paper, comprises 512 pp. measuring 32·8 × 20·3 c. and containing about 53 ll. It begins with a table of contents and ends with 10 pp. of appendices and notes.

The **King's MS.** is undated. See Palmer's *King's Cat.*, p. 8.

249 (p) تأريخ محمود شاه **King's, No. 67**

A history of Maḥmúd Sháh, who ruled over Malwa from 839–873 (1435–1468). See Ethé, *Bodl. Pers. Cat.*, No. 270. The author was 'Alí b. Maḥmúd, called Shiháb-i-Ḥakím.

The MS. is dated 1199/1785. See Palmer's *King's Cat.*, p. 8.

250 (p) تأريخ موسوى **King's, No. 79**

The *Ta'ríkh-i-Músawí*, or "Mosaic History," also entitled *Ta'ríkh-i-Ḥaḍrat-i-Músá*, *Qiṣṣa-i-Múṣawiyya*, and *Mu'jizát-i-Músawí*, by Mu'ínu'd-Dín Muḥammad Amín al-Faráhí al-

Hirawí (d. 907/1501–2). See Ethé's *Ind. Off. Pers. Cat.*, No. 605.

Undated. See Palmer's *King's Cat.*, p. 7.

251 (p) تأريخ مهابت جنگ **King's, No. 111**

Ta'ríkh-i-Mahábat Jang, a history of 'Alí Wirdí Khán Mahábat Jang, completed in 1177/1763–4. See *B.M.P.C.*, p. 312[a].

The MS. is undated. See Palmer's *King's Cat.*, p. 7.

252, 253 (p) تاريخ نادرى موموم بجهان گشا **Christ's, Dd. 3. 3**
King's, No. 101

The *Ta'ríkh-i-Nádirí*, or history of Nádir Sháh, known as *Jahán-gushá* ("the World-Conqueror"), from his rise to his death in 1160/1747, by Muḥammad Mahdí b. Muḥammad Naṣír of Astarábád. See *B. M. P. C.*, pp. 192–5.

The **Christ's MS.**, written in a good clear Persian *ta'líq* at Calcutta, is dated the 14th of Jumáda i, A.H. 1188 (July 23, 1774), and comprises 177 ff. of 25 × 16 c. and 21 ll. with rubrications. The **King's MS.** is undated. See Palmer's *King's Cat.*, p. 8.

254, 255 (p) تأريخ وصّاف **Or. 485 (12)**
King's, No. 95

The *Ta'ríkh-i-Waṣṣáf*, properly entitled *Tajziyatu'l-Amṣár wa tazjiyatu'l-A'ṣár*, a well-known history of the Mongol rulers of Persia from 656–712 (1258–1312) by 'Abdu'lláh b. Faḍlu'lláh of Shíráz, better known as *Waṣṣáfu'l-Ḥaḍrat*, "the Court Panegyrist." See *B.M.P.C.*, pp. 161–164.

Or. 485 comprises the first three volumes only, and contains ff. 267 of 30 × 16·75 c. and 23 ll.; good *nasta'líq* with rubrications; Arabic citations in *naskh*; undated. Bought of Géjou, August 18, 1904. The **King's MS.** contains all five volumes, but the fifth is defective at the end, and comprises ff. 410. See Palmer's *King's Cat.*

256 (p) تأريخ همايونى **King's, No. 84**

Memoirs of the reign of Humáyún, also entitled *Tadhkiratu'l-Wáqi'át*, by Jawhar Áftábchí, who began to write it in

995/1587. See *B.M.P.C.*, p. 246a, Elliot's *Hist. of India*, v, pp. 136–149, and for this MS. Palmer's *King's Cat.*, p. 8.

257 (a) تأويلات القرآن **Or. 492 (10)**

Ta'wílátu'l-Qur'án ("Interpretations of the *Qur'án*"), by Kamálu'd-Dín Abu'l-Ghaná'im 'Abdu'r-Razzáq b. Jamálu'd-Dín al-Káshání as-Samarqandí (d. 887/1482). See Brockelmann, ii, p. 203, and cf. p. 205, l. 2; *B.M.A.C.*, p. 400; and Ḥájji Khalífa (ed. Flügel), vol. ii, p. 175, No. 2358. Ff. 206 of 25·3 × 15 c. and 19 ll.; good, clear, large *naskh*; no date or colophon.

258 (a) تائيّة ابن الفارض مع شرح **Add. 3668 (8)**

The *Tá'iyya*, or "T-poem," of the great mystic poet 'Umar b. al-Fáriḍ (d. 632/1235), with the commentary of Sharafu'd-Dín Dáwúd b. Maḥmúd b. Muḥammad ar-Rúmí al-Qayṣarí (d. 751/1350). See Brockelmann, ii, 231, where, however, this work is not mentioned, and *Ibid.*, i, 263, l. 10.

Ff. 152 of 20 × 13·6 c. and 27 ll.; fair *naskh*, rubrications, dated 10 Rabí'i, 1117 (July 2, 1705). Bought of Sethian, July 17, 1900.

259 (t) التبر المسبوك فى نصيحة الملوك **Trinity, R.13.26**

Naṣíḥatu'l-Mulúk ("Counsels for Kings"), a Turkish translation of *at-Tibru'l-Masbúk fí Naṣíḥati'l-Mulúk*, by the celebrated divine Abú Ḥámid Muḥammad al-Ghazzálí (d. 505/1111).

See Brockelmann, i, 423, No. 30.

Ff. 170, *naskh*, gold margins.

260 (a) التبصرة فى علم الهيئة **Trinity, R.13.10**

At-Tabṣirat fí 'ilmi'l-Hay'at, a work on Geometry and Astronomy by Shamsu'd-Dín Abú Bakr Muḥammad b. Aḥmad b. Abí Bashar al-Marwazí.

Ff. 60, *naskh* handwriting, dated A.D. 1600.

261 (a) التتمّة لكلماتٍ لم يذكرها النّاظم **Add. 3623[4] (7)**

A poem of 32 verses, on ff. 72a–73a of the MS. indicated above, entitled *Tatimma*, or "Supplement to words not mentioned by the versifier." It appears to be of a grammatical character.

Bought of Géjou, Feb. 14, 1900. Dated 891/1486.

262, 263 (a) تجريد العقائد مع شرح **Or. 439 (10) King's, No. 234**

The *Tajrídu'l-'Aqá'id* of Naṣíru'd-Dín Ṭúsí (d. 672/1273–4) with the Commentary of Abu'l-Qásim 'Alá'u'd-Dín 'Alí b. Muḥammad al-Qúshjí as-Samarqandí (d. 879/1474–5). See Brockelmann, i, p. 509, No. 2, *c*.

Or. 439 comprises ff. 192 of 24·5 × 18·5 c. and 21 ll.; good *nasta'líq* with marginal notes; dated 1098/1686–7; bought of Hannan, Watson and Co., August 29, 1903. The **King's MS.** comprises ff. 375 of 25·6 × 15 c., is written in a good scholarly *ta'líq*, and is undated.

تجزية الأمصار و تزجية الاعصار

See above under *Ta'ríkh-i-Waṣṣáf* (تأريخ وصّاف).

264 (a) تحرير العوائد و تفريد العوائد **Or. 213 (10)**

Taḥríru'l-'Awá'id, apparently the commentary of Muḥammad Sharíf al-Ḥusayní on al-Íjí's *al-Fawá'idu'l-Ghiyáthiyya*. See Brockelmann, ii, p. 209, ix, 2.

Ff. 40 of 26·3 × 18 c. and 21 ll., excellent *ta'líq* with rubrications, dated 883/1478–9. Bought of Naaman, Nov. 12, 1902.

265 (p) تحفة الأبرار (ملخّص —) **Or. 430 (6)**

An abridgement, entitled *Wajíza*, of the *Tuḥfatu'l-Abrár* of Muḥammad Ja'far b. Muḥammad Ṣafí al-Fársí, and other tracts.

Ff. 115 of 14·4 × 10·3 c. and 17 lines; small, neat *naskh*; dated 1264/1848; acephalous. Bought of Hannan and Watson, Aug. 29, 1903.

266 (p) تحفة الأحباب، **Jesus College, No. 2**

Tuḥfatu'l-Aḥbáb, "an Essay in Ethics and Morals in the Persian language," in 20 chapters, including also sonnets by various Persian poets, such as Mír Naját, Mírzá Mu'izz of

Mashhad, Mírzá Amín Munshí, Ṭálib, Ṣafí-qulí Beg, Ṭálib-i-Kalím, Wá'iẓ, Shawkat, Mahdí, Humáyún, Adham, Mír Ṣaydí, Shápúr, 'Arshí of Yazd, Nawá'í, 'Urfí, Áqá Ḥusayn, Qudsí, Iḥsán, Mírzá Raḍí, Dánish, etc.

A small neat volume measuring 13·5 × 8·8 c.

267–270 (p) تحفة الأحرار **Add. 3663[1] (10) / Add. 3678 (8) / Christ's, Dd.4.8 / Corpus, No. 237**

Four copies of Jámí's well-known poem the *Tuḥfatu'l-Aḥrár*, or "Gift of the Free."

Add. 3663 comprises ff. 168 (of which this portion fills ff. 1^{b}–63^{a}) of 25 × 16 c. and 15 ll., and is written in excellent *ta'líq*, with headings in blue and gold. Not dated, but probably sixteenth century. Bought of Naaman on June 3, 1900. **Add. 3678** contains the *Tuḥfatu'l-Aḥrár* in the margins and the *Sibḥatu'l-Abrár* in the body of the page. Ff. 94 of 19 × 12·1 c., with 17 ll. in text and 32 ll. in margin; good *ta'líq* with rubrications; dated 1000/1591–2. Bought of Breslauer and Meyer, Aug. 11, 1900. The **Christ's MS.** also contains both poems. It is a fine MS. written in good Persian *ta'líq* on 180 ff. of 24·4 × 17·3 c. and 14 ll., and bearing the seal of Edward Galley. It is undated, but the date 1166/1752–3 occurs with a former owner's name on the fly-leaf. The **Corpus MS.** is undated, and is written in *nasta'líq* on leaves of 19 × 12 c.

271 (t) تحفة الحرمين **Or. 598 (7)**

The *Tuḥfatu'l-Ḥaramayn* of Yúsuf Nábí. See *B.M.T.C.*, p. 113.

Ff. 85 of 18·5 × 11·7 c. and 19 ll.; fair *ta'líq* with rubrications; dated 1092/1681. Bought of Géjou, Oct. 30, 1905.

272 (p) تحفهٔ سامی **Or. 648 (11)**

The well-known biography of Persian poets entitled *Tuḥfa-i-Sámí*, by Sám Mírzá, son of Sháh Isma'íl the Ṣafawí, who was put to death in 984/1576–7. See *B.M.P.C.*, pp. 367–8.

Pp. 213 of 27·5 × 18·8 c. and 19 ll.; poor *ta'líq* with rubrications; copied at 'Azímábád in 1280/1863–4. Bought through Quaritch at the O'Kinealy sale on Jan. 15, 1906.

273 (a) التحفة السّعديّة **King's, No. 228**

At-Tuhfatu's-Sa'diyya, a commentary on the *Kulliyyát*, or General Principles, of the *Qánún* of Avicenna, by Mahmúd b. Mas'úd of Shíráz, known as Qutbu'd-Dín (d. 710/1312). See Brockelmann, ii, p. 212, No. 7.

A bulky volume of which the pages measure 26 × 19·3 c. Copied by 'Alí Naqí Ni'matu'lláhí.

274, 275 (p, t) تحفهٔ شاهدی **Queens', No. 11**
Trinity, R. 13. 28

A well-known rhymed Persian-Turkish vocabulary known as *Tuhfa-i-Sháhidí*, composed by Sháhidí of Broussa in 920/1514–5. See *B.M.P.C.*, pp. 513–514.

The **Trinity MS.** comprises 20 ff. and is vocalized throughout.

276 (p) تحفة الصّدور **Trinity, R. 13. 29**

Tuhfatu's-Sudúr, a work on geometry and mensuration, by Muhammad 'Abdu'l-Karím ad-Dájí al-Ghaznawí, composed in A.D. 1247.

The MS., which comprises ff. 87, was transcribed in A.D. 1526. See Palmer's *Trin. Cat.*, p. 61.

277 (a) تحفة الطّلاب بشرح تحرير تنقيح اللّباب **Add. 3664**

Tuhfatu't-Tulláb, a commentary on the *Tahríru Tanqíhi'l-Lubáb* of Abú Yahyá Zakariyyá al-Ansárí (d. 926/1520), which is itself based on the *Kitábu'l-Lubáb fi'l-Fiqh* of Abú Zur'a al-'Iráqí (d. 826/1423). See Brockelmann, i, 181.

Ff. 144 of 20·2 × 14·6 c. and 23 ll.; good *naskh* with rubrications; dated 1094/1683. Bought of Sethian, July 17, 1900.

278, 279 (p) تحفة العراقيْن خاقانی **Or. 277 (9)**
King's, No. 115

Kháqání's well-known *mathnawí* poem entitled *Tuhfatu'l-'Iráqayn*. See *B.M.P.C.*, p. 560.

Or. 277, copied in 1100/1688, forms part of the Cowell Bequest, and comprises ff. 104 of 23·2 × 14 c. and 17 ll., and is written in a good *ta'líq* with rubrications. The **King's MS.** was transcribed in 1072/1661–2.

280 (p) تحفة الفوائد (—القواعد؟) **Corpus, No. 42**

A work on Medicine called *Tuḥfatu'l-Fawá'id* (or — -*Qawá'id*). There is a lacuna after f. 1, and the colophon has been erased, only the word *Tuḥfa* being legible in it. On the inside of the cover the title is given as *Tuḥfatu'l-Qawá'id.*

281 (p) تحفة الفقه **Corpus, No. 6**

A collection of excerpts on Muslim Law, arranged according to subjects (*e.g.* Marriage, Punishments, Holy War, etc.), apparently for the compiler's own use. In a note on the last leaf the title stands as above, but on the fly-leaf at the beginning as *Bayáḍu'l-Fiqh* (بياض الفقه).

Ff. 135 of 26 × 15 c., undated, *shikasta* hand.

282 (a, p) التحفة فى الأدب **Trinity, R. 13. 62**

An Arabic-Persian Vocabulary of Synonyms, entitled *at-Tuḥfa fi'l-Adab.* See Palmer's *Trin. Cat.*, pp. 150–151.

283 (p) تحفهٔ قاسميّه **Or. 211⁴ (8)**

A Persian lexicographical work entitled *Tuḥfa-i-Qásimiyya*, by Luṭfu'lláh b. Abí Yúsuf Ḥalímí.

Ff. 42^b–65 of 18·8 × 12·3 c. and 12 ll. with interlinear notes; neat, small *nasta'líq*; rubrications; undated. Bought of Naaman, Oct. 12, 1902.

تحفة المأكولات و غيره **Christ's, Dd. 3. 2**

A collection of Cookery-books, containing recipes etc., of which the first is entitled *Tuḥfatu'l-Ma'kúlát.* See *Part II, Untitled MSS., Section vi, ii* (Medicine, *etc.*).

284 (t) تحفة المنازل و تحفة الحفّاظ **Or. 662 (8)**

Two Turkish works in verse, by Ḥájji Sayyid Ḥasan Riḍá'í of Áq-saráy, son of Ḥájji 'Abdu'r-Raḥmán of Qarámán. The first, entitled *Tuḥfatu'l-Manázil*, treats of the stages of the Pilgrimage; the second, entitled *Tuḥfa-i-Ḥuffáẓ-i-Qastamúní*, of those who knew the *Qur'án* by heart.

Ff. 60 of 20·7 × 14·3 c. and 11 ll.; poor *nasta'líq*; dated 1075/1664–5. Bought of Géjou, Feb. 12, 1906.

285, 286 (p) تحفة آلمؤمنين **Add. 3743 (11)**
King's, No. 82

A work on Medicine by Muḥammad Mú'min-i-Ḥusayní, son of Mír Muḥammad Zamán-i-Tunukábuní-i-Daylamí, physician to Sulaymán Sháh the Ṣafawí, entitled *Tuḥfatu'l-Mú'minín*. See *B.M.P.C.*, pp. 476–7, and Palmer, *King's Cat.*, p. 8.

Add. 3743 comprises ff. 414 of 26·5 × 17·3 c. and 21 ll.; written in fair *ta'líq* with rubrications, and undated. It was bought of Géjou on Dec. 2, 1900. The **King's MS.** is dated 1199/1784–5.

287 (a) التحفة الورديّة **Add. 3623^{1-2} (7)**

A grammatical work entitled *at-Tuḥfatu'l-Wardiyya* by Zaynu'd-Dín Abú Ḥafṣ 'Umar b. Muẓaffar b. Muḥammad al-Wardí al-Ma'arrí, with a commentary by the author.

The text with commentary occupies ff. 1^b–51^a, and the text alone ff. 52^a–59^b. The pages measure 17·2 × 13 c. and contain 17 ll. each, written in fair *naskh* with rubrications, and dated, apparently, 891/1486. Bought of Géjou, Feb. 14, 1900.

288 (p) تحفة الهند **King's, No. 119**

The *Tuḥfatu'l-Hind* of Mírzá Muḥammad b. Fakhru'd-Dín Muḥammad, comprising 7 chapters (*Báb*) and a conclusion (*Khátima*). See *B.M.P.C.*, p. 62, Sprenger's *Cat.*, Nos. 1655–6, and Palmer's *King's Cat.*, p. 8. The MS. is undated.

289 (p) تذكرة الأبرار و الأشرار **King's, No. 103**

The *Tadhkiratu'l-Abrár wa'l-Ashrár*, by Ákhúnd Darwíza, composed in 1021/1612–3, a controversial work in which the author gives an account of the true and false doctrines of his own time. See *B.M.P.C.*, p. 28^a, and Palmer's *King's Cat.*, p. 8. The MS. is dated 1199/1784–5.

290 (p) تذکرهٔ اوستادان اهل فارس **Corpus, No. 191[2]**

A fragment, comprising ff. 30, of a work apparently entitled *Tadhkira-i-Ústádán-i-ahl-i-Fárs* ("Memoirs of Persian Masters"). It begins abruptly, without doxology, with the words "Beginning of the Memoirs," and a piece of verse, and ends equally abruptly. The shorter first chapter consists of poetical extracts with remarks on the metres; the second is headed "Explanation of verbal artifices" (دربیان بدایع لفظی).

291 (p) تذکرة الأولياء **King's, No. 75**

A copy of Shaykh Farídu'd-Dín 'Aṭṭár's well-known *Tadhkiratu'l-Awliyá* ("Memoirs of the Saints"), of which the text has been edited in my *Persian Historical Texts Series* (2 vols.) by Dr R. A. Nicholson.

Copied by Núr Muḥammad. See Palmer's *King's Cat.*, p. 9.

292–295 (p) تذکرة الشعراء دولتشاه **Add. 3638 (9)**, **Or. 278 (8)**, **Or. 518 (8)**, **King's, No. 106**

Four MSS. of the well-known Memoirs of the Poets (*Tadhkiratu'sh-Shu'ará*) of Dawlatsháh b. Bakhtísháh of Samarqand, of which the text was published as the first volume of my *Persian Historical Texts Series.*

Add. 3638 comprises ff. 325 of 21·3 × 13·5 c. and 17 ll., defective at end, undated, good *ta'líq* with rubrications. **Or. 278** comprises ff. 146 of 21 × 13·5 c. and 17 ll., poor *ta'líq* with rubrications, dated 1038/1628–9, and forms part of the Cowell Bequest. **Or. 518** comprises ff. 281 of 20·7 × 14 c. and 14 ll., good *ta'líq*, with rubrications, with quite modern supply at end, undated, bought of Hannan and Watson, August 20, 1904. The **King's MS.** comprises ff. 331 and is undated. See Palmer's *King's Cat.*, p. 9.

296 (p) تذکرة الشعراء (کلمات الشعراء) **King's, No. 92**

Notices of poets who flourished during the reigns of the Moghul Emperors Jahángír, Sháhjahán and 'Álamgír. See Palmer's *King's Cat.*, p. 9, Sprenger's *Oude Cat.*, pp. 108–115, and *B.M.P.C.*, p. 369, where the work is entitled *Kalimátu'sh-Shu'ará.* It was compiled by Muḥammad Afḍal, poetically named *Sar-Khush*, in 1093/1682.

297, 298 (t) تذكرة الشعراء لطيفى **Add. 3654 (9) Or. 597 (7)**

Two MSS. of the well-known Biography of Turkish Poets by 'Abdu'l-Laṭíf, poetically surnamed *Laṭífí*, of which the text was printed at Constantinople in 1314/1896–7.

Add. 3654 is acephalous, the missing portion corresponding with the first 48 pages of the Constantinople edition. It comprises ff. 128 of 21·3 × 15 c. and 15 ll., is written in a fair *nasta'líq* with rubrications, and is dated 962/1555. **Or. 597** comprises ff. 139 of 19 × 12·5 c. and 17 ll., is written in a good *ta'líq* with rubrications, is dated 960/1553, and was bought of Géjou on Oct. 30, 1905.

299 (p) تذكرهٔ صيديّه **King's, No. 199**

A treatise on the properties of different animals, entitled *Tadhkira-i-Ṣaydiyya* or *Risála dar Khawaṣṣ-i-Ḥaywánát*, by Ibn Abí Ṭálib az-Záhidí al-Jílání, known as 'Alí, said to be the well-known Shaykh 'Alí Ḥazín (d. 1180/1766–7). See Palmer's *King's Cat.*, p. 14.

300 (p) تذكرهٔ شيخ محمّد على حزين **King's, No. 74**

Memoirs of the above-mentioned Shaykh 'Alí Ḥazín, composed in 1154/1741–2, of which the text with an English translation was published by F. C. Balfour. See *B.M.P.C.*, p. 381*a*. The author was born at Iṣfahán in 1103/1691–2, reached India in 1146/1733–4, and died, as stated above, in 1180/1766–7, at Benares.

301, 302 (a) تذكرة العماد . . فى فضائل دمشق الشّام **Or. 708 (8) Or. 742 (7)**

Two copies of a treatise on the excellence of Damascus and Syria by Shaykh 'Imádu'd-Dín b. Muḥammad al-Ḥanafí (d. 920/1514). See Brockelmann, ii, p. 133, No. 15.

Or. 708 comprises ff. 27 of 20·8 × 15 c. and 19 ll., written in *ta'líq* with rubrications, dated 1160/1747, and bought of

Géjou, Dec. 1906. **Or. 742** comprises ff. 64 of 19 × 12·3 and 13 ll.; good modern *naskh* with rubrications; undated; bought of Géjou, March 27, 1907.

303 (a) التّذكرة فى تفصيل احوال الأمراض **Add. 3754** (9)

A treatise on the diagnosis, aetiology, symptoms and treatment of diseases, the fourth chapter only, defective at the end, undated, and authorship undetermined.

Ff. 136 of 23 × 14·8 c. and 18 ll.; small, neat *naskh*; bought of Géjou, Dec. 8, 1900.

304 (p, h) **Corpus, No. 159**[2]

تذكرهٔ مختصر در حال ريخته گويان هند

An Anthology of Urdú poems, with connecting text in Persian, by Muḥammad Ṣadru'd-Dín. The names of the poets are arranged alphabetically, but the work is incomplete, and breaks of in the middle of the letter ق. Undated.

305 (a) تذهيب التهذيب **King's, No. 83**

A work in six chapters on Logic and Scholastic Theology, entitled *Tadhhíbu't-Tahdhíb*, headed:

هذا قسم الكلام من التهذيب و على السنّة وقع التبويب ,

The author's name does not appear. See Palmer's *King's Cat.*, p. 27. Good, clear, modern *naskh*, undated.

306 (a, p) ترجمة الصّلوة **Corpus, No. 12**[3]

Arabic prayers, with Persian translation and comments, by Muḥsin b. Murtaḍá.

Ff. 16, written in *naskh* and *nasta'líq*, undated.

307 (p) تركيب پختن طعام **Corpus, No. 12**[1]

A Persian Cookery-book, entitled *Tarkíb-i-pukhtan-i-ṭa'ám*, by Qásim 'Alí Khán Bahádur.

Ff. 7, fair *nasta'líq*, undated.

308 (p) تزوكات تيمور **Christ's, Dd. 3. 20**

The *Tuzúkát*, or "Institutes" of Tímúr (Tamerlane). See *B.M.P.C.*, p. 177[b], where the arguments against the genuineness of this work are well set forth.

Written in fair *ta'líq*, with quaint illuminations, and dated the 26th year of the Regnal Era of ...(?). Ff. 113 of 20·8 × 11 c. and 12 ll.

309 (p) تسنيم المقرّبين فى شرح منازل السّائرين **Or. 514** (9)

A commentary on the *Manázilu's-Sá'irín* of the Shaykhu'l-Islám 'Abdu'lláh al-Anṣárí (d. 481/1088–9), by Shaykh Muḥammad b. Shír Muḥammad, entitled *Tasnímu'l-Muqarrabín*.

Ff. 213 of 24·5 × 14 c. and 17 ll., written in clear, coarse Persian *ta'líq*, and dated 1005/1596–7. One of 30 MSS. bought of Hannan and Watson on August 20, 1904.

310 (a) **Trinity, R.13.43**[3]

تسهيل الصّالحى فى جامع اصول الوغ بيگى

The *Tashíl*, a commentary on the *Zíj*, or Astronomical Tables, of Ulúgh Beg (d. 853/1449) the grandson of Sháh-rukh, by 'Abdu'r-Raḥmán aṣ-Ṣáliḥí ash-Sham'í. See Brockelmann, ii, 213*b*.

This work occupies ff. 112–211 of the MS. See Palmer's *Trinity Cat.*, p. 101.

311, 312 (t) تضرّعات (تضرّع نامه) سنان پاشا **Or. 546** (7) **Queens', No. 10**

The *Taḍarru'át*, or Supplications, of Sinán Pasha.

Or. 546 comprises ff. 64 of 17·3 × 9·9 c. and 21 ll., written in fair Turkish *naskh* with rubrications by 'Uthmán al-Jundí in 1027/1618, and bought of Géjou on Jan. 4, 1905. The **Queens' MS.** only bears the last two figures of the year of transcription, '99, and is written in clear *naskh* on pages of 21 × 15·3 c. and 18 ll.

313 (p) تعبيرنامهٔ خواب **Corpus, No. 12**[6]

A *Ta'bír-náma*, or Book of Interpretation of Dreams, ascribed to the Imám Ja'far-i-Ṣádiq.

Ff. 5, written in *ním-shikasta*, and dated 1242/1827.

314 (t) تعبيرنامهٔ روياى مطوّل **Queens', No. 13**

A Turkish work on the Interpretation of Dreams in 53 chapters, written in clear *naskh*, fully pointed, on leaves of 20 × 11·5 c. and 11 lines.

315 (a) تعريقات الجرجانى **Or. 482 (8)**

A MS. of the well-known *Ta'rífát* or "Definitions" of as-Sayyid ash-Sharíf al-Jurjání (d. 816/1413), edited by Flügel in 1845. See Brockelmann, ii, p. 216.

Ff. 79 of 20·25 × 13·25 c. and 21 ll.; dated 969/1561–2. One of 16 MSS. bought of Géjou on August 18, 1904.

316 (p) تعزيهها **Or. 503 (8)**

Poems in mourning (*ta'ziya*) for the Imám Ḥusayn *etc.*, by Mír Aḥmad Riḍá.

Ff. 20 of 21 × 15·3 c. and 15 ll.; excellent modern Persian *naskh*; undated. Bought of Hannan and Watson, August 20, 1904.

317 (a) تعليقات ملّا صدرا الشيرازى **Or. 495 (9)**

The *Ta'líqát*, or Notes, of Mullá Ṣadrá of Shíráz (d. 1050/1640), the most celebrated of the later Persian philosophers.

Ff. 240 of 22 × 13 c. and 23 ll.; small, neat *naskh* with rubrications; dated 1260/1844. One of 30 MSS. bought of Hannan and Watson on August 20, 1904.

318 (a) تعليم المتعلّم لتعلّم طريق العلم **Or. 15 (7)**

A work on Pedagogy, entitled *Ta'límu'l-Muta'allim li-Ta'allumi Ṭaríqi'l-'Ilm*, by Burhánu'd-Dín az-Zarnújí (d. 600/1203). See Ḥájji Khalífa, No. 3134; Brockelmann, i, 462.

Ff. 16 of 18·8 × 12·7 c. and 23 ll.; small and very neat *naskh* with rubrications; dated 1084/1673–4. Bought of Naaman, Feb. 5, 1901.

319 (a) تفسير اورنگزيبى **King's, No. 91**

A Commentary on the *Qur'án*, entitled *Tafsír-i-Awrang-zíbí*, by Mu'ínu'd-Dín b. Ṣadr, one of the disciples of Khwája Kháwand Maḥmúd an-Naqshbandí al-'Alawí al-Ḥusayní.

Fine large *naskh*, text in black, commentary in red, headings in gold and blue. The running commentary is brief. Dated 1075/1664–5. See Palmer's *King's Cat.*, p. 27.

320 (a. **تفسير القرآن** **Or. 477 (8)**

An anonymous and untitled commentary on part of the *Qur'án*, from *Súra* xxxviii to end, defective at beginning and end, and without any indication of title or authorship.

Ff. 201 of 19·7 × 15 c. and 27 ll.; written in clear *naskh* of the fourteenth or fifteenth century of our era, with rubrications.

321 (a) **تفسير القرآن** **Add. 3634**

Explanation of certain verses in the *Qur'án* dealing with the position of women, *etc.* (*Súra* iv, verses 23, 26 and 27).

Ff. 16 of 24·8 × 16·5 c. and 19 ll.; large, clear modern *naskh* with rubrications.

322 (a) **تفسير سورة الفاتحة و سورة البقرة** **Or. 445[1] (9)**

A commentary on the two first chapters of the *Qur'án*, the *Súratu'l-Fátiḥa* and *Ṣúratu'l-Baqara* (*Súra* i, 1—ii, 161), with copious explanations and marginal notes in Persian.

Ff. 89 (of which this portion occupies ff. 1–38), of 22 × 18 c.; poor *naskh*.

323 (a) **تفسير مشكلات القرآن** **Or. 739 (10)**

An explanation of difficult words and passages in the *Qur'án*, by Muḥammad b. Abí Bakr b. 'Abdu'l-Qádir ar-Rázi (d. 720/1320). *Cf.* Brockelmann, ii, 200, where what is almost certainly this work is described under a slightly different title; *B. M. A. C.*[1], p. 227; and Ḥájji Khalífa, i, 296, No. 733.

Copied in 1088/1677–8, by Ibn Muḥammad al-Jurbádhaqání. Ff. 165 of 24·5 × 18·5 c. and 21 ll.; legible *naskh* with rubrications.

324 (h) **تقوية المؤمنين و هداية الرافضيين** **Corpus, No. 150[3]**

This work, entitled *Tuqwiyatu'l-Mú'minín wa Hidáyatu'r-Ráfiḍiyyín*, by Karámat 'Alí the Preacher (*Wá'iẓ*) of Jawnpúr, though placed amongst the manuscripts, is really lithographed. It is undated, and comprises 79 pp.

325–328 (a) **Add. 3648 (8), Or. 450 (10) Or. 590 (7), King's, No. 146**

تلخيص المفتاح مع شروحٍ و حواشٍ

The well-known *Talkhíṣu'l-Miftáḥ* of Jamálu'd-Dín Muḥammad b. 'Abdu'r-Raḥmán al-Qazwíní (d. 739/1338), known as *al-Khaṭíbu'd-Dimashqí*, with various glosses and commentaries. See Brockelmann, i, 294–6.

Add. 3648 contains the glosses or super-glosses on the text of 'Abdu'lláh b. Shihábu'd-Dín al-Yazdí (d. 1015/1606), and comprises ff. 115 of 20·4 × 11·6 c. and 15 ll., written in fair *ta'líq* with rubrications, and dated 1073/1662–3. It was bought of Sethian on May 9, 1900. **Or. 450** contains an acephalous and unidentified commentary on the text, comprises ff. 83 of 25·8 × 13 c. and 18 ll., and is written in good *nasta'líq*, the text overlined with red, and is dated 1023/1614. It was bought of Messrs Hannan and Watson on August 29, 1903. **Or. 590** contains the text of the *Talkhíṣ* in ff. 81 of 17·5 × 14·3 c. and 11 ll., written in large and fairly clear *naskh* with rubrications, dated 734/1334, but the first five leaves supplied in a modern hand. It was bought of Géjou on Oct. 30, 1905. **King's, No. 146** contains the glosses of Mawláná Ḥasan Chelebí, and comprises ff. 293 written in poor *ta'líq* with rubrications.

329 (a) تلويح توضيح التّنقيح **King's, No. 69**

The *Tanqíḥu'l-Uṣúl*, apparently of 'Ubaydu'lláh b. Mas'úd al-Maḥbúbí (d. 746/1346), with the author's commentary entitled *at-Tawḍíḥ*, and the super-commentary entitled *Talwíḥ* of at-Taftázání. Concerning all three, see Brockelmann, ii, 214.

An undated colophon states that the MS. was copied by a student named Sayyid Táju'd-Dín and corrected by 'Abdu'r-Rasúl the lecturer. See Palmer's *King's Cat.*, p. 27.

330 (t) تنقيح تواريخ الملوك **Or. 491 (10)**

A general history in Turkish entitled *Tanqíḥ-i-Tawáríkh-i-Mulúk*, composed in 1081–3/1670–1672 by Ḥusayn "Hazár-Fann."

Ff. 257 of 26 × 16·5 c. and 23 ll.; good clear Turkish *naskh*; bought of Géjou, Aug. 18, 1904.

331 (h) تواریخ مسب نامهٔ قدیم زمانه **Corpus, No. 63**

A Hindustání prose narrative of the sufferings of the two Imáms Ḥasan and Ḥusayn.

The leaves measure 24 × 16 c. and are written in *nasta'líq*. Date of transcription 1243/1827–8 or 1273/1856–7.

332 (h) تواریخ بلند شهر **Corpus, No. 165**

The History of Buland-shahr, by Ráy Mangal Sin, lithographed at Buland-shahr in A.D. 1863. It comprises pp. 192 of 25 × 16 c.

333, 334 (p) توزك جهانگیری **Or. 252 (12)**
King's, No. 88

The *Túzuk-i-Jahángírí* of Muḥammad Hádí, also known as the *Jahángír-náma*. See *B. M. P. C.*, pp. 253–6.

Or. 252 comprises pp. 903 of 29·6 × 16·5 and 15 ll., is written in clear Indian *ta'líq* and dated 1232/1816–7, and forms part of the Cowell Bequest. **King's, No. 88** consists of three volumes, each of which contains about 200 leaves. See Palmer's *King's Cat.*, pp. 9–10.

335–337 (p) توقیعات کسری
Corpus, No. 18[1]
Corpus, No. 65[4]
Corpus, No. 184

Three copies of the *Tawqí'át-i-Kisrá*, or so-called "Institutes of Kisra" (Khusraw) Anúsharwán (Núshírwán) the Sasanian, by Jalálu'd-Dín Ṭabáṭabá'í of Iṣfahán, who came to India in 1044/1634–5. See *B. M. P. C.*, p. 258. This work was published with an English translation by W. Young, under the title of *The Wisdom of Naushirwan*, at Lucknow in 1892.

Of these three Corpus MSS. **No. 18**[1], undated, is written in a clear *nasta'líq*, with glosses, on leaves measuring 25 × 16 c. **No. 65**[4], dated 1256/1840–1, is of the same size and in a similar hand. **No. 184,** undated, is written in a fine large *nasta'líq* on leaves of 29 × 17 c.

338 (a) تهافت التهافت **Or. 165** (8)

The *Tahāfutu't-Tahāfut* ("Destruction of *the Destruction*"), the celebrated refutation of al-Ghazálí's *Tahāfutu'l-Falásifa* ("Destruction of the Philosophers") by al-Walíd b. Rushd, better known as Averrhoes (d. 595/1198). See Brockelmann, i, 425 and 462 and references there given.

Ff. 166 of 21 × 14·3 c. and 23 ll.; small neat *naskh* with rubrications; undated; bought of Naaman, Dec. 6, 1901.

339 (a) تهذيب الأحكام (اجزاء من—) **Or. 447**[2] **(10)**

Portions of the *Tahdhíbu'l-Aḥkám* of Shaykh Muḥammad b. Ḥasan aṭ-Ṭúsí (d. 459/1067). See Brockelmann, i, 405, and for description of the MS. under ارشاد الاذهان, No. **43** *supra.*

340 (a) تهذيب المنطق **King's, No. 251**

A work on Logic entitled *Tahdhíbu'l-Manṭiq*, ascribed to Jamálu'd-Dín Muḥammad b. Maḥmúd al-Ḥusayní ash-Shahristání, but it appears to be in reality the work of this title by Sa'du'd-Dín Mas'úd at-Taftázání (d. 791/1389). See Palmer's *King's Cat.*, p. 17.

341 (p) تيسير البخارى فى شرح صحيح البخارى **King's, No. 100**

A Persian commentary entitled *Taysír* ("the Facilitation") on the well-known Corpus of Traditions known as the *Ṣaḥíḥ* of al-Bukhárí, by Núru'l-Ḥaqq b.'Abdu'l-Ḥaqq of Delhi (d. 1073/1662–3). The MS. comprises two large volumes, dated 1055/1645 and 1153/1740 respectively, and covers about half of the original text. Some account of the author and his father will be found on pp. 223–4 of *B. M. P. C.* See also Palmer's *King's Cat.*, p. 17.

342 (a) تيسير التفسير **Trinity, R. 13. 41**[3]

A small tract (ff. 141–6 of the MS. in question) entitled *Taysíru't-Tafsír* ("the Facilitation of Exegesis"), by Najmu'd-Dín 'Umar an-Nasafí (d. 537/1142). See Palmer's *King's Cat.*, p. 91, and Brockelmann, i, 427–8, where, however, this work is not mentioned.

343 (a) [كتاب] التّيسير فى القرآة **Add. 3719$^{1-2}$ (9)**

The *Kitábu't-Taysír fi'l-Qirá'at*, a guide to the proper reading of the *Qur'án*, by Abú 'Amr 'Uthmán b. Sa'íd ad-Dání (d. 444/1053). See Brockelmann, i, 407, and *B. M. A. C.*², p. 48, No. 84, and references there given.

Ff. 120 (out of 164) of 22 × 15·5 c. and 15 ll., written in clear but clumsy *naskh* with rubrications.

344 (p) تيمور نامه (= ظفرنامهٔ) هاتفى **King's, No. 85**

The versified history of Tímúr-i-Lang known as *Tímúr-náma* or *Ẓafar-náma* by Hátifí (d. 927/1520), nephew of the celebrated poet Jámí. See *B. M. P. C.*, pp. 652–3.

See Palmer's *King's Cat.*, p. 10. The MS. is undated.

345 (a) ثمار القلوب فى المضاف و المنسوب **Or. 828 (8)**

Thimáru'l-Qulúb fi'l-Muḍáf wa'l-Mansúb, by Abú Manṣúr 'Abdu'l-Malik ath-Tha'álibí (d. 429/1038). See Brockelmann, i, 284–6, No. 9.

Ff. 187 of 21·3 × 15·5 c. and 27 ll.; clear *naskh* with copious rubrications; undated; bought of J. J. Naaman, Aug. 12, 1910.

346 (p) جامِ جم **King's, No. 129**

The *Jám-i-Jam* ("Goblet of Jamshíd"), a well-known poem by Awḥadí of Marágha (d. 738/1337–8). See *B. M. P. C.*, p. 619, and Palmer's *King's Cat.*, p. 10.

The MS. is written in a small and elegant *ta'líq* and is undated.

347 (p) جامِ گیتی نما **Queens', No. 6**

The *Jám-i-Gítí-numá* ("Speculum Mundi") of the Qáḍí Mír Ḥusayn-i-Maybudí. See *B. M. P. C.*, p. 812.

Pp. 82 of 19·6 × 10·4 c. and 14 ll., cursive *ta'líq*, undated.

348 (a) جامع الآثار فى مولد النبىّ المختار **Or. 913 (8)**

The first and second parts of a Life of the Prophet Muḥammad entitled *Jámi'u'l-Áthár fí Mawlidi'n-Nabiyyi'l-Mukhtár* by Ibn Náṣiru'd-Dín ad-Dimashqí. Ff. 391 of 20·5 × 13·8 c.

and 29 ll.; undated; poor *naskh* with rubrications. Lynch Bequest, Jan. 1915.

349 (a) الجامع فى الأدوية **Add. 3697 (12)**

A large work on Materia Medica and Pharmacology, defective at end, without indication of authorship.

Ff. 317 of 30 × 20·5 c. and 29 ll.; coarse but legible *naskh*, with rubrications; bought of Sethian, Nov. 5, 1900.

350 (t) جامع الحساب **Trinity, R. 13. 11**

The *Jámi'u'l-Ḥisáb*, a treatise on Arithmetic, by Yúsuf b. Kemál of Broussa. See Palmer's *Trinity Cat.*, p. 23.

Ff. 170; good Turkish *naskh*.

351, 352 (p) جامع عبّاسى **King's, No. 127**
Jesus, No. 3

The well-known manual of Shí'a Law entitled *Jámi'-i-'Abbásí*, by Bahá'u'd-Dín 'Ámilí (d. 1030/1621). See *B.M.P.C.*, pp. 25–26.

The **King's MS.** contains only five of the 20 chapters into which the work is divided. See Palmer's *King's Cat.*, p. 10. The **Jesus MS.** is written in a bad modern Indian *ta'líq*.

353, 354 (p) جامع القوانين (= انشاى خليفه) **Corpus, No. 61**
Corpus, No. 142

The *Jámi'u'l-Qawánín*, an epistolary manual by Khalífa Sháh Muḥammad, also entitled *Inshá-yi-Khalífa*. See Pertsch's *Berlin Cat.*, No. 1058, and Browne's *Camb. Pers. Cat.*, p. 283.

Corpus, No. 61 is written in clear *nasta'líq* on pages of 25 × 16 c. **Corpus, No. 142** comprises ff. 57 of 17 × 11 c. and is written in a cursive *nasta'líq* and dated 1241/1825–6.

355 (p) جذب القلوب الى ديار المحبوب **King's, No. 134**

A Persian abridgement of as-Samhúdí's monograph on al-Madína entitled *Jadhbu'l-Qulúb ila Diyári'l-Maḥbúb*, by 'Abdu'l-Ḥaqq b. Sayfu'd-Dín at-Turk of Delhi. See *B.M.P.C.*, p. 1055[a], xxix, and Palmer's *King's Cat.*, p. 10.

356 (t) جرّاح نامه **Clare, Kk. 3. 10**

The *Jarráḥ-náma*, or "Book of the Surgeon," consisting chiefly of prescriptions supposed to have been given by Hippocrates at the end of his life to one of his disciples named Ya'qúb. See Ḥájji Khalífa, No. 4002. The Turkish is very archaic, as may be seen from the opening words:

قچنکم ابوقرات دنیاسن دکشمل اولدی بر شاگردی وار ایدی آدینه یعقوب دیرلردی '

357 (a) جلاء الصّدی فی سیرة امام الهُدی **Or. 18 (8)**

Jalá'u'ṣ-Ṣadá fí Sírati Imámi'l-Hudá, a work of which I can find no mention, and of which the author's name is not apparent.

Ff. 149 of 20·7 × 15·5 c. and 16 ll.; fair modern *naskh* with rubrications; dated 1311/1893–4. Bought of Naaman, Feb. 5, 1901.

358 (p) جمع مختصر **Or. 542[2] (6)**

A Persian treatise on Prosody which appears to be the *Jam'-i-Mukhtaṣar* of Waḥíd of Tabríz. See *B. M. P. C.*, p. 789. The MS., of which this portion occupies ff. 23b–66a, is described *s.v.* حدایق السحر.

359 (a) جوامع الکلم **King's, No. 126**

A collection of Traditions entitled *Jawámi'u'l-Kalim fi'l-Mawá'iẓ wa'l-Ḥikam*, by 'Alí b. Ḥusámu'd-Dín al-Muttaqí of Burhánpúr in India (d. 975/1567). See Brockelmann, ii, 384–5, and Palmer's *King's Cat.*, p. 27.

Large clear *naskh* with rubrications, leaves not numbered. Copied in Delhi in 1121/1709–1710 by Khwája Muḥammad Gadá of Bukhárá.

360 (p) جواهر الأسرار و زواهر الأنوار **Or. 238 (10)**

That part of the *Jawáhiru'l-Asrár wa Zawáhiru'l-Anwár* of Mawláná Ḥusayn b. Ḥasan al-Khwárazmí which contains the commentary on Book ii of the *Mathnawí* of Jalálu'd-Dín Rúmí. See *B.M.P.C.*, p. 588, and *Camb. Pers. Cat.*, pp. 321–6.

Ff. 295 of 25·5 × 16 c. and 23 ll; copied in 1066/1655-6 in large coarse Indian *ta'líq* with rubrications by Fayḍ Muḥammad. Part of the Cowell Bequest.

361 (p) جواهر الصّنايع (= مجموعة الصّنايع) **King's, No. 130**

An encyclopaedia of arts entitled *Jawáhiru'ṣ-Ṣanáyi'* or *Majmú'atu'ṣ-Ṣanáyi'*. See *B. M. P. C.*, pp. 489-490, and Palmer's *King's Cat.*, p. 10.

Copied by 'Abdu'r-Razzáq in 1195/1781.

362 (a) جواهر الفتاوى (نبذة من—) **Add. 3725² (7)**

An abstract from the *Jawáhiru'l-Fatáwa* of Abú Bakr Muḥammad b. Abi'l-Mafákhir al-Kirmání. See Ḥájji Khalífa, No. 4290.

Ff. 105-134 of 17·5 × 12·5 c. and 19 or 20 ll., dated 1272/1855-6. Bought of Naaman, Nov. 23, 1900.

363 (p) جوگ باششت **King's, No. 128**

A Persian translation of the *Yoga Vásishṭha*, a well-known Sanskrit work on Hindú gnosticism, made from the abridgement of the Kashmírí Pandit Anandan. See *B. M. P. C.*, p. 61, and Palmer's *King's Cat.*, p. 25.

Written at Sháh-Jahán-ábád about A.D. 1766 in a large, coarse Indian *ta'líq*.

364 (p) جوهر صمصام **King's, No. 132**

The *Jawhar-i-Ṣamṣám*, a history of Nádir Sháh's campaigns in India, with an account of the successors of Awrangzíb, composed by Muḥammad Muḥsin b. Muḥsin al-Ḥaníf in 1153/1740-1. See *B. M. P. C.*, p. 941, and Palmer's *King's Cat.*, p. 11.

365, 366 (p) جهانگير نامه **Christ's, Dd. 3. 17**
Trinity, R. 13. 67

Rieu has distinguished (*B. M. P. C.*, pp. 253-5) between the genuine *Jahángír-náma*, begun by the Mughal Emperor Jahángír himself, continued by Mu'tamad Khán, and re-edited and completed by Muḥammad Hádí, and the spurious Memoirs also known as *Ta'ríkh-i-Salímsháhí*. The **Trinity MS.** (see Palmer's *Trinity Catalogue*, pp. 153–4) appears to contain the latter, while the **Christ's MS.,** copied in a good *ta'líq* in 1219/1804–5 contains the third volume of the *Iqbál-náma* of Mu'tamad Khán, beginning like the British Museum MS. **Add. 26,218** (*B.M.P.C.*, p. 255[a]).

367 (p) جنگنامهٔ حضرت سلطان الانبياء **Corpus, No. 181[1]**

A legendary account of the Prophet Muḥammad and a king called Pádisháh Zaqqúm.

Written in a cursive *nasta'líq* on pages of 22 × 14 c. and dated 1203/1788–9.

368 (a) جَنَى الجناس **Or. 56 (8)**

The *Jana'l-Jinás* of that most fertile writer Shaykh 'Abdu'r-Raḥmán as-Suyúṭí (d. 849/1445). See Brockelmann, ii, 156, No 270, and the *Berlin Arabic Cat.*, No. 7334.

Ff. 104 of 20·3 × 14·5 c. and 19 ll.; stiff, legible *nasta'líq* with rubrications, dated 1014/1605–6, but perhaps this date refers only to the supply at the end of the MS., the original portion of which looks older. Bought of Naaman, March 4, 1901.

369 (a) جوهرة الشّرف و جنية التحف **Or. 578[2] (8)**

A work on poetry and rhetoric entitled *Jawharatu'sh-Sharaf wa Janyatu't-Tuḥaf*, of which the author's name is not evident. It comprises ten chapters, of which the subjects are enumerated on f. 233[a].

Ff. 232[b]–297[a] of 21 × 15 c. and 19 ll., written in excellent and clear *naskh* with rubrications, and dated 920/1514. Bought of Géjou, July 14, 1905.

370 (p) جهان الرّمل **Add. 3616[1] (10)**

A work on Geomancy entitled *Jahánu'r-Ramal* (sic), of unknown authorship.

Ff. 2[b]–69[a] of 24 × 17 c. and 21 ll.; fair *ta'líq*; rubrications. Bought of Géjou, 1899.

371, 372 (p) چار شربت **Corpus, No. 67³ Corpus, No. 190¹**

Two MSS. of the *Chár Sharbat* (" Four draughts") of Mírzá Qatíl, a treatise on Prosody, Rhyme, etc. See *B.M.P.C.*, p. 795ᵃ, iv. It was composed in 1217/1802–3.

MS. **67³** is written in *nasta'líq* on pages of 26 × 17 c., and is dated 1252/1836–7. MS. **190¹** is written in small *nasta'líq* on pages of 27 × 17 c.

373, 374 (p) چار عنصر **Christ's, Dd. 4. 1 King's, No. 131**

Two MSS. of the *Chár 'Unṣúr* ("Four Elements") of Mírzá 'Abdu'l-Qádir *Bídil*. See Ethé's *India Office Pers. Cat.*, No. 2115.

The **Christ's MS.** is written within gilt borders in neat, clear Persian *ta'líq* with rubrications; comprises 268 ff. of 29·8 × 14·5 c. and 19 ll., bears on f. 1ᵃ the seal of Archibald Swinton, and is dated 1119/1707. The **King's MS.** (Palmer's *King's Cat.*, p. 11) is dated 1195/1781.

375 (p) چراغ هدايت **King's, No. 125**

The *Chirágh-i-Hidáyat* of Siráju'd-Dín 'Alí Khán, poetically named Árzú, containing explanations of phrases used by contemporary poets like Ṣá'ib, Waḥshí, etc., and forming a supplement to the same author's dictionary entitled *Siráju'l-Lugha*. See *B.M.P.C.*, p. 501, and Palmer's *King's Cat.*, p. 11.

376 (p) چهار چمن **Corpus, No. 94**

Chahár Chiman ("the Four Meadows"), being Memoirs of the life and times of the author, Barahman Chandarbhán, composed about 1057/1647. See *B.M.P.C.*, p. 838ᵇ.

Ff. 104 of 21½ × 14 c., written in *ním-shikasta* and undated.

377 (p) چهار چمن **Corpus, No. 41**

A work bearing the same name as the above, but of different authorship and scope. It is by Ṣádiq Muḥammad 'Áshiq, and contains epistolary models.

Written in *nasta'líq* on leaves of 29·5 × 16 c.; undated.

378 (a, p) **چهل كلمه** **Or. 217** (7)

The *Chahil Kalima*, or "Forty Sayings," of Rashídu'd-Dín Waṭwáṭ, a collection of forty Traditions (*aḥádíth*) in Arabic, each followed by a Persian quatrain paraphrasing the Arabic text. The MS. is a fine specimen of calligraphy, and is written in black, blue and white.

Ff. 9 of 17 × 7 × 11·2 c., and dated Muḥarram, 977 (= June–July, 1569). Bought of Naaman, November 12, 1902.

379 (p) **حالنامهٔ عارفى** **Or. 466**[3] (6)

The *Ḥál-náma* of 'Árifí († 853/1449), known also as *Gúy u Chawgán*. See *B.M.P.C.*, pp. 639–640.

For further description of the MS., which is dated 928/1522, and was bought of Géjou on Jan. 29, 1904, see under the *Laylá wa Majnún* of Hátifí. This portion occupies ff. 98ᵇ–126ᵃ of 16·8 × 12·5 c. and 11 lines; good *ta'líq*.

380 (a) **الحاوى فى الفروع الشافعيّة** **Add. 3636** (7)

A treatise on Sháfi'í Jurisprudence entitled *al-Ḥáwí*, by Najmu'd-Dín 'Abdu'l-Ghaffár b. 'Abdu'l-Karím al-Qazwíní († 665/1266–7). See Brockelmann, i, 394–7; *B.M.A.C.*, p. 134, No. cclii; *B.M.A.S.*, pp. 201–202, No. 315.

Ff. 192 of 16 × 11·3 c. and 11 lines; good, large *naskh*; rubrications. Dated 952/1545; bought of Géjou, April 3, 1900.

381–387 (p) **حبيب السّير** { **Or. 253** (13), **Or. 520** (10), **Or. 917** (15), **Or. 966** (9), **King's, No. 138**, **King's, No. 16**, **King's, No. 104** }

Seven complete or partial copies of Khwándamír's well-known Persian history and biography the *Ḥabíbu's-Siyar*, completed in 930/1524, represented by ten volumes. See *B.M.P.C.*, pp. 98–102, and references there given.

Or. 253, forming part of the Cowell Bequest, comprises ff. 497 of 32·3 × 20·3 c. and 25 ll., and is written in a good, small *ta'líq* with rubrications within gold borders. It was copied in 1095/1684 by Muḥammad Badí' of Iṣfahán, and ends with the defeat of Jalálu'd-Dín Khwárazm-Sháh Mankobirní by Chingíz Khán. **Or. 520,** one of 30 MSS. bought of Hannan and Watson on August 20, 1904, comprises ff. 124, but lacks some 8 or 9 ff. at the beginning, 2 ff. at the end, and ff. 114–122. Each page measures 25·3 × 14·6 c., contains 23 lines, and is written in a small, neat *ta'líq* with rubrications. The MS. is undated, and comprises roughly speaking the years A.H. 549 to 778. **Or. 917,** an undated and defective MS. from the Lynch Bequest, appears to contain the earlier portion of this work down to the assassination of 'Alí. It comprises 190 ff. of 37 × 23 c. and 32 ll., and is written in a fair *ta'líq* with rubrications. **Or. 966** is a translation into English of parts of the *Ḥabíbu's-Siyar* made by Mr G. le Strange at Shíráz in Sept. 1879, and presented by him to the Library in April, 1918. The translation is followed by genealogical tables (p. 540), and by 4 indices (pp. 566–658). Ff. 658 of 20 × 15·8 c. and 16 or 17 ll. to the page. The **King's MS. No. 138** consists of four volumes, the first and second undated, the third dated 966/1558–9, and the fourth 1077/1666–7: see Palmer's *Cat.*, p. 11. The **King's MS. No. 16** is undated; lacks some leaves of the table of contents after f. 1; and contains that portion of the work which deals with the biography of the Prophet. The **King's MS. No. 104** contains part 3 of vol. iii, dealing with the history of Tímúr. The first half of the volume is written in *naskh*, the second in bad *ta'líq*.

388 (p) حجّة الهند **King's, No. 149**

The *Ḥujjatu'l-Hind*, a refutation of Hindúism and defence of Islám, in the form of a dialogue between two birds, compiled in 1055/1645, by Ibn 'Umar Mihrábí. See *B.M.P.C.*, p. 29. Dated 1113/1701–2.

389 (p) حدائق السّحر فى دقائق الشعر **Or. 542[1] (6)**

The *Ḥadá'iqu's-Siḥr*, a well-known work on Rhetoric by Muḥammad b. Muḥammad b. 'Abdu'l-Jalíl al-'Umarí, commonly known as Rashídu'd-Dín Waṭwáṭ (d. 578/1182–3). See *B.M.P.S.*, No. 188, pp. 121–2.

Ff. 1–20 (out of ff. 66) of 16·2 × 9 c. and 13 lines; fair *ta'líq*; incomplete at end; undated. Bought of Géjou, Jan. 4, 1905.

390 (p) حدائق السّحر **Add. 3716 (8)**

The *Ḥadá'iqu's-Siḥr*, ascribed to Sharafu'd-Dín Rámí, but there is probably an error either in the title of the book or the author's name. See *B.M.P.S.*, p. 268, No. 420, where the *Ḥadá'iqu's-Siḥr* of Rashídu'd-Dín Waṭwáṭ (see immediately above) is contained in the same volume as the *Anísu'l-'Ushsháq* of Sharafu'd-Dín Rámí.

Ff. 40 of 19·3 × 12·8 c. and 17 lines; clear *ta'líq*; rubrications. Transcribed in 1137/1724–5. Bought of Naaman, Nov. 23, 1900.

391 (a) حدائق العيان فی مختصر وفيات الأعيان **Or. 166 (8)**

An abridgement of Ibn Khallikán's celebrated biographical dictionary entitled *Ḥadá'iqu'l-'Ayán fí mukhtaṣari Wafayáti'l-'Ayán.* For the original work see Brockelmann, i, 326-8, where, however, this abridgement is not mentioned.

Ff. 132 of 20·4 × 14·3 c. and 19 lines; clear *naskh* with rubrications; defective at end; undated. Bought of Naaman, Dec. 6, 1901.

392–394 (p) حديقة الحقيقة **Or. 254 (8)**
Or. 272 (8)
King's, No. 151

Three copies of the well-known mystical poem entitled *Ḥadíqatu'l-Ḥaqíqat* of Abu'l-Majd Majdúd b. Ádam Saná'í, composed in 524–5/1130–1.

Or. 254 comprises ff. 481, with 7 additional ff. containing Table of Contents, is written in a good, clear *nasta'líq*, and is dated 1067/1656–7. **Or. 272** comprises ff. 276 of 21·8 × 13 c. and 12 ll. in the body of the page, with 23 ll. in margin; good *nasta'líq*; rubrications; dated 1094/1683. Both of these MSS. are from the Cowell Bequest. **King's, No. 151** comprises ff. 456, written in beautiful *ta'líq*. The poem, accompanied by a running commentary, begins on p. 326, and is preceded by an Introduction by 'Abdu'l-Laṭíf entitled *Mirátu'l-Ḥadá'iq*, the author of which died in 1048–9/1639. This MS. was transcribed in Rabí' i, 1102 (= Dec. 1690) by Sa'du'lláh Ibráhímábádí.

395 (a) حديقة الطبّ **Or. 10** (8)

An anonymous work on Medicine in Arabic, with a prefatory note in Persian.

Ff. 214 of 19 × 14 c. and 13 ll.; very poor *nasta'líq*. Bought of Géjou, Jan. 28, 1901.

396, 397 (p) حديقة المتّقين **Or. 507** (8) **Or. 510**[2] (11)

Two copies of a work on Shí'ite theology entitled *Ḥadíqatu'l-Muttaqín fí Ma'rifati Aḥkámi'd-Dín l'Irtiqá'i Madáriji'l-Yaqín* by Mullá Muḥammad Taqí Majlisí of Iṣfahán.

Both MSS. were bought of Messrs Hannan and Watson on August 20, 1904. **Or. 507** comprises ff. 298 of 19·6 × 15 c. and 14 ll., is written in fair *naskh* with rubrications, and is dated 1197/1783. **Or. 510**[2], of which the first portion (ff. 1–44) contains the *Anísu'l-Muwaḥḥidín*, comprises (ff. 45^b–206 of 27·7 × 18·5 c. and 17 ll.) a Preface, 5 chapters and a Conclusion. It is written in a very good, neat, modern *naskh* with rubrications and dated 1219/1804–5, and was copied by Muḥammad Ḥashim al-Ḥusayní, known as Mírzá Bábá.

398 (t) حديقة الوزراء **Or. 670** (9)

The *Ḥadíqatu'l-Wuzará*, containing biographies of eminent ministers of State, by 'Uthmán-záda Tá'ib Aḥmad. See Rieu's *Turkish Cat.*, p. 73.

Ff. 115 of 23·4 × 13·2 c. and 23 ll.; fair Turkish *nasta'líq* with rubrications; dated 1181/1767–8; bought of Géjou, Feb. 17, 1906.

399 (a) حرز الأماني و وجه التّهاني **Trinity, R. 13. 41**[2]

An Arabic *qaṣída* entitled *Ḥirzu'l-Amání wa Wajhu't-Tahání*, or *al-Qaṣídatu'sh-Sháṭibiyya*, by Abú Muḥammad Qásim b. Firróh al-A'má al-Miṣrí (d. 590/1194), accompanied by a commentary entitled *Al-Farídatu'l-Báriziyya fí ḥalli'l-*

Qaṣídati'sh-Sháṭibiyya by the Shaykh al-Maqqarí Abú 'Abdi'lláh al-Maghribí. See Brockelmann, i, pp. 409 and also 407, ll. 13 *et seqq.*

This work occupies ff. 61–137 of the MS.

400–403 (t) حسن و دل **Or. 572 (6)**
Or. 699 (8)
Or. 778 (8)
Emmanuel, 3.2.4

Four copies of the *Ḥusn u Dil* ("Beauty and Heart") of the Turkish poet Áhí (d. 923/1517). See E. J. W. Gibb's *History of Ottoman Poetry*, vol. ii, ch. xi, pp. 286–316, and Pertsch's *Berlin Turk. Cat.*, No. 396 (p. 385).

Or. 572 comprises ff. 124 of 15 × 9·6 c. and 15 ll.; is written in a neat Turkish *naskh* with rubrications and gold punctuation; is dated 873/1468, and was bought of Géjou on July 14, 1905. **Or. 699** comprises ff. 69 of 19·4 × 12·2 c. and 19 ll.; is written in fair *ta'líq* with rubrications; undated. Bought of Géjou, Dec. 1906. **Or. 778** comprises ff. 112 of 20 × 11·7 c. and 17 ll., is written in a good Turkish *naskh* with rubrications, undated; and was bought of Géjou on Jan. 7, 1909. Concerning the Emmanuel College MS. particulars are wanting.

404, 405 (p) حسن و عشق **Add. 3734[3] (9)**
Corpus, 17[3]

Two versions of an allegory entitled *Ḥusn u 'Ishq* ("Beauty and Love"). The first is by Fuḍúlí of Baghdád, and occupies ff. 54^b–62^a of the MS. described under *Siráj-i-Munír*, bought of Sethian on Nov. 28, 1900. Concerning Fuḍúlí (d. 963/1555–6, or 970/1562–3), see Gibb's *History of Ottoman Poetry*, vol. iii, ch. iv, pp. 70–107, where, however, no mention is made of such a poem by this writer. The **Corpus MS.** (ff. 16) contains the *Ḥusn u 'Ishq* of Ni'mat Khán, and is dated 1249/1833, and written in *ním-shikasta*. See *B.M.P.C.*, p. 703^b.

406 (a) **King's, No. 229**

الحصن الحصين من كلام سيّد المرسلين

Al-Ḥiṣnu'l-Ḥaṣín fí Kalámi Sayyidi'l-Mursalín, by Shamsu'd-Dín Abu'l-Khayr Muḥammad al-Jazarí (d. 833/1429). See Brockelmann, ii, pp. 201–3.

The MS. is written in a clumsy but legible *naskh*, and is undated.

حكاية أربعين صُبْحًا و مسآء **Or. 605 (6)**

See under *Qirq Wazír Ḥikáyatí* ("the Story of the Forty Vezírs").

407 (p) **حكاية الصّالحين** **Corpus, No. 228**[6]

Ḥikayatu's-Ṣáliḥín ("Stories of the Just"), a collection of anecdotes about famous Saints and the miracles performed by them, stated to be a translation from the Arabic, and compiled in 1060/1650.

Ff. 121, written in *nasta'líq* and dated 1217/1802–3.

408 (t) **حكايت ورقا و گلشاه** **King's, No. 123**

The Romance of *Warqá and Gulsháh*, a Turkish poem by Ḍiyá'í. See *B.M.T.C.*, p. 185[b]. There is another poem with the same title by the more celebrated Masíḥí: see *B.M.T.C.*, p. 209[a], and Gibb's *History of Ottoman Poetry*, iii, 107.

409 (a) **الحكم العطائيّة** **Trinity, R. 8. 17**

Al-Ḥikamu'l-'Aṭá'iyya, by Shaykh Táju'd-Dín Abu'l-Faḍl Aḥmad b. Muḥammad, known as Ibn 'Aṭá'i'lláh al-Iskandarání (d. 709/1309–10), with commentary by Shihábu'd-Dín Aḥmad b. Muḥammad al-Burnusí al-Fásí. See Brockelmann, ii, 117–8.

Pp. 320; poor African writing; undated.

410 (a) **حكمة العين (شرح —)** **King's, No. 236**

Commentary on a philosophical work entitled *Ḥikmatu'l-'Ayn*, perhaps that of Najmu'd-Dín 'Alí b. 'Umar al-Qazwíní al-Kátibí (d. 675/1276). See Brockelmann, i, 465, but the identification is a mere conjecture.

Ff. 243 of 22 × 13·5 c.; poor *naskh* (different hands) with rubrications; dated 12 Jumáda ii, 1106 (= Jan. 28, 1695).

411 (a) **حكمة العين (حاشية .. على شرح ...)** **King's, No. 142**

A gloss of Mírzá Ján of Shíráz on a commentary on a work entitled like the above *Ḥikmatu'l-'Ayn*.

The MS. is written in a small, cramped *naskh*, and is undated.

412–414 (a) حلبة الكُمَيْت **Or. 17 (8)** / **Or. 594 (8)** / **King's, No. 145**

Two complete copies and one abridged of the *Ḥalbatu'l-Kumayt*, a well-known anthology of poems about wine by Muḥammad b. Ḥasan an-Nawájí (d. 859/1455). See Brockelmann, ii, p. 56.

Or. 17 (the abridgement) comprises ff. 165 of 20 × 14 c. and 13 ll., lacks the concluding portion, is undated, written in a clear but ugly *naskh* with rubrications, and was bought of Naaman on Feb. 5, 1901. **Or. 594** contains ff. 197 of 20·2 × 14·4 c. and 21 ll., is written in good *naskh* with rubrications, is undated, and was bought of Géjou on Oct. 30, 1905. **King's, No. 145** is dated 996/1588, and is written in good *naskh* with rubrications.

415 (a) حلية الأبصار فى فضائل الأنصار . **Trinity, R. 13. 60**

Ḥilyatu'l-Abṣár fí faḍá'ili'l-Anṣár, by Abú 'Abdi'lláh b. Muḥammad al-Anṣárí. See Palmer's *Trin. Cat.*, p. 149.

416 (t) حليهٔ شريفه **Or. 197 (8)**

The *Ḥilya-i-Sharífa*, or description of the Prophet Muḥammad's appearance, by the Turkish poet Kháqání (died about 1015/1606–7), concerning whom see Gibb's *History of Ottoman Poetry*, iii, 193–8. See also *B.M.T.C.*, 257[b]; and Flügel's *Vienna Cat.*, iii, 411, No. 417.

Ff. 29 of 20 × 11·2 c. and 15 ll.; fair *ta'líq* with rubrications; undated; bought of Géjou, Oct. 23, 1902.

417–419 (p) حملهٔ حيدرى **Or. 426 (10)** / **Corpus, No. 52** / **King's, No. 139**

The *Ḥamla-i-Ḥaydarí*, a long *mathnawí* poem in the *Shah-náma* metre (*mutaqárib*) describing the exploits of 'Alí b. Abí Ṭálib, the Fourth Caliph of the Sunnís and First Imám of the Shí'a. See *B.M.P.C.*, p. 704[a]. The author is Mírzá Muḥammad Rafí', poetically surnamed Bádhil.

Or. 426 comprises ff. 134 of 26·3×18 c. and 24 ll.; fair *ta'líq*; undated, but quite modern; bought of Hannan, Watson and Co. on Aug. 29, 1903. **Corpus, No. 52** is dated 1226/1811, and is written in small *nasta'líq* in 4 columns on leaves of 28×18 c. **King's, No. 139** is dated 1198/1783–4.

420 (a) حيوة الحيوان الكُبْرَى للدّميرى **Christ's, Dd. 5. 7–8**

The *Ḥayátu'l-Ḥaywán*, or "Book of Animals," of ad-Damírí (d. 808/1405 at Cairo). See Brockelmann, ii, p. 138. An English translation in 2 vols. by Lieut.-Col. A. S. G. Jayakar was published at Bombay and London in 1906–8.

Ff. 300 and 243 of 29×18·8 c. and 31 ll. Written in coarse, clear *naskh* with rubrications. A note at the end of vol. ii says that the author completed the book in Rajab 773/Jan. 1372.

421, 422 (a, p) حيوة الحيوان **Or. 184 (11)** **King's, Nos. 136–7**

Two more copies of the above-mentioned "Book of Animals" (*Ḥayátu'l-Ḥaywán*) of Kamálu'd-Dín Abú 'Abdi'lláh Muḥammad b. Músá ad-Damírí (d. 808/1405–6), one copy of the first half of the Arabic text, containing the letters ا-ش, and one copy in two volumes of the Persian translation. See Brockelmann, ii, p. 138.

Or. 184 comprises ff. 273 of 29×18·5 c. and 29 ll.; good *naskh*; rubrications; undated; bought of Géjou, Jan. 1, 1902. **King's, 136–7** contain the Persian version in two volumes.

423 (p) خرقه **Add. 3734[4] (9)**

A work on Medicine entitled *Khirqa*, by Murtaḍá-qulí b. Ḥasan Shámlú. For description of MS., see under *Siráj-i-Munír*. This portion occupies ff. 63^b–103^a, and is followed by other treatises on Medicine, the Occult Sciences, etc. The MS. is dated 1255/1839–40, and was bought of Sethian on Nov. 28, 1900.

424 (a) الخريدة البهيّة فى العقائد التوحيديّة **Or. 560 (9)**

Al-Kharídatu'l-Bahiyya fi'l-'aqá'idi't-Tawḥídiyya, by Abu'l-Barakát Aḥmad b. Muḥammad b. Aḥmad ad-Dardír (d. 1201/1786). See Brockelmann, ii, 353.

Ff. 73 of 23·7 × 16·6 c. and 23 ll.; poor, coarse *naskh*; undated. Presented by Khalíl Khálid Efendi.

425 (a) **خزانة الروّايات** **Add. 3730 (12)**

Khizánatu'r-Riwáyát, by the Qáḍí Júkán (or Chakan) al-Hindí. See Brockelmann, ii, 221.

Ff. 251 + 3 of 29·5 × 20·6 c. and 25 ll.; coarse, clear *naskh* with rubrications; dated 1027/1618. Bought of Sethian, Nov. 28, 1900.

426 (a) **خزانة الفقه** **Add. 3725[1] (7)**

Khizánatu'l-Fiqh, by Shaykh Abu'l-Layth Naṣr b. Muḥammad b. Ibráhím as-Samarqandí (d. 383/993). See Brockelmann, i, 195–6; Ḥájji Khalífa, iii, pp. 135–6, No. 4698.

Ff. 1–102 of 17·5 × 12·5 c. and 15 ll., written in excellent *naskh*. Bought of Naaman, Nov. 23, 1900.

427 (p) **خزاين الفتوح** **King's, No. 158**

The *Khazá'inu'l-Futúḥ*, a history of the reign of 'Alá'u'd-Dín Muḥammad Sháh Khiljí from his accession to 711/1311, by Amír Khusraw of Dihlí. See *B.M.P.C.*, p. 240^{b}, and Palmer's *King's Cat.* The MS. is dated 1200/1785-6.

428, 429 (p) **خسرو و شيرين** **Corpus, No. 209**
Corpus, No. 239

The well-known romantic poem of *Khusraw wa Shírín*, by Niẓámí of Ganja. See *infra*, pp. 77–8, s.v. خمسهٔ نظامی.

No. 209 comprises ff. 71 of 20 × 12 c., and is written in minute clear *nasta'líq*, probably about 1000/1591–2. **No. 239** was copied in A.D. 1832, and its pages measure 28 × 20 c.

430 (t) **خسرو و شيرين** **Or. 663 (7)**

The Turkish version of the above-mentioned romance of *Khusraw wa Shírín* by Shaykhí (d. circâ 855/1451). See Gibb's *Hist. of Ottoman Poetry*, i, ch. vi (pp. 299 *et seqq.*).

Pp. 355 of 17 × 11·3 c. and 15 ll., small, neat *naskh*, pointed; dated 908/1502–3. Bought of Géjou, Feb. 17, 1906.

431 (p) **Corpus, No. 218**

خلاصهٔ احوال بانو بیگم مخاطب بممتاز محلّ الخ

An account of the Táj Maḥall, Motí Masjid, Fort of Akbarábád, Fatḥpúr Sikrí, and other famous buildings in India, without any indication of authorship.

Written in fine *nasta'líq* on pages of 24 × 16 c.; undated.

432, 433 (p) **Or. 242 (10)** **King's, No. 155**

خلاصة الأخبار فی بیان احوال الأخیار

The *Khuláṣatu'l-Akhbár* of Ghiyáthu'd-Dín Khwándamír, an abridgement of Mírkhwánd's *Rawḍatu'ṣ-Ṣafá* to the year 905/1499. See *B. M. P. C.*, p. 96b.

Or. 242 comprises ff. 445 of 24·8 × 12·5 c. and 21 ll.; good *ta'líq*; undated: Cowell Bequest. **King's, No. 155** comprises ff. 612.

434 (a) خلاصة الاعراب **Add. 3623⁶ (7)**

Khuláṣatu'l-I'ráb, containing notes (*ḥawáshí*) on the *Miṣbáḥ*, by Ḥájji Bábá b. Ḥájji Ibráhím b. Ḥájji Karím b. 'Uthmán.

Ff. 87b–142a of 17·2 × 13 c. and 21 ll.; cramped *ta'líq*, overlined with red; dated 903/1497–8. Bought of Géjou, Feb. 14, 1900.

435 (a) خلاصة الأفكار فی زبدة الأسرار **Or. 709 (7)**

Khuláṣatu'l-Afkár fí bayáni zubdati'l-Asrár, a commentary on the *Lubbu'l-Albáb*.

Ff. 132 of 18·2 × 12·8 c. and 25 ll.; neat, old-fashioned *naskh* with rubrications. Dated 753/1352. Bought of Géjou, Dec. 1906.

436 (p) خلاصة التّواریخ **King's, No. 156**

The *Khuláṣatu't-Tawáríkh* of Suján Ráy, a general history of India from the earliest times to the accession of 'Álamgír, compiled in 1107/1695–6. There is an Urdú translation entitled *Áráyish-i-Maḥfil*.

Ff. 376.

437 (a) خلاصة الكتاب فى علم الحساب **Or. 436[1] (8)**

A book on Arithmetic entitled *Khuláṣatu'l-Kitáb fí 'ilmi'l-Ḥisab*, by Bahá'u'd-Dín Muḥammad b. Ḥusayn al-'Ámilí.

Ff. 1ᵇ–38ᵇ (out of ff. 89); poor *ta'líq* with rubrications; 12 ll. to page; dated 1245/1829–1830. Bought of Hannan, Watson and Co., Aug. 29, 1903.

438 (p) خلاصة الحساب (ترجمه) **Christ's, Dd. 3. 16**

A Persian translation of an Arabic treatise on Arithmetic entitled *Khuláṣatu'l-Ḥisáb*. Ff. 80 of 22·3 × 13·2 c.

Dated 1124/1712; copied at 'Aẓímábád.

439 (p) خلاصة السّياق **Corpus, No. 54[1]**

A treatise on the cypher known as *Siyáq*, entitled *Khuláṣatu's-Siyáq*, composed in 1115/1703–4, in the 47th year of 'Álamgír's reign.

Written in *shikasta* on pages of 15 × 10·5 c.; undated.

440 (a) خلاصة الوفى بأخبار دار المصطفى **Or. 711 (8)**

The *Khuláṣatu'l-Wafá* of Abu'l-Ḥasan 'Alí as-Samhúdí (d. 911/1505). See Brockelmann, ii, 173–4; and the *Camb. Hand-list*, p. 69.

Pp. 380 of 19·6 × 14·5 c. and 25 ll.; curious cramped *naskh* with rubrications, dated 1042/1632–3. Bought of Géjou, Dec. 1906.

441, 442 (p) خمسهٔ امیر خسرو دهلوی **Or. 259 (8)**
King's, No. 153

Two copies of the *Khamsa*, or Five Romantic Poems, of Amír Khusraw of Dihlí (d. 725/1325). See *B. M. P. C.*, p. 611.

Or. 259 comprises ff. 495 of 17·7 × 11 c. and 19 ll., and is written in a good *ta'líq* and dated 900/1494–5. The five poems occupy the following leaves: *Maṭla'u'l-Anwár*, 1ᵇ–92ᵃ; *Khusraw wa Shírín*, 92ᵇ–213ᵃ; *Laylá wa Majnún*, 214ᵇ–284ᵃ; *Á'ína-i-Sikandarí*, 285ᵃ–404ᵃ; *Hasht Bihisht*, 405ᵇ–495ᵃ. The date of transcription occurs on f. 91ᵇ. This MS. is from the Cowell Bequest. The **King's MS.** is dated 979/1571–2, and contains five or six illustrations.

443 (p) **خمسهٔ جامی** **Trinity, R. 13. 8**

Five of the Seven Poems of the celebrated Persian poet Jámí, collectively known as the *Haft Awrang*, or "Seven Thrones." See *B. M. P. C.*, pp. 644–5. The five are the *Tuḥfatu'l-Aḥrár*, *Sibḥatu'l-Abrár*, *Laylá wa Majnún*, *Yúsuf u Zulaykhá*, and *Khirad-náma-i-Iskandarí*.

Ff. 196; fine *nasta'líq* with some miniatures; dated A.D. 1531.

444 (t) **خمسهٔ عطائی** **Or. 461 (10)**

The *Khamsa*, or Five Poems, of the Turkish poet 'Aṭá'í (d. 1044/1634–5). See Gibb's *History of Ottoman Poetry*, iii, 232–242. The poems are (1) *Sharaf-náma*, (2) *Nafḥatu'l-Azhár*, (3) *Ṣuḥbatu'l-Abkár*, (4) *Haft Paykar*, (5) *Sáqí-náma*.

Ff. 228 of 26·3 × 15 c. and 23 ll.; rather coarse but legible *ta'líq* with rubrications; transcribed by Sulaymán b. Muḥammad ("Muḥarram Efendi-záda") in 1125/1713. Bought of J. J. Naaman, Nov. 27, 1903.

445–456 (p) **خمسهٔ نظامی** **Or. 243 (11), Or. 244 (12)**
Or. 245 (9), Or. 421 (9)
Or. 564 (9), Or. 805 (9)
Or. 964 (12)
Christ's, Dd. 4. 13
King's, 152, 154 and 257
St John's, No. 30

Twelve copies of the *Khamsa*, or Five Romantic Poems of Niẓámí of Ganja. See *B. M. P. C.*, pp. 564 *et seqq.*

Or. 243 comprises ff. 400 of 27·7 × 15·5 c. and 19 ll.; one leaf missing at beginning; undated; from the Cowell Bequest. **Or. 244** comprises ff. 315 of 29·5 × 19 c. and 23 ll.; neat Persian *nasta'líq* with rubrications; dated 996/1588. **Or. 245** comprises ff. 235 of 22 × 14·6 c. and 25 ll.; neat *nasta'líq*, illuminated *'unwáns*; gilt edges and headings; dated 853/1449; from the Cowell Bequest. **Or. 421** seems to have suffered dislocations in many places. It is dated 846/1442–3, and was bought of Hannan and Watson on Aug. 29, 1903. **Or. 564** comprises ff. 418 of 24·4 × 15 c. and 18 ll.; fair, legible *ta'líq* with rubrications; dated 1254/1838–9; bought on July 14, 1905, from Géjou. **Or. 805** contains ff. 423 of 23·7 × 13 c. and 21 ll. in text (3 columns) with 42 or 43 ll. in margin; small, neat *nasta'líq* with rubrications, between gold lines; nine illuminated *'unwáns*; undated, but probably 10th century of the Hijra; presented by C. Marling, Esq. **Or. 964,** a fine old fourteenth century MS., contains the greater part of two of the five poems which constitute the *Khamsa,* to wit the latter portion of *Khusraw wa Shírín* (ff. 1–45) and the whole of the *Haft Paykar* (ff. 46–111). The MS., transcribed in 791/1389 by Ṭayfúr b. Ḥájji Kamál, was bought from J. Whitaker on Nov. 30, 1917. It contains 111 ff. of 27 × 18 c. and 19 ll. (2 *bayts* to the line), and is written in a curious but clear old *naskh,* with headings in gold. **Christ's College, Dd. 4. 13** is undated, and is written in a good, neat, Persian *ta'líq* with rubrications, on 352 ff. of 26 × 15·8 c. and 19 ll. **King's College, No. 152,** is also undated and is written in a good *ta'líq*. **King's College, No. 154,** dated 1140/1727–8, contains selections only. **King's, No. 257** contains only the *Khusraw wa Shírín,* and is undated. The **St John's MS., No. 30,** copied in 947/1540, contains 786 pp. written in good *ta'líq* with thirty miniatures.

457 (a) الخميس فى احوال نفس نفيس **Add. 3687 (11)**

Al-Khamís fí aḥwáli nafs nafís, composed in 926/1520 by Ḥusayn b. Muḥammad b. Ḥasan ad-Diyár-bakrí (d. 966/1558–9). See *B. M. A. C.*, pp. 424 and 584; *B. M. A. S.*, Nos. 517 and 518; Ellis's *Catalogue of printed Arabic books*, i, 701.

Ff. 555 of 27·3 × 18 c. and 33 ll.; small, scratchy *naskh* with rubrications; dated 954/1547–8; bought of Khayyáṭ (late Géjou), Oct. 20, 1900.

458 (p) خواصّ الآيات **Or. 512 (9)**

A Persian treatise on the virtues of certain verses in the *Qur'án,* defective at beginning and end.

Ff. 159 of 22·4 × 18·4 c. and 14 ll.; large, bold, good *naskh* with rubrications; undated. Bought of Hannan and Watson, Aug. 20, 1904.

459 (p) خوان نعمت **King's, No. 157**

A Persian Cookery-book entitled *Khwán-i-Ni'mat.* See Pertsch's *Berlin Catalogue,* No. 320; Palmer's *King's Cat.,* p. 11.

460-462 (t) خیریّهٔ نابی **Add. 3711 (8)** / **Or. 177 (8)** / **Or. 700 (8)**

Three copies of the *Khayriyya* of Nábí, the last containing in addition four other tracts. See Gibb's *History of Ottoman Poetry,* vol. iii, pp. 325–352.

Add. 3711 comprises ff. 50 of 21·2 × 15·3 c. and 17 ll.; transcribed in 1221/1806–7 in clear Turkish *naskh* by 'Abdu'r-Razzáq b. Ṣáliḥ Efendi. Bought of Naaman, Nov. 7, 1900. **Or. 177** comprises ff. 94 of 21 × 13 c. and 17 ll.; transcribed in 1166/1753 in fair Turkish *naskh*; bought of Géjou, Jan. 1, 1902. The *Khayriyya* ends on f. 55ª and is followed by poems illustrating the different metres (ff. 55ᵇ–71ª) and then by models of letters. **Or. 700** comprises ff. 132 of 19·7 × 14 c. and 19–25 ll., was transcribed in 1187/1773–4, and bought of Géjou in Dec. 1906. The *Khayriyya* occupies ff. 2ᵇ–45ª, and contains in addition: (2) a history of Constantinople and of the Mosque of St Sophia (ff. 45ᵇ–76ª); (3) a history of Tiryákí Ḥasan Pasha (ff. 76ᵇ–107ᵇ); (4) the *Manáqib-i-Shamsu'd-Dín* (ff. 109ᵇ–125ª); and (5) the *Manáqib-i-Bashír Chalabí* (ff. 125ª–131ᵇ).

463 (t) خیری نامهٔ نابی افندی **Add. 3714 (8)**

The *Khayrí-náma* of Nábí Efendi.

Ff. 109 of 20·5 × 15·5 c. and 18 ll.; clear Turkish *naskh.* Bought of Naaman, Nov. 23, 1900.

464 (p) داستان امیر قعقاع **Or. 505 (8)**

Dástán-i-Amír Qa'qá', the Story of Amír Qa'qá' and 'Alí the Commander of the Faithful.

Ff. 200 of 20·6 × 16·6 c. and 22 ll.; clear modern Persian *naskh* with rubrications on blue paper; dated 1259/1843–4. One of 30 MSS. bought of Hannan and Watson, August 20, 1904.

465, 466 (h) داستان بینظیر **Or. 526 (9)** **Corpus, No. 19**

A Hindústání poem by Mír Ḥusayn or Ḥasan, entitled *Dástán-i-Bí-naẓír Sháhzáda wa Malik Áftáb wa Badr-i-Munír.*

The **Corpus MS.** is written in a large *nasta'líq* within red borders on pages of 23 × 16 c.; undated. **Or. 526** comprises ff. 91 of 21·8 × 13·6 c. and 13 ll.; written in a large, clear Indian *ta'líq*; a few coarse illustrations. Bought of Luzac, Aug. 27, 1904.

467 (p) داستانِ حاتم طائی **Corpus, No. 228**[1]

The Romance of Ḥátim-i-Ṭá'í.

Ff. 153 of 20 × 13 c., written in cursive *nasta'líq* and dated 1219/1804.

468 (t) داستان خرّم شاه **Or. 749 (7)**

The Story of Khurram Sháh in Turkish.

Ff. 63 of 17·2 × 10·4 c. and 17 ll.; poor Turkish *ta'líq* with rubrications; dated 1117/1705–6. Bought of Géjou, March 27, 1907.

469 (p) دانش آرای **King's, No. 182**

The *Dánish-árá*, a collection of stories in prose and verse, composed in 1159/1746 by Shevanáth. Very illegibly written.

470 (p) دانش نامهٔ جهان **King's, No. 187**

A Persian Encyclopaedia of Sciences, entitled *Dánish-náme-i-Jahán*, by Ghiyáthu'd-Dín 'Alí al-Ḥusayní al-Isfahání (d. 606/1209–10), containing 10 sections (*faṣl*), 20 "origins" (*aṣl*) and a Conclusion (*Khátima*). See *B.M.P.C.*, p. 439[b]. The MS. is dated 1137/1724–5.

471 (p) دُرّة التّاج لغرّة الدّيباج **King's, No. 184**

An Encyclopaedia of Political Science, entitled *Durratu't-Táj li-ghurrati'd-Díbáj*, by Quṭbu'd-Dín Maḥmúd b. Mas'úd b. Muṣliḥ of Shíráz, one of the greatest of the disciples of Naṣíru'd-Dín Ṭúsí, b. 634/1236–7, d. 710/1310–11. The MS. is dated 1050/1640–1.

472–474 (t) دُرّة التّاج فى سيرة صاحب المعراج **Add. 3669 (6) / Or. 489 (8) / Or. 668 (8)**

A Turkish biography of the Prophet Muḥammad, entitled *Durratu't-Táj fí sírati Ṣáḥibi'l-Mi'ráj*, by Waysí (Veysí) Efendi. See *B.M.T.C.*, p. 37.

Add. 3669 comprises ff. 305 of 14 × 9·3 c. and 15 ll.; poor Turkish *nasta'líq*; rubrications; dated 1145/1732–3; bought of Sethian, July 17, 1900. **Or. 489** comprises ff. 182 of 20·6 × 14 c. and 21 ll.; good Turkish *nasta'líq*; rubrications; undated; bought of Géjou, Aug. 18, 1904. **Or. 668** comprises ff. 236 of 20 × 12·5 c. and 17 ll.; fair Turkish *nasta'líq* with rubrications; dated 1029/1620; bought of Géjou, Feb. 17, 1906.

475 (p) دُرّهٔ نادره **Add. 3635 (12)**

The history of Nádir Sháh entitled *Durra-i-Nádira*, by Muḥammad Mahdí b. Muḥammad Naṣír of Astarábád. See *B.M.P.C.*, p. 195.

Ff. 182 of 30·4 × 20·3 c. and 14 ll.; large, clear Persian *naskh* with rubrications; undated; bought of Naaman, March 16, 1900.

476 (p) دُرّ مجالس **Corpus, No. 88**

A collection of legends about Prophets and Saints in 33 chapters, entitled *Durr-i-Majális*, by Sayf-i-Ẓafar Nawbahárí. See *B.M.P.C.*, p. 44[b].

Written on leaves of 22 × 13 c. in *nasta'líq*; considerably wormed; dated 1078/1667–8.

477 (a) الدُرّ المسلوك فى احوال الانبياء...والملوك **Or. 655 (7)**

Ad-Durru'l-Maslúk fí Aḥwáli'l-Anbiyá wa'l-Awṣiyá wa'l-Khulafá wa'l-Mulúk, a compendium of history compiled from a number of books enumerated on ff. 255[b]–256[a] by Aḥmad b. al-Ḥasan.

Ff. 256 of 17·8 × 11·3 c. and 17 ll.; poor *nasta'líq*; dated 1109/1697–8; bought of Géjou, Feb. 12, 1906.

478 (a)   الدُّرّ المكنون   **Or. 208⁶ (8)**

Ad-Durru'l-Maknún, apparently 'Alí b. Aydamur b. 'Alí al-Jildakí's commentary on the *qaṣída* of Dhu'n-Nún. See Brockelmann, ii, 139.

For description of the MS., of which this part occupies ff. 57ᵇ–63, see p. 29 *supra*, s.v. البردة. Bought of Naaman, Nov. 12, 1902.

479 (a)   الدُّرّ المنتخب فى التقريب و شرح المكتسب   **Add. 3688 (8)**

Ad-Durru'l-muntakhab fi't-Taqríb wa Sharḥu'l-Muktasab, commentaries on the *Taqríb* and the *Muktasab,* two works on Alchemy by Shaykh Aydamur b. 'Alí al-Jildakí (d. 743/1342). See Brockelmann, ii, 138–9.

Ff. 187 of 19·7 × 14·4 c. and 15 ll.; poor *naskh* with rubrications; undated; bought of Sethian, Nov. 1, 1900.

480 (a)   الدرر المنثرة فى الشَّجرة و الثَّمرة   **Add. 3624 (8)**

Ad-Duraru'l-munthara fi'sh-Shajarati wa'th-Thamara, a book supposed to be based on a writing of the Prophet Daniel, by 'Uthmán b. 'Alí al-'Umarí al-Mawṣilí.

Ff. 68 (defective at end) of 20·4 × 14·9 c. and 21 ll.; written in a modern *naskh* inclining to *riq'a*; undated; bought of Géjou, Feb. 14, 1900.

481 (a)   الدُّرّ المنظّم فى السرّ الاغطم [يا اسرار العالم]   **Or. 529 (8)**

A Cabbalistic work entitled *ad-Durru'l-Munaẓẓam fi's-sirri'l-a'ẓam,* by Shaykh Kamálu'd-Dín Abú Sálim Muhammad b. Ṭalḥa (d. 652/1254–5). See Ḥájji Khalífa, No. 4886.

Ff. 160 of 20·3 × 15 c. and 13 ll.; bought of Géjou, Nov. 1, 1904.

482 (p)   درود اكبر   **Corpus, No. 183²**

Durúd-i-Akbar; invocations of the Prophet in the form of a kind of litany, undated.

483 (p) دستور شگرف **Corpus, No. 5**

Dastúr-i-Shagarf, a Persian work on style and composition by Pamúpat (?) Rá'o.

Written in large, clear *nasta'líq*; ff. 209 of 25 × 15 c.; dated 1224/1809–10.

484 (p) دستور الصّبیان **Corpus, No. 192**[1]

The *Dastúru'ṣ-Ṣibyán*, by Nundo Ray.

Ff. 35 of 22 × 16 c.; *nasta'líq*.

485 (p) دستور العمل **Corpus, No. 112**

A Persian Grammar entitled *Dastúru'l-'Amal* by 'Abdu'l-Wási' Hánsawí, also the author of a Persian-Urdú Dictionary entitled *Ghará'ibu'l-Lughát*: see *B.M.P.C.*, p. 1096[b], Browne's *Cat. of Cambridge Persian MSS.*, p. 281.

486 (p) دستور العمل **King's, No. 162**

The *Dastúru'l-'Amal* of Rájá Ṭodar Mal, who was Minister of Finance under the Emperor Akbar. See *Ind. Off. Pers. Cat.*, No. 432.

The MS. is dated 1190/1776–7.

487 (p) دستور المبتدی **Corpus, No. 168**

The *Dastúru'l-Mubtadí*, a treatise on Arabic accidence for beginners, by Ṣafí ibn Naṣír.

Written in fair *nasta'líq* on pages of 23·5 × 15 c., and dated 1212/1797–8.

488 (p) دستورنامهٔ کسری **Trinity, R. 13. 68**

The *Dastúr-náma-i-Kisrá*, a Persian translation of the Arabic work entitled *at-Tawqí'átu'l-Kisrawiyya*, composed in 1056/1647. See Palmer's *Trin. Coll. Cat.*, pp. 154–5.

The MS. is dated 1239/1823–4.

489 (t) دقایق الحقایق **Or. 601 (8)**

Daqá'iqu'l-Ḥaqá'iq by Kamál Páshá-záda, preceded, apparently, by a Preface (ff. 1–22). See Rieu's *Turk. Cat.*, p. 141.

Ff. 180 of 21 × 14·8 c. and 15 ll.; large, clear *naskh*. Bought of Géjou, Oct. 30, 1905. Dated 988/1580–1.

490, 491 (a) دلائل الخيرات **Or. 37 (6)**
Or. 559 (8)

Two copies of the well-known Arabic devotional work entitled *Dalá'ilu'l-Khayrát* by Abú 'Abdi'lláh Muḥammad b. 'Abdu'r-Raḥmán al-Jazúlí (d. 807/1404–5). See Brockelmann, ii, 252–3; *Camb. Hand-list*, p. 72.

Or. 37 comprises ff. 98 of 14·3 × 8·5 c. and 11 ll.; good *naskh*; rubrications; dated 1104/1692–3; defective at beginning and end, and followed by a few leaves of a book on the science of the proper reading of the *Qur'án* (تجويد القرآن); dated 1104/1692–3. **Or. 559** comprises ff. 143 of 21·3 × 13·17 c. and 9 ll., written in beautiful *naskh*; richly gilded and illuminated; dated 1197/1783; Sandars Bequest, 1894.

492, 493 (p) ده مجلس **Corpus, No. 194**
King's, No. 185

Two collections of recitations for the month of Muḥarram on the martyrdom of the Imáms, etc., entitled *Dah Majlis* ("the Ten Séances"). For descriptions of similar works, see *B.M.P.C.*, p. 155b, and *Cat. Camb. Pers. MSS.*, No. LXVI.

The **Corpus MS.** is written in large *naskh* on oblong leaves of 12 × 20 c. The **King's MS.** (see Palmer's *King's Cat.*, p. 12) is undated.

494 (p) ديباچهٔ دلکشا **Corpus, No. 98[1]**

Díbácha-i-Dilgushá, a work in ornate prose and verse by Mawlawí Amír 'Alí. Written in *nasta'líq* on leaves of 22 × 14 c.

495 (p) ديباچهٔ سعادت **Corpus, No. 98[2]**

Díbácha-i-Sa'ádat, a work similar to that mentioned above, and copied in the same hand.

496 (p) ديباچهٔ فرح بخش **Corpus, No. 98[3]**

Díbácha-i-Faraḥ-bakhsh, a description of a *bázár* in ornate prose and verse. In the colophon it is described as the *Míná Bázár* of Jámí, but this is certainly incorrect, nor does the book correspond with the homonymous work of Ẓuhúrí. Dated 1241/1825–6.

497 (h) ديوان آبرو **King's, No. 180**

The *Díwán* of a Hindústání poet called *Ábrú*.

A small volume written in very bad *ta'líq*, undated. See Palmer's *King's Cat.*, p. 27.

498 (h) ديوان آتش **Corpus, No. 71**

The *Díwán* of a Hindústání poet called *Átash*.

Ff. 111 of 38 × 18 c.; *nasta'líq*; undated.

499 (p) ديوان آشوب **King's, No. 169**

The *Díwán* of a Persian poet named Muḥammad Bakhsh and poetically entitled *Áshúb*, who died in 1199/1784–5.

The MS. was copied in 1198/1783–4, a year before the poet's death. See Palmer's *King's Cat.*, p. 13.

500 (t) ديوان احمد يَسَوى **Add. 3619** (10)

The Turkish *Díwán* of Khwája Aḥmad Yasawí (Yeseví), also known as *Díwán-i-Ḥikmat*, composed in the twelfth century of the Christian era. See E. J. W. Gibb's *History of Ottoman Poetry*, vol. i, pp. 71, 76, 92, 95, 104 and 169.

Ff. 230 of 26 × 16 c. and 13 ll.; large, clear, sprawling *ta'líq*; rubrications; undated. Bought of Géjou, Feb. 14, 1900.

501 (p) ديوان اديب صابر **Or. 650** (8)

The *Díwán* of the well-known Persian poet Adíb Ṣábir (d. *circ.* 540/1145–6). See *B.M.P.C.*, p. 552.

Pp. 224 of 20 × 15·5 c. and 13 ll., good clear Indian *ta'líq*; copied in A.D. 1878 by Sayyid Ḥusayn of Muẓaffarpúr; bought through Quaritch at the O'Kinealy sale, Jan. 15, 1906.

502, 503 (p) ديوان اسير **Corpus, No. 92**
King's, No. 173

The *Díwán* of Mírzá Jalál Asír of Iṣfahán; d. 1049/1639–40. See *B.M.P.C.*, p. 681[b].

Corpus, No. 92, is written in bad *nasta'líq* on pages of 21 × 11 c.; undated. For **King's, No. 173,** see Palmer's *King's Cat.*, p. 12.

504–506 (p) ديوان امير خسرو دهلوى **Or. 39 (9)**
Or. 757 (9)
Fitzwilliam, No. 199

Three copies of the *Díwán* of the celebrated Persian poet Amír Khusraw of Dihlí (d. 725/1325). See *B.M.P.C.*, pp. 609 *et seqq.*

Or. 39 contains a selection of the *ghazals*; was copied at Herát in 901/1495–6 by Muḥammad 'Alí of Samarqand, and was bought of Naaman on Feb. 5, 1901. **Or. 757** comprises ff. 273 of 24·3 × 14·2 c. and 17 ll.; small, neat *ta'líq*; rubrications; undated; bought of Géjou, May 13, 1907. The **Fitzwilliam MS.** contains ff. 222 of 10 × 6·75 inches and 17 lines in text and 32 in margin; one or more pages missing at the beginning. From the McClean Collection.

507–511 (p) ديوان انورى **Christ's, Dd. 4. 9**
Christ's, Dd. 3. 6
Corpus, No. 113
King's, No. 175
Magdalene, Pepys 1281

Five copies of the *Díwán* of Anwarí (d. 592/1196). See *B.M.P.C.*, pp. 554 *et seqq.*

Of the **Christ's College MSS., Dd. 4. 9** contains also a commentary following the text. It is written in Indian *ta'líq*, comprises 376 ff. of 25·1 × 15·3 and 17 ll., was copied before 1160/1747, and belonged formerly to Archibald Swinton. The second **Christ's MS., Dd. 3. 6,** is written in a good, clear *ta'líq* with headings in blue and borders of blue and gold, is dated 1030/1621, and contains 328 ff. of 24·7 × 14 c. and 17 ll. The **Corpus MS. No. 113** contains many glosses, comprises 241 ff. of 22 × 15 c., and is written in a fair *nasta'líq* hand. It was copied at Sháhjahánábád in the 48th year of Awrangzíb's reign (about 1116/1704–5). For the **King's MS.** see Palmer, p. 12. The **Magdalene MS.,** which I have not seen, was identified by Mr W. H. Mill, and is, as Mr S. Gaselee informs me, "the only Oriental MS. in either of the College Libraries."

512 (p) ديوان آهى **King's, No. 179**

The *Díwán* of Áhí (d. 927/1521). See *B.M.P.C.*, p. 736[a]; *Oude Cat.*, pp. 21, 327; Flügel's *Vienna Cat.*, i, 578; and Palmer, p. 12. The MS. was transcribed at Samarqand, 973/1565–6.

513, 514 (t) دیوان باقی **Or. 218 (9)**
Christ's, Dd. 5. 14

The *Díwán* of the well-known Turkish poet Báqí (d. 1008/1600). See E. J. W. Gibb's *Hist. of Ottoman Poetry*, iii, pp. 133 *et seqq.*

Or. 218 comprises ff. 114 of 21 × 13·3 c. and 21 ll.; is written in a neat *naskh* between gold borders; is undated, but was transcribed before 1232/1817; bought of J. J. Naaman, Nov. 12, 1902. The **Christ's MS.**, presented to the College on Dec. 9, 1898, by the Rev. W. H. Lowe, was transcribed in Constantinople in 1037/1627–8 in a clear Turkish *ta'líq* and comprises 107 ff. of 18·2 × 12·3 c. and 19 ll.

515, 516 (p) دیوان بدر چاچی **Corpus, No. 215**
Jesus, No. 4

Two copies of the *Díwán* of Badr-i-Cháchí (or Sháshí), a poet of Táshkand who flourished in the middle of the 8th century of the *hijra* (14th of the Christian era) and achieved his reputation chiefly in India. See *B.M.P.C.*, p. 1031^b^, iv.

The **Corpus MS.** comprises ff. 86 of 22 × 14 c., is written in *nasta'líq*, and is dated A.D. 1851. The **Jesus MS.**, presented by G. Lewis, is written in fair Indian *ta'líq* and dated 1049/1639.

517 (p) دیوان برهمن **Corpus, No. 114**

The *Díwán* of Brahman, who is probably identical with the author of the *Chahár Chiman* and *Munshá'át*, a Hindú writer of Sháhjahán's reign named Chandarbhán, who flourished in the middle of the 11th century of the *hijra* (17th of the Christian era). See *B.M.P.C.*, pp. 397^b^, 838^b^.

Ff. 58 of 21 × 15 c., written in *ním-shikasta*, undated, incomplete at end. Contains *ghazals* and a few *rubá'ís*.

518 (a) **Trinity, R. 13. 24**

دیوان أبی بكر محمّد بن عبّاس الخوارزمی البكری

The *Díwán* of Abú Bakr Muḥammad b. 'Abbás al-Khwárazmí (d. 383/993 or 393/1002). See Brockelmann, i, 93; and Palmer's *Trin. Cat.*, pp. 55–7.

Ff. 161, good *naskh*, undated.

519 (t) ديوان ثاقب **Or. 459 (9)**

The *Díwán* of the Turkish poet "dervish" Tháqib.

Ff. 146 of 23 × 14 c. and 21 lines; small, neat *nasta'líq* with rubrications; dated 1246/1830–31. Bought of J. J. Naaman, Nov. 27, 1903.

520 (p) ديوان ثاقب **Corpus, No. 225**

The *Díwán* of a Persian poet called Tháqib.

Undated; the leaves measure 16 × 10 c.; written in *nasta'líq*.

521–524 (p) ديوان جامى **Add. 3642 (8), Or. 256¹ (9)**
Or. 291 (9), Or. 466² (6)

Four copies of the *Díwán* of the celebrated Persian poet and mystic Núru'd-Dín 'Abdu'r-Raḥmán Jámí (d. 898/1492–3), or portions of it.

Add. 3642, bought of Sethian, May 9, 1900, comprises ff. 126 of 20·8 × 14·2 c. and 15 ll., and is written in a poor but legible modern *ta'líq* and dated 1248/1832–3. **Or. 256¹** contains "the first of Jámí's three *Díwáns*, omitting the Preface and most of the *qaṣídas*, the *ghazals* beginning on p. 23." It forms part of the Cowell Bequest, contains pp. 701 of 22 × 17 c. and 11 ll., is written in a clear Indian *ta'líq*, and dated 15 Jumáda ii, 1274 (= Jan. 31, 1858). The second part of the volume contains the *Waṣlat-náma* of Shaykh Farídu'd-Dín 'Aṭṭár (*q.v.*). **Or. 291,** incomplete at beginning and end, and without colophon or date, also forms part of the Cowell Bequest, comprises ff. 213 of 21·8 × 15·5 c. and 17 ll., and is written in a poor but legible *nasta'líq*. **Or. 466²,** of which the first and larger portion contains the *Laylá and Majnún* of Hátifí, concludes (ff. 92^b–97^a) with some *ghazals* from the *Díwán* of Jámí. This MS. is dated 928/1522, and was bought of Géjou on Jan. 29, 1904. It is written in a good *ta'líq* on leaves of 16·8 × 12·5 c. and 11 ll.

525, 526 (a) ديوان جرير بن عطيّة التميمى **Christ's, Dd. 5. 11**
Christ's, Dd. 5. 10

The late Dr W. Wright's transcript of the *Díwán of Jarír* (**Dd. 5. 11**), ending with the following note: "Here ends the St Petersburg MS. abruptly, some leaves having been lost.

William Wright. Copied at Dublin, 19 March, 1859. Collated at Cambridge, 6 April, 1884"; followed by other material for an edition in Wright's and other hands. Pp. 211 of 21·1 × 16·8 c. and 19 ll. **Dd. 5. 10** is another copy of the same *Díwán* made for Dr Sachau in March–April 1895 from the Cairo MS. by Aḥmad b. Muḥammad 'Abdu'r-Raḥmán and concluded by him on Dhu'l-Ḥijja 5, 1312 (May 30, 1895). Pp. 1050 of 26 × 18 c. and 10 ll.; large, coarse *naskh* with rubrications and Sachau's autograph on the back.

527–537 (p)	**Or. 249 (10)**	**Jesus, No. 5**
	Or. 261 (8)	**Corpus, No. 25**
	Or. 387 (8)	**Corpus, No. 76**
	Or. 475 (10)	**King's, No. 159**
	Or. 924 (8)	**Trinity, R. 13. 27**
	Christ's, Dd. 3. 11	

ديوان حافظ

Ten copies of the *Díwán* of Ḥáfiẓ, and one volume of English versified translations from the same.

Or. 249 (Cowell Bequest) comprises ff. 250 of 24·4 × 13·4 c. and 15 lines; is written in an excellent Persian *ta'líq* within golden coloured borders, and is dated 1070/1659–60. **Or. 261** (Cowell Bequest) comprises ff. 176 of 20·5 × 13 c. and 15 lines, is written in a poor but legible *ta'líq*, and is incomplete at the end and undated. **Or. 387** (Cowell Bequest) comprises pp. vi + 96 of 20 × 12·5 c. and 28 lines, was transcribed in 1845, and contains English verse translations from Ḥáfiẓ entitled "A Wreath from the Díwán of Ḥáfiẓ." This is preceded by a Dedication and short Preface, and followed by Appendices. **Or. 475,** comprising ff. 269 of 25·8 × 15·8 c. and 13 lines, appears to be, in reality, not a manuscript but a lithograph, though it has been transferred from the class of printed books in which it bore the class-mark **Dd. 3. 8.** The handwriting is a clear but clumsy Indian *naskh*, and it bears the date Muḥarram 2, 1231 (= December 4, 1815). **Or. 924** (Lynch Bequest) is a modern copy transcribed in 1262/1846 in good *ta'líq*. It comprises 143 ff. of 21 × 13 c. and 16 ll. The **Christ's College MS.** (**Dd. 3. 11**), written in a fine *ta'líq* and illuminated, was copied by Maqṣúd 'Alí on Ṣafar 19, 977

(August 3, 1569), contains 188 ff. of 23·1 × 14·8 and 15 ll., and bears on f. 1a the seal of Ghulám Walí 'Alí Quṭbsháh. The **Jesus College MS.** (**No. 5**), written in a good *ta'líq*, was presented to the Library by G. Lewis, and is dated Rajab 26, 1099 (=May 27, 1688). The **Corpus MS.** (**No. 25**) comprises ff. 171 of 24·5 × 14 c., is written in *nasta'líq* and dated 1240/1824–5. The **Corpus MS.** (**No. 76**) is undated and is written in good *nasta'líq* on pages of 18 × 10 c. The **King's MS.** (**No. 159**) comprises ff. 299 written in small but neat *ta'líq*, and is dated 1113/1701–2. The **Trinity MS.** (**R. 13. 27**), copied in the 16th century, comprises ff. 155 written in bad *ta'líq*.

538, 539 (p) دیوان حزین **Or. 524² (9)**
King's, No. 188

Two copies of the *Díwán* of Shaykh 'Alí Ḥazín (d. 1180/1766). See *B.M.P.C.*, 715–717.

Or. 524² (of which the first portion contains an untitled work on Rhetoric) is written in a poor Indian *ta'líq*, becoming worse towards the end, with rubrications. This portion of the volume comprises ff. 59b–113b of 23·8 × 14·8 c. and 15 lines. The MS. was bought of Messrs Luzac on August 27, 1904. The **King's MS. No. 188** is undated. See Palmer's *King's Cat.*, p. 13.

540 (h) دیوان حسرت **Corpus, No. 43**

The Hindústání *Díwán* of a poet named Ḥasrat, transcribed in 1192/1778.

541 (t) دیوان حشمت **Or. 181 (10)**

The *Díwán* of a Turkish poet named Ḥishmat. See *B.M.T.C.*, p. 204.

Ff. 68 of 26·2 × 13·4 c. and 23 lines, written in neat *nasta'líq*, with rubrications, on various coloured paper; undated. Bought of Géjou, Jan. 1, 1902.

542 (p) دیوان خاقانی **King's, No. 167**

The *Díwán* of Kháqání.

See Palmer's *King's Cat.*, p. 13. Undated.

543–545 (h) ديوان درد **Or. 296 (8)**; **Corpus, No. 107⁴**; **Corpus, No. 116³**

The Hindústání *Díwán* of the celebrated poet Mír Dard.

Or. 296 (Cowell Bequest) is dated 2 Rajab, 1273 (Feb. 17, 1858), and comprises ff. 60 of 22 × 16·8 c. and 15 lines, written in legible modern Indian *ta'líq*. Of the **Corpus MSS., No. 107⁴**, copied at Sháhjahánábád in 1228/1813, is written in a clear *nasta'líq* on ff. 45 of 21 × 15 c., while **No. 116³** contains only some selections.

546 (t) ديوان ذكائى **Or. 219 (9)**

The *Díwán* of the Turkish poet Zuká'í (Dhuká'í).

Ff. 48 of 23·6 × 16·5 c. and 17 lines, written in good *naskh* with rubrications, and dated 1245/1829–30. Bought of Naaman, Nov. 12, 1902.

547 (t) ديوان راشد **Or. 458 (8)**

The *Díwán* of the Turkish poet Ráshid.

Ff. 103 of 21·4 × 13 c. and 15 lines; written in neat *nasta'líq* between gold borders, undated. Bought of Naaman, Nov. 27, 1903.

548 (h) ديوان رضا **Corpus, No. 35**

The *Díwán* of a Hindústání poet named Riḍá.

Undated; large *nasta'líq*; pages measuring 28 × 18 c.

549 (a) ديوان [الشريف] الرّضىّ **Or. 212 (9)**

The Arabic *Díwán* of ash-Sharíf ar-Raḍí (d. 406/1015 at Baghdád). See Brockelmann, i, 82.

Ff. 473 of 22·6 × 13·7 and 17 lines; large, clear *naskh*, dated Muḥarram 1090 (Feb.–March, 1679); bought of Naaman, Nov. 12, 1902.

550 (p) ديوان رياضى **Or. 527 (6)**

The Persian *Díwán* of Riyáḍí.

Ff. 69 of 15·4 × 8·8 c. and 10 lines (4 written obliquely); small, neat Persian *nasta'líq*; gilt margins. Bought of Géjou, Nov. 1, 1904. No date.

551 (p) **دیوان سعدی** **Corpus, No. 24**

The *Díwán* of the celebrated Sa'dí of Shíráz.

A modern copy, undated, imperfect at end, written in a *ním-shikasta* hand on leaves of 25 × 15 c.

552 (p) **دیوان سلیم طهرانی** **King's, No. 163**

The *Díwán* of Salím of Ṭihrán (d. 1067/1656–7). See Rieu's *B.M.P.C.*, p 660a; Ethé's *Bodl. P. C.*, col. 309; Palmer's *King's Cat.*, p. 13.

Dated 1081/1670–1.

553, 554 (p) **دیوان سلمان ساوجی** **Or. 61 (11)** **Or. 807 (10)**

Two copies of the *Díwán* of Salmán of Sáwa (d. *circ.* 779/1377–8). See *B.M.P.C.*, pp. 624–6.

Or. 61 comprises ff. 395 of 27·5 × 15·3 c. and 17 ll.; large clear *ta'líq*, copied before 1023/1614; bought of Naaman, May 3, 1901. **Or. 807** comprises ff. 344 of 25·6 × 16 c. and 20 ll.; written in old-fashioned *ta'líq* with rubrications and dated Sha'bán, 858/Sept. 1454; bought of David, May 19, 1909.

555 (h) **دیوان سودا** **Christ's, Dd. 3. 22**

The Hindústání *Díwán* of Sawdá (Mírzá Rafí').

Dated 1194/1780. Ff. 63 of 21 × 14·6 c. and 11 ll.

556, 557 (p) **دیوان شاهی** **Or. 188 (8)** **King's, No. 161**

Two copies of the *Díwán* of Sháhí of Sabzawár? (d. 857/1453). See *B.M.P.C.*, p. 640a.

Or. 188 comprises ff. 37 of 19 × 11·2 c. and 13 lines; good *ta'líq*, within gold borders; illuminated title-page; undated. Bought of Géjou, July 3, 1902. The **King's MS.,** also undated, was copied by one Muḥammad Amín.

558 **دیوان شفیعا** **King's, No. 176**

The *Díwán* of Shafí'á (or Athar) of Shíráz (d. 1113/1701–2). See *B.M.P.C.*, p. 791b. This is followed by the *qaṣídas* of a poet called Rukn, who may be Ruknu'd-Dín Awḥadí or Ruknu'd-Dín Mas'úd of Káshán, or some other.

See Palmer's *King's Cat.*, pp. 13 and 17.

559-561 (p) دیوان شمس تبریز {Or. 273 (8), Or. 284 (11), Or. 806 (12)}

Three copies of the mystical *Díwán* of Shams-i-Tabríz (really the work of Mawláná Jalálu'd-Dín Rúmí, d. 628/1231), two in the Cowell Bequest, the third bought of G. David on May 19, 1909. See *B.M.P.C.*, p. 593, and Dr R. A. Nicholson's *Selected Odes from the Díwán of Shams-i-Tabríz*.

Or. 273 comprises ff. 163 of 21 × 14·4 c. and 19 lines; excellent old *naskh* in earlier part, tending towards *nasta'líq* towards the end, where the MS. is defective; undated; apparently fifteenth century of the Christian era. **Or. 284,** a more extensive collection of the odes, comprises ff. 523 of 27 × 15·8 c. and 27 lines, copied in 1009/1600–1 in a rather poor, scratchy *ta'líq*. It was bought by the late Professor Cowell of one Aḥmad 'Alí in 1864. **Or. 806** comprises 391 ff. of 30·2 × 18 c. with 19 ll. in double columns in the text and 34 half verses in the margins of each page. Many leaves are much damaged and patched. A prose preface occupies ff. 1^b–5^a. Written in good *ta'líq* within red lines. No date or colophon.

562-565 (p) دیوان شوکت بخاری {Or. 543 (9), Trinity, R. 10. 3, Corpus, No. 57[2], Corpus, No. 162}

Four copies of the *Díwán* of Shawkat of Bukhárá (d. 1107/1695-6). See *B.M.P.C.*, p. 698.

Or. 543, copied at Ayyúb in Constantinople in Rabí' ii, 1195/April, 1781, and bought of Géjou, Jan. 4, 1905, comprises ff. 160 of 22·5 × 13·5 c. and 19 lines, and is written in a poor *ta'líq*. The **Trinity MS.** comprises ff. 193, and is written in a small and beautiful *ta'líq* and undated. **Corpus 57[2],** undated, is written in *ním-shikasta* on leaves of 22·25 × 12 c. **Corpus 162,** dated 1247/1831–2, is written in a fair *nasta'líq* on leaves of 22 × 16 c.

566–571 (p) ديوان صائب **Or. 589 (9)** / **Or. 691 (8)** / **Christ's, Dd. 3. 10** / **Corpus, No. 75[4]** / **Corpus, No. 129** / **King's, No. 170**

The *Díwán* of Ṣá'ib of Iṣfahán (d. 1088/1677–8). See *B.M.P.C.*, pp. 693–5.

Or. 589 comprises ff. 115 of 23·2 × 15·2 c. and 15 lines, written in good *ta'líq*, with rubrications, on coloured paper, and dated Dhu'l-Qa'da, 1074 (June, 1664). Bought of Géjou, Oct. 30, 1905. **Or. 691** comprises ff. 248 of 20·7 × 13·4 c. and 17 lines, written in fair *nasta'líq* and undated. Bought of Géjou, Dec. 1906. The **Christ's College MS.**, slightly defective, is written in a good *ta'líq*, and contains 153 ff. of 23·2 × 13·8 c. and 17 ll. **Corpus 75[4]** contains only a fragment of the *Díwán*, filling 41 leaves, and extending from the letter د to ى. It is dated 1071/1660–1, and is written in *nasta'líq* on leaves of 20 × 14 c. **Corpus 129,** undated, contains only the letters ا to د, thus supplementing the preceding MS. It is undated, and is written in fair *nasta'líq* on pages of 30 × 21 c. For the **King's MS.** see Palmer's *Cat.*, p. 13.

572 (a) ديوان الصفىّ الحلّى **Or. 456 (12)**

The Arabic *Díwán* of the poet aṣ-Ṣafí of Ḥilla (Ṣafiyyu'd-Dín Abu'l-Faḍl 'Abdu'l-'Azíz b. Sarájá al-Ḥillí: born 677/1278, d. 750/1349: see Brockelmann, ii, pp. 159–160).

Ff. 301 of 30·4 × 21 c. and 17 ll.; large, clear *naskh* between red lines; titles in red, undated. Bought of Géjou, Nov. 27, 1903.

573 (p) ديوان طالب آملى **King's, No. 172**

The Persian *Díwán* of Ṭálib of Ámul, d. 1035/1625–6. See *B.M.P.C.*, p. 679b, and Palmer's *King's Cat.*, p. 13.

Undated; scribe, Muḥammad Shafí' Qurashí.

574–577 (t) ديوان عرشى دده **Or. 40 (9), Or. 488 (9)** / **Or. 677 (9), Or. 768 (8)**

Four copies of the Turkish *Díwán* of Maḥmúd 'Arshí-Dedé, a poet of the Ḥurúfí sect, concerning which see E. J. W.

Gibb's *Hist. of Ottoman Poetry*, vol. i, pp. 336–388; the description of the *Jáwidán-i-Kabír* in my *Cat. of the Pers. MSS. in the Camb. Univ. Lib.*, pp. 69–86; two articles by me on the *Ḥurúfí Literature and Doctrines* in the *J.R.A.S.* for 1898 (pp. 61–94) and 1907 (pp. 1–49), in the latter of which three of the four Cambridge Univ. Lib. MSS. are described as well as another belonging to myself and yet another belonging to the British Museum. As I have shown at p. 34 of the last-named article, the poet's proper name was Maḥmúd, he was born at Yeñi Bázár in Rumelia, flourished about 964/1556–7, and originally wrote under the name of Chákí which he afterwards changed to 'Arshí. Concerning the Ḥurúfí sect see also vol. ix of the "E. J. W. Gibb Memorial" series, entitled *Textes Ḥouroûfís* by M. Clément Huart and Dr Riḍá Tawfíq.

Or. 40, one of six Ḥurúfí MSS. bought of Naaman on Feb. 5, 1901, comprises ff. 128 of 22·8 × 16·6 c. and 16 or 17 ll. **Or. 488,** which also contains at the end the "Key to the Ḥurúfí books" (مفتاح كتب حروفيان), is one of 16 MSS. bought of Géjou on August 18, 1904, is dated 1272/1855–6, and comprises ff. 129 of 22 × 16·2 c. and 15 ll., written in clear Turkish *nasta'líq* with rubrications. **Or. 677,** bought of Géjou on Feb. 17, 1906, and copied by Darwísh 'Ísá b. Kamálu'd-Dín in 1222/1807–8, comprises ff. 104 of 22 × 15·5 c. and 17 ll., written in a poor Turkish *naskh* within red borders. **Or. 768,** bought of Géjou on Feb. 20, 1908, and dated 1214/1799–1800, comprises ff. 99 of 20·9 × 13·2 c. and 17 ll., and is written in fair *nasta'líq* with rubrications.

578–581 (p) ديوان عرفى **Add. 3708 (8), Corpus, 1 Corpus, 137², King's, 160**

Four copies of the *Díwán* of 'Urfí of Shíráz, who died at Lahore, aged 36, in 999/1590–1. See *B.M.P.C.*, pp. 667–8.

Add. 3708, bought of Naaman on Nov. 7, 1900, comprises ff. 120 of 20 × 11 c. and 21 ll., written in legible Persian *ta'líq* and dated 1053/1643–4. **Corpus 1** comprises ff. 95 of 25 × 17 c., and was copied in 1852 in a negligent *nasta'líq*. **Corpus 137²,** though entitled "*Díwán*" in the colophon, contains only *qaṣídas*. It is dated 1157/1744–5, and is written in *shikasta* on leaves of 28 × 17 c. For the **King's MS.** see Palmer's *Cat.*, p. 13.

582 (a) ديوان عليّ بن أبى طالب **Add. 3706 (7)**

The *Díwán*, or collection of poems, ascribed to 'Alí b. Abí Ṭálib, but generally regarded as spurious. See Brockelmann, i, pp. 43–4. This MS., dated 890/1485, also contains a Persian Introduction and Commentary. Bought of Naaman, Nov. 7, 1900.

583, 584 (a) ديوان عمر بن الفارض **Or. 484 (6)**
Or. 497 (9)

Two copies of the *Díwán* of the celebrated Egyptian mystical poet 'Umar ibnu'l-Fáriḍ (d. 632/1235), the first containing also a commentary on certain verses and the latter a Preface by the poet's grandson 'Alí. See Brockelmann, i, pp. 262–3. **Or. 484,** bought of Géjou on Aug. 18, 1904, comprises ff. 95 of 15·7 × 10·5 c. and 17 ll.; is written in a neat, small *naskh* with rubrications, and is dated 17 Ramaḍán, 1003 (May 26, 1595). At the end are some poems by Ibnu'l-'Arabí. **Or. 497** comprises ff. 105 of 24·2 × 16·5 c. and 14 ll., is written in a large, clear, modern *naskh* with rubrications, undated; and was bought of Messrs Hannan and Watson on August 20, 1904.

585–588 (p) ديوان غنى **Corpus, 22, Corpus, 45**
Corpus, 170, King's, 177

Four copies of the *Díwán* of Muḥammad Ṭáhir Ghaní of Kashmír, who died 1079/1668–9. See *B.M.P.C.*, p. 692. **Corpus 22** is written in wretched *shikasta* on leaves of 22 × 13 c., undated. **Corpus 45** comprises ff. 78 of 27 × 16 c., is written in a large and ugly *nasta'líq*, and is also undated. **Corpus 170,** acephalous, 70 pp. of 23 × 15 c., *shikasta* hand, is dated 1109/1697–8. **King's 177** (Palmer's *King's Cat.*, p. 13) is dated 1186/1772–3.

589 (t) ديوان فضولى بغدادى **Or. 168 (6)**

The *Díwán* of the celebrated Turkish poet Fuḍúlí of Baghdád, who died about 963/1556. See E. J. W. Gibb's *Hist. of Ottoman Poetry*, iii, pp. 70–107. The MS., bought of

Naaman on Dec. 6, 1901, comprises 171 ff. of 14·8 × 10·3 c. and 15 ll.; written in poor but legible *ta'líq*, undated.

590 (p) ديوان فطرت **King's, No. 178**

The *Díwán* of Fiṭrat. There seem to have been at least two poets who wrote under this name, one who died about 1060/1650, and another, Mír Mu'izzu'd-Dín Muḥammad, who died 1106/1694–5. See Ethé's *I. O. Pers. Cat.*, col. 852, No. 1560. This MS. is undated. See Palmer's *King's Cat.*, p. 13.

591, 592 (p) ديوان فغانى **Add. 3707 (7)** **Or. 664 (8)**

Two copies of the *Díwán* of Fighání of Shíráz, who died in 922/1516. See *B.M.P.C.*, p. 651. **Add. 3707,** bought of Naaman on Nov. 7, 1900, is incomplete at end and undated, and comprises ff. 92 of 16 × 7·3 c. and 19 ll. and is written in a minute, neat Persian *ta'líq*. **Or. 664,** bought of Géjou, Feb. 17, 1906, comprises ff. 70 of 19 × 12 c. and 13 ll., and is written in good *ta'líq* between gold lines with ornamentation in gilt and colours, and is dated 968/1560–1.

593 (t) ديوان فهيم **Or. 603 (7)**

The *Díwán* of the Turkish poet Fahím, who died about 1058/1648–9. See Gibb's *Hist. of Ottoman Poetry*, iii, pp. 290–293. The MS., bought of Géjou on Oct. 30, 1905, comprises ff. 58 of 19·4 × 11·4 c. and 19 ll., is undated, and is written in a scratchy Turkish *nasta'líq*.

594 (p) ديوان فيضى **Or. 275 (6)**

The *Díwán* of Fayḍí, who died 1004/1595–6. See *B.M.P.C.*, pp. 670–1. The MS. was given in 1865 by Stanley Leathes to Professor Cowell, by whom it was left to the Library. It comprises 204 ff. of 15 × 9·3 c. and 15 ll., is undated, and is written in a small neat *ta'líq*.

595 (p) ديوان قاسم الانوار **Or. 760 (8)**

The *Díwán* of Qásimu'l-Anwár, who died 837/1433–4. See *B.M.P.C.*, pp. 635–7. This MS., bought of Géjou, May 13, 1907, comprises 185 ff. of 19·5 × 12·2 and 20 ll., is defective at end, undated, and is written in a fair *nasta'líq* with rubrications.

596 (p) ديوان قانع **Corpus, No. 179**

The *Díwán* of a poet named Qání', belonging to the time of Muḥammad Sháh (circ. 1250/1834–5). The *Díwán* is preceded by a prose preface, and followed (on f. 69) by an acephalous *mathnawí* poem.

Ff. 95 of 23 × 16 c.; poor *nasta'líq*; undated.

597 (t) ديوان قائمی **Or. 571 (8)**

The *Díwán* of a Turkish Ḥurúfí poet called Qá'imí. This MS. comprises 63 ff. of 21·2 × 14 c. and 17 ll. and is written in an excellent Turkish *naskh* with rubrications. It was bought of Géjou, July 14, 1905, and is dated 1190/1776.

598 (p) ديوان قتيل **Corpus, No. 78**

The *Díwán* of Qatíl, d. 1233/1817–8. See *B.M.P.C.*, p. 726b. Written in *nasta'líq* on pages of 22 × 12·5 c., undated.

599, 600 (p) ديوان كليم **Add. 3709 (8)**
Corpus, No. 109

The *Díwán* of Abú Ṭálib Kalím of Hamadán, poet-laureate of Sháh Jahán, who died in 1062/1652. See *B.M.P.C.*, pp. 686–7. **Add. 3709,** bought of Naaman on Nov. 7, 1900, comprises 156 ff. of 19·8 × 13·7 c. and 15 ll., is dated 1264/1848, and is written in fair *ta'líq*. The **Corpus MS.** is undated and is written in *ním-shikasta* on leaves of 18 × 10 c.

601, 602 (p) **Christ's, Dd. 3. 4**
King's, No. 171

ديوان كمال الدين اسمعيل اصفهانی

The *Díwán* of the celebrated poet Kamálu'd-Dín Isma'íl of Iṣfahán, who was killed by the Mongols in 635/1237–8. See *B.M.P.C.*, p. 580b. For the **King's MS.,** see Palmer's *King's Cat.*, p. 13. The **Christ's MS.** is a fine copy, written in good *ta'líq*, with a beautiful *'unwán*, and contains 347 ff. of 25 × 14·5 c. and 21 ll.

603, 604 (p) ديوان كمال خجند **Or. 282 (9)**
Or. 780 (8)

The *Díwán* of Kamál of Khujand, who died in 803/1400–1. See *B.M.P.C.*, pp. 632–3. **Or. 282** (Cowell Bequest), rather tattered and worm-eaten, comprises ff. 174 of 22·3 × 12·5 c. and 15 ll., is written in good *ta'líq*, undated and defective at end. **Or. 780,** bought of Géjou, Jan. 7, 1909, comprises ff. 218 of 21·3 × 12·7 c. and 16 ll., is written in excellent *ta'líq* with blue and gold headings, and is dated Sha'bán, 876 (Jan.–Feb., 1472).

605, 606 (h) دیوان گویا **Corpus, No. 20**[3] **Corpus, No. 175**

Two copies of the Hindústání *Díwán* of Faqír Muḥammad Khán *Gúyá*, the second (**175**) being a lithographed edition published at Cawnpore in 1246/1830–1, containing 383 pp. of 28 × 18 c. The other MS. copy is undated, written in *nasta'líq*, and comprises 55 ff.

607 (p) دیوان مسعودِ سعدِ سلمان **Or. 781** (10)

The *Díwán* of Mas'úd-i-Sa'd-i-Salmán, who died in 515/1121–2. See *B.M.P.C.*, pp. 548–9, and a very full critical notice by Mírzá Muḥammad in the *J.R.A.S.* for Oct. 1905 (pp. 693–740) and Jan. 1906 (pp. 11–55). This MS., bought of Géjou on Jan. 7, 1909, comprises 117 ff. of 26·1 × 16·3 c. and 15 ll., is dated Jumádá i, 1283 (= Sept.–Oct. 1866), and is written in large clear *ta'líq* with rubrications. The copyist's name is given as *Wajdí*.

608 (h) دیوان مصحفی **Corpus, No. 59**

The Hindústání *Díwán* of Maṣ-ḥafí, undated and incomplete at end, written in *nasta'líq* on pages of 23 × 18 c.

609, 610 (p) دیوان مظهر **Corpus, No. 171** **King's, No. 166**

Two copies of the *Díwán* of Maẓhar. For the **King's MS.,** undated, see Palmer's *King's Cat.*, p. 13. The **Corpus MS.** is also undated, and is written in *nasta'líq* on pages of 22·5 × 14 c.

611 (p) دیوان مغربی **Or. 565**[1] (8)

The *Díwán* of Maghribí, who died in 809/1406–7. See *B.M.P.C.*, p. 633. This MS., bought of Géjou on July 14, 1905, was transcribed by Muḥammad Sa'íd in 1293/1876, and comprises ff. 1–80 of 20·7 × 14 c. Written in good clear *ta'líq*.

612 (h) دیوان میر تقی **King's, No. 174**

The Hindústání *Díwán* of Mír Taqí. The MS., undated and defective at the end, is written in good *ta'líq*. See Palmer's *King's Cat.*, p. 27.

613 (h) دیوان ناسخ **Corpus, No. 129**

The Hindústání *Díwán* of Shaykh Imám-bakhsh, poetically surnamed Násikh. The MS., dated 1256/1840–1, is written in fair *nasta'líq* on pages of 26 × 16 c.

614–616 (p) دیوان ناصر علی **Christ's, Dd. 3. 28; Corpus, No. 51²; Corpus, No. 157**

The *Díwán* of Náṣir 'Alí, who died in 1108/1696–7. See *B.M.P.C.*, pp. 699–700. The **Christ's MS.,** a small and pretty volume, contains 96 ff. of 13·5 × 7·6 c. and 13 ll. It formerly belonged to Archibald Swinton, "brother of Lord Swynton, one of the Judges of the Court of Session in Scotland, who died at Bath, March 6, 1804." Neither of the **Corpus MSS.** is dated, but **No. 51²** was copied at Jahánábád in the reign of Bahádur Sháh.

617 (t) دیوان نجاتی **Or. 169 (7)**

The *Díwán* of the Turkish poet Najátí, who died in 914/1509. See E J. W. Gibb's *Hist. of Ottoman Poetry*, ii, pp. 93–122, where he is called "the first lyric poet of real distinction to appear among the Ottoman Turks." The MS., bought of Naaman on Dec. 6, 1901, comprises 140 ff. of 18·2 × 12·4 c. and 15 ll., and is written in good *ta'líq* between gold borders with an illuminated *'unwán*.

618 (t) دیوان ندیم **Or. 698 (8)**

The *Díwán* of the Turkish poet Nadím, who flourished in the early eighteenth century. See Gibb's *Hist. of Ottoman Poetry*, iv, pp. 29–57. This MS., bought of Géjou in Dec., 1906, comprises 68 ff. of 21·4 × 13 c., is undated, and is written in good *ta'líq* between gold lines.

619 (t) ديوان نسيمى **Or. 567** (9)

The *Díwán* of the Turkish Ḥurúfí poet Nasímí, who was put to death for heresy in 820/1417–18. See Gibb's *Hist. of Ottoman Poetry*, i, pp. 336–368. The MS., bought of Géjou on July 14, 1905, comprises 214 ff. of 23·3 × 16 c. and 12 ll., is written in a coarse but clear Turkish *naskh* between double red lines, is partly vocalized, and was copied in 1234/1818–19.

620 (t) ديوان نشأت **Or. 178** (8)

The *Díwán* of the Turkish poet Nash'at, who flourished in the second half of the eighteenth century. See Gibb's *Hist. of Ottoman Poetry*, iv, pp. 211–217. This MS., bought of Géjou on Jan. 1, 1902, comprises 100 ff. of 21·7 × 12·5 c. and 17 ll., is undated, and is written in a fair Turkish *nasta'líq* with rubrications.

621 (h) ديوان نصائح **Corpus, No. 129**

The Hindústání poems of Imám-bakhsh, entitled *Díwán-i-Naṣá'iḥ*.

622 (h) ديوان نصير **Corpus, No. 47**

The Hindústání *Díwán* of Naṣír.

623, 624 (p) ديوان نظيرى نيشاپورى **Corpus, No. 79**
King's, No. 165

The Díwán of Muḥammad Ḥasan Naẓírí of Níshápúr, who died in India in 1022/1613–14. See *B.M.P.C.*, pp. 817–8.

The **Corpus MS.**, undated and defective at the beginning, is written in *nasta'líq* on leaves of 21·5 × 13 c. For the **King's MS.**, also undated, see Palmer's *King's Cat.*, p. 13.

625 (p) ديوان شاه نعمة الله كرمانى **Add. 3733** (9)

The *Díwán* of Sayyid (or Sháh) Ni'matu'lláh of Kirmán, who died in 834/1431. See *B.M.P.C.*, pp. 634–5. This MS., bought of Sethian on Nov. 28, 1900, is undated, and comprises 126 ff. of 21 × 15 c. and 12 ll. in text with 21 in margin. It is written in a poor Persian *ta'líq* with rubrications.

626, 627 (p) دیوان واقف **Corpus, No. 34**
Corpus, No. 211

The *Díwán* of Wáqif, who died at Dihlí in 1200/1785–6. See *B.M.P.C.*, 719. Neither MS. is dated. **No. 34** comprises 249 ff. of 29 × 17 c., while **No. 211** measures 22 × 14 c. Both are written in *nasta'líq*.

628 (p) دیوان واله **Add. 3710 (8)**

The *Díwán* of Wálih, probably Muḥammad Káẓim of Iṣfahán, who was seen by Sir Gore Ouseley in 1226/1811, when he was over 80 years of age. See *B.M.P.C.*, pp. 722–3. The MS., undated, was bought of Naaman on Nov. 7, 1900, contains ff. 127 of 20·8 × 15 c. and 9 ll., and is written in a fair Persian *ta'líq*.

629, 630 (h) دیوان ولی **Corpus, No. 40**[2]
King's, No. 164

Two copies of the Hindústání *Díwán* of Walí. The **Corpus MS.**, apparently incomplete, is dated 1212/1797–8, and is written in *ním-shikasta* on pages of 27·25 × 16 c. For the **King's MS.** (undated), see Palmer's *King's Cat.*, p. 27.

631–633 (p) دیوان هلالی **Add. 3679 (8)**
Corpus, No. 30
King's, No. 186

Three copies of the *Díwán* of Badru'd-Dín Hilálí of Astar-ábád, a *protégé* of Mír 'Alí Shír Nawá'í, who was put to death on account of his Shí'a beliefs by the Uzbek 'Ubayd in 939/1532–3. See *B.M.P.C.*, pp. 655–6. **Add. 3679**, bought of Naaman on Aug. 16, 1900, is undated, comprises ff. 51 of 20·5 × 14 c. and 12 ll., and is written in a clear *ta'líq*. The **Corpus MS.**, undated, comprises 66 ff. of 25 × 15 c., and is written in *nasta'líq* and *ním-shikasta*. The **King's MS.** was copied in 937/1530–1 (*i.e.* during the poet's life-time) by Mír 'Alí "the Royal Scribe" (*al-Kátibu's-Sulṭání*). See Palmer's *King's Cat.*, p. 14.

634 (p) دیوان یوسف بیگ شاملو **King's, No. 181**

The *Díwán* of Yúsuf Beg Shámlú. The MS. is dated 1061/1651. See Palmer's *King's Cat.*, p. 14.

635 (t) دواوين متعدّدهٔ عثمانيّه **Add. 3641 (8)**

A MS. containing selections from the Turkish *Díwáns* of Najátí (ff. 1–18), Dhátí (ff. 19–51), Aḥmad or Aḥmadí (ff. 52–61), Masíḥí (ff. 61–71), Fawrí (ff. 72–82), Khayálí (ff. 83–95), Amrí (ff. 95–107), and 'Ubaydí (ff. 108–111). These are followed by a *mathnawí* poem (ff. 112–113) and some quatrains (ff. 114 to end). The MS., bought of Sethian, May 9, 1900, comprises 147 ff. of 19·4 × 11·8 c. and 14 ll., and is written in a fair *nasta'líq*.

636 (h) دواوين منتخبهٔ هنديّه **King's, No. 168**

Selections from the Hindústání *Díwáns* of Yaqín (ff. 34), Sawdá (ff. 18) and Na'ím. The MS. was copied at Sháhjahánábád in the 23rd year of Sháh 'Álam. See Palmer's *King's Cat.*, pp. 14 and 27 *bis*.

637 (a) **Or. 208[4] (8)**

ذخر المعاد (نظير بانت سعاد) لمحمّد البوصيرى

Dhukhru 'l-Ma'ád, an imitation by al-Buṣírí (d. 694/1294) of the well-known *Bánat Su'ád* of Ka'b b. Zuhayr. See Brockelmann, i, p. 267. For description of the MS., of which this portion occupies ff. 38^{b}–53^{a}, see above, p. 29, *s.v. Burda*, **No. 164.**

638 (p) **Christ's, Dd. 3. 18**

ذخيرهٔ خوارزمشاهى (كتاب دهم: قراباذين)

The tenth and last book (in 38 chapters, on Materia Medica) of the great Thesaurus of Medicine entitled *Dhakhíra-i-Khwárazmsháhí* compiled early in the twelfth century for Quṭbu'd-Dín Khwárazmsháh. See *B.M.P.C.*, pp. 466–7; *Camb. Pers. Cat.*, pp. 211–212. The MS. contains 56 ff. of 22 × 16·8 c. and 18 ll., and is undated.

639 (a) ذخيرة الفقه **King's, No. 190**

The second part of a work on Jurisprudence entitled *Dhakhíratu'l-Fiqh*. See Palmer's *King's Cat.*, p. 22. The MS., which is undated, is a large folio volume, incomplete, written in a neat but odd *naskh* hand, with headings in red, blue, and gold.

640 (p) ذخيرة الملوك **King's, No. 189**

A treatise on political ethics entitled *Dhakhíratu'l-Mulúk*, by 'Alí b. Shiháb al-Hamadání, who died in 786/1385. See *B.M.P.C.*, p. 447. The MS. comprises 235 ff. and is dated 1030/1620–1. See Palmer's *King's Cat.*, p. 14.

641–643 (t) ذيل نابى لدرّة التّاج ويسى {**Add. 3646 (8)** / **Add. 3649 (9)** / **Or. 222 (10)**}

Nábí's *Dhayl*, or Appendix, to Waysí's biography of the Prophet entitled *Durratu't-Táj fí sírati Ṣáḥibi'l-Mi'ráj*. See Rieu's *B. M. Turk. Cat.*, p. 37. **Add. 3646,** bought of Sethian on May 9, 1900, comprises 258 ff. of 19 × 12 c. and 21 ll., is written in a good *naskh* with rubrications, and dated 1219/1804–5. **Add. 3649,** bought of Sethian, May 9, 1900, comprises ff. 169 of 20·8 × 15 c. and 21 ll., and is written in a fair Turkish *naskh* and also dated 1219/1804–5. **Or. 222,** bought of Naaman on Nov. 12, 1902, comprises ff. 198 of 24·8 × 14 c. and 27 ll., is undated, and is written in a small, neat *ta'líq* with rubrications.

644 (p) راجاولى **King's, No. 198**

An account of the Kings of Dihlí from Judhishtir to Sháh-jahán, entitled *Rájáwalí*, by Banwálí Dás, secretary of Dárá-Shukúh. See *B.M.P.C.*, p. 855, and for this MS. Palmer's *King's Cat.*, p. 14.

645 (t) رازنامهٔ حسين چلبى الكفوى **Or. 460 (8)**

A Turkish work on the method of taking auguries from the *Díwán* of Ḥáfiẓ (based, apparently, on a Persian original by Shaykh Zaynu'd-Dín Khwáfí) translated by Ḥusayn Chelebi al-Kafawí, containing many anecdotes of appropriate divinations. The MS., bought of Naaman on Nov. 27, 1903, comprises 176 ff. of 20·7 × 12·4 c. and 21 ll., is written in a good Turkish *naskh*, and is dated 1168/1754–5.

646 (p) راك درپن **King's, No. 195**

The *Rág-darpan*, a Persian translation made in 1076/1665–6 by Faqíru'lláh of a Sanskrit treatise on Indian music. See

Ethé, *Bodl. Pers. Cat.*, No. 1847, and *India Office Persian Cat.*, No. 2017, col. 1120–21, and for this MS. Palmer's *King's Cat.*, p. 18.

647, 648 (h) رامايں **King's, No. 196**
King's, No. 197

Two Urdú translations, one in verse, the other in prose, of the *Rámáyana.* The first is written in a clear but ugly Indian *ta'líq*, 3 columns to the page of 31·4 × 20·8 c., rubrications. The second is also undated. See Palmer's *King's Cat.*, p. 14.

649, 650 (p) رُباعيّات عمر خيّام **Add. 4510** (G)
Or. 262 (8)

Two copies, both from the library of the late Professor E. B. Cowell, of the quatrains (*Rubá'iyyát*) of 'Umar Khayyám. **Add. 4510** is Professor Cowell's transcript made in June, 1856, for Edward FitzGerald, of the Bodleian MS. (Ouseley 140 = No. 525 of Ethé's *Catalogue*). Numerous letters interchanged between Cowell and FitzGerald are pasted into the volume, and there is a note in Cowell's hand at the beginning. This MS. comprises 37 ff. of 18 × 11 c. and 18 ll., of which the Persian text fills one half. **Or. 262** is a copy made for Cowell by his Munshí of the old Calcutta lithographed edition published at the *Á'ína-i-Sikandarí* Press in 1252/1836–7. It comprises 70 ff. of 20·3 × 15·3 c. and 11 ll. and is written in a large Indian *ta'líq*. Some particulars concerning these two volumes, furnished by Professor Cowell in 1896 to Mr Edward Heron Allen, will be found on p. xxxiii of the latter gentleman's *Ruba'iyat of Omar Khayyām, a fac-simile of the MS. in the Bodleian Library* (London: H. S. Nichols, 1898).

651 (a) رحمة الأمّة فى اختلاف الائمّة **Or. 561** (8)

A treatise on Sháfi'ite Jurisprudence entitled *Raḥmatu'l-Ummat fí 'khtiláfi'l-A'immat*, composed in 780/1378–9 by Shaykh Muḥammad b. 'Abdu'r-Raḥmán b. al-Ḥusayn al-Qurashí al-'Uthmání ad-Dimashqí, who died in 792/1390. See Brockelmann, ii, p. 91; *Camb. Hand-list*, p. 83. The MS., presented to the Library on March 16, 1905, by Khalíl Khálid Bey, formerly Turkish Teacher in the University of Cambridge, comprises ff. 150 of 20·5 × 15 c. and 25 ll., is written in a poor Egyptian or Sudanese *ta'líq* with rubrications, and is dated 1046/1636–7.

652 (a) الردّ على الوهّابيّة **Or. 738 (9)**

A treatise on the Wahhábí controversy, entitled "Commentary on a book in Refutation of the Wahhábís, being an answer to certain questions which the Wazír Sulaymán Pasha sent to the Author," whose name does not appear. The MS., bought of Géjou on March 27, 1907, is written in a large, clear *naskh*, is dated 1 Dhu'l-Qa'da, 1203 (= July 24, 1789), and comprises 221 ff. of 23·3 × 16·2 c. and 21 ll.

653 (p) رساله در احکام تجارت **Corpus, No. 101**

Risála-i-Aḥkám-i-Tijárat, a treatise on the laws of commerce, of which the author's name does not appear. Copied at Karbalá in 1184/1770–1 in excellent Persian *naskh*.

654 (p) رساله در احکام غالب و مغلوب **Or. 436[6] (8)**

Risála dar Aḥkám-i-Ghálib wa Maghlúb, two or three pages (ff. 88^b–89^b) only of the MS. described on p. 76 above (**No. 437**) under the title *Khuláṣatu'l-Kitáb fí 'Ilmi'l-Ḥisáb*.

655 (p) رساله در استخراج تقویم **King's, No. 203[2]**

Risála dar Istikhráj-i-Taqwím az Zíj-i-muntakhab, a treatise on the Calendar according to the era of Yazdigird used by the Zoroastrians, occupying ff. 79^b–96^a (of 19·3 × 11·5 c.) of the MS., which was copied in 1020/1611–12 by Muḥammad Sharíf b. Sulṭán Muḥammad of Multán.

656 (a) رسالة فى الآلات الفلكيّة و الجيب **Or. 657[2] (6)**

Risála fi'l-Áláti 'l-Falakiyya, a treatise on astronomical instruments in 67 chapters, occupying ff. 28^b–55^b of the MS. described on p. 108 *infra* (**No. 663**) *s.v. Risála fí 'amali'r-Rub'*.

657 (a) رسالة ايوطيوخيوس **Trinity, R.13.35**

A small treatise of 14 ff. ascribed to Eutychius, very badly written by one T. Severne, and accompanied by an interlinear translation in Latin.

658 (p) رساله در بيان الفاظ آلخ **Or. 211³ (8)**

A treatise on simple and compound Arabic words and expressions used in Persian composition and conversation, ascribed to the celebrated poet Rashídu'd-Dín Waṭwáṭ, who died in 578/1182-3. This treatise occupies ff. 21ᵇ–41ᵇ of a MS. bought of Naaman on Nov. 12, 1902. The pages measure 18·8 × 12·3 c., contain 19 lines, and are written in a small, neat *nasta'líq*, not dated.

659 (a) رسالة فى معرفة التقويم **Add. 3700 (8)**

A treatise on the Calendar by Aḥmad b. Muḥammad al-Mahdí ash-Sharíf al-Iṣfahání al-Khátún-ábádí. It comprises ff. 31 of 21·5 × 15 c. and 19 ll., is written in clear modern *naskh* with rubrications, and dated 1126/1714. Bought of Sethian, Nov. 5, 1900.

660 (p) رسالهٔ طغرا **Corpus, No. 188**

Risála-i-Ṭughrá, apparently a selection of the prose writings of Mullá Ṭughrá of Mashhad, who died some time before 1078/1667-8. See *B.M.P.C.*, pp. 742-4 and Ethé's *Bodl. Pers. Cat.*, No. 1389. The MS., undated, comprises 93 ff. of 20 × 11 c. and is written partly in *nasta'líq* and partly in *shikasta*.

661 (a) رسالة فى العروض **Or. 35² (8)**

An Arabic treatise on Prosody by Abú 'Abdi'lláh Muḥammad, known as Abu'l-Jaysh, al-Anṣárí al-Andalusí. It occupies ff. 19ᵇ–27ᵃ of the MS., which was bought of Naaman on Feb. 5, 1901. The pages measure 21 × 15·4 c. and contain each 15 ll. The writing is a fair *ta'líq* with rubrications.

662 (p) رسالهٔ علاج امراض يوسفى **Add. 3737² (7)**

A Persian treatise on Therapeutics by Yúsufí, occupying ff. 26ᵇ–101ᵇ of the MS., which was bought of Sethian on Nov. 28, 1900, is dated 1258/1842-3, and is written in a neat Persian *ta'líq* with rubrications. The pages measure 17·6 × 11 c. and contain 13 ll. each.

663 (a) رسالة فى عمل الربع المجيب **Or. 657**[1] **(6)**

A treatise on the Quadrant, by Shaykh Aḥmad b. Aḥmad b. 'Abdu'l-Ḥaqq as-Sunbáṭí, being an elucidation (توضيح) of a treatise on the same subject by Shaykh Badru'd-Dín al-Márdíní. This treatise occupies ff. 1–25 of the MS., which was transcribed in 1223/1808, and bought of Géjou on Feb. 12, 1906. The pages measure 15·2 × 9·8 c. and each contains 20 ll.

664 (p) رسالهٔ عمليّهٔ فقهيّه **Or. 441 (8)**

A practical treatise on Jurisprudence, defective at the beginning and anonymous. The MS., bought of Messrs Hannan and Watson on Aug. 29, 1903, and dated 1238/1822–3, comprises 210 ff. of 20·6 × 14·2 c. and 15 ll., and is written in a poor *ta'líq* with rubrications.

665 (a) رسالة فى علم الفراسة **Or. 707 (8)**

A treatise on Physiognomy by Muḥammad b. Abí Ṭálib al-Anṣárí aṣ-Ṣúfí ad-Dimashqí. The MS., bought of Géjou in December 1906, comprises 52 ff. of 20 × 13·8 c. and 17 ll., is written in poor *naskh* with rubrications, and is dated 1282/1865–6.

666 (a) رسالة فى الفرائض و الآداب الدينيّة **Add. 3722**[3] **(8)**

A treatise on religious obligations and observances. For description of the MS. (of which this portion occupies ff. 53–72) see further on *s.v. Kitábu'ṣ-Ṣádiḥ wa'l-Bághim.*

667 (p) رسالهٔ قافيه **Corpus, No. 65**[3]

The well-known treatise on rhyme (published by Blochmann in his *Prosody of the Persians*, Calcutta, 1872) by Jámí. Ff. 6 of 26 × 16 c., clear *nasta'líq*, dated 1258/1842.

668 (a) الرسالة القشيريّة **Or. 675 (8)**

The well-known mystical treatise of Abu'l-Qásim 'Abdu'l-Karím al-Qushayrí (died in 465/1074) composed in 437/1045, and called after him *ar-Risálatu'l-Qushayriyya*. See Brockelmann, i, pp. 432–3. The MS., bought of Géjou on Feb. 17,

1906, comprises ff. 189 + 3 of 21·5 × 14·2 c. and 23 ll., and is written in fair *naskh* with rubrications. It was copied in 1131/1718–9 by Ḥasan b. Muḥammad al-Birkawí.

669 (a) رسالة فی علم الكلام **Or. 452 (6)**

An anonymous and untitled treatise on Scholastic Philosophy (*'Ilmu'l-Kalám*), beginning:

فی وجودِ موجودٍ لا شكّ فی وجودِ موجده آلخ

The MS., bought of Messrs Hannan and Watson on Aug. 29, 1903, is undated, and comprises 83 ff. of 16·5 × 10·8 c. and 16–19 ll. It is written in *shikasta* as far as f. 53[a] and *naskh* from thence to the end.

670 (a) **King's, No. 203[1]**

رسالة فی كيفيّة الحكم على تحاويل سنى العالم

A treatise on the determination of the transitions of the years, by Shaykh Muḥiyyu'd-Dín Yaḥyá b. Muḥammad b. Abi'sh-Shukr al-Maghribí al-Andalasí, who flourished in the 13th century of the Christian era. See Brockelmann, i, p. 474. Ff. 79 of 19·3 × 11·6 c.; small, neat *ta'líq* with rubrications. Followed by the *Zíj-i-Ilkhání*, *q.v.*

671 (a) **Add. 3653 (8)**

رسالة لطيفة باهرة كالشّرح فی توضيح ما فی هذه الدائرة

Risála laṭífa báhira...fí Tawḍíḥi má fí hádhihi'd-Dá'ira, a treatise on Cosmogony and Geography, composed for Sháhín, Governor of Aleppo, defective at the beginning. Followed by a poem on the Resurrection entitled *Qiládatu'd-Durri'l-Manthúr*; see below under that title. Ff. 177 of 21 × 15 c. and 19 ll., coarse but legible *naskh*, with rubrications, n. d. Bought of Sethian, May 21, 1900.

672 (p) رسالهٔ مأكول و مشروب **Add. 3737[1] (7)**

A rhymed Persian treatise on foods and drinks by Yúsufí, who is probably Yúsuf b. Muḥammad, the physician of Herát, who died about 950/1543–4. See *B.M.P.C.*, Index, p. 1184 *s.v.* This treatise fills ff. 3^b–26^b of 17·6 × 11 c. and 13 ll.; good Persian *ta'líq*; rubrications. Bought of Sethian, Nov. 28, 1900.

673 (a) رسالة فى بيان المجاز واقسامه **Add. 3665 (8)**

An Arabic translation of a Persian treatise on the different kinds of Metaphor by 'Iṣámu'd-Dín. Ff. 202 of 21·3 × 15 c. and 23 ll.; clear but clumsy *naskh*, dated Ramaḍán, 1133 (= 1721). Bought of Sethian, July 17, 1900.

674 (p) رسالهٔ محمّد زاهد درویش الخ **Corpus, No. 77**

An epistle from a *darwísh* and ascetic named Muḥammad to Khwája Muḥammad Isḥaq Khán, comprising prayer, praise, advice, and a representation of the writer's condition. The leaves measure 21 × 11 c. and are written in a large *nasta'líq*, undated.

675 (p) رسالهٔ محمّد شاه و خاندوران **King's, No. 204**

Memoirs of the *Amíru'l-Umará* Ṣamṣámu'd-Dawla Khán-dawrán and his times. He was killed in battle in 1151/1738–9. See *B.M.P.C.*, p. 277, and for this MS. (dated 1199/1784–5) Palmer's *King's Cat.*, p. 14.

676 (p) رساله در علم مساحت **Or. 436^2 (8)**

A treatise on surveying, without author's name, occupying ff. 39^b–47^b of the MS. described above on p. 76 under *Khuláṣatu'l-Kitáb fí 'Ilmi'l-Ḥisáb* (**No. 437**). The MS. is dated 1245/1829–30, and was bought of Messrs Hannan and Watson on August 29, 1903.

677 (p) رسالة فى معرفة الأهلّة **Or. 436^4 (8)**

A short treatise (ff. 61^b–62^b of the MS. mentioned immediately above) on days of the Muḥammadan months and the feasts and anniversaries which fall on each. Incomplete at end.

678–681 (p) رسالهٔ معمّا **Add. 3674 (9), Add. 3675 (9) Or. 14 (9), Corpus, No. 102^{3-4}**

Several treatises, some long and some short, on riddles or acrostics (*Mu'ammá*). **Add. 3674,** by Shiháb b. Niẓám and Kamál-i-Badakhshí, comprises ff. 50 of 22·9 × 14·8 c. and 12 ll., is written in excellent *ta'líq* with rubrications, is dated 986/

1578–9, and was bought of Naaman on July 23, 1900. The author is mentioned in the *Bábur-náma* (ed. Beveridge, ff. 339 and 378). **Add. 3675,** anonymous, comprises ff. 84 of 21·7 × 13·3 c. and 14 ll. and is written in excellent *ta'líq* with rubrications; undated, but probably copied towards the end of the tenth Muḥammad or sixteenth Christian century. Bought of Naaman, July 23, 1900. **Or. 14** has no title or indication of authorship. It comprises 224 ff. of 22·7 × 14 c. and 21 ll., and is written in good *naskh* with rubrications, probably about the same period as the MS. last mentioned. It was bought of Naaman on Feb. 5, 1901. **Corpus 102,** copied at Bareilly in 1826, contains Jámí's treatise on the *Mu'ammá* (ff. 42), another rhymed treatise on the same subject, and some *Mu'ammás* and chronograms by Ni'mat Khán and others.

682 (p) رساله در باب نجوم **Corpus, No. 12[8]**

A short anonymous treatise of 4 pp. on Astrology, written in *nasta'líq* and undated.

683 (a, t) رسالهٔ نظم لغات **Trinity, R. 13. 65**

A rhymed vocabulary (something like the *Niṣáb* of Abú Naṣr-i-Faráhí) of words occurring in the *Qur'án*, explained in Turkish. Pp. 40. See Palmer's *Trin. Coll. Cat.*, p. 152.

684 (p) رسالهٔ والديّه **Trinity, R. 13. 69**

Risála-i-Wálidiyya ("the Paternal Treatise") of Khwája Aḥrár, who died 895/1489–90, followed by extracts from some *Tadhkira*, or Biography of Poets, on Rúdagí and 'Unṣurí. Ff. 16. See Palmer's *Trin. Coll. Cat.*, pp. 155–6.

685 (a) رسالة فى الوقف للايذجى **Add. 3719[2] (9)**

Risála fi'l-waqf, a treatise on where to pause in reading the *Qur'án*, by al-Ídhají. For description of the MS., of which this portion occupies ff. 121–164, see **No. 343** on p. 60 *supra*.

686 (p) رسالهٔ هيئت (الرّسالة المعينيّة) **King's, No. 200**

Risála-i-Hay'at, a treatise on Astronomy, properly entitled, apparently, *ar-Risálatu'l-Mu'íniyya*, ascribed to Naṣíru'd-Dín Ṭúsí (d. 672/1273–4). Dated 1146/1733–4. See Palmer's *King's Cat.*, p. 15.

687 (p) رساله هيئت **King's, No. 206**

Another treatise on Astronomy, ascribed to 'Alí b. Muḥammad al-Qúshjí, who died at Constantinople in 879/1474–5. See Brockelmann, ii, pp. 234–5; *B.M.P.C.*, p. 458; and Palmer's *King's Cat.*, p. 206.

688 (p) رساله هيئت **Corpus, No. 12⁷**

A short treatise (pp. 5) on Astronomy ascribed to Luqmán.

689 (a) رسائل اخوان الصّفا **King's, No. 2**

Part of the celebrated treatises of the *Ikhwánu'ṣ-Ṣafá*, the celebrated Encyclopaedists of Baghdád in the tenth century of our era. See Brockelmann, i, pp. 213–214. This collection begins with the treatise on Alchemy and opens thus:

الحمد لله الّذى خلق فسوّى و الّذى قدّد و هدى

A small volume of about 6″×4″ comprising ff. 166 (two leaves missing at end), written in good and fairly old *naskh*, undated. See Palmer's *King's Cat.*, p. 19.

690 (a) رسائل الشيخ بهاء الدّين **Trinity, R.13.20**

Thirteen treatises of Shaykh Bahá'u'd-Dín, apparently of the Druzes. Ff. 78, *naskh*, undated. See Palmer's *Trin. Cat.*, pp. 48–50.

691 (a) رسائل فقهيّة حنفيّة لا بن نجيم **Add. 3690 (6)**

Thirty-seven tracts on Ḥanafí Jurisprudence by Shaykh Zayn b. Nujaym, who died in 970/1563. See Brockelmann, ii, pp. 310–311. Ff. 260 of 14·8 × 9·3 and 15 ll., small neat *naskh* with rubrications, undated. Bought of Sethian, Nov. 1, 1900.

692 (a) رشد اللّبيب الى معاشرة الحبيب **Or. 51³ (8)**

A MS. of 230 ff. of 21 × 13·2 and 25 ll., fair modern *riq'a* with rubrications, dated Jumádá ii, 1012 (= Nov.–Dec. 1603), and bought of Naaman, March 4, 1901. The MS. contains three separate works, *viz.* (1) An Anthology without title or indication of authorship (ff. 1–100). (2) Another Anthology compiled for Shaykh 'Abdu'r-Raḥmán as-Suwaydí b. Abu'l-Barakát 'Abdu'lláh as-Suwaydí by his brother (ff. 101–159[a]). (3) The *Rushdu'l-Labíb ila Mu'ásharati'l-Ḥabíb* (ff. 159[b]–230). For the last see Brockelmann, i, pp. 231–2, and the *Cambridge Hand-list*, No. 477, p. 89.

693 (h) رشك پريان (?) **Christ's, Dd. 5. 9**

An English note at the beginning of this MS., which is dated 1077/1666, describes it as "a Gentoo tale in the Hindustani language adorned with paintings," and it is stated to have been written for Muḥammad Náṣir-i-Faqír Abu'l-Faḍl b. Shaykh Abu'l-Faḍl b. Shaykh Dá'úd-i-Ghúrí. Ff. 79 of 27 × 18·6 c. and 15 ll. Begins:

ايك ردن كجبدن سدن بودهه مدن كدن سوت...

and ends:

تمام شده رسالهٔ مسمّى باصلاح هدوى رسك پمريا (*sic*) در علم اشعار هندوى '

694 (p) رقايم كرايم (كلمات طيّبات) **King's, No. 205**

Raqá'im-i-Kará'im, being the letters of 'Álamgír Awrangzíb to Amír Khán Sindhí (d. about 1131/1719), followed by the *Kalimát-i-Ṭayyibát*, another collection of Awrangzíb's letters edited by his secretary 'Ináyatu'lláh Khán (d. 1179/1765–6). For descriptions of both, see *B.M.P.C.*, pp. 400–401, and for mention of this MS., Palmer's *King's Cat.*, pp. 15 and 18. The first portion of the MS., which was copied at Lucknow by Jawádu'lláh Nahánísarí in 1194/1780, comprises 24 ff., and the second part 50 ff.

695 (p) رقعات ابراهيم **King's, No. 208**

Raqa'át-i-Ibráhím, letters on various subjects to persons whose names are not mentioned. The MS., undated and incomplete at end, is mentioned at p. 15 of Palmer's *King's Cat.*

696–698 (p) رقعات ابو الفضل **{Christ's, 13. 4. 22; Corpus, No. 70[2]; Corpus, No. 197}**

The *Raqa'át* or letters of the Emperor Akbar's great minister Shaykh Abu'l-Faḍl-i-'Allámí, also called *Mukátabát-*

i-'Allámí, of which the compilation was finished in 1015/1606–7. See *B.M.P.C.*, p. 396. The **Christ's MS.** is dated Thursday, Rajab 4, but the year is omitted. **Corpus 70**[2] is dated 1263/1847, is written in *ta'líq* and *ním-shikasta*, and contains 147 ff. of 27·5 × 17 c. Mr Ballard has a note: "The private letters of Abu'l-Faḍl are to be distinguished from the *Inshá*, or official correspondence." **Corpus 197** is dated 1172/1758–9, and the leaves measure 23 × 13 c.

699 (p) رقعات امان الله حسينى **King's, No. 202**

Letters of Amánu'lláh-i-Ḥusayní. See Pertsch's *Berlin Pers. Cat.*, No. 62[14], and Palmer's *King's Cat.*, p. 15. The MS., undated, was transcribed by Shaykh Muḥammad Yaqín b. Shaykh Núru'lláh.

700, 701 (p) رقعات بيدل **Corpus, No. 122**
Corpus, No. 160

The Letters of Mírzá Bí-dil, the poet, who died in 1133/1720–21. See *B.M.P.C.*, p. 811[a]. **Corpus 122** comprises 128 ff. of 17 × 12 c., is written in *nasta'líq*, and was copied by one Náṣiru'd-Dín in 1244/1828–9. **Corpus 160** contains besides the letters a running commentary on them, and is written in fair *nasta'líq* on leaves of 29 × 17 c.

702 (p) رقعات جامى **Or. 257**[1] **(8)**

The Letters of the eminent Persian poet Mullá Núru'd-Dín 'Abdu'r-Raḥmán Jámí, in the lithographed Calcutta ed. of 1270/1853–4 bound up with the manuscript. Pp. 179 + 3 of 20·3 × 15 c. and 15 ll.; clear Indian *ta'líq*. Cowell Bequest.

703 (p) رقعات طاهر وحيد **Corpus, No. 4**[1]

The Letters of the poet Ṭáhir Waḥíd, who died about 1120/1708–9, written in *nasta'líq* on leaves of 23 × 12 c. and apparently dated 1261/1845. See *B.M.P.C.*, pp. 810[b] and 842[a].

704, 705 (p) رقعات عالمگير **Corpus, No. 39**[3]
Corpus, No. 190

The familiar letters of 'Álamgír Awrangzíb. See *B.M.P.C.*, p. 801. In **Corpus 190** the lithographed Indian edition of

1261/1845 is bound up with an apparently incomplete MS. transcribed about ten years earlier.

706 (p) رقعات عنایت خانی **King's, No. 194**

Raqa'át-i-'Ináyat Khání, a collection of letters written by or to the Tímúrid Emperors of India (or "Great Moghuls") from the time of Humáyún to that of Bahádur Sháh, and compiled by 'Ináyat Khán Rásikh b. Luṭfu'lláh Khán Ṣádiq. See *B.M.P.C.*, p. 876[b], and Palmer's *King's Cat.* This MS. contains 72 ff. and is undated.

707 (p) رقعات قتیل **Corpus, No. 163**

Letters of Mírzá Qatíl, who died in 1233/1817–18. See *B.M.P.C.*, pp. 794[b], 858[a].

708 (p) رقعات مظفّر حسین **Or. 651[3] (8)**

Letters of Muẓaffar Ḥusayn b. Sayyid Mubárak 'Alí, beginning:

خامهٔ خامکار خارخار آن دارد که بتحریر الخ

The author appears not to be identical with the homonymous writer mentioned in *B.M.P.C.*, p. 1019[b], whose father is differently named. This portion of the MS. occupies ff. 95[b]–131[b] of 19·3 × 11 c. and 13 ll., is written in clear Indian *ta'líq*, and is defective at end. It was bought through Quaritch at the O'Kinealy sale on Jan. 15, 1906.

709 (p) رقعات نصیری **Corpus, No. 236**

Letters of Naṣíru'd-Dín or Naṣírí of Hamadán, who is perhaps identical with the Naṣírá of Hamadán (flourished about 1015/1606–7) mentioned in *B.M.P.C.*, pp. 743[b], xvi, and 1093[b]. Ff. 40 of 20 × 12 c., undated. Written in *shikasta*.

710 (a) رمز الحقایق فی شرح کنز الدقائق **Or. 706 (8)**

Ramzu'l-Ḥaqá'iq, a commentary by Badru'd-Dín Maḥmúd b. Aḥmad b. Músá al-'Ayní al-Ḥanafí (d. 855/1451) on the *Kanzu'd-Daqá'iq* of an-Nasafí, *q.v.* See Brockelmann, ii, p. 197. This MS., copied in 1082/1671–2, was bought of Géjou in December, 1906. It comprises 338 ff. of 20·2 × 14·8 c. and

23 ll., is written in a small, neat *naskh*, and was copied by Aḥmad b. Ḥasan b. Kamál ash-Sháfi'í.

711 (t) روزنامچهٔ حضرت شیخ وفا **Trinity, R. 8. 28**

The *Rúz-námcha*, or Journal, of Shaykh Wafá, dated A.D. 1618 and presented to the Library by J. Wilson. The MS. (bound up with **R. 8. 25**) comprises only 8 ff. and is written in red and black. See Palmer's *Trin. Cat.*, p. 4.

712 (a) **Add. 3752 (11)**

روض الطالب (اسنى المطالب فى شرح —)

Asna'l-Maṭálib, a commentary by Zaynu'd-Dín Abú Yaḥyá Zakariyyá al-Anṣárí ash-Sháfi'í (d. 926/1520) on the *Rawḍu't-Ṭálib*, a work on Sháfi'í jurisprudence by Sharafu'd-Dín Isma'íl al-Muqri' ash-Sháwarí al-Yamaní (d. 837/1433). See Brockelmann, ii, pp. 190–191, No. 10, for the text, and *Ibid.*, pp. 99–100, No. 29, for the commentary. This MS. contains only the first part of the book, and comprises 335 pp. of 26·6 × 17·5 c. and 29 ll. It is undated, written in good *naskh* with rubrications, and was bought of Géjou on Dec. 8, 1900.

713 (a) الروض المريع فى علم البديع **Add. 3621 (9)**

A work on Rhetoric entitled *ar-Rawḍu'l-Murí' fí 'ilmi'l-Badí'* by Shaykh Músá b. Jalál al-Mawlawí. Ff. 91 of 22·5 × 16·8 c. and 15–19 ll., partly *naskh*, partly *ta'líq*, undated. Bought of Géjou, Feb. 14, 1900.

714 (a) روضة الطالبين للنّواوى **Or. 480 (10)**

The *Rawḍatu'ṭ-Ṭálibín wa 'umdatu'l-Muftín* of Shaykh Muḥyi'd-Dín Abú Zakariyyá Yaḥyá b. Sharaf an-Nawáwí, who died in 676/1278. See Brockelmann, i, pp. 394–7, No. vii. The MS., bought of Géjou with 15 others on Aug. 18, 1904, is undated and comprises ff. 209 of 26 × 18 c. and 24 ll.; written in fine large *naskh* with rubrications.

715 (p) **King's, No. 192**

روضة الاحباب فى سير النّبى و الآل و الاصحاب

A Biography of the Prophet Muḥammad and his family and companions entitled *Rawḍatu'l-Aḥbáb fí siyari'n-Nabí* etc., by 'Aṭá'u'lláh b. Faḍlu'lláh Jamál al-Muḥaddithu'l-Ḥusayní, who died in 883/1478-9. See *B.M.P.C.*, pp. 146-149. The MS. is dated 1172/1758-9. See Palmer's *King's Cat.*, p. 15.

716 (p) روضة اولى الالباب **King's, No. 108**

The well-known general history of Abú Sulaymán Dá'úd b. Abu'l-Faḍl Muḥammad-i-Banákití, entitled *Rawḍatu Úli'l-Albáb*, composed in 717/1317-18. See *B.M.P.C.*, pp. 79-80, and Palmer's *King's Cat.*, p. 7. This MS. is dated 980/1572-3.

717 (p) روضة الانوار **King's, No. 210**

A Persian *mathnawí* poem entitled *Rawḍatu'l-Anwár* by Khwájú of Kirmán (died 753/1352). See *B.M.P.C.*, pp. 620-621, 623[a], v, and 855[a], i. The MS. contains ff. 45 and is dated 1194/1780. See Palmer's *King's Cat.*, p. 15.

718 (a) الروضة البهيّة فى شرح اللّمعة الدمشقيّة **Or. 437** (12)

A commentary entitled ar-*Rawḍatu'l-Bahiyya* by Zaynu'd-Dín b. 'Alí b. Aḥmad ash-Shámí al-'Ámilí, who died in 966/1558, on the *Lum'atu'd-Dimashqiyya* of Muḥammad b. Makkí al-'Ámílí, known as "the First Martyr" (*ash-Shahídu'l-Awwal*), who was put to death at Damascus for his Shí'ite proclivities in 782/1382. See Brockelmann, ii, p. 108, and *B.M.A. Suppl.*, No. 334. The MS., bought of Messrs Hannan and Watson on Aug. 29, 1903, is dated 1210/1795-6, contains 135 ff. of 29·9 × 20·2 c. and 22 ll., and is written in a poor *naskh* with rubrications. It contains only the first volume of the work.

719 (p) روضة الشّهدا **Or. 417** (10)

The *Rawḍatu'sh-Shuhadá* ("Mausoleum of Martyrs"), a well-known martyrology by the celebrated writer Ḥusayn b. 'Alí al-Wá'iẓ al-Káshifí, who died in 910/1504-5. See *B.M.P.C.*, pp. 152-153; *Camb. Pers. Cat.*, p. 91. This is followed on f. 251[b] by a genealogy of the Imáms entitled *Nasab-náma-i-A'imma-i-Ma'ṣúmín*. The MS., bought of Géjou on Aug. 29, 1903, was copied in 973/1565-6 by Ruknu'd-Dín b. Muḥammad Shamsu'd-Dín Lárí. It comprises 266 ff. of

25·5 × 16 c. and 17 ll., and is written in a small neat Persian *nasta'líq* with rubrications.

720–724 (p) روضة الصّفا {**Or. 46 (13), Or. 808 (11)**
Add. 3740 (12), King's, No. 26
King's, No. 191

Various volumes of Mírkhwándi's famous universal history the *Rawḍatu'ṣ-Ṣafá*. See *B.M.P.C.*, pp. 87–96. The author died at Herát in 903/1497–8, aged sixty-six. **Or. 46,** containing vol. i, is dated 1067/1656–7, was bought of Messrs E. Parsons and Sons in February, 1901, and comprises 261 ff. of 33·3 × 19·6 c. and 25 ll. **Or. 808,** containing the history of the pre-Islamic kings of Persia, is undated, and was bought of G. David on May 27, 1909. It comprises 122 ff. of 28 × 21·2 c. and 23 ll., and is written on Indian paper in a poor but legible *ta'líq*. **Add. 3740,** containing vol. iv, is dated 1030/1620–21, was bought of Sethian on Nov. 28, 1900, comprises 255 ff. of 31·7 × 19·2 c. and 28 ll., and is written in a clear Persian *naskh* with rubrications. **King's 26** contains selections from the earlier part, dealing with the mythical Bin Jánn and Adam and the Kings of ancient Persia down to the Arab invasion and death of Yazdigird. This MS. is dated 1199/1784–5. **King's 191** is a more or less complete copy of the work in seven volumes, written in various hands. Vols. i and v are dated 1003/1594–5 and 1595–6 respectively. The others are undated. See Palmer's *Pers. Cat.*, pp. 4 and 15.

725 (a) **Trinity, R. 13. 44**

الروضات المزهرات فى العمل بربع المقنطرات

Ar-Rawḍátu'l-Muzhirát fi'l-'amal bi-rub'i'l-Muqanṭarát on the use of Quadrants with parallel circles. See Brockelmann, ii, p. 127, who refers amongst others to this MS. as described in Palmer's *Trin. Cat.*, pp. 101–102. Brockelmann ascribes its authorship to Zaynu'd-Dín Muḥammad b. Aḥmad b. 'Abdu'r-Raḥmán al-Mizzí al-Ḥawafí, who died at Damascus in 750/1349, but I have noted the author's name as 'Alá'u'd-Dín b. Ibráhím b. ash-Sháṭir ad-Dimashqí. This work comprises ff.

22 of the MS., which also contains other astronomical and poetical extracts.

726 (p) **رياض الادويه** **Corpus, No. 85**

A Materia Medica, arranged alphabetically, composed by Yúsufí of Herát in 946/1539–40, and entitled *Riyáḍu'l-Adwiya.* See *B.M.P.C.*, p. 840[b], iv. Transcribed in fair *nasta'líq* in 1237/1821–2 by 'Abdu'lláh Sháh on pages of 21·5 × 14·5 c. This work is followed by 5 ff. of other matter, apparently extracts from a story.

727 (p) **رياض الانشاء** **King's, No. 209**

An epistolary manual entitled *Riyáḍu'l-Inshá*, by Maḥmúd b. Shaykh Muḥammad al-Jílání, who died in 886/1481–2. See *B.M.P.C.*, p. 983[a] and Palmer's *King's Cat.*, p. 18. The MS. is dated 1140/1727–8.

728 (p) **رياض اوليا** **Corpus, No. 126**

A Biography of Saints entitled *Riyáḍ-i-Awliyá.* See *B.M.P.C.*, p. 975[a], i, where a work of this title is ascribed to Bakhtáwar Khán, who completed it in 1090/1679–80. In this MS., however, Niẓámu'l-Dín Awliyá appears to be indicated as the author.

729 (p) **رياض عالمگيرى** **Corpus, No. 193**

The *Riyáḍ-i-'Álamgírí*, a medical work dedicated to 'Álamgír Awrangzíb by Muḥammad Taqí. The work contains only the first of the *Riyáḍ* and appears to be incomplete. It comprises 83 ff. of 21 × 16 c. and is written in a minute *nasta'líq*.

730 (p) **زاد المسافرين** **King's, No. 216**

Zádu'l-Musáfirín ("the Pilgrims' Provision"), an ethical work in 27 chapters (*qawl*) by the celebrated poet, traveller and Isma'ílí missionary Náṣir-i-Khusraw (born 394/1003, died 481/1088). For his life and poetry see an article by myself in the *J.R.A.S.* for April 1905. Of this rare work a MS. formerly belonging to the late M. Charles Schefer is now in the Bibliothèque Nationale in Paris, and is mentioned in Blochet's *Cata-*

logue de la Collection de Manuscrits Orientaux...formée par M. Charles Schefer (No. 1318, p. 66) published by Leroux of Paris in 1900. Of this MS. I possess a transcript made by Mírzá Káẓim-záda.

Ff. 240. See Palmer's *King's Cat.*, p. 15.

731 (p) زاد المسافرين **Add. 3615[2] (9)**

The *Zádu'l-Musáfirín* of Muḥammad b. 'Alí Naqí ash-Sharíf, a work on Medicine, occupying ff. 42–113 of the MS. described further on, *s.v. Kitábu'ṭ-Ṭibbi'l-Jadíd al-Kímiyá'í*. The MS. was copied by Suhráb b. Jahánbakhsh in 1256/1840–1, and was bought of Géjou in 1899. The leaves measure 21·0 × 13·5 c. and contain 19 ll. each.

732 (p) زاد المسافرين **Or. 685[7] (9)**

Extracts from the *Zádu'l-Musáfirín* of Mír Ḥusayní Sádát of Ghúr (d. 718/1318). See *B.M.P.C.*, p. 608. The MS., of which this portion occupies ff. 141–179, is undated, and was bought of Géjou on May 10, 1906.

733 (p) زبدة التواريخ **Corpus, No. 220**

Zubdatu't-Tawáríkh, a history of the Muslim dynasties of India founded on the *Ta'ríkh-i-Ḥaqqí* of the author's father, by Núru'l-Ḥaqq b. 'Abdu'l-Ḥaqq of Dihlí, who died in 1073/1662–3. See *B.M.P.C.*, p. 224. The MS., dated 1118/1706–7, comprises 186 ff. of 29 × 18 c., and is written in *nasta'líq*.

734 (p) زبدة الحقايق **Or. 685[8] (9)**

The *Zubdatu'l-Ḥaqá'iq* of 'Azíz b. Muḥammad an-Nasafí. The MS., undated, was bought of Géjou on May 10, 1906.

735 (p) زبدة الرمل **Corpus, No. 177**

Zubdatu'r-Ramal, a versified treatise on Geomancy, with geometric tables. Ff. 59 of 25 × 16 c., undated.

736 (p) زبدة اللّغات **King's, No. 215**

A lexicon entitled *Zubdatu'l-Lughát* by Muḥammad Ṭáhir b. al-Ḥusayn of Sabzawár, who flourished about 1014/1605.

See *B.M.P.C.*, pp. 119–121. The MS. is dated 1049/1639–40. See Palmer's *King's Cat.*, p. 15.

737 (a, m) **Or. 642 (10)**

زهد الطلب فی الكشف عن قواعد الاعراب

Zuhdu't-Ṭalab (? -*Ṭulláb*) and other works on Arabic grammar, with explanations in Malay. The MS., undated, comprises 40 ff. of 24·5 × 19·3 c. and 7 ll., is written in large clumsy *naskh*, and was bought of B. Jolley on June 3, 1905.

738–741 (p) زیج اُلُغ بیگ **Or. 566 (11) / Corpus, No. 210 / King's, No. 214 / King's, No. 233**

The *Zíj* or astronomical tables of Ulugh Beg, the grandson of Tímúr, who was born in 796/1393–4, ascended the throne in Herát in 852/1448–9, and was killed by his son 'Abdu'l-Laṭíf in the following year. See *B.M.P.C.*, pp. 455–7. **Or. 566** is undated and was bought of Géjou on July 14, 1905. It comprises 206 ff. of 28 × 18·2 c. and 21 ll., and is written in an excellent scholarly *naskh* which cannot be much later than the author's time. **Corpus 210,** undated and defective at end, comprises 17 ff. of 24 × 15 c. and is written in a small cursive *nasta'líq*. For **King's 214** and **King's 233** see Palmer's *King's Cat.*, pp. 16 and 17. The latter contains the commentary of 'Abdu'l-'Alí b. Muḥammad b. Ḥusayn of Birjand, composed in 929/1522–3. See *B.M.P.C.*, pp. 457–8.

742 (p) زیج محمّدشاهی **King's, No. 212**

The *Zíj-i-Muḥammad Sháhí* compiled by the Rájpút Jay Singh Sawá'í in 1140/1728. See *B.M.P.C.*, pp. 460–461 and Palmer's *King's Cat.*, p. 15. The MS. comprises 26 ff.

743 (p) زین الاخبار **King's, No. 213**

A copy of the very rare and valuable historical and ethnological work entitled *Zaynu'l-Akhbár* of Abú Sa'íd b. 'Abdu'l-Ḥayy b. ad-Ḍaḥḥák al-Kurdízí (or -Gurdízí), a pupil of the celebrated Abú Rayḥán al-Bírúní. There is another MS. in the Bodleian Library. See Ethé's *Pers. Cat.*, No. 15.

744 (p) زين الرّمل **Add. 3616[3] (10)**

A work on Geomancy entitled *Zaynu'r-Ramal* by Zaynu'l-'Ábidín b. Qásim-i-Rammál ("the Geomancer") of Iṣfahán. The MS. was bought of Géjou in 1899, and is undated. This portion occupies ff. 118^b–151^b of 24 × 17 c. and 21 ll.; fair *ta'líq*; rubrications.

745 (p) زينة المجالس **Or. 862 (12)**

The *Zínatu'l-Majális* of Majdu'd-Dín Muḥammad al-Ḥusayní (or al-Ḥasaní), poetically surnamed Majdí, composed some time after 1004/1595–6. See *B.M.P.C.*, pp. 758–9; *Camb. Pers. Cat.*, p. 94. The MS., bought of Messrs Luzac in May, 1911, comprises 236 ff. of 30·3 × 19 c. and 25 ll., is written in a small neat *ta'líq* between gold and blue borders with rubrications, and is undated.

746 (p) ساقی نامهٔ ظهوری **Corpus, No. 50[1]**

The *Sáqí-náma* of Ẓuhúrí, who died in 1024/1615. See *B.M.P.C.*, pp. 678–9. Ff. 117 of 33 × 23 c., written in *nasta'líq* in four columns and dated 1276/1859–60.

747 (p) ساقی نامهٔ طغرای مشهدی **King's, No. 122**

The *Sáqí-náma* of Ṭughrá of Mashhad, who died in 1070/1659–60. See *B.M.P.C.*, p. 742, and Ethé's *I. O. Pers. Cat.*, col. 868, No. 1586. This MS., undated, is mentioned at p. 18 of Palmer's *King's Cat.*

748 (p) ساقی نامه **Or. 251 (9)**

Another short anonymous *Sáqí-náma* transcribed in fine large *ta'líq* in album form by Yúsuf an-Núrí at Sanándij in Kurdistán in 1273/1856–7 for Áqá 'Alí of Iṣfahán. Ff. 19 of 23·5 × 15 c.: one large and two small *bayts* to the page; leather Persian binding. Cowell Bequest.

749 (t) سالنامه (١١٤٩–١١٥٠) **Or. 225 (12)**

A Turkish *Sál-náma* or Year-book for A.H. 1149–1150 (= A.D. 1736–7), transcribed, apparently, in that year, and bought of Naaman on Nov. 12, 1902. Ff. 13 of 29·2 × 17·5 of about

26 ll.; excellent *naskh*, gold borders, rubrications and coloured headings, with numerous tables.

750 (a, p) السّامى فى الأسامى **Add. 3657** (10)

A dictionary of Arabic words explained in Persian, entitled *As-Sámí fi'l-Asámí*, perhaps that of al-Maydání. See Brockelmann, i, p. 289. The MS., bought of Sethian on May 21, 1900, comprises 122 ff. of 24·6 × 19·6 c. and 18 ll., clear *naskh*, pointed, with rubrications. The date Ṣafar 654 (=March, 1256) occurs in the colophon, but as the writing is of a much later period this is presumably the date of the MS. from which it was copied.

751–754 (p) سبحة الابرار جامى **Add. 3663**[2] (10), **Add. 3677** (9), **Add. 3678** (8), **Or. 247** (6)

Four copies of Jámí's *Sibḥatu'l-Abrár*. See *B.M.P.C.*, pp. 644–6. In **Add. 3663** this poem occupies ff. 65^b–168^b of 25 × 16 c. and 15 ll. The MS., written in excellent *ta'líq* but undated, was bought of Naaman on June 3, 1900. **Add. 3677,** bought of Naaman on July 23, 1900, is dated 970/1562–3, is written in excellent *ta'líq* with rubrications, and comprises 104 ff. of 22·8 × 12·4 c. and 15 ll. **Add. 3678** contains the *Sibḥatu'l-Abrár* in the text and the *Tuḥfatu'l-Aḥrár* (*q.v.*) in the margins. It was bought of Breslauer and Meyer on Aug. 11, 1900, is dated 1000/1591–2, and comprises 94 ff. of 19 × 21·1 c. and 17 ll. in text and 32 in margin; good *ta'líq* with rubrications. **Or. 247** (Cowell Bequest) was apparently given to Cowell by Edward FitzGerald on Feb. 26, 1856, and was copied by Aḥmad b. Muḥammad 'Alí of Shíráz in A.H. 1242 and completed on 12 Rabí'i in that year (= Oct. 14, 1826). It is written in a modern Persian *ta'líq* with rubrications, and comprises ff. 141 of 15 × 10 c. and 11 ll.

755 (p) سبع سموات **Corpus, No. 195**

Sab'u Samáwát ("the Seven Heavens"), a work on astrology and divination by Abu'l-Fatḥ Fatḥí, an author who lived in the Sháhpúr district of Behár in India, and whose name is more fully given as Faṭḥu'lláh b. Shaykh Muṣṭafá b. Shaykh 'Abdu 'sh-Shukúr al-Fárúqí al-Isḥáqí, who wrote it in 1067/1656–7. The MS. is dated 1168/1754–5, comprises ff. 161 of 21·5 × 14 c., and is written in *shikasta*.

756 (p, h)   سحر البيان   **Or. 899 (8)**

Siḥru'l-Bayán ("the Magic of Utterance"), a versified treatise in mixed Hindustání and Persian ascribed to Amír Ḥasan of Dihlí (d. 727/1327), and apparently composed in 711/1311. Ff. 113 of 20·3 × 13·3 c. The colophon is obliterated. Begins:

کرون پهلی توحید یزدان رقمِ، جهکا جسکی سجده مین اوّل قلمِ،

757 (a)   سراج الملوك للطّرطوشی   **Or. 206 (11)**

The *Siráju'l-Mulúk* of Abú Bakr Muḥammad aṭ-Ṭurṭúshí (d. 520/1126). See Brockelmann, i, 459. Ff. 224 of 27·8 × 20 c. and 21 ll. The work is divided into 64 chapters, of which a complete list is given on ff. 1ᵃ–3ᵇ, and it begins abruptly without doxology or introduction. The title only occurs on the fly-leaf in a modern hand. Bought of Naaman, Nov. 12, 1902.

758 (p)   سراج مُنیر   **Or. 522 (8)**

The *Siráj-i-Munír*, a collection of moral anecdotes, divided into twenty sections called *Lum'as*. See *B.M.P.C.*, pp. 861–2, where the author's name is given as Ibn Shamsu'd-Dín Muḥammad Sharíf. In this MS. the author is merely described as *'Alláma-i-Shírází*. Ff. 38 of 21·2 × 15 c. and 14 ll.; fine Persian *ním-shikasta*, dated Ṣafar 13, 1274 (Oct. 3, 1857) at Ṭihrán. Bought of Hannan and Watson, Aug. 20, 1904.

759 (t)   سعادت نامه   **Or. 45 (7)**

A Turkish Ḥurúfí work (one of six bought from Naaman on Feb. 5, 1901) in prose, entitled *Sa'ádat-náma*. Ff. 42 of 18·7 × 11 c. and 13 ll., dated Dhu'l-Ḥijja, 995 (Nov. 1587). F. 1 is supplied in a modern hand.

760 (a, m) سفر الخليقة **Or. 193 (14)**

Sifru'l-Khalíqa, an Arabic-Malay translation of the Book of Genesis, dated Anno Mundi 7587. The Malay version appears as an interlinear translation, and is written in a smaller and lighter character than the Arabic. The numbers of the chapters are written at the top of each page and the numbers of the verses in the margins. The MS., bought of Quaritch on Sept. 8, 1902, is bound in vellum, was copied in the seventeenth century, and comprises 232 ff. of 32 × 20·5 c. and 8 ll. of Arabic with 8 ll. Malay.

761 (t) سفينة الرؤساء (ذيل) **Or. 573 (9)**

The *Safínatu'r-Ru'asá* (Supplement) by Sulaymán Fá'iq, a biography of ministers of state, etc., composed in 1229/1814. The MS., undated, was bought of Géjou on July 14, 1905, and comprises 152 ff. of 23·8 × 17 c. and 15 ll.; good Turkish *riq'a* with rubrications.

762 (t) سفينهٔ لطائف و مجموعهٔ معارف **Or. 575 (6)**

The *Safína-i-Laṭá'if wa Majmú'a-i-Ma'árif* of Lámi'í, a copy made in 947/1540–41, and bought of Géjou on July 14, 1905. Concerning the author, who died in 937/1530–1 or 938/1531–2, at the age of about fifty, see Gibb's *Hist. of Ottoman Poetry*, vol. iii, pp. 20–44. The MS. comprises 63 ff. of 15 × 10 c. and 15 ll.

763–766 (p) سكندرنامهٔ نظامى **Add. 3736 (10)**
Christ's, Dd. 5. 12
Corpus, No. 212
Corpus, No. 213

The well-known *Sikandar-náma* of Niẓámí of Ganja, who died about 600/1203–4. See *B.M.P.C.*, pp. 564–575. **Add. 3736,** bought of Sethian on Nov. 28, 1900, comprises 103 ff. of 23·9 × 17·5 c. and 17 ll.; good *ta'líq* with rubrications. The **Christ's MS.** is written in clear, neat *ta'líq*, with rubrications and many glosses in the margin, on 209 ff. of 22·8 × 13 c. and 17 ll. It was presented to the College by the Rev. W. M. Lowe, and belonged in 1803 to H. George Keene of Sidney Sussex College. **Corpus 212,** written in *ta'líq* on leaves of

24 × 18 c., is dated 1247/1831–2. **Corpus 213,** an anonymous commentary on the poem, is written in plain *ta'líq* on leaves of 30 × 17 c. and is dated 1246/1830–31.

767 (p) سلسلة الذهب **Or. 425 (12)**

The *Silsilatu'dh-Dhahab*, or "Chain of Gold," a well-known poem by Jámí. See *B.M.P.C.*, pp. 643–9. The MS., undated, was bought of Hannan and Watson on August 29, 1903, and comprises 78 ff. of 29 × 20 c. and 21 ll., written in a poor but legible *ta'líq* with rubrications.

768 (a) سُلّم العلوم **King's, No. 249**

The *Sullamu'l-'Ulúm*, or "Ladder of Sciences," commentated by Qiwámu'd-Dín al-Anṣárí al-Márahrawí for his son Iftikháru'd-Dín. The book, but not this commentary, is mentioned by Brockelmann, ii, 420–21, who gives the author's name as Muḥibbu'lláh b. 'Abdu'sh-Shukúr, who died in 1119/1708. The MS., transcribed in A.D. 1785 by Ḥáfiẓ Muḥammad Sa'ádatu'lláh Khán, is written in a large, clear, coarse *ta'líq* on leaves of 23·8 × 15·5 c. with rubrications.

769 (a) سلوان المطاع **Trinity, R. 13. 55**

The *Sulwánu'l-Muṭá'* of Abú 'Abdi'lláh Muḥammad aṣ-Ṣaqalí who died in 565/1169. See Brockelmann, i, pp. 351–2; *Camb. Hand-list*, p. 97; and for this MS., which contains 65 ff., Palmer's *Trin. Cat.*, pp. 144–6.

770 (p) سمر الفلاسفه **King's, No. 222**

Samaru'l-Falúsifa ("Tales of the Philosophers" of Greece and Rome), by 'Abdu's-Sattár b. Qásim, a pupil of the celebrated Jesuit missionary Xavier from whom he learned Latin at Akbar's command. See *B.M.P.C.*, pp. 177[b] and 1077[a], and Palmer's *King's Cat.*, p. 22. The MS. was transcribed in 1197/1783.

771 (a) سند صحيفة المجون فى علم الفرفير **Or. 16 (6)**

A refutation of the Shaykhí sect (the followers of Shaykh Aḥmad b. Zaynu'd-Dín al-Aḥsá'í) entitled *Sanadu Ṣaḥífati'l-Mujún fí 'ilmi'l-Firfír*, composed by Muḥammad b. 'Abdu'l-Wahháb b. Dá'úd in 1275/1858–9. Concerning Shaykh Aḥmad, who died in 1242/1826–7 at the age of 85 years, and his peculiar doctrines, see my translation of the *Traveller's Narrative written to illustrate the Episode of the Báb*, vol. ii, pp. 234–8. This MS., bought of Naaman on Feb. 5, 1901, contains 34 ff. of 15·5 × 11 c. and 10 ll., and is written in an excellent *naskh*.

772 (h) سندر سنکار **King's, No. 224**

A poem in Hindí written in a large, clear *ta'líq* with rubrications on leaves measuring 21·9 × 12·3 c., copied at Sháhjahán-ábád in the month of Rajab in the 1st year of Muḥammad Sháh (1132/1720).

773, 774 (p) سنگهاسن بتیسی **Corpus, No. 106**
King's, No. 221

Two copies of a Persian translation of the *Singhásan Battísí*, or [32] "Tales of the Throne." See *B.M.P.C.*, p. 763; *Camb. Pers. Cat.*, p. 398. The **Corpus MS.**, undated but modern, and written in *shikasta* on leaves of 18 × 12 c., contains a metrical version. The **King's MS.** comprises 105 pp., is undated, and is mentioned in Palmer's *Pers. Cat.*, p. 25.

775 (t) سؤال از نظام الملك **Or. 673 (13)**

Su'ál az Niẓámu'l-Mulk, an account of the organization, administrative divisions, etc., of the Ottoman Empire, with copious Tables and Indices. Ff. 60 of 33 × 18 c. and 21 ll.; neat Turkish hand with rubrications; undated. Bought of Géjou on Feb. 17, 1906.

776 (p) سؤال و جواب دارا شکوه با بابا لال **King's, No. 14[1]**

Questions put by Dárá-Shikúh to Bábá Lál as to points of Hindú doctrine, with the latter's answers. Prince Dárá-Shikúh was put to death in A.D. 1659. This MS. (Palmer's *King's Cat.*, p. 16) contains 5 tracts, of which this, the first, occupies 13 ff. See *B.M.P.C.*, p. 1034[a].

777 (h) سهس رس **King's, No. 218**

Sahas Ras, translated (from the Sanskrit, presumably) by Bakhshú Náyik and dedicated to Sháh Jahán. Written in large clear *ta'líq* with rubrications on leaves of 24·6 × 15·8 c. The date of the month only and not of the year is given.

778 (p) سیاست نامهٔ نظام الملك **King's, No. 219**

The great minister Niẓámu'l-Mulk's *Siyásat-náma*, or Treatise on Government, of which the text and French translation were published by the late M. Charles Schefer in Paris in 1891–3. The author was assassinated at Niháwand in 485/1092–3. See *B.M.P.C.*, pp. 444–6. This MS., copied by 'Abdu'l-Waḥíd in 1020/1611–12, comprises 358 pp. See Palmer's *King's Cat.*, p. 16.

779 (t) سيف العزّت **Or. 216 (9)**

A Turkish treatise on Politics entitled *Sayfu'l-'Izzat*, containing an Introduction, 8 Sections and a Conclusion, composed in the time of Sulṭán Salím for Ḥájji 'Izzat Muḥammad Pasha. The MS., undated, was bought of Naaman on Nov. 12, 1902.

780–783 (a) الشافية لابن الحاجب **Jesus, No. 13[1]; Or. 579 (6); Or. 540 (9); King's, No. 133**

The well-known work on Arabic Grammar entitled *ash-Sháfiya* by Ibnu'l-Ḥájib (died 646/1248). See Brockelmann, i, pp. 303 and 305. Of these four MSS. the **Jesus MS.,** given to the College by Samuel Lyde, Fellow, who died in 1860, and transcribed in 1269/1852–3, contains only the text. The other three MSS. also contain the commentary of al-Járibardí, who died 746/1345. **Or. 579,** dated 712/1312–3, was bought of Géjou on July 14, 1905. It comprises 202 ff. of 16·1 × 12·2 c. and 19 ll., the first 4 ff. supplied in a modern *nasta'líq*, the remainder in fine old *naskh*. **Or. 540,** dated 759/1358, and bought of Géjou on Jan. 4, 1905, comprises 118 ff. of 24 × 17 c. and 21 ll., and is written in clear *naskh* with rubrications. **King's 133,** undated, is written in a large, clear Indian *naskh*.

784 (p, t) شامل اللّغات **Trinity, 5.13.17[1]**

The *Shámilu'l-Lughát*, a Persian-Turkish lexicon by Ḥasan b. Ḥusayn 'Imád of Qará-Ḥiṣár. This work occupies ff. 2^a–83^a

of the MS., concerning which see Palmer's *Trin. Cat.*, pp. 39-40.

785-789 (p)	شاهنامهٔ فردوسی	Or. 420 (13) Corpus, No. 202 Corpus, No. 203 King's, No. 135 Corpus, No. 148

The famous *Sháh-náma* ("Book of Kings") of Firdawsí. **Or. 420,** bought of Hannan and Watson on August 29, 1903, seems to be dated 841/1437-8, and contains the first part of the poem from the beginning to the end of Kay-Khusraw's reign. It comprises 281 ff. (each folio containing about 100 *bayts*) of 32·2 × 20 c. and 25 ll. **Corpus 202** is a fairly written copy of the second part, beginning with the reign of Luhrásp, without preface, and containing several illustrations of considerable merit, and dated 1053/1643-4. **Corpus 203** is a fragment of a finely-written copy, which, however, is hopelessly destroyed by worms, while the fine binding is also in a very bad state of preservation. **Corpus 148** is an Urdú translation of the well-known Persian abridgement known as *Ta'ríkh-i-Shamshír Khání* or *Muntakhab-i-Sháh-náma*, concerning which see *B.M.P.C.*, pp. 539-540. The MS., dated 1267/1850-1, comprises 170 ff. of 26 × 17 c., and is written in a cursive *nasta'líq* in four columns. The Indian translator's name is given as Munshí Múlchand. **King's 135** is a long strip of paper containing 35 *bayts* from the *Sháh-náma*, with illuminated borders and at the end two well-executed pen-sketches. See Palmer's *King's Cat.*, p. 10.

790 (p)	شاهنامهٔ شاه اسمعیل	King's, No. 238

The *Sháh-náma-i-Sháh Isma'íl*, an imitation of the *Sháh-náma* describing the achievements of the founder of the Ṣafawí dynasty, by Qásimí, who was flourishing about 975/1567-8. See *B.M.P.C.*, pp. 660-661, and Palmer's *King's Cat.*, p. 16.

791, 792 (p)	شاه جهان نامه	King's, No. 252 King's, No. 253

Two separate works bearing the same title of *Sháh-Jahán-náma*. The first (**King's 252**) was completed in 1070/1659-60 by Muḥammad Ṣáliḥ Kanbú, and is written in a bad Indian *shikasta*. The second, in verse, is by the poet Kalím of Hamadán (died 1062/1652), is undated, and contains about 500 ff. See *B.M.P.C.*, pp. 686–7, and p. 454 of the *Oude Catalogue*.

793, 794 (t) شاه و گدا **Add. 3694 (8)**
Or. 769 (7)

Two MSS. of the Turkish poem *Sháh u Gadá* ("the King and the Beggar") by Yaḥyá Bey, who died in 983/1575–6. See Gibb's *Hist. of Ottoman Poetry*, vol. iii, pp. 116–132, and for an analysis of the poem pp. 368–370 of the same volume. **Add. 3694** comprises 50 ff. of 20·5 × 11·3 c. and 21 ll., is undated, written in fair Turkish *nasta'líq*, and was bought of Sethian on Nov. 5, 1900. **Or. 769,** bought of Géjou on Feb. 20, 1908, and dated 1022/1613, comprises 61 ff. of 18·5 × 10·7 c. and 17 ll. and is written in fair *ta'líq* with rubrications.

795 (p) شبستان خيال **King's, No. 256**

The *Shabistán-i-Khayál*, or *Shabistán-i-Nukát wa Gulistán-i-Lughát* of Yaḥyá Síbak of Níshápúr, poetically surnamed Fattáḥ, who died in 852/1448-9. The MS. is dated 1021/1612–3.

796 (p) شجاع حيدرى **Corpus, No. 135**

Shujá'-i-Ḥaydarí, a work treating of the curiosities and wonders of various countries by Muḥammad Ḥaydar. See *B.M.P.C.*, p. 427. The MS. comprises 101 ff. of 31 × 21 c. and is written in *nasta'líq*.

797, 798 (p) شجرة الامانى **Corpus, No. 67[1]**
Corpus, No. 137[1]

Two copies, both defective, of the *Shajaratu'l-Amání* of Mírzá Qatíl. See *B.M.P.C.*, pp. 794–5.

799 (a) الشذور الذهبيّة و القطع الاحمديّة **Trinity, R. 13. 38**

Ash-Shudhúru'dh-Dhahabiyya, a work on the Turkish language by Mawláná Ibn Muḥammad Ṣáliḥ. See Palmer's *Trin. Cat.*, pp. 85–6. Ff. 61, good Turkish *naskh*.

800 (a) شرح تصريف الزّنجانى **King's, No. 220**

The commentary of Sa'du'lláh b. Mas'úd b. 'Umar at-taftázání (d. 792/1390) on the well-known Arabic grammar entitled *Kitábu't-Taṣríf* of 'Izzu'd-Dín az-Zanjání (d. 655/1257). See Brockelmann, vol. i, p. 283. The MS. is undated and is written in a large clear *naskh* on leaves of 20·4 × 12·9 c.

801 (a) شرح التصوّرات **Or. 541 (8)**

The commentary of Ḥasan Efendi of Áq-Hiṣár on the *Taṣawwurát*. The MS. comprises 33 ff. of 20 × 12·4 and 17 ll., and is written in clear *naskh* with rubrications. It was bought of Géjou on Jan. 4, 1905, and is undated.

802 (a) شرح مقدمة الانصارى على البسملة **Add. 3628 (9)**

An anonymous commentary on the Introduction of Shaykh Zaynu'l-'Ábidín Zakariyyá al-Anṣárí to the *Bismi'lláh*. The MS. is dated 1098/1686–7, and contains 76 ff. of 21 × 15·5 c. and 21 ll., written in poor but legible *naskh* with rubrications.

803, 804 (a) شرح ملّا جامى **King's, No. 141**
King's, No. 143

Sharḥu Mullá Jámí, the commentary of the celebrated Persian poet Mullá Núru'd-Dín 'Abdu'r-Raḥmán Jámí (d. 898/1492) on the *Káfiya* of Ibnu'l-Ḥájib: two super-commentaries (*Ḥáshiya*) on the same, *viz.* that of Jámí's pupil 'Abdu'l-Ghafúr of Lár (d. 912/1506); see Brockelmann, i, p. 304, No. 13; and that of al-Ḥáfiẓ Sulṭán Muḥammad. For both MSS. see Palmer's *King's Cat.*, p. 21. **King's 143** is dated 1002/1593–4, and is written in a clear Indian *naskh* with rubrications. **King's 141** is written in a similar hand but is undated.

805 (a) الشرح الشريف فى الفقه الامامى **Or. 435 (8)**

A gloss (*ta'líqa*) by Muḥammad Káẓim b. Muḥammad Naṣír of Astarábád and Hazár-jaríb on Sayyid 'Alí's *Sharḥu'sh-Sharíf* (Commentary) on Imámí Jurisprudence. Ff. 104 of 20·9 × 14·1 c. and 25 ll.; neat *naskh*; defective at end; undated. Bought of Hannan, Watson and Co., Aug. 29, 1903.

806 (a) شرح العنوان **Or. 667 (12)**

Sharhu'l-'Unwán, a commentary by Shaykh Rashídu'd-Dín Abú Muḥammad b. aẓ-Ẓáhir b. Abu'l-Makárim Nashwán b. 'Abdu'ẓ-Ẓáhir ar-Rúḥí as-Sa'dí (died 649/1251–2) on the *'Unwán fi'l-Qirá'at* of Abú Ṭáhir Isma'íl b. Khalaf al-Muqrí al-Anṣárí al-Andalusí (died 455/1063). See Ḥájji Khalífa, vol. iv, pp. 274–5. The MS., copied in Dhu'l-Qa'da 1001 (= Aug. 1593) by 'Abdu'lláh al-Málikí al-Miṣrí, contains 250 ff. of 30 × 19·5 and 27 ll., and is written in a poor but legible *naskh* with rubrications. Bought of Géjou, Feb. 17, 1906.

807 (a) شرح ما وقع من اسماء الادوية باليونانيّة **Or. 528 (9)**

This appears to be an account of drugs which have retained their Greek names in Arabic, by Yúsuf b. Isma'íl al-Khúbí, known as Ibnu'l-Kabír, who died in 711/1311–12. See Ḥájji Khalífa, vol. v, No. 11278. This MS., bought of Géjou on Nov. 1, 1904, is undated, contains 54 ff. of 23 × 15·8 c. and 25 ll., and is written in good *naskh* with rubrications.

808 (p) شفاء المريض (يا طبّ شفائى) **Corpus, No. 29**

A treatise on Medicine in verse entitled *Shifá'u'l-Maríḍ* or *Ṭibb-i-Shifá'í*. The MS. comprises 80 ff. of 24 × 15·5 c., followed by a few pages of scribbled prescriptions, the first pages in *naskh*, the remainder in *ním-shikasta*, and is undated.

809 (a) شفيعات الحسنيّة فى مدح خير البريّة **Or. 31 (8)**

Poems in praise of the Prophet Muḥammad, on the model of the *Witriyyát*, entitled *Shafí'átu'l-Ḥasaniyya*, by Ḥasan b. 'Abdu'l-Fattáḥ al-A'ẓamí al-Ḥanafí al-Qádirí. The MS., bought of Naaman on Feb. 5, 1901, and undated, contains 45 ff. of 21 × 15·3 c. and 21 ll., and is written in a coarse *naskh* with rubrications.

810 (a) الشقائق النعمانيّة فى علماء الدولة العثمانيّة **Or. 187 (8)**

The well-known Biography of Turkish doctors and theologians entitled *ash-Shaqá'iqu'n-Nu'mániyya*, a work to which Gibb constantly refers under the title of "the Crimson Peony" in his *History of Ottoman Poetry* (*e.g.* vol. i, p. 139). Though several Turkish translations exist, the original of Aḥmad b. Muṣṭafá Tásh-kyúpri-záda, composed in 965/1557–8, is in Arabic. See Brockelmann, ii, pp. 425–6; *Camb. Hand-list*, p. 112. The MS., bought of Géjou on July 3, 1902, is dated 968/1560–1, contains 190 ff. of 19·4 × 10·6 c. and 19 ll., and is written in a small, neat *nasta'líq* with rubrications.

811 (a) الشمائل الشريفة النبويّة **Or. 201 (10)**

The *Shamá'il*, or Personal Characteristics of the Prophet, by Abú 'Ísá Muḥammad at-Tirmidhí (d. 279/892–3), beginning like the British Museum MS. (*B.M.A.C.*[1], p. 98). See also Brockelmann, i, pp. 161–2. The MS., bought of Géjou on Oct. 23, 1902, was transcribed in 1083/1672–3, is written in a poor but clear *naskh* with rubrications and some marginal notes, and contains 72 ff. of 24·5 × 14 c. and 19 ll.

812–817 (a) [الرسالة] الشمسيّة **Trinity, R. 13. 54[1]**
Or. 584 (8)
Add. 3627 (8)
Or. 443 (8)
King's, No. 183
Add. 3689 (10)

The well-known treatise on Logic entitled *ar-Risálatu'sh-Shamsiyya* by Najmu'd-Dín 'Alí al-Kátibí al-Qazwíní, who died in 675/1276. See Brockelmann, i, p. 466. The **Trinity MS.** (ff. 1–28) contains the original treatise. See Palmer's *Trin. Coll. Cat.*, pp. 141-4. **Or. 584** contains the commentary of Quṭbu'd-Dín ar-Rází, who died in 766/1364. This MS., undated, was bought of Géjou on July 14, 1905, and comprises 124 ff. of 19·8 × 13·7 c. and 16 ll., and is written in fair *naskh* with rubrications. **Add. 3627** contains the gloss (*ḥáshiya*) of as-Sayyid ash-Sharíf al-Jurjání on the above, as does **Or. 443** The former MS., dated 1088/1677–8, was bought of Géjou on Feb. 14, 1900, and contains 96 ff. of 20·7 × 13·3 c. and 15 ll. The first 7 ff. contain a short tract entitled *Sharḥu Ádábi'l-Ḥanafiyya*. **Or. 443** contains besides al-Jurjání's gloss (ff. 2ᵇ–71ᵃ) another commentary on the *Shamsiyya* entitled *Taḥríru'l-Qawá'idi'l-Manṭiqiyya fí Sharḥi'r-Risálati'sh-Sham-*

siyya. This MS., dated 1232/1816–7, was bought of Messrs Hannan and Watson on August 29, 1903, and contains 224 ff. of 21 × 15 c. and 19 ll., written in good *naskh.* **King's 183** contains a gloss and a super-gloss on the commentary on the *Shamsiyya* by Mullá Dá'úd. The MS., a vile scrawl in several different hands, is undated and contains 79 ff. See Palmer's *King's Cat.*, p. 22. **Add. 3689,** undated, bought of Sethian on Nov. 1, 1900, contains 90 ff. of 24 × 12·5 c. and 18 ll., written in a small, neat *ta'líq* with rubrications and many interlinear and marginal comments and glosses.

818 (a) شواهد الربوبيّة **King's, No. 255**

The *Shawáhidu'r-Rubúbiyya*, or "Evidences of Divinity," a well-known philosophical work by Mullá Ṣadrá of Shíráz, who died in 1050/1640. See Gobineau's *Les Religions et les Philosophies dans l'Asie Centrale* (ed. 1866), pp. 80–91. This MS., written in an excellent Persian *naskh* with blue and gilt *'unwáns* within gold borders, was copied by Ibn Muḥammad Ibráhím 'Azízu'lláh at the end of Sha'bán, 1119 (= Nov. 1707). Its pages measure 20 × 12 c.

819, 820 (p) شواهد النبوّة **King's, No. 254**
Corpus, No. 240

The *Shawáhidu'n-Nubuwwa*, or "Evidences of the Prophetic Function," by Mullá Núru'd-Dín 'Abdu'r-Raḥmán Jámí, who composed it about 885/1480–1. See *B.M.P.C.*, p. 146. Neither MS. is dated. For the **King's MS.** see Palmer's *King's Cat.*, p. 24. The **Corpus MS.** contains 314 ff. of 22 × 13 c., and is written in cursive *nasta'líq.*

821 (a) الشهب اللامعة فى السياسة النافعة **Or. 607 (8)**

A work on Politics entitled *ash-Shuhabu'l-Lámi'a fi's-Siyásati'n-Náfi'a* by Abu'l-Qásim b. Riḍwán, who wrote about 600/1203. See Brockelmann, i, p. 463. This MS., undated but copied about the 18th century, was bought of Khalíl Khálid Bey, formerly Turkish Lecturer in this University, who obtained it in Constantine, Algeria, about April 1905. It contains 162 ff. of 21·2 × 15·8 c. and 19 ll., and is written in a Maghribí hand.

822 (a) [كتاب] الصادح و الباغم **Add. 3722[1] (8)**

The *Kitábu's-Ṣádiḥ wa'l-Bághim* of Abú Ya'lá Muḥammad b. al-Habbáriyya, who died in 504/1110–11. See *B.M.A.S.*, p. 712, No. 1131, and Brockelmann, i, p. 252. The MS., undated, was bought of Naaman on Nov. 23, 1900, and contains 86 ff. (of which this portion fills 40 ff.) of 19·7 × 15 c. and 25 ll. It is written in fair *nasta'líq* with rubrications and is incomplete at the end.

823 (a) صاعقة الرابية على الفرقة الصابية الكذّابية **Or. 26[2] (8)**

A refutation of the Wahhábí heresy, entitled *Ṣa'iqatu'r-Rábiya*, by Shaykh Dá'úd b. Sulaymán al-Baghdádí al-Khálidí an-Naqshbandí. This MS., undated, was bought of Naaman on Feb. 5, 1901. This portion of it occupies ff. 75[a]–87[b] of 19·3 × 14·5 c. and 12 ll.

824 (a) الصافية فى شرح الشافية **Jesus, No. 12[2]**

Aṣ-Ṣáfiya, a commentary on the *Sháfiya* of Ibnu'l-Ḥájib (d. 646/1248) by Yúsuf b. 'Abdu'l-Malik, dated 1270/1853–4.

825 (a, p) الصحاح العجميّة **Trinity, R. 13. 50**

Aṣ-Ṣiḥáḥu'l-'Ajamiyya, a Persian grammar in Arabic, by Muḥammad b. Pír 'Alí al-Birkawí (or Birgilí), who died in 981/1573. See Brockelmann, ii, 442, l. 2, and Palmer's *Trin. Coll. Cat.*, p. 138. Ff. 73.

826 (a) صحيح مسلم **Or. 68 (7)**

The seventeenth of the thirty parts into which the *Ṣaḥíḥ* of Muslim (d. 261/875) is divided. See Brockelmann, i, p. 160. Ff. 88 of 18 × 13·6 c. and 11 ll.; large clear *naskh* with rubrications; no date.

827 (a) صحيفة سجاديّة **Corpus, No. 141**

A collection of prayers arranged by Muḥammad b. al-Ḥasan al-'Ámilí entitled *Ṣaḥífa Sajjádiyya*. The MS., undated, is written in a neat *naskh*, fully pointed, on pages of 13 × 19 c.

828 (a) صحيفة علويّة **Add. 3729 (8)**

A collection of prayers entitled *Ṣaḥífa 'Alawiyya*. The MS., dated 1238/1822–3, was bought of Naaman on Nov. 23, 1900, and contains 103 ff. of 18·8 × 13 c. and 13 ll., written in good *naskh* with rubrications.

829, 830 (a, p) **الصحيفة الكاملة** **Or. 433** (9) **Or. 581** (5)

Aṣ-Ṣaḥífatu'l-Kámila, a collection of prayers ascribed to the fourth Imám of the Shí'ites, 'Alí Zaynu'l-'Ábidín, with interlinear Persian translation. **Or. 433,** undated, bought of Hannan and Watson on Aug. 29, 1903, contains 182 ff. of 23·6 × 14 c. and 10 ll. of text with another 10 ll. of interlinear translation. **Or. 581,** bought of Géjou on July 14, 1905, also undated, contains 164 ff. of 12·7 × 7·5 c. and 12 ll., written in good *naskh* with rubrications.

831, 832 (p) **صد پند لقمان** **Corpus, No. 12**[9] **Corpus, No. 115**[4]

The "Hundred Counsels" (*Ṣad Pand*) supposed to have been given by the Sage Luqmán to his son. This occupies only 5 pp. in the first MS. and ff. 159–160 in the second.

833 (p) **صد كلمهٔ بطليموس** **King's, No. 239**

The "Hundred Words" (*Ṣad Kalima*) of Ptolemy, a Persian commentary on his καρπὸς or *Liber Fructus*, by Muḥammad Shamsu'd-Dín. See *B.M.A.C.*, pp. 197[b], 773[a]. The text was prepared by the celebrated Naṣíru'd-Dín Ṭúsí for Bahá'u'd-Dín Juwayní. See Palmer's *King's Cat.*, p. 23.

834 (p) **صدر الكتاب** **Corpus, No. 130**

Ṣadru'l-Kitáb, a collection of epistolary models of Shukr 'Alí.

835 (a) **الصّراح فى الصّحاح** **Or. 868** (9)

Aṣ-Ṣuráḥ, an abridgement by Abu'l-Faḍl Muḥammad... al Jamál al-Qurashí (d. 681/1282) of the well-known Arabic lexicon *aṣ-Ṣiḥáḥ* of al-Jawharí (d. 393/1002). See Brockelmann, i, pp. 128 and 296; *Camb. Pers. Cat.*, pp. 239–240.

This MS., from the late Professor Robertson Smith's library, is dated 1091/1680–1, and contains ff. of 22·7 × 13·8 c. and 23 ll., and is written in fair *naskh* and *ta'líq* with rubrications.

836 (a) صفوة الزُّبَد فى فقه الامام الشّافعى **Or. 24 (8)**

A metrical treatise on Sháfi'ite Jurisprudence entitled *Ṣafwatu'z-Zubaḍ* by Shaykh Abu'l-'Abbás Aḥmad b. Arslán. See Brockelmann, ii, p. 96. The MS., undated, was bought of Naaman on Feb. 5, 1901, and comprises 38 ff. of 20·2 × 14·9 and 15 ll.

837 (p) صفوة الصّفى (الصّفا) **King's, No. 87**

Ṣafwatu'ṣ-Ṣafí (or *-Ṣafá*), an account of the life and miracles of Shaykh Ṣafiyyu'd-Dín Isḥáq, the ancestor of the Ṣafawí kings of Persia, originally composed by Darwísh Tawakkul b. Isma'íl, called Ibn Bazzáz, and edited in the time of Sháh Ṭahmásp by Abu'l-Fatḥ al-Ḥusayní. See *B.M.P.C.*, pp. 345–6, No. 1842 of Ethé's *India Office Cat.*, and Palmer's *King's Cat.*, p. 9.

838 (a) **Or. 660 (8)**

الصواعق المحرقة فى الردّ على اهل الزيغ و الزّندقة

A refutation of heretics entitled *aṣ-Ṣawá'iqu'l-muḥriqa fi'r-radd 'ala ahli'z-ziyagh wa'z-Zindiqa*, by Abu'l-'Abbás Aḥmad...b. Ḥajar al-Haythamí as-Sa'dí al-Anṣárí, who died in 973/1565. See *B.M.A.S.*, p. 117, No. 192; Brockelmann, ii, pp. 387–8; and Wüstenfeld's *Geschichtschreiber d. Araber*, p. 247, No. 529. The MS., bought of Géjou on Feb. 12, 1906, is dated 1082/1671–2, contains 167 ff. of 20·3 × 12·7 c. and 23 ll., and is written in a neat *naskh* with rubrications.

839 (p) صور الاقاليم **Or. 947 (11)**

A Persian geographical work entitled *Ṣuwaru'l-Aqálím* by Abú Zayd Aḥmad ibn Sahl al-Balkhí, acquired by G. le Strange in 1913 from the library of the late Sir Houtum-Schindler and presented by him to the Library in March 1916. The MS., dated 1083/1672–3, comprises 99 ff. of 29 × 20·5 c. and 20 ll., and is written in a good clear *ta'líq* with rubrications.

840 (p) ضياء القلب **King's, No. 37[2]**

The *Ḍiyá'u'l-Qalb* ("Light of the Heart") of Mullá Muḥsin of Káshán, who died about 1105/1693–4. The MS. (see Palmer's *King's Cat.*, pp. 5 and 25) is dated 1057/1647–8.

841 (a, p) طبّ النّبى و غيره **Or. 516 (8)**

Ṭibbu'n-Nabí ("The Medical Art of the Prophet"). See Brockelmann, i, p. 362 and ii, p. 48. This MS., one of thirty bought of Hannan and Watson on Aug. 20, 1904, is dated 1241/1825–6, and contains 76 ff. of 20·2 × 13·8 c. and 16 ll. The first and second parts, *viz.* the *Ṭibbu'n-Nabí* (ff. 1^b–17^a) and a letter to a Caliph on foods and drinks (ff. 18^b–28^b) are written in a good *naskh*, while the third part, containing various medical notes and prescriptions, is written in a bad and irregular *ta'líq*.

842 (a) طبقات الشافعيّة لابن السّبكى **Trinity, R.13.5**

The *Ṭabaqátu'sh-Sháfi'iyya*, in the medium-sized recension known as *al-Wusṭá*, by 'Abdu'l-Wahháb...b. Táju'd-Dín as-Subkí, who died in 771/1370. See Brockelmann, ii, pp. 89–90. This volume, transcribed in A.D. 1455, contains the first half only, *viz.* the letters *alif—sín*.

843 (a) طبقات الشافعيّة **Or. 842 (8)**

The *Ṭabaqátu'sh-Sháfi'iyya* of Shaykh Jamálu'd-Dín 'Abdu'r-Raḥím b. Ḥasan al-Isnawí, who died in 772/1370. See Brockelmann, ii, pp. 90–91. The MS., dated 814/1411–12, was bought of Naaman on Feb. 11, 1911, contains 208 ff. of 21·3 × 13·8 c. and 23 ll., and is written in good *naskh* with rubrications.

844 (a) طوالع الأنوار من مطالع الأبصار آلخ **Corpus, No. 401**

The *Ṭawáli'u'l-Anwár min Maṭáli'i'l-Abṣár* of the celebrated commentator al-Bayḍáwí (d. 685/1286): see Brockelmann, i, pp. 416–418; with the commentary of Shamsu'd-Dín Abu'th-Thaná Maḥmúd al-Iṣfahání (d. 749/1348): see Brockelmann, ii, 110–111. The MS., dated 940/1533–4, is written in a Maghribí hand, and at the beginning are bound in four leaves, cut across transversely, in an archaic Maghribí hand, which appear to contain part of a commentary on the *Qur'án*, followed by two similar leaves.

845 (p) طوطی نامه **Corpus, No. 68**

A fairly good copy of the well-known *Ṭúṭí-náma*, or "Tales of a Parrot," of Ḍiyá-i-Nakhshabí, completed in 730/1329–1330. See *B.M.P.C.*, pp. 753–754. This is the complete work, not the abridgement. The MS. contains about 290 ff. of 23 × 14 c., is defective at end and undated, but is apparently fairly old.

846 (h) طوطی کهانی **Or. 880 (13)**

The *Ṭúṭí-Kaháne*, or Hindustání version of the "Tales of a Parrot." The MS., dated 1245/1829–30, comprises 50 ff. of 32·5 × 20·4 c. and 16 ll., and is written in a good Indian *ta'líq* hand with rubrications. It was bought of G. David on July 3, 1912.

847 (p) ظفرنامهٔ شرف الدین **Christ's, Dd.4.4**

The well-known history of Tímúr by Sharafu'd-Dín 'Alí Yazdí entitled *Ẓafar-náma*. The author died in 858/1454. See *B.M.P.C.*, pp. 173–7. This MS., copied in clear Indian *ta'líq* by one Muḥammad 'Ábid, is dated October 29, 1774, and comprises 489 ff. of 28·9 × 18·6 c. and 21 ll.

848 (p) ظفرنامه **Corpus, No. 115[3]**

A collection of wise counsels said to have been composed for the Sásánian king Anúsharwán (Núshírwán) by his minister Buzurjmihr and Aristotle (!). It only fills ff. 149–157 of the MS.

849 (p) عالم آرای عبّاسی **Christ's, Dd.4.6**

The second *Ṣaḥífa* of the *'Álam-árá-yi 'Abbásí* of Iskandar Munshí, containing the reign of Sháh 'Abbás the Great (A.H. 996–1038 = A.D. 1588–1628). See *B.M.P.C.*, pp. 185–188. Ff. 564 of 34·7 × 20·7 c. and 21 ll.; clear Indian *ta'líq*.

850, 851 (p) عالمگیر نامه **Or. 239 (10)**
Trinity, R.10.2

Two copies of the *'Álamgír-náma* of Munshí Muḥammad Káẓim, containing the history of the first ten years of the reign of Awrangzíb 'Álamgír (A.H. 1068–1078 = A.D. 1658–1668). See *B.M.P.C.*, pp. 266–7. **Or. 239,** from the Cowell Bequest, is undated, and contains 356 ff. of 23·6 × 15 c. and 13 ll. The **Trinity MS.** was presented to the Library in 1754 and contains 216 ff. See Palmer's *Trin. Cat.*, pp. 5–6.

852 (p) عبرت ارباب بصر **Corpus, No. 102[2]**

A rhymed chronicle of the events of the year 1170/1756–7. Cf. *B.M.P.C.*, p. 965. The author of this versified rendering appears to be called Ráy Bálakmand. The MS., which contains 37 ff., was copied at Bareilly in 1826.

853 (a) عجائب البلدان **Or. 902 (6)**

'Ajá'ibu'l-Buldán ("Wonders of the Lands"), composed, apparently, about 514/1120–1 by Abú Ḥámid Muḥammad b. 'Abdu'r-Raḥmán al-Andalusí for the Wazír Yaḥyá b. Hubayra. It contains the following four chapters:

الباب الاوّل فى صفة الدنيا و سكّانها من انسها و جانّها ' الباب الثانى فى صفة عجائب البلدان و غرائب البنيان ' الباب الثالث فى صفة البحار و عجائب حيوانها ' الباب الرابع فى صفة الحفائر و القبور ' الخاتمة '

Ff. 53 of 15·2 × 11·9 c. and 19 ll.; written in an ancient Maghribí hand; undated. Bought of Naaman, Aug. 1914.

854–856 (p) عجائب المخلوقات **Or. 486 (10), Or. 538 (9), Or. 911 (11)**

Three copies of the Persian translation of Zakariyyá b. Muḥammad b. Maḥmúd al-Qazwíní's *'Ajá'ibu'l-Makhlúqát*, or "Wonders of Creation." See Broçkelmann, i, pp. 481–2 and *B.M.P.C.*, pp. 462 and 995. **Or. 486,** undated, was bought of Géjou, August 18, 1904, contains 207 ff. of 26·7 × 15 c. and 19 ll., and is written in a good small Persian *ta'líq* with illustrations. **Or. 538,** dated 1022/1613–14, was bought of G. Grahame, Esq., Nov. 9, 1904, contains 207 ff. of 23·2 × 15 c. and 21 ll., and is written in a good Persian *ta'líq* with illustrations and rubrications. **Or. 911,** from the Lynch Bequest, is undated, written in a clear, modern *naskh* with rubrications, and comprises 184 ff. of 29·3 × 19 c. and 27 ll.

857 (a) عجائب المقدور فى نوائب تيمور **Or. 577 (12)**

The well-known history of Tímúr by Abu'l-'Abbás Aḥmad ...Ibn 'Arabsháh, who died in 854/1450. See Brockelmann, ii, pp. 28–30; *Camb. Hand-list*, pp. 120–121. The MS., dated 1267/1850–1, was bought of Géjou on July 14, 1905, comprises 182 ff. of 30 × 19·5 c. and 17 ll., and is written in a large, clear *naskh*.

858, 859 (p) عروض سيفى **King's, No. 207** **Corpus, No. 23**[2]

Two copies of the '*Urud-i-Sayfí*, the treatise on Prosody of Sayfí of Bukhárá, who died in 909/1503–4, edited and translated into English by Blochmann (Calcutta, 1872), together with Jámí's Treatise on Rhyme. See *B.M.P.C.*, p. 525. For the **King's MS.**, dated 1199/1784–5, see Palmer's *King's Cat.*, p. 14. The **Corpus MS.**, written in careless *nasta'líq*, is undated and contains 36 ff.

860–862 (t) عشق نامهٔ فرشته زاده **Or. 44 (7)** **Or. 531 (6)** **Or. 702 (8)**

The '*Ishq-náma*, a well-known Ḥurúfí treatise originally composed in Persian in 833/1429–1430, by 'Abdu'l-Majíd Firishta-záda 'Izzu'd-Dín, and subsequently translated into Turkish. See my *Further Notes on the Literature of the Ḥurúfís* in the *J.R.A.S.* for July 1907, pp. 12, 26 (the lithographed edition), 27, 38–9, 42 and 46. **Or. 44,** bought of Naaman on Feb. 5, 1901, is dated 996/1588, contains 131 ff. of 18·7 × 10·8 c. and 13 ll., and is written in *naskh* with rubrications. **Or. 531,** bought of Naaman on Nov. 1, 1904, is dated 1215/1800–1, was copied by 'Umar b. 'Uthmán, contains 198 ff. of 16·7 × 11·5 c. and 11 ll., and is written in fair *nasta'líq* with rubrications. **Or. 702,** dated 1217/1802–3, was bought of Géjou in Dec. 1906, contains 126 ff. of 20·1 × 14 c. and 19 ll., and is written in a large, coarse *naskh*.

863 (t) عقائد اسحق افندى **Or. 208**[2] **(8)**

The '*Aqá'id*, or Articles of Faith, of Isḥáq Efendi, beginning: گليدر بسمله گلزارِ علمك '

For description of the MS., which was bought of Naaman on Nov. 12, 1902, and of which this portion occupies ff. 19b–31a, see *s.v.* البُرْدَة, No. **164**, p. 29 *supra*.

864–867 (a) العقائد النسفيّة **Or. 12 (7)** **Or. 478 (7)** **King's, No. 150** **Trinity, R.13.46**

The *'Aqá'id* of Najmu'd-Dín 'Umar...an-Nasafí, who died in 537/1142, with the commentary of Sa'du'd-Dín at-Taftázání (d. 791/1389). See Brockelmann, i, pp. 427–8. **Or. 12,** undated, was bought of Naaman on Feb. 5, 1901, contains 30 ff. of 17·8 × 11·6 c. and 21 ll., and is written in a small, neat *nasta'líq*. It also contains the super-gloss of Siyálkútí (d. 1060/1650). **Or. 478,** copied by Sa'íd b. 'Aynu'd-Dín b. Míká'íl of Marágha in 789/1387, and bought of Géjou on August 18, 1904, comprises 68 ff. of 18·3 × 13·5 c. and 17 ll. The **King's MS.,** dated 1029/1620, contains 172 ff. See Palmer's *King's Cat.*, p. 11. The **Trinity MS.,** undated, contains 91 ff. and concludes with a short essay on the means to knowledge (اسباب العلم). See Palmer's *Trin. Cat.*, p. 124.

868 (a) العقد الفاخر..فى..اعيان..اليمن **King's, No. 72**

Part 2 of a biography of notable personages of Yaman, entitled *al-'Iqdu'l-Fákhiru'l-Ḥasan fí Ṭabaqáti A'yáni Ahli'l-Yaman*, by Shaykh Shamsu'd-Dín 'Alí b. al-Ḥasan al-Khazrají, who died in 812/1409. See Brockelmann, ii, pp. 184–5, where a work apparently identical with this is described under a somewhat different title. This volume contains chs. xvii–xxx, from the letter ظ to the end of the alphabet, ending with notices of eminent women of Yaman. The MS., written in a fine, clear and rather old *naskh* with rubrications, is undated. See Palmer's *King's Cat.*, p. 27.

869 (a) عقد الفرائد فيما نظم من الفوائد **Or. 57 (8)**

The *'Iqdu'l Ferá'id fímá naẓama mina'l-Fawá'id*, by 'Alá'u'd-Dín b. 'Abdu'l-Báqí al-Khaṭíb, who died in 1005/1596. See Brockelmann, ii, 378. The MS., dated 1009/1600–

1601, was bought of Naaman on March 4, 1901, contains 74 ff. of 23·3 × 14·2 c. and 19 ll., and is written in a good *naskh* with rubrications.

870 (a) **عقود الجواهر** **Trinity, R. 13. 43²**

The '*Uqúdu'l-Jawáhir* of Shaykh 'Alí al-Qúshjí, who died in 879/1474. See Brockelmann, ii, pp. 234–5, where, however, this work is entitled '*Unqúd* instead of '*Uqúd*. See also Palmer's *Trin. Cat.*, pp. 100–101. This portion of the MS. occupies ff. 92–111.

871 (p) **عقود الجواهر** **Or. 211. b. (8)**

A rhymed Persian-Arabic glossary in 650 verses and 51 *qiṭ'as*, composed by Aḥmad-i-Dá'í, for the Ottoman Sulṭan Murád II. Concerning the author see Gibb's *History of Ottoman Poetry*, vol. i, pp. 256–9. The MS., bought of Naaman on Nov. 12, 1902, and dated 1184/1770–1, comprises 20 ff. of 18·8 × 12·3 c. and 19 ll., and is written in a small neat *nasta'líq* with interlinear glosses.

872 (a) **العقيدة الكبرى (شرح)** **Add. 3625 (9)**

A commentary on *al-'Aqídatu't-Kubrá* of Muḥammad b. Yúsuf as-Sanúsí, who died in 892/1486. See Brockelmann, ii, pp. 250–2. The MS., dated 1115/1703–4, was bought of Géjou on Feb. 14, 1900, and contains 61 ff. of 20·9 × 15·2 c. and 19 ll., and is written in a large, clear *naskh* with rubrications.

873 (a) **عمدة الطالب فى نسب أبى طالب** **Add. 3655 (10)**

'*Umdatu'ṭ-Ṭalib fí nasabi Abí Ṭálib* by Jamálu'd-Dín Aḥmad known as ibn 'Uqba, who died in 825/1422. See Brockelmann, ii, p. 199, and *B.M.A.C.*, pp. 167–8. The MS., dated 945/1538–9, was bought of Sethian on May 21, 1900, comprises 142 ff. of 25 × 17·4 c. and 19 ll., and is written in an excellent clear *naskh* with rubrications. Some other genealogical and other tables are prefixed and affixed to the text.

874 (p) **عنايت نامه** **Corpus, No. 49**

The '*Ináyat-náma*, a collection of Persian epistolary models, compiled by 'Ináyat Khán Rásikh b. Shamsu'd-Dawla

Luṭfu'lláh Khán Ṣádiq. The above is the title given by the author himself to the work on f. 1ᵇ, but in the colophon it is called *Majma'u'l-Jawáhir*. It was composed in 1163/1750, and this copy was transcribed in 1257/1841. It is written in *ním-shikasta* on pages of 28·5 × 15·5 c. See *B.M.P.C.*, pp. 876ᵇ–877ᵃ under **Or. 1410.**

875 (a) العنوان العجيب فى رؤياء الحبيب **Or. 209 (9)**

Al-'Unwánu'l-'Ajíb, a commentary on the Apocalypse of St John, composed in A.D. 1713, by Yúsuf b. Jirjíṣ of Aleppo, a Maronite priest of the Church of Rome. The book comprises a Preface (pp. 1–9), a Table of Contents (pp. 10–19), an Introduction in six sections (pp. 20–61), the text (written in red) of the 22 chapters of the Apocalypse (pp. 63–729) with commentary, and a Conclusion (pp. 729–739). The MS. contains 739 pp. of 22·8 × 16·5 c. and 21 ll. and the transcription was completed at Constantinople on August 15, 1819, by Gregory, an Armenian priest of Aleppo, from a correct MS. written by Antún ibnu'l-Khúrí Búlus in A.D. 1769. Bought of Naaman, Nov. 12, 1902.

876 (a) عوارف المعارف **Or. 67 (7)**

The *'Awárifu'l-Ma'arif*, a well-known mystical treatise by Shaykh Shihábu'd-Dín Abú Ḥafṣ 'Umar as-Suhrawardí, who died in 632/1234. See Brockelmann, i, pp. 440–441. The MS., which is undated, was bought of Géjou on May 11, 1901, comprises 80 ff. of 17 × 11 c. and 25 ll., is written in a small, clear *naskh* with rubrications, and contains 43 out of the 63 chapters which constitute the work.

877 (p) عيار دانش **Corpus, No. 58**

The well-known story-book entitled *'Iyár-i-Dánish* by Abu'l-Faḍl composed for the Emperor Akbar in 996/1588. See *B.M.P.C.*, pp. 756–7. The title of the book is here given as *Kalíla wa Dimna*, but though it wants the Preface it is almost certainly the *'Iyár-i-Dánish*. Ff. 98 of 24 × 14 c., written in a cursive *nasta'líq* and dated 1246/1830–1.

878 (p) عين الجنان **Or. 525** (9)

The *'Aynu'l-Janán*, or *Waqáyi'-i-Nawwáb Khán dar lashkar-i-Awrangzíb* ("Adventures of Nawwáb Khán in the army of Awrang-zíb"). The MS., bought of Luzac on Aug. 27, 1904, contains 97 ff. of 21·3 × 11·7 c. and 9 ll., and is written in good *ta'líq* in mixed prose and verse.

879 (p) عين الحيوة (فى عقائد الشيعة) **Or. 182** (10)

The *'Aynu'l-Ḥayát*, a treatise on Shí'a dogmatics, by Muḥammad Báqir b. Muḥammad Taqí al-Majlisí al-Iṣfahání, who died in 1098/1686–7. See Cambridge *Pers. Cat.*, pp. 64–69. The MS., bought of Géjou on Jan. 1, 1902, is dated 1073/1662–3, comprises 379 ff. of 24·6 × 15 c. and 21 ll., and is written in a small, neat *naskh*.

880 (a) عيون الحكمة (شرح) **King's, No. 225**

A commentary by Abú 'Abdi'lláh Muḥammad b. 'Umar b. Ḥusayn ash-Shírází on the *'Uyúnu'l-Ḥikmat*, perhaps the work of that name by Avicenna. See Brockelmann, i, p. 455, No. 23. The MS., undated, is a bulky volume written in a very cursive *nasta'líq* with very few diacritical points, on pages of 23 × 12·7.

881 (a) **Add. 3720** (7)

غاية تهذيب الكلام فى تحرير المنطق و الكلام

A work on Logic entitled *Gháyatu tahdhíbi'l-Kalám fí taḥríri'l-Manṭiq wa'l-Kalám*. The MS., undated, was bought of Naaman on Nov. 23, 1900, comprises 11 ff. of 18 × 11 c. and 11 ll., and is written in a small, neat *naskh* with rubrications.

882 (h) غزليّات خورشيد **Corpus, No. 66**[6]

The *ghazals*, or Odes, of a Hindustání poet named Khurshíd. This portion of the MS., copied in 1251/1835–6, comprises only 5 ff. of 25 × 15·5 c., and is written in *ním-shikasta*. The title is illegible.

883 (p) غزليّات ظهورى **Corpus, No. 50**[2]

Selected *ghazals* from the *Díwán* of Ẓuhúrí, who died in 1025/1616. The MS., dated 1276/1859–60, contains only 6 ff. in this portion and is written in four columns in *nasta'líq*.

884 (p) غنية المنية **Corpus, No. 219**

A treatise on Indian music, entitled *Ghunyatu'l-Munyat*, by an unknown author, composed in the 14th century. See Ethé's *I.O.Pers.Cat.*, col. 1116–17, No. 2008. The MS., undated, is written in good *naskh*, and is defective at the beginning. The pages measure 24 × 16 c.

885 (a) غنيمة السفر فى احوال الشيخ جعفر **Or. 33** (7)

Ghanímatu's-Safar fí aḥwáli'sh-Shaykh Ja'far, by Muḥammad b. 'Abdu'l-Wahháb al-Hamdání. The MS., copied about 1292/1875, was bought of Naaman on Feb. 5, 1901, and contains 34 ff. of 16·5 × 12·3 c. and 14 ll.

886 (a) فتاوى ابن نجيم **Add. 3724** (8)

The *fatwás*, or legal decisions, of Ibn Nujaym, who died in 970/1563. See Brockelmann, ii, p. 310. The MS., bought of Naaman on Nov. 23, 1900, comprises 185 ff. of 20·6 × 12·2 c. and 24 ll., and is written in a neat *nasta'líq* with rubrications.

887 (p) فتحيّهٔ عبرتيّه (تاريخ آشام) **Christ's, Dd. 3. 7**

A history of events in Assam during the period A.H. 1068–73 (= A.D. 1657–1663), in which last year it was concluded, by Shahádatu'd-Dín Ṭálish. See *B.M.P.C.*, p. 266. Copied at Murshidábád. Ff. 121.

888 (p) فتوح الحرمين **Corpus, No. 235**

The *Futúḥu'l-Ḥaramayn*, here ascribed to Jámí, but probably the work of that name described in *B.M.P.C.*, p. 655, which is by Muḥíy of Lár. The MS., copied at Agra in 1019/1610–11, contains 43 ff. of 20 × 12 c., and is written in poor *nasta'líq* with crude drawings.

889 (a) فتوح الشّام للواقدى **Or. 665-666** (10)

The *Futúḥu'sh-Shám*, or "Conquest of Syria," ascribed to Abú 'Abdi'lláh Muḥammad b. 'Umar al-Wáqidí. See Brockelmann, i, pp. 135–6 and references there given. Vol. i comprises 95 and vol. ii 115 ff. of 25·5 × 17 c. and 23 ll. The MS., written in an excellent *naskh* with rubrications and transcribed in 832/1428–9, was bought of Géjou on Feb. 17, 1906.

890 (p) فتوح ابن اعثم كوفى **King's, No. 105**

The *Futúḥ* (or *Ta'ríkh*) of Muḥammad b. 'Alí b. A'tham of Kúfá, who died about 314/926. The Arabic original is not known to exist, and the book is only known through the Persian version made in 596/1199 by Muḥammad al-Mustawfí al-Hirawí. See Brockelmann, i, 516, *B.M.P.C.*, pp. 151–2; Ethé's *Bodl. Pers. Cat.*, No. 126; and Palmer's *King's Cat.*, p. 6. This MS. is in 2 vols., of which the first contains 338 ff. and the second 191 ff.

891 (t) فرقت نامهٔ خليلى ديار بكرى **Or. 748 (6)**

The *Furqat-náma*, or "Book of Parting," a Turkish poem by Khalílí of Diyár Bakr, composed in 866/1461–2. See Gibb's *Hist. of Ottoman Poetry*, vol. ii, pp. 379–383. The MS., bought of Géjou on March 27, 1907, is undated, and contains 53 ff. of 15 × 11 c. and 14 ll., and is written in good *naskh*, fully pointed.

892 (p) فرمان جعفرى **Corpus, No. 67[5]**

Farmán-i-Ja'farí, a treatise on Logic and Metaphysics written by Mírzá Qatíl for the Nawwáb Mírzá Ja'far 'Alí Khán. The MS. is written in *nasta'líq* on pages of 26 × 17 c. and is dated 1252/1836–7.

893 (p) فرهاد و شيرين **Or. 276 (6)**

The Romance of Farhád and Shírín in *mathnawí* verse, begun by *Waḥshí* (d. 991/1583) and finished by Wiṣál in 1265/1848–9. See *B.M.P.C.*, pp. 663–4. The MS., dated Rabí' ii, 1285 (July–Aug. 1868), was given to the late Professor Cowell by the late Dr Bumsted on Jan. 4, 1897, and forms part of the Cowell Bequest. It contains 135 ff. of 16 × 10·3 c. and 9 ll. and is written in a fair Persian *ta'líq* with rubrications.

894 (p) فرهنگ لغات بهار دانش و غيره **Corpus, No. 214**

Two Persian glossaries, the first of the words contained in the *Bahár-i-Dánish* of Shaykh 'Ináyatu'lláh (see Nos. **190–192** *supra*), the second of the works of Abu'l-Faḍl. The MS. is written in *nasta'líq* on pages of 25 × 15 c., and is dated 1212/1797–8.

895 (p) فرهنگ مکاتبات ابو الفضل **Corpus, No. 189**[1]

A glossary of the words occurring in the Letters of Abu'l-Faḍl, probably identical with the second part of the MS. described above. This MS. is dated 1250/1834–5, and is written in *nasta'líq* on 20 ff. (numbered 41–61) of 20·5 × 15 c.

896 (h) فسانهٔ عجائب **Corpus, No. 155**[2]

A collection of Hindustání tales entitled *Fasána-i-'Ajá'ib* ("the Tale of Wonders"), but in the colophon *Nuskha-i-anjuman-árá wa Malika Mihr-nigár*. The MS., dated 1258/1842, is written in large, clear *nasta'líq*.

897 (a) فصول بقراط (شرح) **Trinity, R. 13. 42**

A commentary on the Aphorisms of Hippocrates by Abu'l-Qásim 'Abdu'r-Raḥmán b. 'Alí b. Abí Ṣádiq of Níshápúr, who died in 460/1068. See Brockelmann, i, p. 484, and Palmer's *Trin. Cat.*, pp. 91–2. Ff. 214.

898 (a) الفضائل السنيّة فى معرفة الاجرام الاثيريّة **Add. 3652 (8)**

A treatise on Astronomy entitled *al-Faḍá'ilu's-Saniyya fí ma'rifati'l-Ajrámi'l-Athíriyya wa 'l-'Unṣuriyya* by 'Alí [b.] Muḥammad b. Aḥmad al-Ḥalál ash-Sháfi'í. The MS., dated 906/1500–1, was bought of Sethian on May 21, 1900, contains 138 ff. of 21·2 × 14·6 c. and 15 ll., and is written in a clear, old-fashioned *nasta'líq*.

899, 900 (a) الفقه الاكبر (شرح) **Add. 3626 (9)**
Add. 3630 (6)

The *Fiqhu'l-Akbar*, ascribed to the Imám Abú Ḥanífa (d. 150/767), with commentaries. See Brockelmann, i, pp. 169–171. **Add. 3626** contains the commentary of al-Qárí al-Hirawí (d. 1014/1605). It is undated, was bought of Géjou on Feb. 14, 1900, is written in a small neat *naskh*, and comprises 108 ff. of 21·1 × 13·4 c. and 26 ll. **Add. 3630** contains the commentary of Abu'l-Muntahí composed in 939/1532, was bought at the same time and place as the last-mentioned MS., is written in a good *naskh*, and comprises ff. 36 of 15·7 × 9·9 c. and 15 ll.

901 (a) فقه القلوب و معراج الغيوب **Or. 9¹ (8)**

The *Fiqhu'l-Qulúb wa Mi'ráju'l-Ghuyúb* of Muḥammad b. Aḥmad b. Sa'íd, commonly called Ibn 'Aqíla, who died at Mecca in 1150/1737. See Brockelmann, ii, p. 386, where, however, this work is not mentioned. The MS., undated, was bought of Géjou on Jan. 28, 1901, and is written in clear, coarse *naskh* with rubrications. This portion occupies ff. 2ᵇ–87ᵃ of 21·8 × 15·6 c. and 13 ll.

902 (a) فقه اللّغة و سرّ العربيّة **Jesus, No. 13²**

The *Fiqhu'l-Lugha wa Sirru'l-'Arabiyya* of Abú Manṣúr ath-Tha'álibí, who died in 429/1038. See Brockelmann, i, pp. 284–286. This MS. was presented to the College by Samuel Lyde, Fellow, who died in 1860.

903 (p) فوائد الانسان **Or. 683 (7)**

A versified treatise on Pharmacology in Persian, with preface in prose, composed by one Fidá'í for the Emperor Akbar, and entitled *Fawá'idu'l-Insán*. Ff. 136 of 18·8 × 12·5 c. and 13 ll., good *ta'líq*, undated: bought of Géjou, June 13, 1906.

904 (a) الفوائد الشنشوريّة **Add. 3750 (8)**

Al-Fawá'idu'sh-Shinshawriyya, a commentary by the Sháfi'ite preacher ash-Shinshawrí, who died in 999/1590 on the *Manẓúmat* [or *Urjúzat*]*u'l-Raḥbiyya* of ar-Raḥbí, who died in 579/1183. See Brockelmann, i, pp. 390–391, and ii, pp. 320–321. The MS., bought of Naaman on Dec. 8, 1900, is dated 1264/1848, and contains 134 pp. of 20·7 × 16·3 c. and 18 ll., and is written in a legible *naskh* with rubrications.

905 (p) فوائد المبتدى **Corpus, No. 145**

An epistolary manual entitled *Fawá'idu'l-Mubtadí*. The MS. contains [92 ff., of which this portion occupies 74 ff. of

23 × 14 c., the remaining leaves containing poetical extracts. It is dated 1239/1823–4, and is written in *ta'líq* and *shikasta.*

906, 907 (a) فوائد وافية بحلّ مشكلات الكافية **King's, No. 230 Or. 865 (8)**

A commentary by Jámí, who died in 898/1492, composed for the use of his son Ḍiyá'u'd-Dín, on the *Káfiya* of Ibn Ḥájib, who died in 646/1248. See Brockelmann, i, pp. 303–304, and ii, p. 207. This commentary is better known as *al-Fawá'idu'd-Ḍiyá'iyya*. The **King's MS.,** undated, is written in a good, legible *ta'líq*, on pages of 24·8 × 14·4 c., and is collated and annotated. See Palmer's *King's Cat.*, p. 24. **Or. 865,** wanting the first leaf and dated 897/1491, contains 201 ff. of 19·2 × 12·8 c. and 17 ll., and is from the late Professor Robertson Smith's library. It is written in a fair *nasta'líq* with rubrications, the text in rather a larger hand.

908 (h) **Corpus, No. 40[1]**

فيصلجات صدر ديوان عدالت ممالك مغربى

This appears to contain a Hindustání translation of the decisions of Western (? British) High Courts, written in 1848. These are followed by the Hindustání *Díwán* of Walí. Written in *ta'líq* on leaves of 27·5 × 16 c.

909, 910 (a) القاموس للفيروزابادى **Add. 3608 (10) Or. 444 (9)**

Two portions of the well-known Arabic lexicon entitled *al-Qámús* of al-Fírúzábádí, who died in 817/1414–15. See Brockelmann, ii, pp. 181–3. **Add. 3608** contains from the section *sín* of the chapter *rá* to the section *yá* of the chapter *shín*. This MS. was bought of Géjou in 1899, and is undated. It contains 166 ff. of 23·3 × 15·6 c. and 25 ll., ends abruptly without colophon, and is written in a clear old *naskh* described in a note as the author's autograph (خطّ المصنّف). **Or. 444,** containing only the letters *lám* and *mím*, is dated 1099/1687–8, was bought of Hannan and Watson on Aug. 29, 1903, comprises 322 ff. of 24 × 13·4 c. and 15 ll., and is written in a poor but legible *ta'líq* with rubrications.

911 (a) القانون **Add. 3639** (**11**)

The 10th *Fann* of the 3rd Book of the *Qánún* of Ibn Síná (Avicenna), who died in 428/1037. See Brockelmann, i, pp. 452–8. This MS., undated, but apparently of the 13th or 14th century, comprises 209 ff. of 19·8 × 15 c. and 17 ll. and is written in a fine old *naskh*, fully pointed. Bought of Géjou, April 3, 1900.

912 (t) قانون الرشاد **Or. 469**[3] (**8**)

A Turkish work entitled *Qánúnu'r-Rashád*, dated 1160/1747, and bought of Géjou on Jan. 29, 1904. This portion of the MS. occupies ff. 119^b–161^b of 21·1 × 11·7 c. and 23 ll., and is written in a fair *nasta'líq* with rubrications.

913 (p) قانون مجدّد **Corpus, No. 67**[4]

The *Qánún-i-Mujaddad*, a treatise on Arabic grammar by Mírzá Qatíl. See *B.M.P.C.*, p. 795. The MS. is written in cursive *nasta'líq* on pages measuring 26 × 17 c.

914–916 (a, p) قانونچه فی الطبّ **Or. 6 (7)**; **King's, No. 107**; **Corpus, No. 42**

The *Qánúncha*, an abridgement of the *Qánún* by al-Jaghmíní, who died in 745/1344. See Brockelmann, i, p. 457. **Or. 6** contains the commentary of Ḥusayn b. Muḥammad al-Astarábádí. See Brockelmann, *loc. cit.*, and Ḥájji Khalífa, No. 9347. This MS. contains 200 ff. of 16·7 × 10 c. and 16 ll., and is written in a small bad *ta'líq* with some Persian interlinear glosses. It is undated, and was bought of Géjou on Jan. 28, 1901. The **King's MS.** is a Persian translation apparently made in the reign of Sháhrukh (A.H. 807–850=A.D. 1404–1446). The MS. is undated. See Palmer's *King's Cat.*, pp. 9, 18. The **Corpus MS.** contains an anonymous commentary dedicated to the Ottoman Sultan Sulaymán *al-Qánúní*, known in Europe as "the Magnificent." The MS., undated, is written in *nasta'líq* on leaves of 26 × 18 c.

917 (a) قانوننامهٔ سلطان سليمان **Or. 537** (**12**)

The *Qánún-náma*, or Code of Laws, of Sultan Sulaymán "the Magnificent," compiled by the Shaykhu'l-Islám Abu's-

Su'úd, who died at 87 years of age in 982/1574. See Gibb's *Hist. of Ottoman Poetry*, vol. iii, p. 116. The MS., dated 1126/1714, was bought of Géjou on Nov. 1, 1904, contains 75 ff. of 30 × 16·2 c. and 31 ll., and is written in a fair *ta'líq* with rubrications. It concludes with some notes on various legal points by the same Abu's-Su'úd. Copyist, Muṣṭafá Qaṣṣáb-záda.

918, 919 (p) قرابادين **Corpus, No. 33**
Corpus, No. 90

Two separate works on Materia Medica entitled *Qarábádín*. **Corpus 90** is the work of Shifá'í, who died in 963/1555–6. See *B.M.P.C.*, pp. 473–4. It is undated, and is written in *nasta'líq* on pages of 20 × 14 c. **Corpus 33,** by Muḥammad Arzání, was lithographed at Dihlí in 1271/1854–5, and ought not to have been placed amongst the MSS.

920, 921 (p) قران السعدَيْن **Corpus, No. 14**
Corpus, No. 97

The *Qiránu's-Sa'dayn*, or "Conjunction of the Two Fortunates," a well-known poem by Amír Khusraw of Dihlí, composed in Ramadán 688 (= Aug.–Sept. 1289). See *B.M.P.C.*, pp. 611–612. **Corpus 14,** undated, contains 258 pp. of 23 × 14 c. and is written in *nasta'líq*. **Corpus 97,** also undated but fairly old, is also written in *nasta'líq* on pages of 22 × 16 c., and contains many glosses, but seems to be incomplete at the end.

922–934 (a) القرآن
Or. 882 (5), Trin. R. 8. 7
Or. 916 (13), Trin. R. 8. 12
Clare, c. 7. 12, Trin. R. 13. 4
Emmanuel, 4. 2. 19, Trin. R. 13. 7
Fitzwilliam, No. 194, Trin. R. 14. 59
Fitzwilliam, No. 200, Trin. R. 14. 60
Trin. R. 15. 50

Thirteen complete copies of the *Qur'án*. **Or. 882,** presented by Lady Scott in 1912, is a nearly square case of 13 × 12·8 × 2 c. containing a quantity of unnumbered and disarranged leaves of the *Qur'án* of 11·5 c. square, written in a clumsy African hand with rubrications and primitive ornamentation in colours, each page containing from 9 to 11 lines.

The text appears to be complete but needs arrangement, if it were worth the time required. **Or. 916,** one of the Lynch MSS. acquired in January 1915, is a modern undated copy of 232 ff. of 33·5 × 22 c. and 15 ll., written in large clear *naskh* and fully pointed. **Clare, c . 7 . 12** is undated and written in a plain modern *naskh*. **Emmanuel, 4 . 2 . 19** was "picked up at Delhi after the capture of the town in 1857 by Captain Lionel Francis Wells of the Bengal Army, then serving with Hodson's horse, by whom it was presented to the College through his brother, then a student." **Fitzwilliam 194,** undated, contains 30 ff. of 31·6 × 19·2 c. and 42 ll., and is written in a small neat *nashk* with rubrications and gold within richly illuminated borders. **Fitzwilliam 200,** dated 15 Dhu'l-Qa'da, 1074 (= June 9, 1664), contains 272 ff. of 18·5 × 11 c. and 15 ll., and is written in a good, clear, modern *naskh*, pointed, with rubrications. **Trin. R . 8 . 7,** presented by Richard Duke, Fellow of the College, in 1682, is undated, contains 243 ff., and is written in a plain *naskh* with rubrications. **Trin. R . 8 . 12,** undated, is described in Latin as "rescued in 1622 by the English from the flames at Ormus[1]; presented by Adam Bowen, 1628." It is written in fine Persian *naskh* and is undated. **Trin. R . 13 . 4,** presented by the above-mentioned Adam Bowen in 1632, is written in a Maghribí hand, undated, and contains 232 ff. **Trin. R . 13 . 7,** transcribed at Fez (Fás) in Morocco in A.D. 1643 by 'Abdu'lláh Raḥmúní, contains 164 ff. **Trin. R . 14 . 59,** containing 400 ff, is carelessly written in what appears to me a Malay hand. **Trin. R . 14 . 60,** copied by one David Clerk, contains 375 ff. **Trin. R . 15 . 50** contains 326 ff.

935–946 (a)
القرآن (اجزاء)

Or. 410 (12),	**Christ's, Dd . 3 . 29**
Or. 476 (5″ × 8″),	**Fitzwilliam, No. 188**
Or. 636 (8),	**Jesus, No. 11**
Or. 652 (8),	**Trinity, R . 13 . 22**
Or. 770 (10),	**Pembroke, No. 289**
Or. 771 (13),	**Pembroke, No. 290**

Portions of the *Qur'án*, Kúfic, Maghribí etc. **Or. 410,** badly written in an African hand on coarse brown paper,

[1] *i.e.* the Island of Hormuz or Ormuz in the Persian Gulf, which was taken from the Portuguese in 1622 by a combined Anglo-Persian force.

wanting some leaves at the end, contains 352 ff. of 24·5 × 16 c. and 15 ll. It ends with *súra* xci, 10. Presented by Deputy Surgeon-General A. M. Dallas, Feb. 27, 1903. **Or. 476** contains the end of the 13th and the whole of the 14th and 15th Portions of the *Qur'án* (xiv, 32 to xviii, 73), written in gold in a fine large Kúfic hand with diacritical and vowel points in red. Ff. 52 of 12 × 19·8 c. (oblong form) and 7 ll.; bought of Géjou, August 18, 1904. **Or. 636,** a fragmentary African *Qur'án*, the leaves all separate from one another and in great disorder. They measure 19 × 16 c. and contain 11 ll. each. The writing is large and coarse, the vocalization in red and the punctuation in yellow. The following account is given of its acquisition. "This Koran was taken out of a burning hut in the stockaded town of Saba, at Badibas, in the river of Gambia, West Coast of Africa, when it was stormed and taken by the Naval Brigade from H.M. Ships 'Arrogant,' 'Falcon' and 'Torch,' the 1st and 2nd West Indian Regiments, Gambia Military Artillery, and 500 Native Allies in February, 1861. Wm. J. Cunningham, 2nd Master, H.M.S. Torch, and Beachmaster to the Expedition." **Or. 652,** portions of the *Qur'án*, with some prayers, obtained, according to a note on the fly-leaf in Spanish, at Ciudad Real, and written in a Maghribí hand with rubrications. It begins abruptly in the middle of verse 71 of *súra* xxxvi, which is immediately followed on the same leaf by verse 18 of *súra* lix. The passages of the *Qur'án* seem to be arranged with no regard to sequence, while here and there prayers and other extraneous matters are interpolated. Ff. 10–31 contain, with a few omissions, *súras* lxxvii–cxiv, which are followed by *súra* lv. After this (f. 34^b) what follows is in some African language written in the Arabic character and fully pointed. The MS., which is written in a Maghribí hand with rubrications, contains 60 ff. of 20·7 × 14 c. and 12 ll., and is undated. **Or. 770** consists of 37 ff. of an old Kúfic *Qur'án*, containing most of the 27th Portion or *Juz'* (*súra* li, 31–lv, 56). Each leaf measures 22 × 14 c. and contains 5 ll. of large Kúfic writing with red and gold diacritical points. **Or. 771** is another fragment of a Kúfic *Qur'án* consisting of 36 ff. of 31 × 22·3 c. and 17 ll., and written in a fine large Kúfic hand with headings and diacritical points in red. It contains the following *súras* and verses:—viii, 62–ix, 49; xvii, 63–xviii, 23; xviii, 40–81; xviii, 102–xix, 13; xix, 36–77; xxi, 64–xxii, 44; xlviii, 11–l, 6; liv, 32–lix, 24. **Christ's, Dd. 3. 29,** a small volume of 212 ff. of 10·3 × 7·8 c., contains extracts from the *Qur'án* and prayers in a Maghribí hand with vowels in red. **Fitzwilliam 188** consists of two volumes, the first containing the 16th *Juz'* and the second the 23rd *Juz'* of the *Qur'án*, both in Kúfic writing. The first contains 94 ff. of 14 × 9·8 c. and 5 ll.; the second 73 ff. of 15·3 × 10·3 c. and 5 ll. **Jesus 11** contains the 27th *Juz'* of the *Qur'án*, and is dated Ṣafar 22, 1047 (= July 16, 1637). It was presented to the College by Samuel Lyde, Fellow, who died in A.D. 1860. **Trinity, R. 13. 22,** comprising 18 ff., contains some of the shorter *súras*. **Pembroke 289** comprises 304 ff. of 21·2 × 15 c. and 15 ll., and is written in a poor but clear *naskh* with rubrications. It was copied in Rabí' ii, 1038 (Dec. 1628) by 'Abdu'r-Raḥmán b. al-Mu'allim 'Umar b. al-Mu'allim 'Abdu'r-Raḥman Abú 'Izzán. The text of the *Qur'án* is followed (on ff. 301–304) by a prayer. F. 1ª bears the name "Mr ffuller." It was given to the College by Edward Tines c. 1633. **Pembroke 290** comprises 260 ff. of 20·6 × 15 c. and 19 ll.; is written in a Maghribí hand with rubrications and titles of *súras* in yellow; and is dated 18 Jumáda 1, 1064 (April 6, 1654). The title-page bears the following Latin inscriptions: (1) "*Donum Joannis de Vado, missum ex urbe Marroco anno* 1598"; (2) "*Francisci Junii Biturigis. A Francisco Patre ad Franciscum filium, jure et merito pervenit: Ab Illius verò munificâ manu ad me Christophorum Wren. A° 1622*"; (3) "*Ipsis kal: Ian: MDCXXVI. Christophorus Wren Matthæi germanissimus frater Arabem hunc sacerrimum mancipio dedit civitati Dei in celeberrimo cœtu Pembrochianorum Cantabrigiæ; Quem et aliorum aliquot ex ingenuâ Gente anteambulonem esse voluit jussit.*"

947 (a) قرّة العيون فى اخبار يمن الميمون **Or. 226 (10)**

Qurratu'l-'Uyún fí Akhbári Yamani'l-Maymún, a history of Yaman from the time of the Prophet to 923/1517, by Ibn Dayba'. See the description of **Add. 2894** in the *Cambridge*

Hand-list, No. 842, p. 150; *B.M.A.S.*, Nos. 587 and 591[1]; and Brockelmann, ii, pp. 400–401. This MS. is undated and was bought of Naaman on Nov. 12, 1902. Ff. 242 of 25 × 16·5 c. and 19 ll.

948, 949 (t) قرق وزير **Or. 605 (6)**
Trinity, R. 13. 34

Two copies of the well-known Turkish story-book entitled *Qirq Wazír* ("the Forty Wazírs") by Aḥmad-i-Miṣrí. See *B.M.T.C.*, pp. 216 and 219. **Or. 605,** dated Rajab 1150 (= Oct.-Nov. 1737), was bought of Géjou on Oct. 30, 1905, is written in a neat Turkish *naskh* with rubrications, and contains 141 ff. of 16·5 × 10·7 c. and 19 ll. The **Trinity MS.,** written in a small, neat *naskh*, contains 172 ff., and was copied in A.D. 1552.

950 (a) القصائد السبع العَلَويّات **Add. 3748[1] (8)**

Al-qaṣá'idu's-sab'u'l-'Alawiyyát, poems in praise of 'Alí b. Abí Ṭálib by the Shí'ite poet 'Izzu'd-Dín 'Abdu'l-Ḥamíd b. Abi'l-Ḥadíd, who died in 656/1258. See Brockelmann, i, pp. 249–250, with anonymous commentary. The MS., dated 1258/1842–3, was bought of Naaman on Dec. 6, 1900, and contains 141 ff. of 22 × 15 c. and 14 ll., written in a fair *naskh* with rubrications. This portion of the MS. occupies ff. 1–72. The remainder (ff. 73–141) contains an untitled and acephalous work of theological contents composed in 904/1498–9.

951 (p) قصائد و مقطّعات سلمان ساوجی **Or. 649 (9)**

The *qaṣídas* and fragments of the eminent Persian poet Salmán of Sáwa, who died about 779/1377–8. See *B.M.P.C.*, pp. 624–626. This MS., undated, was bought at the O'Kinealy sale on Jan. 15, 1906. It contains 226 ff. of 22 × 13·5 c. and 17 ll., and is written in a good, clear *ta'líq*.

952 (p) قصائد عراقی و قصائد انوری **Corpus, No. 191[1]**

Selected *qaṣídas* from the poems of 'Iráqí and Anwarí, of whom the former died about the beginning of the 14th and the latter about the end of the 12th century of the Christian era. See *B.M.P.C.*, pp. 593–4 and 555–6. The MS., undated, is written in clear *nasta'líq* on leaves of 23 × 15 c.

953 (p) قصائد عرفی و قصائد اهلی **Corpus, No. 149**

Selected *qaṣídas* of 'Urfí (died 999/1590–1591) and Ahlí (died 942/1535–6). See *B.M.P.C.*, pp. 667–8 and 657–8. A modern and defective MS. written in *nasta'líq* on pages of 27 × 16 c. and considerably wormed.

954 (p) قصائد عنصری **Or. 236 (10)**

The *qaṣídas* of 'Unṣurí, the well-known contemporary of Firdawsí at the court of Sulṭán Maḥmúd of Ghazna. This copy was made (in 1884) for the late Professor E. B. Cowell from MS. No. 615 of the Bengal Asiatic Society. It comprises 88 ff. of 25 × 17·5 c. and 15 ll., and is written in a fair modern *ta'líq*. Added at the end are 10 ff. more of 20·6 × 16·5 and 18 ll. containing more *qaṣídas* of the same poet, collated by E. G. Browne in June 1887 with **Or. 1858** of the British Museum.

955 (p) قصائد متفرّقهٔ کلیم **Add. 3643 (9)**

A selection of the poems of Kalím, who died about 1062/1652. See *B.M.P.C.*, pp. 686–7. The MS., defective at the beginning and elsewhere, was bought of Sethian on May 9, 1900, and contains 232 ff. of 22 × 11·5 c. and 15 ll.; headings in red.

956, 957 (p) قصص الانبیاء **Add. 3731 (9)**
Corpus, No. 217

Qiṣaṣu'l-Anbiyá ("Stories of the Prophets"). Two anonymous Persian works of this name which may or may not be identical. **Add. 3731** begins with Adam and Idrís and comes down to 'Uthmán. It is dated 1074/1663–4 and was bought of Sethian on Nov. 28, 1900. Ff. 235 of 22·8 × 12·5 c. and 19 ll.; good Persian *ta'líq* with rubrications. **Corpus 217**, undated, is written in good *nasta'líq* on pages of 26 × 20 c. It is described by Mr Hillelson as "apparently identical with the work described in Ethé's *India Office Pers. Cat.*, No. 593, where the correct title is said to be *Majma'u'l-Ḥasanát*."

958 (p) قصّهٔ ابو مسلم مروزی **Trinity, R. 13. 2**

Qissa-i-Abú Muslim-i-Marwazí, the Story of Abú Muslim, by Abú Ṭáhir b. 'Alí b. Isma'íl aṭ-Ṭarsúsí. The work is incomplete, containing only Books 20 and 24–28. Ff. 240; copied in Herát in 895/1489–90 by 'Alá'u'd-Dín b. Maḥmúd b. Ḥusayn Sháh-i-Tír-andáz in a very poor hand.

959 (h) قصّهٔ اوزشاه اور سمن رخ بانو **Corpus, No. 16**

A tale translated from Persian into Hindustání, entitled in English *Naw Ratan*, but in Persian *Qiṣṣa-i-Úzsháh wa Samanrukh Bánú*. Undated; *ním-shikasta*; 23 × 14 c.

960 (h) قصّهٔ بدر منیر **Corpus, No. 2**

A romantic *mathnawí* poem in Hindustání concerning the loves of Prince Bí-Naẓír and the Lady Badr-i-Munír, by Mírzá Ḥasan. Ff. 101 of 23 × 13 c.; careless *nasta'líq*; dated 1222/1807–8.

961–963 (h) قصّهٔ چار درویش **Corpus, No. 11**; **Corpus, No. 128**; **Corpus, No. 151**

Qiṣṣa-i-Chár Darwísh, the Story of Four Dervishes. For the Persian original see *B.M.P.C.*, p. 762. The last of these three MSS. is dated 1257/1841; contains ff. 123 of 25 × 16 c.; and gives the author's or translator's name as Mír Muḥammad 'Aṭá Ḥusayn.

964 (p) قصّهٔ حمزه امیر المؤمنین **Trinity, R. 13. 3**

The Romance of Amír Ḥamza, uncle of the Prophet Muḥammad. See *B.M.P.C.*, p. 760. This MS. contains 291 ff. written in good *ta'líq*, and was copied in A.D. 1660.

965–969 (p) قصّهٔ خضر خان و دول رانی **Or. 167 (8)**; **Or. 235 (10)**; **Or. 240 (12)**; **Or. 260 (7)**; **Christ's, Dd. 3. 12**

The metrical Romance of Duwal (or Deval) Rání and Khiḍr Khán, by the celebrated poet Amír Khusraw of Dihlí, who died in 725/1325. See *B.M.P.C.*, p. 612. **Or. 167,** bought of Naaman on Dec. 6, 1901, contains 153 ff. of 20·5 × 12·7 c. and 15 ll.; is undated, written in a good *naskh* with rubrications; first and last leaves damaged. **Or. 235,** obtained by the late Professor E. B. Cowell on May 18, 1886, and left by him to the Library, is dated 1112/1700–1, contains 156 ff. of 25 × 12·5 c. and 11 ll., and is written in a good *ta'líq*, much faded in places, with rubrications. **Or. 240,** copied in Sept. 1885 for Professor Cowell from a MS. belonging to the Asiatic Society of Bengal at Calcutta, contains 280 ff. of 31·3 × 20·8 c. and 17 ll., and is written in a clear, legible Indian *ta'líq* between red lines. **Or. 260,** undated, also belonged to Professor Cowell, and contains 189 ff. of 17·2 × 10 c. and 12 ll.; good *ta'líq* with rubrications. The **Christ's MS.,** illuminated but undated, is written in a good *ta'líq* and formerly belonged to Archibald Swinton. It comprises 155 ff. of 22·7 × 15 c. and 15 ll.

970 (h) قصّهٔ سوداگر **Corpus, No. 66**[10]

Qiṣṣa-i-Sawdágar ("the Story of the Merchant"), a *mathnawí* poem in Hindustání. Ff. 13 of 25 × 15·25 c., *ním-shikasta*, dated 1247/1831–2.

971 (p) قصّهٔ سودامان جی صاحب **Corpus, No. 39**[4]

Qiṣṣa-i-Súdámán-jí Ṣáḥib, a narrative *mathnawí*, apparently translated from the Sanskrit or Hindí, and transcribed about 1820.

972 (h) قصّهٔ عاشق شدن شخصی بر پسر زرگر **Corpus, No. 66**[7]

The story of how one became enamoured of a young goldsmith, another narrative poem in Hindustání. Ff. 7 of 25 × 15·5 c.

973, 974 (p) قصّهٔ مسعود شاه و عزیز شاه **Corpus, No. 89**
Corpus, No. 224

The story of Mas'úd Sháh and 'Azíz Sháh, a Persian prose romance, possibly identical with that described under the same title in *B.M.P.C.*, p. 773, and Ethé's *Bodl. Pers. Cat.*, No. 484.

In **Corpus 89** the first page is so much stained as to be illegible, and the MS. is defective at the end, besides being very badly written. **Corpus 224** is dated the 42nd year of Sháh 'Álam (= 1215/1800).

975 (p) قصّهٔ قاضی **Corpus, No. 102[5]**

Qiṣṣa-i-Qáḍí ("the Story of the Judge"), apparently identical with the well-known "Story of the Thief and the Judge." See *B.M.P.C.*, p. 773, and Ethé's *Bodl. Pers. Cat.*, No. 484, copied at Bareilly, 1826.

976 (p) قصّهٔ کامروپ **Christ's, Dd.3.27**

The Story of Kámrúp and Kámlatá, a prose version agreeing with that described in *B.M.P.C.*, pp. 763–4. Ff. 181 of 18·5 × 10·5 c. and 11 ll.; good *ta'líq*.

977 (p, h) قصّهٔ گلِ بکاولی **Corpus, No. 26**

The Story of the Rose of Bakáwalí, a Persian version of an Indian romance, followed by two short pieces in Hindustání entitled *Ṣanam-náma-i-Girdáb* and *Urdú-yi-Khayálí*. See Browne's *Cambr. Pers. Cat.*, No. cccxxxv, p. 422 and references. The MS. is dated 1255/1839–40.

978 (p) قصّهٔ ماه و مشتری **Corpus, No. 10**

Qiṣṣa-i-Máh u Mushtarí by Turáb 'Alí. Ff. 200 of 23 × 15 c., large *nasta'líq*, imperfect at end and undated.

979–981 (p) قصّهٔ مهر و ماه **Corpus, No. 74**
Corpus, No. 181[2]
Corpus, No. 182

Qiṣṣa-i-Mihr u Máh. These three MSS. apparently represent as many different versions of the story. The first, in *mathnawí* verse, ascribed to 'Áqil Khán-i-Rází, was copied about the end of the 18th century. The two others are in prose, but are entirely different. Cf. *B.M.P.C.*, p. 765.

982–984 (a, t) قصّهٔ يوسف **Add. 3629 (9)**, **Trinity, R. 15. 51**, **Or. 676 (9)**

The Story of Joseph in one Turkish and two Arabic versions. **Add. 3629** is defective at the beginning and end and has no proper title or indication of authorship. It is undated, was bought of Géjou on Feb. 14, 1900, contains 58 ff. of 22×15 c. and 15 ll., and is written in fair *naskh* with rubrications. The **Trinity MS.,** which seems to contain simply the Arabic version of the Old Testament story, contains 50 ff. written in Indian *naskh*, and is described in Palmer's *Trin. Cat.*, p. 176. **Or. 676** contains the Turkish verse rendering, composed by a poet called Ḥamídí, whose full name is given as

محمّد الحميد الملقّب ابن اسمعيل ابن اجير امام چچن زاده

The date of composition is expressed by the chronogram:

مصردا دولتی بولدی یوسف علیه السّلام،

I presume that the two last words "upon whom be peace" do not form part of the chronogram, which without them gives 993/1585, but with them would yield a date still fifty years ahead of us. The MS., bought of Géjou on Feb. 17, 1906, contains 149 ff. of 23·8×17 c. and 15 ll., and is written in a large, coarse *naskh*, with rubrications.

985 (a) قصيدة الامالى (شرح) **Add. 3702 (8)**

The *Qaṣídatu'l-Amálí*, or *Bad'u'l-Amálí* of Siráju'd-Dín 'Alí b. 'Uthmán al-Úshí al-Farghání, who wrote about 569/1173, with commentary, beginning:

الحمد لله المنزّه عن سمات النّقص و الزّوال الخ،

See Brockelmann, i, p. 429. The MS., undated, was bought of Naaman on Nov. 7, 1900, and contains 37 ff. of 21·2 × 15·8 c. and 16 ll., and is written in a clear thick *naskh* with rubrications.

986 (a) قصيدة بَانَتْ سُعَاد **Or. 580 (5)**

The famous *qaṣída* of Ka'b b. Zuhayr (a contemporary of the Prophet Muḥammad) known, from its opening words, as

Bánat Su'ád, with commentary. See Brockelmann, i, pp. 38–9. The MS., dated Rajab, 822 (=July–Aug. 1419), was bought of Géjou on July 14, 1905, contains 67 ff. of 13·4×9 c. and 22 ll., and is written in a small, neat *naskh* with overlines in red. For another copy see **Or. 208⁷**, ff. 73–7.

987 (a) قصيدة ابن عبدون مع شرح **Or. 921 (8)**

The celebrated *qaṣída* of Ibn 'Abdún (died 529/1134) with the historical commentary of Ibn Badrún (circ. 560/1164). See Brockelmann, i, p. 271. The MS., completed on Ṣafar 3, 1045 (July 19, 1635), by Muḥammad...al-'Akkárí al-Qádirí, forms part of the Lynch Bequest. It contains 115 ff. of 20·8 × 13·8 c. and 25 ll., and is written in a clear *naskh* with rubrications.

988 (a) القصيدة المضريّة و غيرها **Or. 208[7] (8)**

A "fivesome" (*takhmís*) of the *Qaṣídatu'l-Muḍariyya* of al-Búṣírí (died 694/1294) in praise of the Prophet. See Brockelmann, i, p. 267. This poem occupies ff. 65^b–69^a of the MS., and is followed by the *Qaṣídatu'n-Naḍída* (ff. 69^a–70^a), the *Bánat Su'ád* of Ka'b b. Zuhayr (see above, **No. 986**), etc. The MS., undated, was bought of Naaman on Nov. 12, 1902.

989 (a) القصيدة المقصورة **Add. 3738 (7)**

The *Qaṣídatu'l-Maqṣúra* of Ibn Durayd, who died in 321/934, with the commentary of al-Lakhmí. See Brockelmann, i, pp. 111–112. The MS., dated 1027/1618, was bought of Sethian on Nov. 28, 1900, contains 85 ff. of 18·1 × 10·3 c. and 13 ll., and is written in a good *naskh* with rubrications.

990 (a) القصيدة المنفرجة **Or. 208[5] (8)**

A *qaṣída* ascribed to Táju'd-Dín as-Subkí (d. 771/1370: see Brockelmann, ii, pp. 89–90) and entitled *al-Munfarija*, filling only 4 pp. (ff. 54^b–56^b) of a MS. described on p. 29 above, *s.v.* البردة, **No. 164,** bought of Naaman on Nov. 12, 1902.

991 (a) قصيدة نضيدة **Or. 889 (9)**

A poem of about 28 stanzas, each rhyming in successive letters of the alphabet, and dedicated to "our lord and master"

(افندينا) Sulaymán Pasha. The MS. formerly belonged to M. Vidal, dragoman to the French Consulate at Baghdád, who sold it on July 24, 1822, to Dr Joseph Wolff the missionary. It is undated, and was bought of G. David on November 22, 1912. It contains 37 ff. of 23·2 × 14·6 c. and 13 ll., and is written in a coarse, clear *naskh* with rubrications. A prose preface occupies ff. 2b–5a.

992–994 (a) قطر النّدَى و بلّ الصّدَى **Add. 3656 (9), Add. 3718 (8), Or. 2 (9)**

The well-known Arabic grammar of Ibn Hishám (died 761/1360) entitled *Qaṭru'n-Nadá wa ballu'ṣ-Ṣadá*, with various commentaries and glosses. See Brockelmann, ii, pp. 23–5. **Add. 3656** contains the author's own commentary. This MS. is dated 1231/1816, was bought of Sethian on May 21, 1900, comprises 128 ff. of 22 × 15·8 c. and 13 ll., and is written in a clear, modern *naskh* with rubrications. **Add. 3718** contains glosses on the text. It is undated, was bought of Naaman on Nov. 23, 1900, and contains 84 ff. of 23 × 14·8 c. and 16 ll. written in fair modern *naskh*. **Or. 2,** dated 1203/1788–9, was bought of Géjou on Jan. 28, 1901, contains 90 ff. of 22 × 16 c. and 17 ll., and is written in fair *naskh*, the text in red, and the commentary on the *Shawáhid* by Jamálu'd-Din b. 'Ulwán al-Qabání in black.

995 (a) قلادة الدّرّ المنثور فى ذكر البعث و النّشور **Add. 3653 (8)**

Qiládatu'd-durri'l-manthúr fí dhikri'l-Ba'thi wa'n-Nushúr, a poem on the Last Day and the Resurrection, by 'Izzu'd-Dín ad-Díríní, who died in 694/1295. See Brockelmann, i, pp. 451–2. This is preceded by a treatise entitled:

رسالة لطيفة باهرة كالشرح فى توضيح ما فى هذه الدائرة

The MS., undated, was bought of Sethian on May 21, 1900, contains 177 ff. of 21 × 15 c. and 19 ll., and is written in a clear *naskh* with rubrications.

996 (a) قلائد العقيان فى محاسن الأعيان **Fitzwilliam, No. 190**

Qalá'idu'l-'iqyán fí maḥásini'l-A'yán, a biographical work by Abú Naṣr b. al-Fatḥ b. Kháqán, who was murdered in

Morocco in 529/1134. See Brockelmann, i, p. 339. The MS., dated 1049/1639–40, contains 120 ff. of 19 × 14 c. and 21 ll., and is written in poor but clear *naskh*.

997 (a) القلائد و الفرائد **Fitzwilliam, No. 189**

Al-Qalá'id wa'l-Fará'id by Abu'l-Ḥasan (or, according to Brockelmann, i, p. 407, Abu 'Alí al-Ḥasan)...al-Ahwází, who died in 446/1055. See Ḥ. Kh., No. 9572 and *B.M.A.S.*, No. 85. The MS. contains 78 ff. of 18·7 × 17·3 c. and 7 ll.; excellent *naskh* within gold borders.

998–1000 (p) كارستان **Christ's, Dd. 3. 25; Corpus, No. 21; Corpus, No. 105**

The *Káristán* or *Kár-náma* (wrongly entitled *Kháristán* in the **Christ's MS.**) of Abu'l-Barakát Munír, composed in 1050/1640–41. See Ethé's *I. O. Pers. Cat.*, Nos. 2083–87, cols. 1150–51. These three MSS. are all of mediocre quality. The **Christ's MS.** contains 172 ff. of 22·3 × 11 c. and 12 ll. and is written in a bad Indian *ta'líq*.

1001 (a) الكافى فى علم العروض و القوافى **Jesus, No. 12[1]**

An Arabic treatise on Prosody and Rhyme entitled *al-Káfí fí 'ilmi'l-'Arúḍ wa'l-Qawáfí*, by Abu'l-'Abbás Aḥmad al-Qiná'í, who died in 858/1454. See Brockelmann, ii, p. 27. This MS. is dated 1269/1852–3, and was presented to the College by Samuel Lyde, Fellow, who died in 1860.

1002 (a) الكافية فى علم النّحو **Christ's, Dd. 3. 23**

The well-known Arabic grammar of Ibn Ḥájib entitled *al-Káfiya*. See *Camb. Hand-list*, pp. 160–161. Pp. 224 of 22·6 × 12·6 c. and 5 ll., written in large *naskh* with interlinear glosses, undated.

1003 (a) كامل المبرّد **Or. 934 (12)**

The late Dr W. Wright's own transcript of the *Kámil* of al-Mubarrad, published at Leipzig in 1864–1892, fully collated and annotated throughout, presented by his widow. On June

15, 1889 it was lent by the late Professor W. Robertson Smith to the late Professor de Goeje of Leyden. It comprises 49 chapters, 72 quires, and 596 pp. See Brockelmann, i, pp. 108–109.

1004 (a) كتاب ارسترخوس فى جُرْمَى النيّرين **Trinity, O.5.15[2]**

An Arabic translation, probably by Naṣíru'd-Dín Ṭúsí, of a Greek astronomical treatise on the sun and moon by Aristarchus, illustrated with 17 diagrams. See Palmer's *Trin. Cat.*, p. 180, and Brockelmann, i, p. 512.

1005 (a) **Fitzwilliam, No. 193[1]**

كتاب الاعجاز فى القرآن العظيم

The *Kitábu'l-I'jáz fi'l-Qur'áni'l-'Aẓím*, a work on the miraculous quality of the *Qur'án* by the Qáḍí Muḥammad ibnu't-Ṭayyib al-Báqilání, a pupil of al-Ash'arí, who died 403/1012. See Brockelmann, i, 197. For the other work contained in this volume, see *infra, s.v.* نهاية الايجاز. This volume contains 139 ff. of 26·3 × 17·8 c. and 21 ll., and is dated 681/1282–3.

1006 (a) كتاب الاعلاق النّفيسة **Or. 920 (8)**

The *Kitábu'l-A'láqi'n-nafísa* of Abú 'Abí Aḥmad b. 'Umar b. Rusta, who wrote in 290/903 in Iṣfahán. This appears to be only one volume (probably the seventh, on Geography) out of the seven which constitute the work, being the one published by de Goeje in his *Biblioth. Geograph. Arab.* See Brockelmann, i, p. 227. The MS. comprises ff. 201 of 20·5 × 15 c. and 15 ll., is undated and defective at the end, and is written in a good modern *naskh* with the titles in a larger hand. It forms part of the Lynch Bequest.

1007 (a) كتاب [مختصر] الاغانى **Or. 907 (13)**

An abridgement of the *Kitábu'l-Aghání* of Abu'l-Faraj al-Iṣfahání, but by whom is not clear, though allusion is made at the beginning to one by ar-Rashíd Abu'l-Ḥusayn Aḥmad b. az-Zubayr. See Brockelmann, i, p. 146. The MS. contains 596 ff. of 32·3 × 19·5 c. and 43 ll., is written in clear *naskh* with rubrications, and was copied by Muḥammad b. 'Uthmán b. Muḥammad b. Rajab... known as Ibnu'sh-Shum'a and completed on the 5th Jumádá i, 1167 (= Feb. 28, 1754). Lynch Bequest.

1008 (a) كتاب الافصاح عن احاديث النّكاح **Or. 32 (9)**

The *Kitábu'l-Ifṣáḥ 'an aḥádíthi'n-Nikáḥ*, a collection of fifty traditions respecting Marriage, by Jalálu'd-Dín as-Suyúṭi. See *B.M.A.S.*, p. 550, and for the author Brockelmann, ii, pp. 143–158. The MS. contains 29 ff. of 24·2 × 14 c. and 17 ll., and is written in a clear *naskh* with rubrications. Scribe, 'Abdu'l-Ghaffár b. al-Faqíh 'Ísá al-Qiwámí at-Taláwí al-Azharí; dated Thursday, Muḥarram 9, but the year is omitted. Bought of Naaman, Feb. 5, 1901.

1009 (p) كتاب الاكرّ **King's, No. 13**

An Arabic translation of the *Sphærica* of Theodosius by Qusṭá b. Lúqá and Thábit b. Qurra, containing three *Maqálas* and 59 diagrams. See Brockelmann, i, p. 204, and Palmer's *King's Cat.*, p. 20. The MS. contains 47 ff.

1010 (a) كتاب الانساب **Or. 927 (12)**

Part of the *Kitábu'l-Ansáb* (or more probably an abridgement of it) by Abú Sa'd 'Abdu'l-Karím...as-Sam'ání, who died in 562/1167, containing the letters ا to ح. See Brockelmann, i, pp. 329–330. The MS. contains 157 ff. of 30·1 × 20·6 c. and 29 ll., and is defective at end and undated. Lynch Bequest, Jan. 1915.

1011 (a) كتاب اوقليدس **King's, No. 117**

An Arabic translation of Euclid, completed, as stated in the colophon, in 646/1248, and therefore probably that made by Naṣíru'd-Dín Ṭúsí in the same year. See Brockelmann, i, p. 510. The MS. contains 178 ff. and is written in clear, neat *naskh*, with rubrications and numerous geometrical figures.

1012 (a) كتاب بَدْو الخلق **King's, No. 63**

The *Kitábu Badwi'l-Khalq*, or more properly *Badw* (or *Khalq*)*i'd-Dunyá wa Qiṣaṣi'l-Anbiyá*, of Abú Bakr Muḥammad al-Kisá'í. See Brockelmann, i, p. 350. Palmer has omitted this MS. from his list. It is written in a large clear *naskh*, and is dated Jumádá i, 975 (= Nov. 1567).

1013 (a) كتاب البرهان فى علامات مهدىّ آخر الزّمان **Or. 52 (8)**

The *Kitábu'l-Burhán fí 'alámáti Mahdiyyi ákhiri'z-zamán*, by Shaykh 'Alí b. Ḥusámu'd-Dín...al-Muttaqí al-Hindí, who died in 975/1567. It is based on a similar work by as-Suyúṭí. See Brockelmann, ii, p. 384. The MS. contains 77 ff. of 20·2 × 14·2 c. and 15 ll., is written in a large, clumsy *naskh* with rubrications and is defective at end and undated. It was bought of Naaman on March 4, 1901. The volume also contains another work by as-Suyúṭí, for which see *infra*, p. 172, **No. 1042**, *s.v.* الكشف.

1014 (a, heb.) كتاب الترجمان **Christ's, Dd. 5. 13**

A MS. containing Hebrew prayers in the Samaritan character with interlinear Arabic translation, 11 lines of each to the page of 22·8 × 17 c. Copied out in 1188/1774–5.

1015 (a) كتاب التوحيد **Add. 3651 (10)**

The *Kitábu't-Tawḥíd* of Abú Manṣúr Muḥammad b. Maḥmúd al-Máturídí, who died in 333/944. See Brockelmann, i, p. 195, where, however, no work with this title is mentioned. The MS. contains 215 ff. of 24·2 × 15·8 c. and 21 ll., is undated but fairly ancient, and was bought of Sethian on May 21, 1900.

1016 (a) كتاب خير الزاد فى المبدأ و المعاد **Or. 9[2] (8)**

Khayru'z-Zád fi'l-Mabda' wa'l-Ma'ád ("the Best Provision for this life and the next"), without author's name. For description of the MS., which is dated 1144/1731–2, and was bought of Géjou on Jan. 28, 1901, see p. 149, **No. 901** *supra*, *s.v.* فقه القلوب. This portion fills ff. 87^b–106^b, and is written in a large, coarse, clear *naskh* with rubrications.

1017 (a) كتاب السُّبْعيّات فى مواعظ البريّات **Or. 592 (8)**

The *Kitábu's-Sub'iyyát fí mawá'iẓi'l-bariyyát*, a treatise on the virtues and properties of the number Seven, by Shaykh

Abu'n-Naṣr Muḥammad...al-Hamadání, who died in 966/1558. See Brockelmann, ii, p. 412. The MS., undated, was bought of Géjou on Oct. 30, 1905, contains 81 ff. of 20 × 14·4 c. and 17 ll., and is written in a large clear *naskh* with rubrications.

1018 (a) كتاب الشّفا فى حقوق المصطفى **Or. 415 (10)**

The *Kitábu'sh-Shifá fí Ḥuqúqi'l-Muṣṭafa* by the Qáḍí Abu'l-Faḍl 'Iyáḍ...al-Yaḥsubí, who died in 544/1149. See Brockelmann, i, p. 369 and *B.M.A.S.*, No. 159, p. 94. The MS., bought of Géjou on June 3, 1903, is undated, contains 155 ff. of 25·7 × 17 c. and 27 ll., and is written in a fine old *naskh* with modern supply.

1019 (t) كتاب شير دلير و مهر منير **Or. 604 (8)**

A Turkish romance by Báqí of Broussa, described as an autograph copy (با خط مؤلّف), entitled *Kitáb-i-Shír-i-dilír wa Mihr-i-munír* ("the Book of the brave Lion and the bright Sun"). The MS., dated 1101/1689–90, was bought of Géjou on Oct. 30, 1905, comprises 87 ff. of 20·4 × 14 c. and 21 ll., and is written in a good Turkish *naskh*, pointed, with rubrications.

1020 (p) كتاب الصحّة و المرض **Or. 695 (8)**
كتاب رند و زاهد

Two prose works in Persian by the Turco-Persian poet Fuḍúlí of Baghdád who, according to his contemporary townsman 'Ahdí, died in 963/1555–6. See Gibb's *Hist. of Ottoman Poetry*, vol. iii, pp. 70 *et seqq*. The MS., bought of Géjou in December, 1906, comprises 40 ff. of 21·3 × 15·3 and 15 ll., and is written in a good *ta'líq*. The *Kitábu'ṣ-Ṣiḥḥat wa'l-Maraḍ* ("Book of Health and Disease") occupies ff. 1b–12a, and the *Kitáb-i-Rind u Záhid* ("Book of the Wastrel and the Zealot"), ff. 12b–40a. The MS. was copied in 993/1585, and bought of Géjou in December, 1906.

1021 (a) كتاب الضّعفاء **King's, No. 98**

The *Kitábu'ḍ-Ḍu'afá* of Jamálu'd-Dín Abu'l-Faraj 'Abdu'r-Raḥmán...ibnu'l-Jawzí, who died in 597/1200. See Brockelmann, i, pp. 499–506, especially p. 503, No. 25, under *Ḥadíth*. See Palmer's *King's Cat.*, p. 24.

1022, 1023 (a) كتاب الضّؤ فى شرح المصباح **Or. 582 (7)** **King's, No. 10**

The *Kitábu'd-Ḍaw'*, a commentary by Tájú'd-Dín al-Isfará'iní, who died in 684/1285, on the *Miṣbáḥ fi'n-Naḥw* of al-Muṭarrizí, who died in 610/1213. See Brockelmann, i, pp. 293 and 296. **Or. 582,** which is dated 867/1462–3, and was bought of Géjou on July 14, 1905, contains 117 ff. of 17·7 × 13·2 c. and 13 ll., and is written in a good *nasta'líq*, the text being overlined with red. The **King's MS.** is a very poor one, copied at Ajmír in India by Khwájá Bakhsh and undated.

1024, 1025 (a) **Add. 3615[1] (9)** **Add. 3735 (9)**

كتاب الطبّ الجديد اكيميائى الخ

Kitábu't-Ṭibbi'l-Jadíd, the Book of the New or Alchemic Medicine invented by Paracelsus, by Ṣáliḥ b. Naṣru'lláh b. Salám al-Ḥalabí, who died in 1080/1669. See Brockelmann, ii, p. 365. **Add. 3615[1]**, copied by Suhráb-i-Jahánbakhsh and completed on the 25th of Rabí' ii, A.H. 1255 (=July 8, 1839), was bought of Géjou in 1899 and has been partly described above, p. 120, **No. 731,** *s.v.* زاد المسافرين. This portion comprises ff. 1–41 of 21 × 13·5 c. and 21 ll., and is written in a minute *ta'líq* with rubrications and many marginal notes in a clumsy hand. **Add. 3735** is dated 1238/1822–3, was bought of Sethian on Nov. 28, 1900, contains 63 ff. of 22·1 × 15·5 and 21 ll., and is written in a coarse modern *naskh* with rubrications.

1026 (a) كتاب الفرح **Or. 9[3] (8)**

Kitábu'l-Faraḥ. For description of the MS., which is dated 1146/1733–4 and was bought of Géjou on Jan. 28, 1901, see above, p. 149, **No. 901,** *s.v.* فقه القلوب. This portion occupies ff. 107ᵃ–112ᵇ of 21·8 × 15·6 c. and 19–21 ll.

1027 (a) كتاب الفلاحة (مختصر) **Or. 608 (8)**

An abridgement of the *Kitábu'l-Faláḥa* ("Book of Agriculture") of Ibnu'l-'Awwám al-Andalusí, who flourished in the first half of the sixth century of the Christian era. See Brockelmann, i, p. 494. The MS. was bought in Constantine (Algeria), in April, 1905, by Khalíl Khálid, formerly Turkish lecturer in the University of Cambridge, is dated 1269/1853, is written in a Maghribí hand, and contains 60 ff. of 21·7 × 16·3 c. and 21 ll.

1028 (a) كتاب القواعد المقرّرة فى علم القرآة **Or. 21² (9)**

Kitábu'l-qawá'idi'l-muqarrara fí 'ilmi'l-qirá'at, a treatise on the proper reading of the *Qur'án*, by Muḥammad b. Qásim al-Baqarí, who died in 1111/1699. See Brockelmann, ii, p. 327. The MS., dated 1211/1796–7, was bought of Naaman on Feb. 5, 1901, and this portion comprises 11 leaves (ff. 73–83) at the end of the volume.

1029 (a) كتاب ما رواه الواعون فى اخبار الطاعون **Or. 172² (8)**

Kitábu má rawáhu'l-Wá'ún fí akhbári'ṭ-Ṭa'ún, a history of the Plague, by the celebrated polygraph Jalálu'd-Dín as-Suyúṭí, who died in 911/1505. See Brockelmann, ii, pp. 143–158, especially p. 146, No. 32. For description of the MS. see below, p. 172, **No. 1041**, *s.v.* كشف الصّلصلة. This treatise occupies ff. 29ᵇ–50ᵇ, and is followed by a short poem in praise of the Prophet by 'Umar ibnu'l-Wardí.

1030 (a) كتاب المحاكمات **Or. 867 (9**

The *Kitábu'l-Muḥákamát*, described in a note as "Commentaires sur la philosophie de la nature," beginning:

لقد اتينا على المنطق من شرح الشرح موفين حقّه من التحرير الخ

The MS., from the late Professor W. Robertson Smith's library, contains 173 ff. of 24 × 13·8 c. and 19 ll., and is written in a modern *ta'líq* with rubrications, undated.

1031 (a) كتاب مشارع و مطارحات **Trinity, R. 13. 37**

The *Kitábu Masharí' wa Muṭáraḥát*, by the celebrated mystic Shaykh Shihábu'd-Din Yaḥyá b. Ḥabash as-Suhrawardí, who was put to death at Aleppo in 587/1191. The work is divided into six parts and comprises 146 ff. See Brockelmann, i, pp. 437–8, and Palmer's *Trin. Cat.*, pp. 84–85.

1032–1037 (a) كشّاف الزّمخشرى **Or. 163, 164 (13)**
King's, No. 86
King's, No. 70
King's, No. 140
Or. 740
King's, No. 147

The *Kashsháf* of az-Zamakhsharí, who died in 538/1143. See Brockelmann, i, pp. 289–293. **Or. 163, 164** contain the whole commentary, the division being between *Súras* xviii and xix. Vol. i comprises 290 ff. of 28 × 19 c. and 31 ll., and is written in a fairly good *nasta'líq* with rubrications. Vol. ii comprises 302 ff. of 31 × 22·5 c. and 31 ll. and is written in a good, clear *naskh*, with rubrications. Neither volume is dated. **King's 86** is the second half only (from the *Súratu Maryam* to the end). It comprises 294 ff. and is written in a curious small *nasta'líq*, with some notes at the end which appear to be in Malay. **King's 70,** beautifully written in fine *naskh* with rubrications between borders ruled in gold, and transcribed at Damascus in 980/1572–3, contains the *Kashsháf* in the margins and the *Anwáru't-Tanzíl* of al-Bayḍáwí in the body of the text. **King's 140,** defective at end and undated, and written in a clear Indian *naskh* with rubrications, contains the glosses of Sa'du'd-Dín at-Taftázání (d. 792/1389) on the *Kashsháf*. **Or. 740,** described in a note on the fly-leaf as the *Kashfu'l-Kashsháf*, is again Sa'du'd-Dín at-Taftázání's explanation of the *Kashsháf* as far as the *Súratu Yúnus* (*Súra* x), this, according to Ḥ. Kh., vol. v, p. 187, being all that was written. It comprises 367 ff. of 26 × 18 c. and 21 ll., is written in a small, fairly legible, modern *naskh* with rubrications, and is undated. **King's 147** contains a gloss by Khayálí on the commentary of al-Járabardí (d. 746/1345) on the same work. It is defective at end and undated, and is written in a poor *ta'líq* with rubrications.

1038 (p) كشايش نامه **Corpus, No. 56**

Kusháyish-náma, a collection of stories, compiled in 1110/1698–9, by Rájkarn, and followed by a glossary of Arabic words. See *B.M.P.C.*, p. 767. Written in good *ta'líq* on pages of 23 × 14 c., undated.

1039 (a) كشف الاسرار عن لسان حال الطيور و الازهار **Add. 3746** (8)

Kashfu'l-Asrár 'an lisáni ḥáli't-Ṭuyúri wa'l-Azhár, on the "language of Birds and Flowers," by Shaykh 'Izzu'd-Dín b. 'Abdu's-Salám b. Aḥmad b. Ghánim al-Wá'iẓ, who died about 678/1279. See Brockelmann, i, pp. 450–1; Ḥ. Kh., No. 10,659; *Camb. Hand-list*, pp. 178–9. This MS., dated 1205/1790–1, was bought of Naaman on Dec. 8, 1900, and comprises 22 ff. of 20·7 × 14·8 c. and 21 ll., and is written in a clear *naskh* with rubrications.

1040 (a) كشف الاسرار النورانيّة القرآنيّة آلخ **Or. 214** (9) **Or. 215** (9)

Kashfu'l-Asrári'n-Núrániyyati'l-Qur'ániyya fí-má yata-'alliqu bi'l-Ajrámi's-Samáwiyya ("Disclosure of the luminous Qur'ánic mysteries in respect to what is connected with the Heavenly Bodies"), by Muḥammad b. Aḥmad al-Iskandarání, in two volumes, the first containing 206 ff. and the second 182 ff. of 21·5 × 16·7 c. and 27 ll., written in a clear modern *naskh* with rubrications, undated. Bought of Naaman Nov. 12, 1902.

1041 (a) كشف الصّلصلة عن وصف الزلزلة **Or. 172**[1] (8)

The *Kashfu'ṣ-Ṣalsala 'an Waṣfi 'z-zalzala* of Shaykh Jalálu'd-Dín as-Suyúṭí, who died in 911/1505. See Brockelmann, ii, pp. 143–158, especially p. 147, No. 42. The MS., undated, contains 51 ff. of 21·5 × 15·5 c. and 21 ll., and is written in good, legible *naskh* with rubrications. This portion fills pp. 1–28. Bought of Naaman, Dec. 6, 1901.

1042 (a) الكشف عن مجاوزة هذه الامّة الالف **Or. 52**[2] (8)

Al-Kashf 'an mujáwazati hádhihi'l-Ummati'l-Alf by Jalálu'd-Dín as-Suyúṭí. See Brockelmann, ii, p. 151, No. 135 and for description of the MS. p. 167, **No. 1013** *supra*.

1043 (a) كشف اللّثام فى شرح قواعد الاسلام **Or. 438** (12)

Kashfu'l-lithám fí sharḥi qawá'idi'l-Islám by al-'Allámatu'l-Ḥillí, perhaps identical with the work by Ḥusayn b Aḥmad al-Maḥallí described by Brockelmann, ii, p. 323. The MS., dated 1211/1796–7, was bought of Hannan Watson and Co., on August 29, 1903, and contains 346 ff. of 30·1 × 20·9 c and 30 ll., written in poor *naskh* with rubrications.

1044 (a) کشکول **Or. 183** (11)

The *Kashkúl* of Shaykh Bahá'u'd-Dín al-'Ámilí (died 1030/1621). See Brockelmann, ii, pp. 414–415. The MS., dated 1052/1642–3, was copied in Shíráz, and was bought of Géjou on Jan. 1, 1902. It comprises 229 ff. of 28·2 × 17·3 c. and 34 ll., is written in an excellent Persian *naskh* with rubrications and some marginal notes, and comprises five books or volumes bound in one.

1045 (t) کشور درون **Or. 224** (8)

A Turkish mystical work entitled *Kishwar-i-Darún* ("the Kingdom Within"), beginning:

حکمای متقدّمین و عقلای متأخّرین نیجه دورلردن برو قوّهٔ محاکمهٔ قلبیّه‌دن بحث ایلمشلر

The MS., undated, was bought of Naaman on Nov. 12, 1902, and comprises 32 ff. of 19·5 × 12·6 c. and 11 ll., and is written in a good *naskh*.

1046 (p) كفاية التعليم فى علم التنجيم **Add. 3612** (8)

A Persian manual of Astronomy entitled *Kifáyatu't-Ta'lím fí 'ilmi 't-Tanjím*, by Abu'l-Maḥámid Muḥammad b. Mas'úd Muḥammad Zakí al-Ghaznawí.

The MS., dated 10 Rabí' ii, 1219 (= July 19, 1804), was bought of Géjou in 1899, is written in a clear *nasta'líq* with rubrications, and contains 166 ff. of 20·8 × 13·3 c. and 19 ll. Copyist, Muḥammad Ibráhím.

1047–1050 (p) کفایت مجاهدیّهٔ منصوری {**Add. 3613** (11), **Add. 3614**[1] (10), **Add. 3737**[3] (7), **Or. 47** (9)}

Four copies of the *Kifáyat-i-Mujáhidiyya-i-Manṣúrí*, a well-known medical work by Manṣúr b. Muḥammad b. Aḥmad b. Yúsuf b. Ilyás, composed about the middle of the 9th century of the Muḥammadan (15th of the Christian) era. See *B.M.P.C.*, pp. 470–1, and Ethé's *Bodl. Pers. Cat.*, No. 1587, col. 958. **Add. 3613**, undated, was bought of Géjou in Dec.

1899, contains 261 ff. of 25·8 × 12·5 c. and 17 ll., is defective at the beginning and end, and is written in a fair *ta'líq* with rubrications. **Add. 3614**[1], also undated, contains 181 ff., of which this work (which is followed by the *Ikhtiyárát-i-Badí'í* and the *Yádigar-i-Ḥusayní*) occupies ff. 1–140, of 24·7 × 17·4 c. and 22 ll., and is written in a clear *naskh* with rubrications. **Add. 3737**[3], bought of Sethian on Nov. 28, 1900, is a portion of the work occupying ff. 102ª–113ª of 17·6 × 11 c. and 13 ll., and is written in a small, neat Persian *ta'líq* with rubrications. **Or. 47,** dated 1070/1659–1660, was bought of E. Parsons and Sons in Feb. 1901, contains 268 ff. of 22·7 × 13 c. and 17 ll., and is written in a neat *ta'líq* with rubrications.

كلمات طيّبات

Letters of the Moghul Emperor 'Álamgír Awrangzíb. See p. 113 *supra*, **No. 694**, *s.v. Raqá'im-i-Kará'im.*

1051 (p) كلّيّات امير خسرو دهلوى **Emmanuel, 4.2.1 (formerly 3.2.17)**

The *Kulliyyát* or complete poetical works of Amír Khusraw of Dihlí, who died in 725/1325. See *B.M.P.C.*, pp. 609–617.

1052–1055 (p) كلّيّات انورى **Or. 27 (10)**, **Or. 258 (10)**, **Or. 279 (8)**, **Or. 283 (10)**

The *Kulliyyát* of Anwarí, who died in the latter part of the sixth century of the Muḥammadan (twelfth of the Christian) era. See *B.M.P.C.*, pp. 554–7. **Or. 27,** defective both at beginning and end, and undated, was bought of Naaman on Feb. 5, 1901, and contains 113 ff. of 24 × 14·25 c. and 17 ll., and is written in a good, modern Persian *ta'líq*. **Or. 258,** from the Cowell Bequest, is dated 1024/1615, comprises 347 ff. of 24·2 × 13·5 c. and 17 ll., and is written in a good *nasta'líq*. **Or. 279,** also from the Cowell Bequest, is defective both at beginning and end and undated, contains ff. 21–385 of 20 × 12·5 c. and 15 ll., and is written in a good *ta'líq* with rubrications. **Or. 283,** also from the Cowell Bequest, was originally presented to Professor Cowell by Mr Sidney Churchill on Jan. 12,

1887. It comprises 222 ff. of 24·4 × 15 c. and 21 ll., is written in a good *nasta'líq*, and is placed by Mr Churchill in the ninth century of the *hijra*, but the figures ١١٦ at the end would suggest that it was transcribed either in 1016/1607–8 or 1116/1704–5.

1056 (p) **كلّيّات بيدل** **Add. 3632** (12)

The *Kulliyyát* of Mírzá Bí-dil, who died in 1133/1720–1. See *B.M.P.C.*, p. 706. The MS. was bought of Naaman on March 5, 1900, and comprises 965 pp. of 29·3 × 16·2 c., 23 ll. in text and 34 in margin, borders ruled in gold and colours.

1057, 1058 (t) **كلّيّات ثابت (علاءالدين افندى)** **Or. 473** (9) **Or. 762** (8)

Two MSS. of the *Kulliyyát* of Thábit (Sábit), whose personal name was 'Alá'u'd-Dín, and who died in 1124/1712–13. See Gibb's *Hist. of Ottoman Poetry*, vol. iv, pp. 14–29, and *B.M.T.C.*, p. 202. **Or. 473** is undated, was bought of Géjou on Jan. 29, 1904, contains 174 ff. of 23 × 12·5 c. and 23 ll., and is written in a small, neat *nasta'líq* between gold borders. **Or. 762,** undated, was bought of Géjou on May 13, 1910, contains 195 ff. of 21·7 × 13·2 c. and 17 ll., and is written in a good Turkish *ta'líq* with rubrications between gold borders.

1059 (p) **كلّيّات جامى** **Add. 3685** (10)

The *Kulliyyát* of the great Jámí, who died in 898/1492–3. See *B.M.P.C.*, pp. 643–9. This fine MS. was copied in 891/1486, during the author's life-time, and contains the three *Díwáns* known as *Fátiḥatu'sh-Shibáb*, *Wásiṭatu'l-'Iqd* and *Khátimatu'l-Ḥayát*. It was bought of Naaman in Sept. 1900, contains 321 ff. of 24·3 × 14·5 c. and 19 ll., and is written in excellent Persian *ta'líq* between gold borders.

1060–1062 (p) **كلّيّات خاقانى** **Or. 250** (12) **Or. 255** (9) **Jesus, No. 6**

The *Kulliyyát* of Kháqání, who died in 595/1198–9. See *B.M.P.C.*, pp. 558–562. **Or. 250** contains a commentary on the poems of Kháqání by 'Abdu'l-Wahháb b. Muḥammad al-Ḥasaní al-Ma'múrí, poetically surnamed Fanáʼí. This MS., which forms part of the Cowell Bequest, is dated 1235/1819–1820, contains 250 ff. of 29·2 × 18 c. and 19 ll., and is written in a poor but clear *ta'líq* with rubrications. **Or. 255,** also from the Cowell Bequest, is undated and defective both at beginning and end. It contains 505 ff. of 23 × 15·25 c. and 13 ll. and is written in a clear *ta'líq* with rubrications. **Jesus 6** was presented by Captain Edward Thurlow Hibgane through his cousin Ed. Hibgane to the College, of which he was a Fellow. It is a fine MS. containing a very full text, and comprising 447 ff. of 16·7 × 8·7 c.

1063 (p) كلّيّات الرّمى **Corpus, No. 216**

Kulliyyátu'r-Ramy, a treatise on Archery, by Amínu'd-Dín b. Mír Muḥammad Háshim b. Sayyid Aḥmad of Najaf, completed in 1132/1719–1720. See Ethé's *Ind. Off. Pers. Cat.*, col. 1497, No. 2771.

1064–1070 (p) كلّيّات سعدى شيرازى

Or. 246 (10)
Or. 422 (9)
Or. 502 (8)
Or. 941 (11)
King's, No. 201
Trinity, R. 13. 101
Trinity, R. 15. 52

The *Kulliyyát* of Sa'dí of Shíráz, who died in 690/1291. See *B.M.P.C.*, pp. 595–605. **Or. 246,** dated 1249/1833–4, is from the library of the late Professor Cowell, who received it from the late Dr Bumsted, who received it from Doria, to whom it was given on Jan. 2, 1849, in Ṭihrán. It contains 221 ff. of 24 × 14 c. and 25 ll., and is written in a minute *ta'líq* hand between gilt and blue lines. **Or. 422,** undated, was bought of Hannan and Watson in 1903. It contains 216 ff. of 22 × 11·5 c. and 21 ll. in text, with 36 in the margin, and is written in a small, neat *nasta'líq* with rubrications. **Or. 502,** undated, also bought of Hannan, Watson and Co., on Aug. 20, 1904, contains 240 ff. of 20·3 × 12·5 c. and 15 ll. in text, with 26 in the margin, and is written in a small neat *ta'líq* with rubrications. **Or. 941,** copied in 1236 or 1237 (1820–22) by Asadu'lláh of Maḥallát, and presented to the Library by Mr G. Le Strange in Feb. 1916, contains 237 ff. of 28·7 × 19 c., is written in a neat Persian *ním-shikasta*, 15 ll. (15 *bayts*) to each page in the text, and 30 ll. (= 15 *bayts*) in the margins. **King's 201,** undated, contains only the five prose treatises prefixed to Sa'dí's *Kulliyyát*, and is written in a very large *ta'líq*. See *B.M.P.C.*, p. 596^{b}, and Palmer's *King's Cat.*, p. 14. **Trin. R.13.101** contains 381 ff. and is described at great length in Palmer's *Trin. Coll. Cat.*, pp. 158–170. **Trin. R.15.52** contains 343 ff., is written in a fine *ta'líq* with numerous miniatures, and is dated, according to Palmer (*op. cit.*, pp. 176–180), A.D. 1578.

1071 (p) کلّیّات سوزنی **Or. 563 (8)**

The *Kulliyyát* of Súzaní, who died in 569/1173–4. See *B.M.P.C.*, p. 868^{b}. The MS., undated, was bought of Géjou on July 14, 1905, contains 272 ff. of 21·3 × 15 c. and 17 ll., and is written partly in a small, neat *ta'líq*, partly in a coarser hand, with rubrications.

1072 (p) کلّیّات غنی **Corpus, No. 169**

The *Kulliyyát* of Ghaní of Kashmír, who died in 1079/1668–9. See *B.M.P.C.*, p. 692. The MS., transcribed by Naráyan Dás in 1250/1834–5, contains 76 ff. of 19 × 12 c. and is written in *nasta'líq*.

1073 (p) کلّیّات فرید الدّین عطّار **Or. 500 (10)**

The *Kulliyyát* of Shaykh Farídu'd-Dín 'Aṭṭár, who was killed in the sack of Níshápúr by the Mongols in 627/1229–30. *B.M.P.C.*, pp. 344 and 576–580. This MS. was one of 30 bought of Messrs Hannan and Watson on August 20, 1904. It is undated and incomplete at end, contains 282 ff. of 24·8 × 17 c. with 21 ll. in the body of the text and 56 in the margin, and is written in a fairly good *nasta'líq* with rubrications.

1074 (t, p) کلّیّات فصیح **Or. 535 (8)**

The *Kulliyyát* of Faṣíḥ Efendi, professedly an autograph, comprising (1) his Turkish *Díwán*; (2) his Persian *Díwáncha*; (3) the *Qalamiyya*; (4) the dispute (*munázara*) between

Gul-i-Ra'ná ("the Beauteous Rose") and *Mul-i-Ḥamrá* ("the Red Wine"). The MS., dated Rajab 1090 (= August, 1679), was bought of Géjou on Nov. 1, 1904, contains 108 ff. of 21·4 × 10 c. and 21 ll., and is written in a rather involved *ta'líq* with rubrications.

1075 (h) كلّيّات نثار **Corpus, No. 185**

The *Kulliyyát* of the Hindustání poet Mír Abu'l-Qásim *Nithár*, comprising (1) a Compendium of Indian history; (2) Odes (*Ghazaliyyát*); (3) a verse-translation of a story from the *Bústán* of Sa'dí; (4) a *tarjí'-band* and some *qaṣídas*, several of which are in praise of William Augustus Brooke; (5) Threnodies (*Maráthí*). The MS. was copied in Calcutta in 1215/1800–1, and is written in *nasta'líq* on leaves of 23 × 15·5 c.

1076 (a) كليلة و دمنة **Corpus, No. 123**

A fine old MS. of the Book of *Kalíla and Dimna*, translated into Arabic from the Pahlawí about the middle of the 8th century of the Christian era by 'Abdu'lláh b. al-Muqaffa'. See Brockelmann, i, pp. 151–2. The MS. is written in a fine old *naskh* with many vowel-points and a large number of coloured illustrations, which, however, have no great artistic merit. In the colophon the words preceding "and seven hundred" (و سبعمائة) are lost, but the MS can at any rate be assigned to the 14th century of the Christian era.

1077 (p) كنز التّحف **King's, No. 211**

An anonymous treatise on music, composed in the 8th century of the Muḥammadan (fourteenth of the Christian) era, and entitled *Kanzu't-Tuḥaf*. See *B.M.P.S.*, p. 115[b], v, and Palmer's *King's Cat.*, p. 14.

1078–1081 (a, p) كنز الدقائق **Add. 3747 (7)**
Corpus, No. 199
Christ's, Dd. 4. 3
Emmanuel, 3. 2. 3

The *Kanzu'd-Daqá'iq*, a well-known legal work composed in 684/1285–6 by Abu'l-Barakát 'Abdu'lláh an-Nasafí, who died in 710/1310. See Brockelmann, ii, pp. 196–7; *B.M.A.S.*,

p. 188. **Add. 3747** comprises 43 ff. of 18·2 × 10·2 c. and 15 ll., is incomplete at the end and undated, and was bought of Naaman on Dec. 8, 1900. It contains at the end fragments of two other treatises. **Corpus 199** contains the Persian translation of this work by Náṣir b. Muḥammad al-Kirmání. See Pertsch's *Berlin Pers. Cat.*, No. 200, p. 250, and my *Cambridge Pers. Cat.*, pp. 51–52. This MS. is dated 1143/1730–1 and is written in various *ta'líq* hands on pages of 26 × 17 c. The **Christ's MS.**, containing the Arabic original, was copied at Damascus in 904/1498–9, and is written in a good, clear *naskh* with headings in red on 145 ff. of 26·3 × 17 c. and 13 ll. The **Emmanuel MS.** (Arabic original) is dated Ṣafar 1051 (May–June, 1641). See also p. 115 *supra*, under رمز الحقايق.

1082 (a) كنوز الحقائق فى حديث خير الخلائق **Or. 204 (9)**

The *Kunúzu'l-Ḥaqá'iq fí ḥadíthi Khayri'l-Khalá'iq*, a collection of some 10,000 traditions about the Prophet arranged alphabetically, by 'Abdu'r-Ra'úf al-Munáwí, who died in 1031/1622. See Brockelmann, ii, pp. 305–7. The MS. contains 100 ff. of 24 × 16·2 c. and 25 ll. and is written in a small and legible *ta'líq* with rubrications. It was copied by Báyazíd al-Mardashtí and is undated. Bought of Géjou, October 23, 1902.

1083 (p) كيمياى باسليقا **Add. 3672 (8)**

A work on Medicine, entitled, apparently, *Kímiyá-yi-Básilíqá*, of which the contents are elaborately set forth on ff. 2b–8b. The MS., undated, was bought of Sethian on July 17, 1900, contains 126 ff. of 20·2 × 14·2 c. and 19 ll., and is written in a large, clear *naskh* with rubrications. It also contains 17 ff. besides those enumerated above scribbled over with prayers and other fragments, and seven loose leaves from another work, an Arabic-Persian glossary.

1084 (h) گلزار ابراهيم **Corpus, No. 159**[1]

Biographies of Hindustání poets arranged alphabetically and entitled *Gulzár-i-Ibráhím* by 'Alí Ibráhím Khán, originally written in Persian, and translated into Urdú at the request of Mr J. Gilchrist. Cf. Ethé's *Ind. Off. Pers. Cat.*, No. 703, col.

361. The MS. is undated and is written in good *nasta'líq* on pages of 30 × 16 c.

1085–1098 (p)
گلستان سعدی

Or. 741[1] (9),	**Corpus, No. 70[1]**
Or. 750 (7),	**Corpus, No. 173**
Or. 751 (8),	**Jesus, No. 7**
Or. 752 (8),	**Queens', Nos. 3 & 4**
Or. 939 (8),	**Trinity, R. 13. 36**
Christ's, Dd. 4. 14,	**Trinity, R. 13. 107**
Corpus, No. 20[1],	**Trinity, R. 13. 108**

Fourteen or fifteen copies of the well-known *Gulistán* of Sa'dí of Shíráz and its various translations and commentaries. **Or. 741[1]** contains the commentary on difficult words and passages in the text by Muḥammad b. Shihábu'd-Dín b. Shaykh 'Abdu'lláh b. Shaykh Ḥasan al-Qurashí al-Háshimí. The MS., bought of Géjou on March 27, 1907, contains 15 ff. of 24 × 17 c. and 32 ll., comprises 5 sections, and is written in a poor *nasta'líq* with the text overlined. **Or. 750** contains the text with the Arabic commentary of Surúrí. The MS., copied at Amásiya in 957/1550, was bought of Géjou on March 27, 1907, and contains 291 ff. of 19 × 11·5 c. and 19 ll. It is written in a clumsy *nasta'líq* with rubrications, and the text is overlined with red. **Or. 751,** dated 934/1528, was bought of Géjou on March 27, 1907, contains 149 ff. of 19·4 × 14 c. and 17 ll., and is written in a clumsy Turkish *nasta'líq* with rubrications and overlinings in red. It contains the text with the Arabic commentary of Ya'qúb b. Sayyid 'Alí. **Or. 752** contains the text with the Turkish commentary of Sham'í. It is undated, was bought of Géjou on March 27, 1907, comprises 162 ff. of 20·6 × 13 c. and 23 ll., and is written in a small *nasta'líq* with rubrications. **Or. 939,** containing the Persian text, comprises 109 ff. of 20·3 × 13·7 c. and 15 ll., is undated, and is written in a poor Turkish *ta'líq* with rubrications. The date of its acquisition by the Library is unrecorded, but it belonged to Claudius J. Rich in Jan. 1804, and afterwards to Adam White, who gave it to Henry Gough on Sept. 11, 1858. The **Christ's MS.** contains the text written in a clear Indian *ta'líq* on 87 ff. of 28·2 × 20 c. and 15 ll. **Corpus 20[1]** contains a Hindustání translation. It is dated 1268/1852 and comprises 70 ff. written in *ta'líq*. **Corpus 70**[1] contains a Persian commentary by Muḥammad 'Abdu'r-Rasúl b. Shihábu'd-Dín b. 'Abdu'lláh. It is dated 1262/1846, comprises 66 ff. of 27·5 × 17 c., and is written in a modern *ta'líq*. **Corpus 173,** dated 1253/1837–8, is written in a negligent *nasta'líq* on pages of 22 × 16 c. **Jesus 7,** dated 1096/1685, is well written and bears the seal of George Lewis with the date A.D. 1707. **Queens' 3** and **4** are two undated Indian copies, the second containing at the end some verses in praise of God, etc. Of the three Trinity MSS. the first (**R . 13 . 36**), described on pp. 83–4 of Palmer's *Trin. Cat.*, contains 106 ff. and was copied in A.D. 1594. The second (**R . 13 . 107**) contains 153 ff. and four illustrations, has the *Bústån* written in the margins, and is described on p. 173 of the *Trin. Cat.* The third (**R . 13 . 108**) contains 96 ff., is undated, and is described on p. 174 of the *Trin. Cat.*

1099 (p) گلستان شعور **Corpus, No. 178**[1]

Gulistán-i-Shu'úr, an epistolary manual by the Nawwáb Muṣṭafá Khán. The MS. is dated 1222/1807–8, is written in *shikasta*, and contains 26 ff. of 20 × 12 c.

1100–1103 (p)
گلشن ابراهیمی (=تاریخ فرشته)

Christ's, Dd . 5 . 1
Christ's, Dd . 5 . 2
Christ's, Dd . 5 . 4
King's, No. 102

Four copies of the *Gulshan-i-Ibráhímí* or *Ta'ríkh-i-Firishta*, the well-known general history of India from the earliest times to 1015/1606–7 by Muḥammad Qásim Hindúsháh of Astarábád, commonly called *Firishta*. See *B.M.P.C.*, pp. 225–8; *Camb. Pers. Cat.*, Nos. lxxxii–lxxxiii, pp. 155–7. Of the three Christ's MSS. **Dd . 5 . 1** is written in a rather scratchy *ta'líq* on 274 ff. of 28·6 × 21·3 c. and 19 ll., but has a full Index prefixed; **Dd . 5 . 2,** copied in Ḥaydarábád, is written in a fine *naskh* on 450 ff. of 29·2 × 18·5 c. and 19 ll. with the titles and headings in red; and **Dd . 5 . 4,** undated, is written in an Indian *ta'líq* on 308 ff. of 32 × 21·6 c. and 17 ll. The **King's MS.** comprises 2 vols. of 243 and 308 ff. respectively, and was copied in 1198/1783–4 by a certain Imám-bakhsh.

1104, 1105 (t) گنجینهٔ راز **Or. 180 (8)**
Or. 777 (7)

The *Ganjína-i-Ráz* ("Treasure of Mystery"), a Turkish poem in 38 cantos (*maqálas*) preceded by a short prose preface, by Yaḥyá Bey of Dúqagín, who died in 983/1575–6. See Gibb's *Hist. of Ottoman Poetry*, vol. iii, pp. 116–132; *B.M.T.C.*, p. 181. **Or. 180,** dated 1024/1615, was bought of Géjou on Jan. 1, 1902, contains 85 ff. of 19·5 × 13·6 c. and 19 ll., and is written in a poor *naskh* with rubrications. **Or. 777,** dated 997/1589, was bought of Géjou on Jan. 7, 1909, contains 110 ff. of 18·3 × 11·7 c. and 15 ll., and is written in a neat *naskh*, pointed, with rubrications.

1106 (p, t) لغت حلیمی **Or. 596 (8)**

The *Lughat-i-Ḥalímí*, properly entitled *Baḥru'l-Ghará'ib*, a well-known Persian-Turkish lexicon by Luṭfu'lláh b. Abí Yúsuf, commonly called Ḥalímí Chelebi, who died in 923/1516. See Gibb's *Hist. of Ottoman Poetry*, ii, p. 267 *ad calc.* The MS. is undated and was bought of Géjou on Oct. 30, 1905. It contains 145 ff. of 20·5 × 13·4 c. and 19 ll. and is written in a fair Turkish *naskh*, the Persian words in red.

1107 (p) لمعات عراقی **Corpus, No. 75[3]**

A fragment of 8 leaves of 20 × 14 c. from the *Lama'át* of Fakhru'd-Dín 'Iráqí, a well-known Persian mystic and poet, who died about 686/1287. See *B.M.P.C.*, pp. 593–4.

1108 (p) لوامع الاشراق فی مکارم الاخلاق **Or. 467 (7)**

The well-known ethical work commonly known as *Akhláq-i-Jalálí*, but properly entitled as above *Lawámi'u'l-Ishráq fí Makárimi'l-Akhláq*, by Jalálu'd-Dín Dawání, who died in 908/1502–3. See *B.M.P.C.*, pp. 442–3. The MS., copied at Constantinople in 946/1539–1540, was bought of Géjou on Jan. 29, 1904, and contains 210 ff. of 17·6 × 10·5 c. and 13 ll. Written in a very neat *naskh* with rubrications.

1109 (p) لوائح جامی **Or. 565[2] (8)**

The *Lawá'iḥ* of Jámí (d. 898/1492-3). See *B.M.P.C.*, p. 44. This portion of the MS., written in clear, good *ta'líq* and dated 1293/1876, comprises ff. 81–94. Bought of Géjou, July 14, 1905: copyist, Muḥammad Sa'íd.

1110 (p) ليلى و مجنون نظامى **Or. 13 (6)**

The romantic poem of *Laylá wa Majnún* by Niẓámí of Ganja, with selections from his *Khusraw wa Shírín*, *Haft Paykar*, and *Ghazaliyyát*. See above *s.v.* خمسهٔ نظامى. The MS., undated, was bought of Naaman on Feb. 5, 1901, is defective at both ends, and contains 94 ff. of 14·2 × 9·3 c. and 11 ll., written in different *ta'líq* hands.

1111 (p) ليلى و مجنون امير خسرو دهلوى **Corpus, No. 111**

The *Laylá wa Majnún* of Amír Khusraw of Dihlí, who died in 725/1325. See *B.M.P.C.*, pp. 608-617, especially 611[b], ix The MS., undated, is written in fair *ta'líq* with some miniatures of no great merit.

1112, 1113 (p) ليلى و مجنون هاتفى **Or. 466[1] (6)**
Corpus, No. 107

The *Laylá wa Majnún* of Hátifí, Jámí's nephew, who died in 927/1520–21. See *B.M.P.C.*, pp. 652–3. **Or. 466,** dated 928/1521–2, was bought of Géjou on Jan. 29, 1904, and comprises 92 ff. of 16·8 × 12·5 and 11 ll. written in excellent *ta'líq* with rubrications. The **Corpus MS.,** copied about 1228/1813, is written in *ta'líq* on pages of 21 × 15 c.

1114, 1115 (h) ليلى و مجنون هوس **Corpus, No. 64**
Corpus, No. 66[8]

The *Laylá wa Majnún* in Hindustání verse by Muḥammad Taqí 'Alí Khán poetically named Hawas. **Corpus 64** is dated 1248/1832–3, and is written in clear *ta'líq* on pages of 26 × 16 c. **Corpus 66**[8], undated, contains 53 ff. of 25 × 15·5 c., and is written in *ním-shikasta*.

1116 (h) ليلى و مجنون تجلّى **Corpus, No. 107[3]**

The *Laylá wa Majnún* in Hindustání verse by Mír Tajallí. The MS., copied at Shahjahánábád in 1228/1813, contains 96 ff. of 21 × 15 c., and is written in good *ta'líq*.

1117 (h) ليلى و مجنون **Corpus, No. 125**

The *Laylá wa Majnún* in Hindustání verse by Naẓír, followed by other poems in the same language. The MS. is dated 1260/1844, and is written in *shikasta-ámíz* on pages of 22 × 15 c.

1118 (p) مأتمكدهٔ محمّد شريف **Corpus, No. 178^3**

An elegy in prose on the death of Muḥammad Sharíf, entitled *Mátamkada*, "the House of Mourning." See Ethé's *Ind. Off. Pers. Cat.*, col. 1149, No. 2078, 5. The MS., of which this portion occupies ff. 119–129, is dated 1222/1807–8.

1119 (a) المباحث الطبيعيّة فى شرح الاشارات **Or. 205** (10)

Al-Mabáḥithu'ṭ-Ṭabí'iyya, a commentary on the *Kitábu'l-Ishárát wa't-tanbíhát* of Avicenna, apparently ascribed to al-Muḥaqqiq [Naṣíru'd-Dín] aṭ-Ṭúsí and al-Quṭb [Fakhru'd-Dín] ar-Rází. See Brockelmann, i, p. 454, No. 20 to bottom of page. The MS. contains 168 ff. of 25·1 × 18·5 c. and 23 ll.; clear modern ***naskh*** to f. 82^b, thence onwards ***ním-shikasta***, undated, bought of Géjou Oct. 23, 1902.

1120–1132 (p)
مثنوئ جلال الدّين رومى

Add. 3691 (10), **Or. 685^1** (9)
Or. 285 (10), **Or. 938** (10)
Or. 286 (10), **Corpus, No. 221**
Or. 287 (10), **Corpus, No. 222**
Or. 288 (10), **Corpus, No. 223**
Or. 423 (10), **King's, No. 121**
Or. 424 (16),

Thirteen complete or partial copies of the Mystical *Mathnawí* of Jalálu'd-Dín Rúmí, who died in 672/1273. See *B.M.P.C.*, pp. 584–593. **Add. 3691** contains Books iv, v and vi (the second half of the poem), was copied in 1011/1602–3 from an original dated 712/1312–3, and was bought of Sethian on Nov. 1, 1900. It comprises ff. 81–300 of 25·5 × 15·8 c. and 19 ll., and is written in a poor but legible *ta'líq* with rubrications. **Or. 285,** dated 848/1444–5, is from the Cowell Bequest. It contains 426 ff. of 25 × 16·7 c. and 17 ll. and is written in a good Persian *ta'líq* with headings in gold. **Or. 286,** also from the Cowell Bequest, is dated 1120/1708–9 and was acquired by Professor Cowell on July 25, 1846. It comprises 410 ff. of 27 × 16·4 c. and 19 ll., and is written in a fair *naskh* with rubrications. **Or. 287,** also from the Cowell Bequest, contains Books iii and iv only, and is undated. It comprises 282 ff. of 24 × 13 c. and 19 ll. and is written in a clear *ta'líq* with rubrications, with many marginal notes and glosses in a minute hand. **Or. 288,** also from the Cowell Bequest, contains Books v and vi and is undated. It contains 161 ff. of 24·2 × 13·2 c. and 19 ll., and is written in a good *ta'líq* with rubrications and glosses like the volume last described, of which it forms the continuation. **Or. 423** contains Books iv, v and vi (the second half of the poem), is undated but probably of the sixteenth century, and was bought of Hannan and Watson on August 29, 1910. It contains 138 ff. of 24·8 × 16 c. and 25 ll. and is written in a good small *ta'líq*. **Or. 424,** dated 1098/1686–7, was acquired from the same source and on the same occasion as the last. It comprises 214 ff. of 40 × 21·5 c. and 35 ll., and is written in a poor but legible *ta'líq* with rubrications. **Or. 685**[1], undated, was bought of Géjou on May 10, 1906, contains on ff. 1–82 a selection of 3333 *bayts* from the *Mathnawí*, preceded by an acephalous prose preface. The verses are divided into *bands*, or strophes, separated by the recurrent verse:

جمله معشوقست و عاشق پردهٔ زنده معشوقست و عاشق مردهٔ

Or. 938, containing Books ii, iii and iv, is undated and was bought of G. David on Nov. 5, 1915. It contains 172 ff. of 25 × 16·8 c. and 21 ll. in quadruple columns (two *bayts* to the line), and is written in good, clear *ta'líq* with marginal notes and glosses. **Corpus 221,** dated 1041/1631–3, contains the poem without the prose prefaces, and is written in a small, neat *nasta'líq* on pages of 31 × 19 c. **Corpus 222,** undated, contains Books i, ii and iii (the first half of the poem) with the prefaces. It is well written in small *nasta'líq* on pages of 28·5 × 18 c., rather badly stained. **Corpus 223,** containing only Book i without the preface, was copied in 1135/1722–3 by Muhammad-i-Dihlawí, and is written in a large, clear *nasta'líq* on pages of 27 × 17 c. **King's 121,** dated 1081/1670–1, contains only the first half of the poem (Books i, ii and iii) and comprises 484 ff.

1133 (h) مثنوی ضمیر (قصّهٔ سوداگر) **Corpus, No. 66³**

The Story of the Merchant (*Qiṣṣa-i-Sawdágar*), a Hindustání *mathnawí* poem by Ḍamír. The MS. is dated 1243/1827–8 and is written in *ním-shikasta* on leaves of 25 × 15·25 c. This portion comprises ff. 7–13.

1134 (h) مثنوئ میرزا لطف **Corpus, No. 66⁴**

A Hindustání *mathnawí* poem by Mírzá Luṭf, following that mentioned above and occupying the next 10 ff. It is dated 1251/1835–6.

1135 (h) مثنوی مصحفی **Corpus, No. 66²**

Another Hindustání *mathnawí* poem by Muṣḥafí, being an imitation of a poem entitled *Daryá-yi-'Ishq* ("the Ocean of Love"). It fills the 6 ff. preceding **No. 1133** *supra*, and bears the same date, 1243/1827–8.

1136 (h) مثنوی ملکهٔ سیمتن **Corpus, No. 55**

Another Hindustání *Mathnawí* relating in a very much Persianized Urdú the adventures of Prince Máh-paykar and Queen Sím-tan. The MS. is undated but quite modern, comprises 379 pp. of 20 × 15 c., and is written in a good, clear *nasta'líq*.

1137, 1138 (h) مثنوی میر حسین **Corpus, No. 38**
Corpus, No. 66¹

Another Urdú poem entitled *Mathnawí-i-Mír Ḥusayn*. **No. 38,** dated A.D. 1812, comprises 87 ff. of 24 × 14·5 c., is written in *nasta'líq*, and ends with 7 ff. of medical prescriptions written in *shikasta*. **No. 66¹** consists of the first 98 ff. of the MS. mentioned above (**Nos. 1133–5**).

1139 (p) مثنویّات شیخ علی حزین **King's, No. 124**

The *mathnawí* poems of Shaykh 'Alí Ḥazín, who died in 1180/1766. See *B.M.P.C.*, pp. 372, 715–717, and Ethé's *Bodl.*

Pers. Cat., col. 1185. The seven poems contained in this MS. are:—(1) *Wadí'atu'l-Badí'a*; (2) *Ṣifr-i-Dil*; (3) *Kharábát*; (4) *Chiman u Aujuman*; (5) *Maṭmaḥu'l-Anẓár*; (6) *Farhang-náma*; (7) *Tadhkiratu'l-'Áshiqín*.

1140 (p) مجالس العشّاق **Or. 761 (8)**

The *Majálisu'l-'Ushsháq*, a pseudo-biography of some 76 eminent and saintly persons and their love-affairs, generally ascribed to Sulṭán Ḥusayn b. Bayqará, but according to Bábur (*Bábur-náma*, ed. Ilminsky, p. 221) really written by Kamálu'd-Dín Ḥusayn Gázargáhí. See *B.M.P.C.*, pp. 351–353. The MS., which is undated, was bought of Géjou on May 13, 1907. It contains 140 ff. of 20·5 × 12·7 c. and 19 ll., and is written in a small, neat Persian *ta'líq* with rubrications.

1141 (p) مجرّبات اکبری **Corpus, No. 12[5]**

Mujarrabat-i-Akbarí, a treatise on compound medicaments by Muhammad Akbar, known as Sháh Arzání, the author of several medical works, who wrote between A.H. 1112 and 1130 (A.D. 1700–1718). See *B.M.P.C.*, p. 480. This MS. is dated 1242/1826–7.

1142, 1143 (a) مجمع البحرَيْن و ملتقى النيّرَيْن **Add. 3639 (11)** **Or. 189 (10)**

Two copies of the *Majma'u'l-Baḥrayn wa Multaqa'n-Nayyirayn*, a work on Ḥanafí law by Aḥmad b. 'Alí...as-Sá'átí al-Ba'labakkí, who died in 696/1296. See Brockelmann, i, pp. 382–3; *B.M.A.S.*, p. 186, No. 284. **Add. 3639,** undated, was bought of Géjou on April 3, 1900, contains 168 ff. of 27 × 18 c. and 13 ll., and is written in a large, clear *naskh* with rubrications. **Or. 189,** dated 758/1357, was bought of Géjou on July 3, 1902, contains 117 ff. of 24·50 × 16·5 c. and 15 ll., and is written in an excellent old *naskh* with rubrications.

1144, 1145 (p) مجمع الصّنایع **Corpus, No. 23[1]** **Corpus, No. 28**

Two copies of the *Majma'u'ṣ-Ṣanáyi'*, a treatise on the Ars Poetica compiled in 1060/1650 by Niẓámu'd-Dín Aḥmad b. Muḥammad Ṣáliḥ aṣ-Ṣiddíqí al-Ḥusayní. See *B.M.P.C.*,

p. 814[b], xiii. Of these two MSS., **No. 28** is fuller and richer in poetical quotations. Both are undated. **No. 23**[1] comprises 81 ff. and is written in a careless *ta'líq*: **No. 28** is written in *ním-shikasta* on pages of 24·5 × 16 c.

1146 (p) مجمع الفرس **Or. 914 (12)**

The *Majma'u'l-Furs*, a well-known Persian lexicon compiled in 1008/1599–1600 by Muḥammad Qásim b. Ḥájji Muḥammad of Káshán, poetically surnamed Surúrí. See *B.M.P.C.*, pp. 498–500, and Ethé's *Bodl. Pers. Cat.*, col. 1342, No. 2478. This MS., from the Lynch Bequest, contains 237 ff. of 31·5 × 22·5 c. and 19 ll., and was transcribed in 1083/1672–3, by Aḥmad b. Ni'matu'lláh of Iṣṭahbánát in Shabánkára of Fárs.

1147 (t) مجمع اللّطائف **Or. 471 (8)**

The *Majma'u'l-Laṭá'if*, a theological work by Siráj b. 'Abdu'lláh. See *Camb. Hand-list*, p. 195. The MS., dated 1024/1615, was bought of Géjou on Jan. 29, 1904, is divided into five chapters, comprises 132 ff. of 20·7 × 14·5 c. and 17 ll., and is written in a large, clear, good Turkish *naskh*.

1148 (p) مجموع خانی **Corpus, No. 36**

Majmú'-i-Khání, a manual of Sunní law by Kamál Karím, dedicated to a certain Bahrám Khán. Cf. Ethé, *Bodl. Pers. Cat.*, No. 1782, and *Ind. Off. Pers. Cat.*, Nos. 2572–4. The MS. contains about 100 ff. of 23 × 19 c., is written in a very neat *naskh*, and is undated.

1149 (a) مجموع المستلقطات آلخ **Or. 940 (9)**

A collection of dialogues in Arabic on ancient mythology and other general topics with a long descriptive title beginning as above. It seems to have been prepared for press, and a note on f. 1[b] implies that it was printed, or was to be printed, in A.D. 1780 at Verona (فيرنا) at a Press called بوندشيا. The compiler appears to have been a priest named Rafaël Zachariah, who was a professor of Arabic in Paris in A.D. 1807. On the title-page are pencilled the following words: "*Mahometis*

Abdallae fillii (sic) *Antologia, Dialogo explicata.*" The MS. was presented to the Library by Mr S. Gaselee, Fellow of Magdalene College, Cambridge, in 1915, and contains 56 ff. of 22 × 15·1 c. and 19–20 ll.

1150 (h) مجموع هفت رساله **Corpus, No. 151**[1]

This portion of the volume is not a MS., but a collection of religious poems entitled *Faḍá'il-náma, Núr-náma, Shamá'il-náma*, etc, lithographed at Dihlí in 1272/1855–6, and comprising 48 pp.

1151 (p) مجموعة من تصانيف مير محمّد باقر داماد **King's, No. 8**

A collection of three treatises by the celebrated theologian and philosopher Mír Muḥammad Báqir Dámád, who died in 1040/1630–1. See *B.M.P.C.*, p. 835[a], xxviii. This collection professes to contain (i) *Nuskha-i-Taqwímát*; (ii) *Ímáḍát*; (iii) *Aṣ-Ṣiráṭu'l-Mustaqím*, but the second appears to be missing. The MS. is undated.

1152 (p) محشرنامه **Corpus, No. 100**

The *Maḥshar-náma*, an account of the signs of the Last Day, entitled *Qiyámat-náma* on the fly-leaf, but as above in the colophon, by Rafí'u'd-Dín. The MS. contains 36 ff. of 22 × 13 c., is written in a cursive *ta'líq*, and is dated 1231/1816.

1153 (t) محمّديّه **Or. 959 (7)**

A Turkish poem in praise of the Prophet Muḥammad, for recitation at religious festivals, untitled and defective at beginning. Ends:

بونجه نعمت حاضرلنمش قولونه ' مولد اوقودنلر يسون ديلر '

The MS., dated 1228/1813, contains 30 ff. of 19·3 × 14·2 c. and 15 ll., and is written in clear but coarse Turkish *nasta'líq*, fully pointed; copyist, Mullá 'Ísá b. Muḥammad. Presented in Feb. 1917 by 2nd Lieut. R. H. Aldis, who found it in a deserted house near Karakli, east of Lake Doiran.

1154–1156 (p) محمود و اياز **Or. 863 (10)**
Corpus, No. 50[1]
Corpus, No. 104

The Story of Sulṭán Maḥmúd and his favourite Ayáz in verse, by Zulálí, completed in 1024/1615. See *B.M.P.C.*, pp. 677–8. **Or. 863** was transcribed by Ghulám Ḥusayn of Qandahár at the end of 1253 (Feb. 1838), and was bought of Luzac in May, 1911. It contains 185 ff. of 24·3 × 14·3 c. and 19 ll., and is written in good *ta'líq* with rubrications, between red, blue and gold borders. **Corpus 50** only contains selections from the poem, is dated 1276/1859–1860, and comprises 22 ff. written in *nasta'líq* in four columns. **Corpus 104,** dated 1120/1708–9 and written in cursive *ta'líq*, contains 242 ff. of 21 × 11 c.

1157, 1158 (p) محمود نامه **Corpus, No. 166**
Corpus, No. 190[4]

Maḥmúd-náma, a collection of *ghazals* by a poet named Maḥmúd. **Corpus 166** is not a MS., but was lithographed at Lucknow in 1264/1848, and contains 16 pp. of 24 × 15 c. **Corpus 190** contains four unbound works tied together in a bundle. The fourth part of this appears to be identical with the lithograph mentioned above. It comprises 12 ff. of 21 × 16 c. and is written in *ta'líq*.

1159 (t) محيط **Or. 747 (8)**

A work on cosmography, navigation and travel, entitled *Muḥíṭ*, translated into Turkish by the celebrated Turkish admiral Sídí 'Alí b. Ḥusayn *Ra'ís* in 961/1554. A similar work by the same writer is mentioned by Rieu, *B.M.T.C.*, p. 120, under the title of *Khuláṣatu'l-Hay'at*. This MS., dated 1104/1692–3, was bought of Géjou on March 27, 1907.

1160–1162 (a) مختار الصّحاح **Add. 3673 (10)**
Or. 483 (8)
Or. 710 (7)

Three copies of the well-known abridgement of the *Ṣiḥáḥ* of al-Jawharí (died 393/1002) by Muḥammad b. Abí Bakr b. 'Abdu'l-Qádir ar-Rází (died 720/1320) entitled *Mukhtáru'ṣ-*

Ṣiḥáḥ. See Brockelmann, i, p. 128, and ii, pp. 200–201, *Camb. Hand-list*, p. 198, and *B.M.A.C.*, p. 227, No. ccccIxix. **Add. 3673,** dated 930/1524, contains 140 ff. of 25·9 × 18 c. and 29 ll., is written in a fair *nasta'líq* with rubrications, and was bought of Sethian on July 17, 1900. **Or. 483,** dated 995/1587, is one of 16 MSS. bought of Géjou on Aug. 18, 1904, contains 251 ff. of 20·7 × 14 c. and 23 ll., and is written in a good *nasta'líq* with rubrications. **Or. 710,** undated, was bought of Géjou in December, 1906, contains 270 ff. of 17·6 × 12·7 c. and 21 ll., and is written in a poor *nasta'líq* with rubrications.

1163 (a) المختار للفتوى **Or. 8** (8)

Al-Mukhtár li'l-Fatwá (or *li'l-Fatáwa*), with its commentary *al-Ikhtiyár*, both by Majdu'd-Dín al-Mawṣilí, who was born in 599/1202 and died in 683/1284. See Brockelmann, i, p. 382; *B.M.A.S.*, No. 282, pp. 185–6. Ff. 117 of 21·2 × 15 c. and 14 ll.; large coarse *naskh*; rubrications; dated 1120/1708–9. Bought of Géjou, Jan. 28, 1901.

1164 (p) مختصر البيان **Corpus, No. 51**[3]

Mukhtaṣaru'l-Bayán, excerpts from various medical works made by Muḥammad Badru'd-Dín b. Khwája Jamálu'd-Dín. Three leaves of 29 × 19 c. written in neat *nasta'líq*, dated 1268/1851–2.

1165 (a), **1166** (p) مختصر فى الطبّ **Or. 202** (8) **Add. 3658** (8)

Or. 202 (Arabic) purports to be an abridgement (*mukhtaṣar*) of the *Shifá* of Avicenna, but this seems doubtful. It comprises 75 ff. of 20·4 × 11·5 c. and 17 ll., is dated 843/1439–1440, is written in fair *naskh* and at the end in *ta'líq*, and was bought of Géjou on Oct. 23, 1902. **Add. 3658** contains portions of a Persian treatise on Medicine in four parts (*fann*), without title or author's name. It begins with ch. ii (on Antidotes), divided into four sections (*faṣl*), and ends in the middle of ch. xxxix. The title *Mukhtaṣar dar Ṭibb* occurs on f. 4[a]. Ff. 304 of 20 × 14·5 c. and 17 ll., poor but clear *naskh* with rubrications, undated, bought of Sethian, May 21, 1900.

1167, 1168 (a) مختصر القدوری **Add. 3728 (9)**
Or. 576 (10)

The *Mukhtaṣar* of al-Qudúrí, who was born in 362/972 and died in 428/1036. See Brockelmann, i, pp. 174–5, *Camb. Hand-list*, p. 199. **Add. 3728,** containing the text, comprises 166 ff. of 21·3 × 16 c. and 13 ll., is written in large, clear *naskh* with rubrications, is undated, and was bought of Naaman on Nov. 23, 1900. **Or. 576** contains a commentary on the second half of the same work by Abú Naṣr Aḥmad b. Muḥammad al-Baghdádí, commonly known as al-Aqṭa'. It contains 195 ff. of 27·2 × 18 c. and 21 ll., is written in good *naskh* with rubrications and completed on the 15th of Ṣafar, 851/May 1, 1447 by Ṭáhir b. Ibráhím b. Jibra'íl b. Aḥmad b. 'Abdu'lláh b. Ibráhím of Diyár Bakr, and was bought of Géjou on July 14, 1905.

1169 (a) مختصر المنتهی **Or. 451 (9)**

The *Mukhtaṣaru'l-Muntahá*, the abridgement of Ibnu'l-Ḥájib's *Muntahá* by the Qáḍí 'Aḍudu'd-Dín al-Íjí (d. 756/1355) with the glosses of as-Sayyidu'sh-Sharífu'l-Jurjání. Ff. 152 of 21·9 × 12·4 c. and 23 ll., written in good small *naskh* and dated 989/1581–2. Copied by Sa'd b. Muḥammad al-Jazá'irí al-Asadí, and bought of Hannan and Watson on August 29, 1903.

1170 (a) مختصر فی النّحو **King's, No. 243**

A compendium of Arabic grammar by Shihábu'd-Dín b. Shamsu'd-Dín b. 'Umar az-Záwulí ad-Dawlatábádí, who died in 849/1445. See Brockelmann, ii, p. 220. This MS. appears to be identical with the work entitled *Irshád* there described, and to contain a commentary on it by Siráju'd-Dín...al-Íjí. The MS. is written in clear *naskh* on pages of 23·2 × 14·5 c. and was transcribed on Rajab 9, 1044/Dec. 29, 1634.

1171, 1172 (p) مخزن الاسرار نظامی **Corpus, No. 161**
Corpus, No. 234

Two copies of the *Makhzanu'l-Asrár* of Niẓámí of Ganja. See above *s.v.* خمسهٔ نظامی. **No. 161** comprises 62 ff. of

24 × 15 c., is written in fair *nasta'líq*, and was copied by one Aḥmad about 1023/1614–5. **No. 234,** undated, is written in cursive *nasta'líq* on leaves of 22 × 13 c.

1173 (af.) مخزن الاسلام **Or. 606** (9)

The *Makhzanu'l-Islám*, a Pushtú or Afghán work on Islám by Ákhúnd Darwíza (d. A.D. 1638) amplified by his son Karímdád. Other copies exist in the British Museum and elsewhere. Ff. 195 of 25 × 14·5 c. and 13 ll.; large, clear *naskh* with rubrications; undated. Presented by Professor A. A. Bevan on Oct. 5, 1905.

1174 (p) مخزن افغانی **Christ's, Dd. 3. 1**

The *Makhzan-i-Afghání* of Ni'matu'lláh Bey, composed at the end of 1021 (Feb. 1613). See *B.M.P.C.*, pp. 210–212. The MS. contains 430 ff., is written in a large, clear Indian *ta'líq*, and was copied near Oude in 1181/1767–8.

1175 (a) مدارك الأحكام فی شرح شرایع الاسلام **Or. 440** (11)

The *Madáriku'l-Aḥkám*, a commentary by Sayyid Muḥammad b. 'Alí b. Ḥusayn b. Abi'l-Ḥasan al-Ḥusayní on the *Sharáyi'u'l-Islám*, a well-known work on Shí'ite jurisprudence by Najmu'd-Dín Ja'far al-Muḥaqqiqu'l-Ḥillí. See Brockelmann, i, p. 406, and the *Berlin Arab. Cat.*, No. 4647. The MS., written in a small *naskh* with rubrications, contains 240 ff. of 28·7 × 18·3 c. and 29 ll., and was bought of Hannan and Watson on Aug. 29, 1903.

1176, 1177 (a) مراح الارواح **Or. 419** (6)
Or. 922 (6)

Two MSS. of the *Maráḥu'l-Arwáḥ*, a well-known manual of Arabic grammar composed about the beginning of the 8th (fourteenth Christian) century by Aḥmad b. 'Alí b. Mas'úd. See Brockelmann, ii, p. 21. **Or. 419** comprises ff. 113 of 16·5 × 10·5 c. and 13 ll.; good *naskh*; rubrications; undated. Bought of Géjou, Aug. 29, 1903. **Or. 922,** copied in 1098/1687, contains ff. 32 of 19·4 × 13 c. and 16 ll., and is written in a clear *naskh* with rubrications. Lynch Bequest.

1178, 1179 (a) **Or. 908 (12)**
Or. 839 (6)

مراة الجنان و عبرة اليقظان فى معرفة حوادث الزّمان

The *Mirátu'l-Janán* of al-Yáfi'í, born in 698/1298, died in 768/1367. See Brockelmann, ii, pp. 176–7. **Or. 908** contains the years A.H. 1–750 and appears to be complete. It is undated and forms part of the Lynch Bequest. It contains 399 ff. of 30·5 × 21 c. and 31 ll., and is written in a good, clear *naskh*, the last few leaves supplied in a modern hand. **Or. 839** only contains an abridgement of the work (filling ff. 1–76) by Ya'qúb b. Sayyíd 'Alí. This is followed by (2) the *Iṣláḥu's-saqaṭat* (on errors of speech) of Kamál Páshá-záda, who died in 940/1533 (ff. 81–95). See Brockelmann, ii, p. 452, No. 107. (3) *Ráḥatu'l-Arwáḥ fí raf'i'l-Ashbáḥ* (ff. 96–101) by the same. See Brockelmann, *loc. cit.*, No. 102. (4) Commentary on the *Khamriyya* of Ibnu'l-Fáriḍ (ff. 102–117), who died in 632/1235. See Brockelmann, i, pp. 262–3. (5) A few more short tracts (ff. 117–127), including one or two more by Kamál Páshá-záda. This MS., which was bought of Naaman on Feb. 8, 1911, comprises 127 ff. of 15·5 × 10·4 c. and 17 ll., and is written in a small, neat *nasta'líq* with rubrications, undated, probably 16th century.

1180 (p) (مرات جهان نما (تاريخ سلاطين دهلى **King's, No. 109**

The *Mirát-i-Jahán-namá* of Muḥammad Baqá (died in 1094/1683), edited by his brother Muḥammad Riḍá. See *B.M.P.C.*, pp. 890–891, and Palmer's *King's Cat.*, p. 7.

1181 (t) مراة الكائنات **Or. 599 (8)**

The *Mirátu'l-Ká'inát* of Nishánjí-záda Muḥammad b. Aḥmad. See *B.M.T.C.*, pp. 29–30. The MS., dated 17 Jumáda ii, 1164 (May 13, 1751), was bought of Géjou on Oct. 30, 1905. It contains 481 ff. of 20·7 × 14·7 c. and 21 ll., and is written in a fair Turkish *nasta'líq* with rubrications.

1182 (a) مراتع الغزلان فى وصف الغلمان **Add. 3620 (8)**

Marátí'u'l-Ghizlán fí waṣfi'l-Ghilmán, by the Qáḍi 'Alá'u'd-Dín 'Alí b. Muḥammad as-Sa'dí, commonly called Ibn 'Abdu'ẓ-

Ẓáhir, who died in 717/1317–1318. See Ḥájji Khalífa, No. 11756. The MS. is dated 1083/1672–3, and was bought of Géjou on Feb. 14, 1900. It contains 168 ff. (f. 1 missing) of 20·4 × 13 c. and 19 ll. and is written in good *naskh*, pointed, with rubrications.

1183 (a) مروج الذهب و معادن الجوهر **Or. 909** (12)

Part of al-Mas'údí's *Murúju'dh-Dhahab*. See Brockelmann, i, pp. 143–145. The MS., incomplete and undated, belongs to the Lynch Bequest, is written in a good *naskh*, and contains 310 ff. of 29·3 × 18·3 c. and 30 ll.

1184–1187 (a) مزامير داود {**Or. 878** (7), **Or. 929** (10), **Trinity, R.13.12**, **Trinity, R.13.57**}

The Psalms (*Mazámír*) of David in Arabic. **Or. 878,** copied at Iṣfahán in 1095/1684 and collated by Muḥammad Zamán the physician, was bought of G. David on Feb. 28, 1912. It contains 260 ff. of 17 × 10·8 c. and 9 ll., and is written in good *naskh* with rubrications within gold borders. **Or. 929,** forming part of the Lynch Bequest, is a polyglot Psalter in Arabic, Syriac, Greek, and Hebrew. It includes the Psalms from xvii, 15 to the end, besides a fragment (1 leaf) of Exodus xv, and a fragment (1 leaf) of Deuteronomy xxxii. Mr Leo Jung, who kindly examined the text, says that the Syriac version is not the Peshitto text, but agrees with the Syriac Psalms edited by Caietanus Bugatus in the Bibliotheca Ambrosiana (1820). The MS. contains 185 ff. of 25 × 17 c., defective at the beginning and end. **R.13.12** was copied in A.D. 1595 at the Maronite College at Rome in a bad European hand with rubrications, and contains 204 ff. **R.13.57** contains 226 ff. For these two last MSS. see Palmer's *Trin. Cat.*, pp. 23–24 and 146–7.

1188 (a) **Add. 3623**[3] (7)

مساعد الطلّاب فى الكشف عن قواعد الاعراب

A brief treatise on Arabic grammar entitled *Musá'idu'ṭ-Ṭulláb* ("the Student's Aid") by Jamálu'd-Dín Muḥammad al-Marjání. The MS. was bought of Géjou on Feb. 14, 1900, is dated 891/1486, and is written in a large, clear *naskh* with rubrications. This portion occupies ff. 60–71.

1189 (a) المسلك السّهل (شرح على التوشيح البديع) **Or. 890 (9)**

Al-Maslaku's-Sahl, a commentary on at-*Tawshíhu'l-Badí'*, by Ibráhím b. Sahl. The MS., dated 1256/1840–1, was bought of G. David on Dec. 20, 1912. It contains 231 pp. of 22·2 × 17·6 c. and 19 ll., is written in a Maghribí hand, pointed, with rubrications, and is punctuated in red and white.

1190 (p) مشابهات ربيعى **Corpus, No. 91**

Mushábahát-i-Rabí'í ("Vernal Similitudes"), one of the minor works of Mullá Ṭughrá of Mashhad, one of the Court poets of Sháh-Jahán. See *B.M.P.C.*, p. 743, xii. The MS., undated, contains 68 ff. of 21 × 12 c., and is written in *nasta'líq*.

1191 (a) المشارب الهنئيّة و الموارد الشمسيّة **Trinity, R. 13. 43[1]**

Al-Mashāribu'l-Haní'iyya wa'l-Mawáridu'sh-Shamsiyya, by Burhánu'd-Dín al-Qayruwání. See Palmer's *Trin. Cat.*, pp. 92–100. This portion of the MS. occupies pp. 1–91.

119 (t) مشاقّ العُشّاق **Or. 469[2] (8)**

The *Masháqqu'l-'Ushsháq* ("Lovers' troubles"), by Nargisí, who died in 1044/1634–5. See Flügel's *Vienna Cat.*, vol. ii, pp. 264–5; Pertsch's *Berlin Turkish Cat.*, No. 145, pp. 163–4. This MS. was bought of Géjou on Jan. 29, 1904, and appears to be dated 1160/1747. This portion occupies ff. 72–118, and is written in a small, neat *nasta'líq* on pages of 21 × 11·5 c. and 23 ll.

1193 (p) **Or. 521 (8)**

المصابيح السلطانيّة فى الابعاد النجوميّة و الاجرام البسيطة

A Persian work on Astronomy entitled *al-Maṣábíḥu's-Sulṭániyya etc.* The MS. is one of thirty bought of Hannan and Watson on August 20, 1904; is dated 1250/1834–5; comprises 88 ff. of 21 × 14·8 c. and 20 ll., and is written in a poor *ta'líq* with rubrications.

1194 (a, p) مصابيح القلوب Corpus, No. 200

Maṣábíḥu'l-Qulúb ("Hearts' Lamps"), a collection of traditions in Arabic with Persian translation and commentary, in 53 chapters, by al-Ḥasan ash-Shí'í (?) of Sabzawár. The MS. was transcribed by 'Alí b. Riḍá of Dínpúr (?) in 1183/1769–1770, and is written in *naskh* on pages of 25 × 16 c.

1195 (a) المصباح المنير فى غريب الشرح الكبير Or. 496 (8)

Al-Miṣbáḥu'l-munír fí gharíbi'sh-Sharḥi'l-Kabír, by Aḥmad b. Muḥammad b. 'Alí al-Muqrí al-Fayyúmí, who died in 770/1368. See Brockelmann, ii, p. 25; *B.M.A.S.*, p. 587, Nos. 867–9. This MS., undated, is one of thirty bought of Messrs Hannan and Watson on Aug. 20, 1904, and comprises 255 ff. of 21 × 15 c. and 27 ll. It is written in fair *naskh* with rubrications, is incomplete at the end, and is undated.

1196 (p) مصباح طريق Or. 434 (6)

A Persian mystical work entitled *Miṣbáḥ-i-Ṭaríq* ("the Lamp of the Path") by Abu'l-Ḥasan b. Muḥammad 'Alí of Yazd. This MS., bought of Hannan and Watson on Aug. 29, 1903, comprises 169 ff. of 15 × 10·25 c. and 12 ll. and is defective at the end.

1197 (p) مصباح المبتدى Corpus, No. 196

A Persian grammar entitled *Miṣbáḥu'l-Mubtadí* ("the Beginner's Lamp"), by Muḥammad Raḥím 'Alí Khán, who lived at Sikandarpúr in the time of Khán Muẓaffar Jang Bahádur. The MS., undated, is written in cursive *nasta'alíq* on pages of 24 × 15 c.

1198 (p) مصيبت نامهٔ عطّار Or. 685³ (9)

A few selections from the *Muṣíbat-náma* of Shaykh Faríd'd-Dín 'Aṭṭár occupying ff. 100–113 of the MS. described under **Nos. 732** and **734** *supra* and **1265** *infra*, which was bought of Géjou on May 10, 1906.

1199 (a) مطالع الانظار فى شرح طوالع الانوار Or. 7 (10)

The *Maṭáli'u'l-Anẓár*, a commentary by Maḥmúd b. 'Abdu'r-Raḥmán b. Aḥmad b. Muḥammad b. Abí Bakr al-

Iṣfahání, who died in 749/1348, on the *Ṭawáli'u'l-Anwár* (see **No. 844,** pp. 138–9 *supra*) of the Qáḍí 'Abdu'lláh b. 'Umar al-Bayḍáwí, who died in 685/1286. See for the former Brockelmann, ii, pp. 110–111, and for the latter, *Ibid.*, i, 416–418. The MS., bought of Géjou on Jan. 28, 1901, contains 208 ff. of 26·5 × 16·3 c. and 21 ll., and is written in a poor *nasta'líq* and undated.

1200–1203 (a) مطالع الانوار **Add. 3741 (7) / Or. 656 (9) / King's, No. 148 / King's, No. 247**

The *Lawámi'u'l-Asrár*, a commentary by Quṭbu'd-Dín Muḥammad...ar-Rází at-Taḥtání (d. 766/1364) on the *Maṭáli'u'l-Anwár* of Siráju'd-Dín Maḥmúd b. Abí Bakr al-Urmawí (d. 682/1283). See for the latter Brockelmann, i, p. 467, and for the former *Ibid.*, p. 209. **Add. 3741,** bought of Sethian on Nov. 28, 1900 and dated 1014/1605–6, contains only the second half of the commentary. It comprises 238 ff. of 18·3 × 12·2 c. and 21 ll., and is written in a small, neat *naskh*. **Or. 656** contains a gloss (*ḥáshiya*) on the above-mentioned *Lawámi'* by as-Sayyidu'sh-Sharífu'l-Jurjání (d. 816/1413). It was transcribed by Maḥmúd b. Ḥasan al-Múqání in 889/1484; bought of Géjou on Feb. 12, 1906; comprises 142 ff. of 24 × 14·3 c. and 21 ll.; and is written in a poor *nasta'líq* with rubrications. **King's 148** contains the gloss of al-Jurjání mentioned above, was transcribed in 994/1586 by 'Abdu'l-Jalíl, and is written in an excellent *naskh*, the text overlined with red. **King's 247,** undated, also contains a commentary on the *Maṭáli'*.

1204 (p) مطالع الانوار **Corpus, No. 205[2]**

An anonymous Persian biography of the Prophet Muḥammad entitled *Maṭáli'u'l-Anwár*, followed by a number of chapters on Muslim eschatology. The MS. was transcribed in the 23rd year of Muḥammad Sháh (= 1153/1740–1).

1205 (a) مطلع خصوص الكلم فى معانى فصوص الحكم **Or. 494[1] (9)**

Maṭla'u Khuṣúṣi'l-Kalam fí ma'ání Fuṣúṣi'l-Ḥikam, a commentary on the celebrated *Fuṣúṣu'l-Ḥikam* of Ibnu'l-

'Arabí (d. 638/1240) by his disciple Ṣadru'd-Dín al-Qúnyawí (d. 673/1274). See Brockelmann, i, pp. 441–448. The MS., of which this treatise forms the first portion (ff. 1–36) is undated, and is one of thirty MSS. bought of Hannan and Watson on Aug. 20, 1904. It is written in good *naskh* with rubrications on pages of 22·75 × 15 c. and 19 ll.

1206, 1207 (p) مطلع السَّعْدَيْن **Or. 267, 268 (10) Christ's, Dd. 3. 5**

Two copies of the *Maṭla'u's-Sa'dayn* of 'Abdu'r-Razzáq b. Isḥáq of Samarqand, the first in two volumes. See *B.M.P.C.*, pp. 181 *et seqq.*; Ethé's *Bodl. Cat.*, col. 91. **Or. 267** (vol. i) contains 569 ff. of 24·8 × 16 c. and 15 ll., is written in a clear, modern Indian *ta'líq* with rubrications, and is undated. **Or. 268** (vol. ii) contains 341 ff. of 22 × 12·4 c. and 22 ll., and is written in a neat Persian *ta'líq*. It is defective at the end and undated. Both of these volumes form part of the Cowell Bequest. The **Christ's MS.**, written in a good neat *ta'líq* with rubrications, is dated 27 Dhu'l-Ḥijja, 989 (= Jan. 22, 1582), and contains 532 ff. of 23·6 × 17 c. and 22 ll.

1208, 1209 (a) المطوّل على تلخيص المفتاح **Or. 199 (12) King's, No. 242**

The *Muṭawwal*, a well-known commentary by Sa'du'd-Dín at-Taftázání (d. 791/1389) on the *Talkhíṣu'l-Miftáḥ* of al-Khaṭíbu'd-Dimashqí (d. 739/1338), which is itself an abridgement of Part III of the *Miftáḥu'l-'Ulúm* of as-Sakkákí (d. 626/1229). See Brockelmann, i, pp. 294–6; *B.M.A.C.*, p. 254; *B.M.A.S.*, p. 621, No. 983. **Or. 199,** dated 1092/1681, was bought of Géjou on Oct. 23, 1902, contains 254 ff. of 30·3 × 20·5 c. and 21 ll., and is written in a good Persian *ta'líq* with rubrications. **King's 242** contains a commentary by Ḥusayn b. Shihábu'd-Dín ash-Shámí on the verses cited in the *Muṭawwal*. It is written in a large legible *ta'líq* hand, with the text overlined in red, on pages of 21·8 × 14 c., and is undated.

1210 (p) مظهر العجائب **Or. 651[1] (8)**

The *Maẓ-haru'l-'Ajá'ib*, one of the *mathnawí* poems of Shaykh Farídu'd-Dín 'Aṭṭár. See *B.M.P.C.*, p. 579. The MS., dated 17 Rabí'i, 1201 (= Jan. 17, 1787) was copied at Lucknow, and was bought at the O'Kinealy sale on Jan. 15, 1906. It is written in a clear *ta'líq* with rubrications on ff. 1–82 of 19·3 × 11 c. and 15 ll.

1211 (p) معارج النبوّة فی مدارج النبوّة **King's, No. 76**

The *Ma'ariju'n-Nubuwwa fí Madáriji'n-Nubuwwa*, a history of the Prophet Muḥammad by Mu'ínu'd-Dín b. Ḥájji Muḥammad al-Faráhí, who died at Herát in 907/1501–2. See *B.M.P.C.*, pp. 149–150; Ethé's *I. O. Pers. Cat.*, col. 138; and Dorn in vol. vii of the *Mélanges Asiatiques* (1874), p. 400, where the latter part of the title is better given as *Madáriji'l-Futuwwa.*

1212 (p) معالجات شفائی (= خلاصهٔ شفائی) **Add. 3753 (10)**

The *Mu'álaja* or *Khuláṣa-i-Shifá'í*, a work on Materia Medica probably identical with the *Ṭibb-i-Shifá'í.* See *B.M.P.C.*, pp. 473–4, Ethé's *I. O. Pers. Cat.*, col. 1264, etc. The MS., dated 1076/1665–6, was bought of Géjou on Dec. 8, 1900, contains 138 ff. of 24·5 × 19 c. and 20 ll., and is written in a coarse Persian *naskh* with rubrications.

1213, 1214 (p) المعجم فی آثار ملوك العجم **Or. 519 (9)**
King's, No. 116

The *Mu'jam fí áthári Mulúki'l-'Ajam*, a history of the pre-Islamic kings of Persia by Faḍlu'lláh al-Ḥusayní. See *B.M.P.C.*, pp. 811–812 and 1065; Ethé's *Bodl. Cat.*, No. 285. **Or. 519,** defective both at beginning and end, was bought of Hannan and Watson on Aug. 20, 1904, and comprises 140 ff. of 21·9 × 13 c. and 15 ll. It is written in a clear *ta'líq* with rubrications. The beginning corresponds with p. 67 of the lithographed edition. **King's 116,** written in a small *ta'líq*, comprises 178 ff. and is undated.

1215, 1216 (a) المعلّقات السبع (شرح) **Trinity, R. 13. 13**
Or. 501 (8)

Two copies of the seven *Mu'allaqát* with commentaries. The **Trinity MS.** contains the commentary of az-Zawzaní, is dated A.D. 1316, and comprises 102 ff. written in a legible hand. See Palmer's *Trin. Cat.*, pp. 24–26. **Or. 501** contains a commentary by Aḥmad b. Muḥammad b. 'Abdu'l-Karím al-Músawí, entitled *Miftáḥu'l-Mughlaqát fí Sharḥi'l-Mu'allaqát.* It is dated 1273/1856–7 and is one of thirty MSS. bought of Hannan and Watson on August 20, 1904. It comprises 190 ff. of 21·2 × 15·5 c. and 16 ll., and is written in a good *naskh* with rubrications, the text in rather a larger hand.

1217–1219 (a) مُغْنى اللبيب عن كتب الاعاريب **{Or. 65 (10) Or. 66 (8) Fitzwilliam, No. 191**

Three copies of the *Mughni'l-Labíb*, a well-known work on Arabic grammar composed in 749/1348 by 'Abdu'llah...b. Hishám. See Brockelmann, ii, pp. 23–5. **Or. 65** and **66** were both bought of Géjou with four other MSS. on May 11, 1901. The former is dated 1086/1675–6, comprises 224 ff. of 24·3 × 12·2 c. and 27 ll., and is written in a neat *naskh* with rubrications and copious marginal notes. **Or. 66,** undated, contains 162 ff. of 20·3 × 14·8 c. and 27 ll., and is written in a small, neat *naskh*. The **Fitzwilliam MS.,** dated 1077/1666–7, comprises 377 ff. of 19·8 × 15 c. and 19 ll., and is written in a fair *naskh* with rubrications.

1220 (t) مفتاح الجنّة **Trinity, R.13.40**

Miftáḥu'l-Jannat ("the Key of Paradise"), by Aḥmad aṭ-Ṭawíl. See Palmer's *Trin. Cat.*, pp. 87–88.

1221–1224 (a) مفتاح العلوم (القسم الثالث) **{Or. 176 (7) Or. 659 (10) Or. 705 (10) Trinity, R.13.6**

Four MSS. of the third part of the well-known *Miftáḥu'l-'Ulúm* of as-Sakkákí. See *B.M.A.S.*, p. 620, No. 981; Brockelmann, i, pp. 294–6, etc. **Or. 176,** dated 894/1489, and bought of Géjou on Jan. 1, 1902, comprises 132 ff. of 18 × 11·2 c. and 15 ll., and is written in a cramped but clear *ta'líq* with rubrications and marginal notes. **Or. 659,** dated 1087/1676, contains the shorter commentary of Sa'du'd-Dín at-Taftazání. It was bought of Géjou on Feb. 12, 1906, contains 162 ff. of

24·3 × 12·3 c. and 22 ll., and is written in a good *naskh*, the text overlined in red. **Or. 705** contains the commentary of as-Sayyidu'sh-Sharífu'l-Jurjání, and was bought of Géjou in December, 1906. It comprises 243 ff. of 25 × 15·2 c. and 25 ll., and is written in a fair *nasta'líq* with rubrications. The **Trinity MS.** also contains the commentary of Sa'du'd-Dín at-Taftazání entitled *Miftáḥu'l-Miftáḥ*. See Palmer's *Trin. Cat.*, pp. 15–16.

1225 (a) مفتاح الغيب **Or. 494² (9)**

The *Miftáḥu'l-Ghayb* of Shaykh Ṣadru'd-Dín al-Qunyawí (d. 672/1273). See Brockelmann, i, pp. 449–450. This part of the MS., which is one of thirty bought of Hannan and Watson on Aug. 20, 1904, comprises ff. 38–105 of 22·75 × 15 c. and 19 ll. It is undated.

1226 (a) مفتاح الفلاح **Or. 171 (8)**

The *Miftáḥu'l-Faláḥ* of Shaykh Bahá'u'd-Dín al-'Ámilí, who died in 1030/1621. See Brockelmann, ii, pp. 414–415. Ff. 116 of 18·6 × 12·1 c. and 15 ll.; fair *naskh* with rubrications. Bought of Naaman, Dec. 6, 1901. The colophon contains the absurd date 785!

1227 (p) مفتاح القلوب **Christ's, Dd.4.6**

The third volume of an anonymous history in Persian containing an account of Chingíz Khán and his successors, Tímúr, the Ottoman Sultans, the "Black" and "White Sheep" dynasties, the Uzbeks, etc. Ff. 564 of 26·7 × 15·7 c. and 21 ll.

1228 (p) مفتاح الكنوز **Add. 3616² (10)**

The *Miftáḥu'l-Kunúz* ("Key of Treasures"), a treatise on Geomancy etc., by Muḥammad b. Jalál b. 'Abdu'lláh al-Ḥusayní, who appears to have compiled it in 968/1560–1 from an original composed in Yazd in 735/1334–5. The MS., dated 1099/1688, was bought of Géjou in 1899. This part of it occupies ff. 70–117 of 24 × 17 c. and 21 ll., and is written in a fair *ta'líq* with rubrications.

1229, 1230 (p) مفرّح القلوب **Corpus, No. 96**
Jesus, No. 8

Two copies of a Persian version of the Sanskrit *Hitopadesa* entitled *Mufarriḥu'l-Qulúb* ("the Gladdener of Hearts"), both fairly modern. See *B.M.P.C.*, p. 757; *Camb. Pers. Cat.*, pp. 404–6.

1231 (a) مقالات فى الطبّ **Add. 3742** (8)

Anonymous "Discourses on Medicine" (*Maqálát fi'ṭ-Ṭibb*), three in number, dealing with Pathology and Therapeutics. The MS., bought through Géjou from one Khayyáṭ on Dec. 2, 1900, is undated. It contains 263 ff. of 19·2 × 11·6 c. and 19 ll., and is written in a small and neat but rather illegible Persian *nim-shikasta*.

1232 (a) مقامات الحريرى **Or. 919** (8)

The *Maqámát* of al-Ḥaríri (ff. 1–314), followed by the criticisms of Ibnu'l-Khashsháb. See Brockelmann, i, pp. 276–8. The MS., forming part of the Lynch Bequest of January, 1915, was transcribed by Muḥammad Ṣalíḥ in 1179–1180/1765–7, and comprises 333 ff. of 21·6 × 15 c. and 9 ll. It is written in a clumsy *naskh*, fully pointed, with rubrications and interlinear notes, and contains (ff. 315–317) a biography of al-Ḥaríri.

1233 (a) المقامة اللطيفة **Or. 35³** (8)

Al-Maqámatu'l-Laṭífa, one of the *Maqámát* of Jalálu'd-Dín as-Suyúṭí (d. 911/1505). See Brockelmann, ii, p. 158, No. 302. This MS., dated 1253/1837–8, was bought of Naaman on Feb. 5, 1901. This portion comprises ff. 29–52 of 21 × 15·4 c. and 23 ll., and is written in fair *naskh*.

1234 (t) المقدّمة الهاشميّة فيما يتعلّق باللّغة الفارسيّة **Or. 59** (10)

Al-Muqaddamatu'l-Háshimiyya, an anonymous Turkish treatise on Persian grammar and Rhetoric. The MS., undated, was bought of Naaman on March 4, 1901, comprises 134 ff. of 25·4 × 13 c. and 25 ll., and is written in a good modern Turkish *naskh* with rubrications.

1235 (p) مقصد اقصی **Or. 697 (8)**

The *Maqṣad-i-Aqṣá* of ʻAzíz b. Muḥammad an-Nasafí. See *B.M.P.C.*, p. 834, xxv. The MS., which is apparently incomplete at the end and undated, was bought of Géjou in Dec. 1906. It contains 65 ff. of 20 × 12·6 c. and 19 ll., and is written in a good *naskh* with rubrications.

1236, 1237 (p) مقطّعات ابن يمين **Or. 257[4] (8)**
Or. 504 (8)

Two MSS. of the "Fragments" (*Muqaṭṭaʻát*) of the poet Ibn Yamín, who died in 745/1344–5. See *B.M.P.C.*, p. 825b, iii. Neither MS. is dated. **Or. 257** forms part of the Cowell Bequest, contains ff. 40 of 20·3 × 15 c. and 13 ll., and is written in a good *taʻlíq*. **Or. 504,** one of thirty MSS. bought of Hannan and Watson on Aug. 20, 1904, contains 86 ff. of 20·8 × 13·6 c. and 15 ll., is written in a Persian *shikasta-ámíz*, and appears to be incomplete at the end.

1238 (a) المقفّى **Or. 935 (8)**

A fragment of al-Maqrízí's *Muqaffá* copied by the late Professor M. J. de Goeje and so certified by his note and signature. Presented by the late Mrs Wright, but no record of date. See Brockelmann, ii, p. 39, No. 4. Ff. 12 of 21 × 17 c. and 20 ll.

1239 (p) مكاتبات عبد الله قطب بن محيى **Or. 517 (7)**

Persian letters (*Mukátabát*) of ʻAbdu'lláh Quṭb b. Muḥiy, mostly on religious topics, addressed to various persons. The MS., dated 1280/1863–4, was bought of Hannan and Watson on August 20, 1904, contains 262 ff. of 17·6 × 11·2 c. and 12 ll., and is written in a poor but legible Persian *naskh*.

1240 (p) مكاشفات رضوى (شرح مثنوى) **King's, No. 241**

A commentary on the *Mathnawí* of Jalálu'd-Dín Rúmí by Muḥammad Riḍá, composed in 1084/1673–4. See Ethé's *India Office Pers. Cat.*, No. 1105. The MS. is dated 1130/1718.

1241 (a)   ملتقى الأَبْحُر   Or. 203 (8)

Multaqa'l-Abḥur, a manual of Ḥanafí law by Burhánu'd-Dín Muḥammad al-Ḥalabí, who died in 956/1549. See Brockelmann, ii, p. 432. The MS., dated 1111/1699–1700, was bought of Géjou on Oct. 23, 1902, contains 199 ff. of 20·8 × 11·9 c., and is written in a good *ta'líq* with rubrications.

1242 (a)   ملحة الاعراب و سبحة الآداب   Add. 3623⁵ (7)

The *Mulḥatu'l-I'ráb* of al-Ḥarírí, who died in 515/1122. See Brockelmann, i, p. 277, No. vii. The MS., dated 891/1486 was bought of Géjou on Feb. 14, 1900. This portion occupies ff. 74–86 of 17·2 × 13 c. and 17 ll., and is written in a large, clear *naskh* with rubrications.

1243, 1244 (a) الملخّص فى الهيئة البسيطة Or. 593 (7)
                                        Trinity, R.13.21

The *Mulakhkhaṣ*, a compendium of Astronomy by al-Jaghmíní, who died in 618/1221. See Brockelmann, i, p. 473. The **Trinity MS.**, which contains also a commentary on the text, comprises 109 ff. and is written in *naskh*. See Palmer's *Trin. Cat.*, pp. 50–52. **Or. 593,** dated 764/1362–3, was bought of Géjou on Oct. 30, 1905, contains 38 ff. of 18·5 × 13·5 c. and 15 ll., and is written in a clear old *naskh* with rubrications.

1245, 1246 (p)   ملفوظات امير تيمور   King's, No. 93
                                        King's, No. 93*

Two separate copies (not, as appears from the numbering, one copy in two volumes) of the *Malfúzát* or so-called Memoirs of Tímúr, against the authenticity of which Dr Rieu has produced such cogent arguments. See *B.M.P.C.*, pp. 177–180; Ethé's *India Office Pers. Cat.*, col. 84–6, etc. The first MS., dated 1126/1714, contains 193 ff.; the second, undated, 148 ff.

1247 (a)   من لا يحضره الفقيه   Or. 493 (11)

Man lá yaḥḍuruhu'l-Faqíh (a title which may be paraphrased as "Every man his own Lawyer") by the notable Shí'ite jurisconsult and theologian Ibn Bábawayhi (or Bábúya) of Qum, who died in 381/991. See Brockelmann, i, p. 187. This MS., which is only the third volume of the work, is dated 1110/1698–9, was bought of Hannan and Watson on Aug. 29, 1904, and contains 311 ff. of 29·1 × 17·6 c. and 21 ll.

1248 (a) منار الانوار (حاشية على—) **Add. 3609** (8)

The gloss (*háshiya*) of 'Azmí-záda (d. 1040/1630) on the *Manáru'l-Anwár* of Abu'l-Barakát 'Abdu'lláh...an-Nasafí (d. 710/1310). See Brockelmann, ii, p. 196. The MS., dated 1067/1657, was bought of Géjou in 1899, contains 160 ff. of 21 × 14 c., and 23 ll., and is written in a legible *naskh* with rubrications.

1249 (t) مناسك الحجّ **Or. 536** (8)

A Turkish poem by Bakhtí on the Rites of the Pilgrimage (*Manásiku'l-Ḥájj*), beginning:

احمد لله على كلّ حال، كيف يؤدّيه لسان المقال،

بر در آنك شبه و نظيرى عديم، موهبهٔ لطفى جهانه عديم،

The MS., dated 1056/1646, was one of eleven bought of Géjou on Nov. 1, 1904, contains 39 ff. of 21·8 × 12·9 c. and 15 ll., and is written in a good *ta'líq*.

1250 (p) مناظر الانشاء **Or. 779** (8)

A Persian treatise on the art of literary composition, entitled *Manáziru'l-Inshá*, by Maḥmúd b. Shaykh Muḥammad of Gílán (d. 886/1481–2). See *B.M.P.C.*, pp. 527–8. The MS., copied at Constantinople in 926/1520, was bought of Géjou on Jan. 7, 1909, contains 171 ff. of 19·3 × 13 c. and 11 ll., and is written in a fair *nasta'líq* with rubrications.

1251 (t) مناقب ثواقب **Trinity, R. 13. 1**

The *Manáqib-i-Thawáqib*, a Turkish version of Aflákí's *Manáqibu'l-'Árifín*. This latter was abridged in Persian by 'Abdu'l-Wahháb b. Muḥammad Ṣábúní of Hamadán, and the Turkish version was made from the abridgement by Darwísh Maḥmúd. See Palmer's *Trin. Cat.*, pp. 7–9.

1252 (p) منتخب التواريخ **King's, No. 77**

The *Muntakhabu't-Tawáríkh*, a well-known history of India from the Muḥammadan conquest to the fortieth year of Akbar's reign (1004/1595–6) by 'Abdu'l-Qádir b. Mulúksháh-i-Badá'úní. See *B.M.P.C.*, pp. 222–3.

1253, 1254 (p) منتخب اللّباب **Or. 241 (13)** **Or. 271 (10)**

The *Muntakhabu'l-Lubáb*, a history of India from the time of Bábur to the accession of Muḥammad Sháh, by Muḥammad Háshim, commonly known as Kháfí Khán. See *B.M.P.C.*, pp. 232–6. Both MSS. form part of the Cowell Bequest. **Or. 241**, undated, contains the reign of Awrang-zíb. **Or. 271**, copied in 1237/1821–2 from an original dated 1183/1769–1770, begins with the eleventh year of the same reign (= vol. ii, p. 211 of the printed edition). It contains 330 ff. of 24·8 × 16 c. and 14 ll.

1255 (p) منتخبات اشعار فارسيّه **Or. 170 (7)**

Selections (*Muntakhabát*) of Persian verses by Ṣá'ib and other poets, mostly modern. The MS., undated but quite modern, was bought of Naaman on Dec. 6, 1901, and contains 157 ff. of 18·6 × 12·2 c. and 15 ll., written in a careless Persian *ním-shikasta*.

1256 (a) المنتظم فى اخبار الامم **Or. 910 (10)**

The first part (down to the year 11/632–3) of the *Muntaẓam fí Akhbári'l-Umam* of Jamálu'd-Dín Abu'l-Faraj 'Abdu'r-Raḥmán...b. al-Jawzí, who died in 597/1200. See Brockelmann, i, pp. 499–506. The MS., forming part of the Lynch Bequest of January 1915, is undated, but written in a fine old *naskh*, probably of the 13th century of the Christian era, with rubrications. It is defective at the beginning and end, and contains 176 ff. of 26·2 × 16·7 c. and 27 ll.

1257 (t) منزل العارفين **Or. 211ᵃ (8)**

A Turkish mystical work entitled *Manzilu'l-'Árifín* by Shaykh Shamsu'd-Dín, beginning:

حمد و ثنا اول بارگاه اعلایه لائق و روا در که آلخ

The MS., dated 1193/1779, was bought of Naaman on Nov. 12, 1902, and contains 40 ff. of 20·25 × 15 c. and 21 ll., written in a fair Turkish *naskh* with rubrications.

1258 (p) منشآت برهمن **Corpus, No. 83**

Munsha'át-i-Brahman, a collection of letters by Chandarbhán Brahman, author of a *Díwán*, the *Chahár Chaman*, etc. See Ethé's *Bodleian Pers. Cat.*, No. 1385. Copied at Lahore in 1813.

1259 (p) منشآت طاهر وحيد **Or. 684 (9)**

Munsha'át-i-Ṭáhir Waḥíd, who died about 1120/1708–9. See *B.M.P.C.*, p. 810; Ethé's *Bodl. Pers. Cat.*, No. 1387, col. 845, etc. The MS., dated 1271/1854–5, was bought of Géjou on June 13, 1906, and contains 274 ff. of 22 × 13·8 c. and 11 ll., written in a poor *ta'líq* with rubrications.

1260 (p) منشآت طغرا **Corpus, No. 155[1]**

The *Munshá'át*, or Letters, of Ṭughrá of Mashhad, who died some time before 1078/1667–8. See *B.M.P.C.*, p. 742. This MS., dated 1258/1842–3, is written in a cursive *nasta'líq* on pages of 26 × 17 c.

1261 (p) منشآت عالمگيری **Christ's, Dd. 5. 3**

This work is properly entitled not, as here, *Munshá'át* but *Ádáb-i-'Álamgírí*. The letters which it contains were written not by but for Awrangzíb 'Álamgír by Shaykh Abu'l-Fatḥ Qábil Khán, and edited by Shaykh Muḥammad Ṣádiq, who died at the beginning of A.H. 1129 (Dec. 16, 1716). See *B.M.P.C.*, pp. 399–400. This MS. is dated 22 Ramaḍán in the 14th year of Muḥammad Sháh, and contains 424 ff. of 28·9 × 17 c. and 19 ll.

1262–1266 (p) منطق الطير **Or. 190 (7)**, **Or. 195 (7)**, **Or. 264 (8)**, **Or. 685[2] (9)**, **Corpus, No. 231**

Five MSS. of the *Manṭiqu't-Ṭayr* of Shaykh Farídu'd-Dín 'Aṭṭár. See *B.M.P.C.*, p. 576 etc. **Or. 190,** dated 925/1519, was bought of Géjou on July 3, 1902, contains 138 ff. of 17·3 × 12·5 c. and 19 ll., and is written in a large, clear *naskh* with rubrications. **Or. 195,** dated 852/1448–9, was bought of Géjou on Oct. 23, 1902. Ff. 191 of 17 × 10·6 c. and 15 ll., defective at beginning, small, neat *naskh* between gold borders. **Or. 264,** dated 900/1495 was bought from Quaritch on March 27, 1889 by the late Professor Cowell, by whom it was left to the Library. It contains 173 ff. of 19·5 × 10·5 c. and 14 ll., and is written in a good Persian *ta'líq* with gold headings. **Or. 685**[2], undated, bought of Géjou on May 10, 1906, contains on ff. 83–99 selections from the poem. **Corpus 231,** dated 1239/1823–4, is written in *ta'líq* on pages of 18 × 12 c.

1267 (p) منظومة فى الطبّ و المعالجة **Add. 3693 (9)**

A rhymed treatise (*Manẓúma*) on Medicine and Therapeutics by Muḥammad Báqir b. 'Abdu'r-Raḥmán of Tabríz, composed in 1283/1866–7, autograph copy by the author made in the following year. Bought of Sethian, Nov. 1, 1900. Ff. 102 of 21 × 15·4 c. and 17 ll., Persian *ta'líq*, rubrications.

1268 (p) منقول الحكمة **Corpus, No. 228**[2]

A treatise on Alchemy, entitled *Manqúlu'l-Ḥikmat*, composed by Muḥammad Ḥaníf, apparently in 1185/1771–2. This MS. is apparently an autograph.

1269 (a) منهاج الصّحّة **Or. 445**[2] **(9)**

A Shí'ite treatise on Prayer entitled *Minháju'ṣ-Ṣiḥḥat* The MS., of which this portion fills ff. 39–89 of 22 × 18 c., was copied in 1229/1814 by Ghulám Ḥusayn b. Mírzá Muḥammad Khashja-Rúdí in a poor *naskh*, and was bought of Hannan and Watson on Aug. 29, 1903.

1270–1272 (a) منهاج الطالبين **Add. 3622 (10)**
Or. 4 & 5 (8)
Or. 479 (8)

The *Minháju'ṭ-Ṭálibín*, a well-known manual of Sháfi'í Jurisprudence by Abu Zakariyyá Yaḥyá...an-Nawawí, who died in 676/1278. See Brockelmann, i, pp. 394–7, *Camb. Hand-*

list, p. 223. **Add. 3622,** bought of Géjou on Feb. 14, 1900, is the second volume only, with the commentary of al-Maḥallí (Brockelmann, i, p. 395, No. 15), and lacks the last leaf and the colophon. It comprises 149 ff. of 23 × 16 c. and 25 ll., and is written in a legible *naskh*, the text in red, the commentary in black. **Or. 4** and **5,** in two vols., contain the text and the same commentary, are undated, and were bought of Géjou on Jan. 28, 1901 Both vols. contain 427 ff. of 21 × 15 c. and 19 ll., and are written in a large, clear *naskh*, the text in red, the commentary in black. **Or. 479,** dated Muḥ. 873/Aug. 1468, was bought of Géjou on Aug. 18, 1904, comprises 251 ff. of 20·5 × 15·3 c. and 15 ll., and is written in a fine, large, legible *naskh*.

1273 (a) منهج الطُّلاب **Add. 3727 (8)**

The abridgement of the above entitled *Manhaju'ṭ-Ṭulláb* by Abú Yaḥyá Zakariyyá al-Anṣárí, with the gloss (*Ḥáshiya*) of Núru'd-Dín az-Ziyádí. See Brockelmann, i, end of p. 395, and ii, p. 99; also *B.M.A.S.*, No. 314, p. 200. The MS., undated, was bought of Naaman on Nov. 23, 1900, contains 367 ff. of 20 × 15 c. and 23 ll., and is written in a fair *naskh* with rubrications.

1274 (a) منهل الهداة الى معدّل الصّلاة **Add. 3749 (8)**

The *Manhalu'l-Hudát*, apparently a commentary by Abu'l-Ḥasan b. Muḥammad aṣ-Ṣádiq al-Musnadí on the *Mu'addilu'ṣ-Ṣalát* of Muḥammad b. 'Alí al-Birkawí (Birgilí), concerning whom see Brockelmann, ii, pp. 440–442. See also Ḥájji Khalífa, vol. v, p. 630, No. 12391. The MS., dated 1187/1773–4, was bought of Naaman on Dec. 8, 1900, contains 94 ff. of 20·8 × 12 c. and 17 ll., and is written in a good *ta'líq* with rubrications.

1275, 1276 (a) المواقف **King's, No. 9**
King's, No. 235

The *Mawáqif* of 'Aḍudu'd-Dín 'Abdu'r-Raḥmán al-Íjí, who died in 756/1355, with the commentary of as-Sayyidu'sh-Sharífu'l-Jurjání (d. 816/1413). See Brockelmann, ii, pp. 208–

209. **King's 9,** undated, is incomplete at both ends and has many other lacunae. **King's 235,** also undated, contains 518 ff. of 23·8 × 14 c.

1277 (p) مواهب الهى **Fitzwilliam, No. 198**

The *Mawáhib-i-Iláhí*, a history of the Muẓaffarí dynasty by Mu'ín-i-Yazdí. See *B.M.P.C.*, pp. 168–169; *B.M.P.S.*, No. 50, p. 33. This MS., dated 15 Ramaḍán, 778 (= Jan. 26, 1377) was written eleven years before the author's death It contains 98 ff. of 24·3 × 15·4 c. and 21 ll., and is written in an archaic *nasta'líq* with rubrications.

1278, 1279 (p) مواهب عليّه **Or. 963 (10)**
King's, No. 113

The *Mawáhib-i-'Aliyya*, a well-known Persian commentary on the *Qur'án* by Ḥusayn Wá'iẓ-i-Káshifí, composed in 897–9/1492-4. See *B.M.P.C.*, pp. 9–11. **Or. 963** contains only part of the work, from *Súra* vii, 198 to the end of *Súra* xvii. It is undated, was bought of J. Whitaker on Nov. 30, 1917, and comprises 102 ff. of 24·8 × 18·1 c. and 25 ll., written in a legible *ta'líq*. The **King's MS.,** in two volumes, divided after *Súra* xviii, is undated, and was copied by Fírúz b. 'Abdu'l-Ḥamíd.

1280 (p) موائد الاسحار **Or. 509 (6)**

Mawá'idu'l-Asḥár, a work on Shí'ite Theology by Muḥammad b. Abí Ṭálib (Ḥazín), who died in 1180/1766–7. The MS., undated but quite modern, was bought of Hannan and Watson on August 20, 1904, contains 110 ff. of 15·6 × 10·3 c. and 15 ll., and is written in a small, neat *naskh* with rubrications.

1281–1286 (a)
موجز القانون فى علم الطبّ
Add. 3650 (12)
Add. 3744 (9)
Or. 1 (8)
Or. 539 (7)
King's, No. 237 (2 vols)
King's, No. 248 (3 vols)

The *Mújiz*, or Compendium, of the *Qánún* of Avicenna by 'Alá'u'd-Dín Abu'l-Ḥasan 'Alí...al-Qarshí ibnu'n-Nafís, who died in 687/1288, or 696/1296. See Brockelmann, i, pp. 457 and 493; *Camb. Hand-list*, p. 227; *B.M.A.S.*, p. 546. **Add. 3650,** dated 1190/1776, was bought of Sethian on May 21, 1900, contains 253 ff. of 29·7 × 18·5 c. and 21 ll., and is written in a clear *naskh* with rubrications. **Add. 3744,** dated 841/1437–8, was bought of Géjou on Dec. 2, 1900, contains 189 ff. of 22 × 15 c. and 21 ll., and is written in an excellent *naskh* with rubrications. **Or. 1,** dated 1124/1712, was bought of Géjou on Jan. 28, 1901, contains 265 ff. of 20·2 × 15·3 c. and 14 ll., and is written in a poor *naskh* with some Persian glosses in the margin. **Or. 539,** dated 824/1421, was bought of Géjou on Jan. 4, 1905, and contains 211 ff. of 18·4 × 13·8 c. and 15 ll., written in a good *naskh* with rubrications. **King's 237** consists of two volumes, containing al-Kázarúní's commentary, of which the first contains 178 ff. of 23 × 14 c., and was transcribed in Multán in 1108/1697. The second, more modern, is not dated. Both are written in a clumsy *ta'líq* with rubrications. **King's 248** consists of 3 vols. (the 1st, 2nd and 4th of the work), and like the previous MS. contains the commentary of al-Kázarúní. Vol. i is dated 1005/1596-7; the others are undated. All are written in a large, clear *naskh* on pages averaging 28 × 17 c. in size.

1287 (a) مونس الوحيد **Trinity, R.13.8**

The *Múnisu'l-Waḥíd* of Abú Manṣúr 'Abdu'l-Malik ath-Tha'álibí (died 429/1038). See Brockelmann, i, pp. 284–6 and Palmer's *Trin. Cat.*, pp. 43–44.

1288 (p) مهذّب الاخلاق **Corpus, No. 17[1]**

An anonymous Persian treatise on Ethics entitled *Muhadhdhibu'l-Akhláq*. The MS., dated 1249/1833–4, comprises 69 ff. and is written in *ním-shikasta*.

1289–1291 (p) مهر و مشترى **Or. 265 (9)**
Or. 274[2] (8)
Or. 281 (8)

Three MSS. of *Mihr u Mushtarí*, a well-known Persian poem by 'Aṣṣár of Tabríz, who died in 779/1377–8 or 784/1382–3. See *B.M.P.C.*, pp. 626–7. **Or. 265,** undated, contains 151 ff. of 22·7 × 14·3 c. and 17 ll., and is written in a good *ta'líq* with rubrications. **Or. 274**², dated Nov. 20, 1857, is written in a fair Indian *ta'líq* with rubrications. This portion of the MS. comprises ff. 25–196 of 21·3 × 16 c. and 15 ll., and is followed by two Sanskrit texts, the *Srútabodha* of Kálidása, and the *Dhúrtasamayana Nátak*. **Or. 281**, dated 790/1388 and copied by Jalálu'd-Dín Muḥammad, comprises 192 ff. of 19·5 × 10·8 c. and 14 ll. and is written in a small, neat *naskh*. All three MSS. form part of the Cowell Bequest.

1292 (p) میزان **Corpus, No. 189**²

A Persian treatise on the inflection of the Arabic verb. See Ethé's *Bodl. Pers Cat.*, No. 1669. This part of the MS., which is dated 1250/1834–5, comprises ff. 62–83.

1293 (t) میزان الازهار **Or. 671**¹ **(8)**

The *Mízánu'l-Azhár* (? = *Risálát-i-Narjisiyya*) of Shaykh Muḥammad Lála-zárí. The MS., undated, contains 36 ff. (of which this portion occupies ff. 1–18) of 20·7 × 12 c. and 15 ll.; poor *ta'líq*; rubrications. Bought of Géjou, Feb. 17, 1906.

1294 (p) میزان الطبّ **Corpus, No. 60**

A Persian manual of Medicine entitled *Mízánu'ṭ-Ṭibb*, by Muḥammad Arzání, known as Muḥammad Akbar, who wrote several medical works about 1112–1130/1700–1718. See *B.M.P.C.*, p. 479. The MS., dated 1213/1798–9, is written in *ním-shikasta* on pages of 23 × 14·5 c.

1295, 1296 (p) مینا بازار **Corpus, No. 117**
Corpus, No. 190²

Míná Bázár, by Ẓuhúrí of Turshíz. See *B.M.P.C.*, p. 678 for the author's biography and p. 742 for the present work. Both MSS. are undated and written in *nasta'líq*.

1297, 1298 (p) نان و حلوا **Add. 3676 (8)**
Or. 266 (10)

Nán u Ḥalwá ("Bread and Sweetmeats"), a poem by Shaykh Bahá'u'd-Dín 'Ámilí, who died in 1030/1620–1. See *B.M.P.C.*, p. 679. **Add. 3676**, undated, was bought of Naaman on July 23, 1900, contains 76 ff. of 19·2 × 12 c. and

14 ll., and is written in a fair *ta'líq* with rubrications. The first 12 ff. contain fragments of other poems. **Or. 266,** from the Cowell Bequest, formerly belonged to H. G. Keene of Sidney Sussex College, and is dated 1057/1647. It contains 24 ff. (of which this portion occupies ff. 1–14, and the popular *Qiṣṣa-i-Duzd u Qáḍí* ff. 17–23) of 24·4 × 15 c. and 13 ll., and is written in legible *nasta'líq* with rubrications.

1299 (a) نتائج الافكار فى شرح اظهار الاسرار **Or. 962 (6)**

Natá'iju'l-Afkár, a commentary by Muṣṭafá b. Ḥamza (composed in 1085/1674) on the *Iẓháru'l-Asrár* of al-Birkawí (d. 981/1573). See Brockelmann, ii, p. 441. The MS., undated, was bought of J. Whitaker on Nov. 30, 1917, and contains 156 ff. of 16 × 11 c.

1300–1302 (t) نتائج الفنون **Or. 470 (8)**, **Or. 545 (6)**, **Or. 744 (6)**

Natá'iju'l-Funún, a Turkish Encyclopaedia of twelve sciences by the poet Naw'í (Nev'í), who died in 1007/1599. See *B.M.T.C.*, pp. 114–115, and Gibb's *Hist. of Ottoman Poetry*, vol. iii, p. 173. **Or. 470,** undated, was bought of Géjou on Jan. 29, 1904, contains 103 ff. of 16·2 × 9·9 c. and 19 ll., and is written in a good *ta'líq* with rubrications. **Or. 545,** dated 1030/1620–1, was bought of Géjou on Jan. 4, 1905, contains 168 ff. of 12·9 × 7·5 c. and 15 ll., and is written in a small, neat *naskh* with rubrications. **Or. 744,** dated 1106/1694–5, was bought of Géjou on March 27, 1907; contains 100 ff. of 14·3 × 9·5 c. and 19 ll., and was copied by Ḥajji Yúsuf b. 'Abdu'lláh.

1303 (a) نخبة الفكر فى مصطلح اهل الأثر (شرح) **Add. 3703 (8)**

The *Nukhbatu'l-Fikar fí muṣṭalaḥi ahli'l-athar* of Ibn Hajar al-'Asqalání (d. 852/1449), with running commentary. See Brockelmann, ii, bottom of p. 68, and i, p. 359; Ḥájji Khalífa, vol. vi, p. 316, No. 13,634; *Camb. Hand-list*, p. 232. The MS., undated, was bought of Naaman on Nov. 7, 1900, contains 66 ff. of 19·7 × 13·7 c. and 13 ll., and is written in a clear modern *naskh* with rubrications.

1304 (p) نزهة الارواح **Corpus, No. 156**

The *Nuzhatu'l-Arwáḥ*, a Ṣúfí work by Amír Ḥusayní, who died in 718/1318–1319. See *B.M.P.C.*, p. 40. The MS., dated 1126/1714, is written in a fair *nasta'líq* with many glosses on pages of 21 × 13 c.

1305 (a) نزهة الزّمان فى حوادث عربستان **Or. 63 (9)**

Nuzhatu'z-Zamán fí Ḥawádithi 'Arabistán, a history of events in the Lebanon from 1109–1215 (= A.D. 1697–1800), by Amír Ḥaydar ash-Shihábí. The MS., dated 1266/1849, was bought of Naaman on May 3, 1901. It contains 136 ff. of 20·8 × 15·5 c. and 18 ll., and is written in a good, clear modern *naskh*.

1306–1309 (p) نزهة القلوب **Or. 647 (11), Or. 915 (12), Or. 945 (10), Or. 946 (9)**

The *Nuzhatu'l-Qulúb*, a well-known geographical work by Ḥamdu'lláh Mustawfí of Qazwín compiled in 740/1339–1340. See *B.M.P.C.*, pp. 418–420, and concerning the author *Ibid.*, pp. 80–82. The text, edited by G. le Strange, was published in 1915 in the "E. J. W. Gibb Memorial Series," vol. xxiii, and was followed in 1919 by the translation. **Or. 647,** undated, was bought at the O'Kinealy sale on Jan. 15, 1906. It contains 198 ff. of 28·2 × 19·8 c. and 18 ll., and is written in a large, clear Persian *nasta'líq* with rubrications. **Or. 915,** from the Lynch Bequest, is dated 1084/1673–4. It contains 313 ff. of 31 × 19·8 c. and 17 ll., and is written in a clear *ta'líq* with rubrications. **Or. 945,** transcribed by Ibn Karbalá'í Ḥaydar 'Azíz in 1119/1708, was acquired by G. le Strange in July, 1904, and presented by him to the Library in March, 1916. It contains 229 ff. of 26·8 × 16 c. and 19 ll., and is written in a small, neat *ta'líq* with rubrications. **Or. 946,** undated, was acquired and presented by G. le Strange at the same time as the MS. last mentioned. It contains 210 ff. of 21·2 × 18·2 and 23 ll., some maps, and a full table of contents at the end in le Strange's handwriting, and is written in clear *nasta'líq* with rubrications.

1310 (a) النزهة المبهجة فى...تعديل الامزجة **Add. 3723 (8)**

A work on Medicine entitled *an-Nuzhatu'l-mubhija fí tashḥídhi'l-adhhán wa ta'dílí'l-amzija*, by Ḍá'úd al-Anṭákí, who died in 1008/1599. See Brockelmann, vol. ii, p. 364. The MS., bought of Naaman on Nov. 23, 1900, contains 221 ff. of 20 × 14·5 c.

1311 (a) نزهة المجالس [و منتخب النفايس] **Emmanuel, 3.2.2**

The *Nuzhatu'l-Majális* [*wa Muntakhabu'n-Nafá'is*] by 'Abdu'r-Raḥmán b. 'Abdu's-Salám...aṣ-Ṣaffúrí, who died in 884/1479. See Brockelmann, ii, p. 178; Ḥájji Khalífa, vi, No. 13,725; *Berlin Arab. Cat.*, Nos. 8827–31. The MS. is dated 1059/1649.

1312 (p) نسخهٔ منشعبه **Corpus, No. 189³**

A Persian treatise on Arabic verbs, similar to if not identical with No. 1664² of Ethé's *Bodleian Pers. Cat.* This tract, occupying ff. 62–75 of the MS., which was transcribed in 1250/1834–5, is here absurdly ascribed to the great Sa'dí of Shíráz.

1313, 1314 (a, p) نصاب الصبيان **Christ's, Dd.4.5**
Corpus, No. 227³

Two copies of the *Niṣábu'ṣ-Ṣibyán*, a well-known rhymed Arabic-Persian Vocabulary by Abú Naṣr-i-Faráhí, composed about 617/1220–1. See *B.M.P.C.*, p. 504. The **Christ's MS.**, written in a good *ta'líq*, was copied in 1184/1770–1 at Ḥaydarábád by 'Izzat 'Alí and contains 33 ff. of 27·5 × 16·8 c., 9 ll. in text and marginal notes. The **Corpus MS.** lacks the two most important figures of the date. This part of it comprises only 29 ff.

1315 (a, p) نصاب مثلّث **Corpus, No. 227²**

Niṣáb-i-Muthallath, another rhymed vocabulary, occupying 8 ff. of the **Corpus MS.** mentioned immediately above.

1316 (a) نظام الغريب **Trinity, R.13.30–31**
(2 vols in one)

A MS. of 114 ff. of which ff. 1–13 and 83–114 contain Arabic *qaṣídas* by Ibn Muqrab, Ibn Majíd and other poets, while the body of the volume (ff. 13–83) contains the *Niẓámu'l-Gharíb* of 'Ísá b. Ibráhím ar-Raba'í, who died in 480/1087. See Brockelmann, i. p. 279, and Palmer's *Trin. Cat.*, pp. 62–5.

1317 (t) نظامنامهٔ اصلاحات **Or. 574 (8)**

The *Niẓám-náma-i-Iṣláḥát*, or Turkish Code of Reforms compiled in 1190/1776–7. The MS., dated 1249/1833–4, was bought of Géjou on July 14, 1905. It contains 65 ff. of 21·2 × 13·7 c. and 15 ll., and is written in a poor *naskh*.

1318 (a) نظم اللآلی (تعليقة على —) **Or. 3 (8)**

A gloss (*ta'líqa*) by Badru'd-Dín Muḥammad al-Márdíní on the *Naẓmu'l-La'álí*, a versified manual of Sháfi'ite law by Abú Muḥammad Ṣáliḥ al-Ja'barí, who died in 706/1306. See Brockelmann, ii, p. 163; *B.M.A.S.*, No. 436. The MS., dated 1069/1658–9, was bought of Géjou on Jan. 28, 1901, and contains 142 pp. of 20·7 × 15·2 c.

1319 (t) نظم و نثر ويرانى بابا وغيره **Or. 568 (7)**

The Turkish verse and prose writings (*Naẓm u Nathr*) of Wírání (Vírání) Bábá, of the Ḥurúfí sect and Bektáshí order, followed by the *'Uyúnu'l-Hidáya* of Ra'ís Efendi al-Ḥurúfí. The MS., dated 1249/1833–4, was bought of Géjou on July 14, 1905, and contains 148 ff. of 17·3 × 11·7 c. and 15 ll., written in a fair Turkish *naskh* with rubrications.

1320 (p) نفائس الفنون و عرائس العيون **Corpus, No. 208**

Part of the great Encyclopaedia entitled *Nafá'isu'l-Funún wa 'Ará'isu'l-'Uyún* of Muḥammad b. Maḥmúd of Ámul, who flourished in the early part of the 8th Muḥammadan (14th Christian) century. See *B.M.P.C.*, pp. 435–8. This MS., undated and written in good *nasta'líq* on leaves of 22 × 14 c., contains only the fourth and fifth *Fanns* of the fourth *Maqála* of the second *Qism*, treating of the interpretation of dreams and physiognomy.

1321, 1322 (p) نفحات الانس **Or. 468 (10)**
King's, No. 118

Two MSS. of Jámí's *Nafaḥatu'l-Uns*. See *B.M.P.C.*, pp. 349–351, and, for the author's life, *Ibid.*, p. 17. **Or. 468,** dated 1100/1688–9, was bought of Géjou on Jan. 29, 1904, contains 228 ff. of 26 × 16 c. and 27 ll., and is written in a good *naskh* with rubrications. **King's 118** is undated, but fairly old.

1323, 1324 (a) نقائض جرير و الفرزدق **Christ's, Dd. 5. 15**
Christ's, Dd. 5. 16

Dr William Wright's transcripts of the Bodleian and the Strassburg MSS. of the *Naqá'iḍ* of Jarír and al-Farazdaq, presented to the Library by Professor A. A. Bevan after the completion of his edition, published in 3 vols. in 1905–1912 by Messrs Brill of Leyden. **Dd. 5. 15** is described in Professor Bevan's hand as the "copy made by William Wright of a MS. in the Bodleian Library (Pococke 390)," and has a note at the end "revised and compared with the original MS. at intervals ending on 6 Jan. 1882. W. W." Ff. 399 of 21 × 16·7 c. and 18–19 ll. **Dd. 5. 16** is described by Professor Bevan as the "copy of a MS. in the University of Strassburg (Spitta'sche Sammlung, No. 36)," and has a note at the end "transcript finished by me on Wednesday, 6 Oct. 1886, at 5.45 p.m. Wm. Wright, St Andrew's, Station Road, Cambridge." The pages, unnumbered, measure 27 × 21·8 c. and comprise 29 ll. each.

1325 (t) نقش خيال **Or. 602 (9)**

Naqsh-i-Khayál ("Fancy's Picture") by Ádharí (Ázerí), who died in 994/1586. See *B.M.T.C.*, p. 184, and Ḥájji Khalífa, No. 13,967 (vol. vi, pp. 379–380). His proper name was Ibráhím b. Aḥmad. The MS., dated 987/1579, was bought of Géjou on Oct. 30, 1905, contains 80 ff. of 23·3 × 11·8 c. and 21 ll., and is written in fairly good legible *naskh*.

1326 (p) نكات بيدل **Corpus, No. 232**

Nukát-i-Bí-dil. A note by the late Professor E. B. Cowell describes this as "a work discussing certain problems in morals and metaphysics." Written in good *ta'líq* on pages of 21 × 12 c., and undated.

1327 (p) نگارستان **Corpus, No. 3**

The *Nigáristán*, a well-known collection of biographical anecdotes by Qáḍí Aḥmad Ghaffárí, who died in 975/1567–8. See *B.M.P.C.*, p. 106. The MS. is undated and written in *ta'líq* on pages of 24 × 16 c.

1328 (p) نگارنامهٔ منشی **Trinity, R.13.106**

The *Nigár-náma-i-Munshí*, by Munshí Malik-záda, composed in 1095/1684. See *B.M.P.C.*, p. 985; Ethé's *Bodleian Pers. Cat.*, No. 1395, col. 848; and Palmer's *Trin. Cat.*, p. 172.

1329–1331 (p) نل و دمن **Christ's, Dd.3.8; Corpus, No. 87; Corpus, No. 186**

Three copies of *Nal u Daman*, the Persian verse-translation of the Sanskrit romance of Nala and Damayanti, by Fayḍí, who died in 1004/1595–6. See *B.M.P.C.*, pp. 670–1. The **Christ's MS.**, undated, is beautifully written in a fine *ta'líq* between gold borders, on pages decorated with gold, and contains 143 ff. of 23·4 × 14·8 c. and 15 ll. **Corpus 87,** dated 1247/1831, is written in *nasta'líq* on pages of 21 × 15 c. **Corpus 186,** date illegible, contains 161 ff. and is written in minute *nasta'líq* on pages of 19 × 11 c.

1332 (a) نوابغ الكلم **King's, No. 46[3]**

The *Nawábighu'l-Kalim* of az-Zamakhsharí, who died in 467/1074. See Brockelmann, i, pp. 289–293, and Palmer's *King's Catalogue*, p. 46. This is preceded in the same volume by the *Aṭbáqu'dh-Dhahab* and the *Aṭwáqu'dh-Dhahab* of the same author. The MS. is dated 1141/1728–9 and 1147/1734–5.

1333, 1334 (p) نوباوه (= انشای ملّا منیر) **King's, No. 17; Corpus, No. 178[2]**

The *Naw-Báwa* ("First fruits"), a collection of letters compiled at Jawnpúr in 1051/1641–2 by Abu'l-Barakát Munír of Lahore, son of 'Abdu'l-Majd of Multán. See Ethé's *Bodl.*

Pers. Cat., Nos. 2078, 2079. The **Corpus MS.** is dated 1222/1807–8, and this portion of it fills ff. 27–117.

1335 (p) نو بهار عشرت **Corpus, No. 44**

The *Naw-Bahár-i-'Ishrat* of Munshí Shív Naráyan..., described as an autograph copy. Ff. 434 of 29 × 17 c., written in a very illegible *shikasta*. Several pages are blank, others are filled with medical prescriptions, etc.

1336 (a) نور العين فى شرح سلك العين **Or. 64 (7)**

Núru'l-'Ayn, a commentary by Shaykh 'Alawán (d. 936/1529) on the *Silku'l-'Ayn*, a mystical poem by Abu'n-Najá'ib 'Abdu'l-Qádir aṣ-Ṣafadí (d. 915/1509). See Brockelmann, ii, p. 123. This is followed by the *Mubashshirát* of Shaykh Muḥiyyu'd-Dín ibnu'l-'Arabí. The MS. contains 199 ff. of 17·25 × 12·75 c. and 21 ll., is undated, and was bought of Géjou on May 11, 1901.

1337 (h) نو طرز مرصّع (قصّهٔ چار درويش) **Corpus, No. 128**

Naw Ṭarz-i-Muraṣṣa', apparently substantially identical with the well-known "Story of the Four Darwíshes," by 'Aṭá Ḥusayn Khán. The MS., undated, contains 125 ff. of 25 × 16 c., and is written in *ta'líq*.

1338, 1339 (t) نهالستان **Or. 469[1] (8)**
Or. 474 (8)

Two copies of the *Nihálistán*, a Turkish imitation of the well-known *Gulistán* of Sa'dí, divided into 5 chapters, each entitled *Nihál*.

Both MSS. were bought of Géjou on Jan. 29, 1904. **Or. 469,** dated 1160/1747, contains 251 ff. of 21 × 11·5 c. and 23 ll., of which this portion fills ff. 1–71. It is written in a small, neat *nasta'líq*. **Or. 474,** undated, contains 110 ff. of 21·5 × 13·3 c. and 21 ll., and is written in a good, clear Turkish *naskh* with rubrications.

1340 (a) نهاية الايجاز فى دراية الاعجاز **Fitzwilliam, No. 193[2]**

The *Niháyatu'l-Íjáz fí dirấyati'l-I'jáz*, a work on rhetoric by Fakhru'd-Dín Rází, who died in 606/1209. See Brockelmann, i, pp. 506–8. For fuller description of the MS., which is dated 681/1282–3, see **No. 1005**, p. 165 *supra*, *s.v.* *Kitábu'l-I'jáz*.

1341, 1342 (a, p) نهج البلاغة **King's, No. 90** / **King's, No. 246**

The *Nahju'l-Balágha*, professedly containing homilies and sayings of 'Alí b. Abí Ṭálib, compiled by ash-Sharífu'l-Murtaḍá or his brother ar-Raḍí. See Brockelmann, i, pp. 404–5. **King's 90** contains the Arabic text, followed, paragraph by paragraph, by the Persian translation of the son of Qáḍí 'Abdu'l-'Azíz, completed in 1028/1619. **King's 246,** dated 1078/1667–8, contains the Persian commentary on the text by Fatḥu'lláh b. Shukru'lláh of Káshán. The MS. is divided into two sections, containing 419 and 220 ff. respectively.

1343–1345 (p) نهر الفصاحة **Corpus, No. 65[1]** / **Corpus, No. 67[2]** / **Corpus, No. 174**

Three copies of the *Nahru'l-Faṣáḥa* ("River of Eloquence") of Mírzá Qatíl. See *B.M.P.C.*, p. 520. These 3 MSS. are nearly of the same size, *viz.* 26 × 16 c., and are all written in *nasta'líq*. Only the first is dated 1258/1842.

1346–1348 (p) نیرنگ عشق **King's, No. 120** / **Corpus, No. 31[1]** / **Corpus, No. 73**

Three copies of the *Nírang-i-'Ishq* ("Witchery of Love"), a *mathnawí* poem by Muḥammad Ikrám, poetically named *Ghanímat*, composed in 1096/1685. The author died in 1107/1695–6. See *B.M.P.C.*, p. 1034, and Ethé's *India Office Pers. Cat.*, No. 1649.

1349 (t) واردات الهيّه **Or. 570 (9)**

Wáridát-i-Iláhiyya, a Turkish mystical treatise by 'Alí of Crete (Kirídí 'Alí). The MS., undated, was bought of Géjou on July 14, 1905, and contains 52 ff. of 23·9 × 15·8 c. and 13 ll.

1350 (h) وا سوخت سودا **Corpus, No. 66[5]**

A Hindustání poem of the kind called *Wá-súkht* by Mírzá Rafí', poetically surnamed Sawdá. The MS. is dated 1251/1835–6. This portion occupies ff. 11–19 of 25 × 15·25 c.

1351 (p) واقعات بابری **King's, No. 96**

The *Wáqi'át-i-Báburí*, or Persian version of the Emperor Bábur's Turkí memoirs, generally known as the *Bábur-náma*. The Persian translation was made by Mírzá Páyanda Ḥasan of Ghazna and Muḥammad-qulí Mughúl-i-Ḥiṣárí. See *B.M.P.C.*, p. 799. The MS., undated, ends with the year 935/1528–9, and contains 166 ff.

1352 (p) وامق و عذرا **Or. 280** (8)

The romantic poem of *Wámiq and 'Adhrá* by Námí, copied for the late Professor E. B. Cowell from the Bengal Asiatic Society's MS. It is undated, contains 110 ff. of 20·5 × 16 c. and 13 ll., and is written in a legible Indian *ta'líq* with rubrications.

1353 (a) (الوجيز (شرحه المسمّى بالعزيز **Or. 53, 54, 55** (10)

The commentary entitled *al-'Azíz* of 'Abdu'l-Karím al-Qazwíní ar-Ráfi'í (d. 623/1226) on the *Wajíz* of al-Ghazálí. See Brockelmann, i, p. 424, No. 50. These 3 volumes contain not more than half the work, and are wrongly arranged. They are nearly uniform, the page containing 22 or 23 ll., and having an average measurement of 25 × 17 c. The 7th vol., **Or. 53**, is dated 640/1242–3. It contains 409 ff. **Or. 54** (ff. 443), dated in the same decade as the last, is the 4th vol., and **Or. 55** (ff. 340) the 6th. They were bought of Naaman on March 4, 1901.

1354 (p, t) وسيلة المقاصد الى حسن المراصد **Trinity, R.13.17**[2]

A handbook of the Persian language for Turks entitled *Wasílatu'l-Maqáṣid ila Ḥusni'l-Maráṣid* (pp. 85–159 of the MS.), followed by two Arabic vocabularies by 'Alá'u'd-Dín of Qasṭamúní (pp. 161–206 and 207–261). See Palmer's *Trin. Coll. Cat.*, pp. 40–42.

1355 (p) وصلت نامهٔ عطّار **Or. 256**[2] (9)

The *Waṣlat-náma*, a poem by Shaykh Farídu'd-Dín 'Aṭṭár, copied for the late Professor E. B. Cowell from the Bengal Asiatic Society's MS. in Feb. 1858. See *B.M.P.C.*, p. 579. The MS. contains 72 ff. of 22 × 17 c. and 11 ll., and is written in a clear Indian *ta'líq* with rubrications.

1356, 1357 (t) وصيّت نامهٔ برکوی **Or. 449 (8)**
Trinity, R. 13. 59

The *Waṣiyyat-náma*, or "Testament," of Muḥammad b. Pír 'Alí al-Birkawí (or Birgilí), who died in 981/1573. **Or. 449,** undated, was bought of Hannan, Watson and Co. on Aug. 29, 1903, contains 185 ff. of 20·8 × 13·1 c. and 15 ll., and is written in a large clear Turkish *naskh* with rubrications. The **Trinity MS.** contains 105 ff.: see Palmer's *Trin. Cat.*, pp. 148–9.

1358 (a) وفاء الوفا بأخبار دار المصطفى **King's, No. 99**

The *Wafá'u'l-Wafá bi-akhbári Dári'l-Muṣṭafá*, composed in 886/1481–2 by 'Alí b. 'Abdu'lláh...as-Samhúdí, who died in 911/1505. See Brockelmann, ii, pp. 173–4. The MS. was copied in 1004/1595–6 by 'Abdu'r-Raḥmán b. Muḥammad b. Ádam al-Jabartí. See Palmer's *King's Cat.*, pp. 25, 27.

1359 (t) وفيات الاعيان (ترجمهٔ فارسی) **King's, No. 110**

The Persian translation of Ibn Khallikán's famous biographical dictionary the *Wafayátu'l-A'yán* made for Sulṭán Salím (A.H. 918–926 = A.D. 1512–1520) by Kabír b. Uways b. Muḥammad Laṭífí. See Brockelmann, i, p. 328; Ḥájji Khalífa, vol. vi, p. 455. The MS. is in two parts (422 ff. in all), of which the first is the translator's autograph, and was written at Constantinople in 926/1520, while the second, dated 1019/1610–1611, was copied from his autograph.

1360–1364 (a, p)
وقاية الرّواية فى مسائل الهداية
Add. 3751 (7), King's, No. 244
Add. 3610 (8), King's, No. 226
Add. 3666 (8)

The *Wiqáyatu'r-Riwáya fí masá'ili'l-Hidáya*, a well-known commentary on the *Hidáya* of al-Marghínání (d. 593/1197) by Burhánu'd-Dín Maḥmúd (7th century of the *hijra*, 13th of the Christian era). See Brockelmann, i, pp. 376–7; *B.M.A.C.*, p. 119; *B.M.A.S.*, p. 187, Nos. 285, 286. **Add. 3751,** dated end of 954/Feb. 1548, was bought of Naaman on Dec. 8, 1900, contains 287 ff. of 17·5 × 12 c. and 9 ll., and is written in a good *ta'líq* with rubrications and glosses. It contains the text of the *Wiqáya.* The next 3 MSS. contain the commentary of 'Ubaydu'lláh b. Mas'úd al-Maḥbúbí. **Add. 3610,** undated, was bought of Géjou in Dec. 1899, contains 280 ff. of 20 × 12·5 c. and 21 ll., and is written in a fair *naskh,* the text overlined in red. **Add. 3666,** dated 1065/1654–5, was bought of Sethian on July 17, 1900, contains 240 ff. of 20·4 × 14·5 c. and 25 ll., and is written in a legible *ta'líq* with rubrications. **King's 244,** dated 1160/1747, is written in a large and legible but poor *ta'líq* with rubrications, on pages of 30 × 20·3 c. **King's 226** contains a Persian version of the *Wiqáya* by 'Abdu'l-Ḥaqq...of Sirhind, completed in 1076/1665–6. See Ethé's *India Office Pers. Cat.,* No. 2590. The MS. is dated 1114/1702–3.

1365 (p) **Corpus, No. 102[1]**

وقايع بدايع احوال محاربات بنگاله

Waqáyi'-i-Badáyi', a rhymed chronicle of the wars in Bengal in 3 parts, each with separate pagination, dealing respectively with the years 1156/1743–4, 1158/1745–6, and 1161/1748, by Afḍalu'l-'Ulamá Afáq Sháh Wifáq (?) of 'Aẓímábád. The MS. is written in good *nasta'líq* on pages of 18 × 11 c., and was copied at Bareilly in 1826. The 3 parts contain respectively 48, 30 and 35 ff.

1366 (t) ولايت نامهٔ حاجی بکطاش **Or. 41 (10)**

The *Wiláyat-náma* of Ḥájji Bektásh b. Sayyid Muḥammad of Khurásán, the founder of the Bektáshí Order of darwíshes, one of 6 Ḥurúfí MSS. bought of Naaman on Feb. 5, 1901. For description of this and other MSS. see my article on the *Literature of the Ḥurúfís* in the *J.R.A.S.* for July 1907, pp. 29, 34–6 and 37. The MS., dated 1274/1857–8, contains 130 ff. of 24·3 × 16·8 c. and 17 ll., and is written in a fair Turkish *nasta'líq.*

1367 (p) الهداية (شرح فارسی) **King's, No. 245**

A Persian paraphrase and explanation of the *Hidáya* of al-Marghínání (d. 593/1197: see Brockelmann, i, p. 376) by 'Abdu'l-Ḥaqq of Sirhind, who began it in 1082/1671–2, and finished it in 1087/1676–7. See Ethé's *India Office Pers. Cat.,* No. 2593, col. 1397. The MS. contains 239 ff.

1368 (a) هداية المَيْبُذى **Or. 591 (7)**

The *Hidáya*, a well-known Introduction to the study of Philosophy, still used as a text-book in Persia, by Ḥusayn b. Mu'ínu'd-Dín al-Maybudhí, who died about 890/1485. See Brockelmann, ii, p. 210. This MS., dated 881/1476–7, was bought of Géjou on Oct. 30, 1905, contains 133 ff. of 18·4 × 9·6 c. and 15 ll., and is written in a neat *nasta'líq* with rubrications.

1369, 1370 (p) هشت بهشت امیر خسرو دهلوی **Or. 248 (8)** **Or. 257² (8)**

The *Hasht Bihisht*, one of the five *mathnawís* which make up the *Khamsa*, or "Quintet," of Amír Khusraw of Dihlí, composed by him in imitation of the *Khamsa* of Niẓámí. See *B.M.P.C.*, pp. 611–615; Ethé's *India Office Pers. Cat.*, col. 691–2, etc. This poem, the "parallel" to Niẓámí's *Haft Paykar*, was composed in 701/1301. Both MSS. are from the Cowell Bequest. **Or. 248,** undated, contains 114 ff. of 21·5 × 13·3 c. and 15 ll., and is written in a clear *ta'líq*. **Or. 257²**, copied for Professor Cowell (presumably at Calcutta) in 1857, contains 231 pp. of 20·3 × 15 c. and 15 ll., and is written in a large, clear Indian *ta'líq*. See **Nos. 702, 177** and **1236** *supra.*

1371 (p) هفت اورنگ جامی **Or. 292 (11)**

The *Haft Awrang*, or seven *mathnawí* poems (*Sab'a*) of Jámí (d. 898/1492). See *B.M.P.C.*, pp. 645–6; Ethé's *India Office Pers. Cat.*, col. 746–8 and 755, etc. This MS. contains only five of the seven poems, and lacks the *Laylá and Majnún*, and *Salámán and Absál*. It is from the Cowell Bequest, is undated, contains 224 ff. of 28·8 × 17·8 c. and 21 ll., and is written in a good *ta'líq* with rubrications.

1372 (p) هفت پیکر نظامی **Corpus, No. 229**

An undated MS. of the *Haft Paykar* of Niẓámí of Ganja. See under *Khamsa-i-Niẓámí*, pp. 77–8 *supra*, especially **No. 451.**

1373 (p) هفت منظر هاتفی **Or. 237 (10)**

The *Haft Manẓar* of Hátifí, Jámí's nephew, who died in 927/1521. See *B.M.P.C.*, p. 653. This copy was made for

Professor Cowell (presumably in Calcutta) in 1857, and has been collated with a MS. dated 942/1535–6. It contains 68 ff. of 25 × 15·6 c. and 16 ll., and is written in a poor Indian *ta'líq* with rubrications.

1374 (t) همايون نامه **Or. 221 (11)**

The *Humáyún-náma*, the Turkish verse-translation of the well-known *Book of Kalíla and Dimna*, made by 'Alí Chelebí early in the 16th century. See Gibb's *History of Ottoman Poetry*, vol. iii, p. 90, n. 1 *ad calc.* The MS., dated 1000/1591, was bought of Naaman on Nov. 12, 1902, contains 361 ff. of 27·8 × 17·5 c. and 23 ll., and is written in an excellent *naskh* with rubrications.

1375 (a) هياكل النّور **Or. 840 (6)**

Haykilu'n-Núr ("Temples of Light"), a mystical work by Shaykh Shihábu'd-Dín Suhrawardí, called *al-Maqtúl*, because he was put to death for alleged heresy at Aleppo in 587/1191. See Brockelmann, i, pp. 437–8. The MS., dated 1014/1605, was bought of Naaman on Feb. 8, 1911, and contains besides the text, which is overlined with red, the commentary of Jalálu'd-Dín Dawání (d. 907/1501). It comprises 92 ff. of 15·3 × 10·5 c. and 17 ll., and is written in a neat *nasta'líq*.

1376 (p) يادگار حسينى **Add. 3614³ (10)**

Yádigár-i-Ḥusayní, a short medical treatise occupying ff. 172–181 of the MS. described above (**Nos. 26** and **1048**) under *Ikhtiyárát-i-Badí'í* and *Kifáya-i-Mujáhidiyya*.

1377–1380 (p) يوسف و زليخاى جامى **Trinity, R.13.104; Trinity, R.13.105; Corpus, No. 81; Or. 741² (9)**

The well-known romantic poem of *Yúsuf and Zulaykhá* by Jámí (d. 898/1492). See Ethé's *India Office Pers. Cat.*, col. 743 *et seqq.* The two Trinity MSS. are described in Palmer's *Trin. Cat.*, pp. 170–172. **R.13.104** was copied in 1722, and contains 165 ff. **R. 13. 105** contains 140 ff. and some coloured illustrations. **Or. 741,** bought of Géjou on March 27, 1907, contains the commentary on the poem by 'Abdu'l-Wásiʻ Hánsáwí. This portion of the MS. occupies ff. 16–44. It is written in poor Turkish *nastaʻlíq* with rubrications on pages of 24 × 17 c. and 32 ll. **Corpus 81** contains 114 ff. of 22 × 14 c. and is written in a careless *nastaʻlíq*.

1381 (p) يوسف و زليخا **Or. 487 (7)**

Another Persian metrical rendering of the *Story of Yúsuf and Zulaykhá*, beginning:

خدايا چون بسپهرم سينه بكشاى ، دلم طوطى كن و آئينه بنماى ،

This MS., one of 16 bought of Géjou on August 18, 1904, is dated 1266/1849–50, comprises 204 ff. of 19·2 × 12 c. and 13 ll., and is written in a poor but legible *taʻlíq*.

1382 (t) يوسف و زليخا (تركى) **Add. 3695 (9)**

Another versified rendering of the *Romance of Yúsuf and Zulaykhá* in Eastern Turkí. The MS., undated, was bought of Sethian on Nov. 1, 1900, contains 83 ff. of 22 × 12·6 c. and 14 or 15 ll., and is written on coarse paper in clumsy but legible *taʻlíq*.

1383–1386 (t) يوسف و زليخاى حمدى **Or. 58 (8) / Or. 179 (8) / Or. 534 (6) / Or. 763 (7)**

The Ottoman Turkish metrical version of the *Romance of Yúsuf and Zulaykhá* of Ḥamdí, who died in 914/1509. See a long account of him in Gibb's *History of Ottoman Poetry*, vol. ii, ch. vii (pp. 138–225). **Or. 58,** copied in 999/1591 by Darwísh Muṣṭafá of Belgrade, and bought of Naaman on March 4, 1901, contains 217 ff. of 19·7 × 12·3 c. and 15 ll., and is written in an excellent *taʻlíq* with rubrications. **Or. 179,** not dated, was bought of Géjou on Jan. 1, 1902, contains 225 ff. of 20·5 × 12 c. and 15 ll., and is written in a poor Turkish *taʻlíq* with rubrications. **Or. 534,** also undated, was bought of Géjou on Nov. 1,

1904, contains 190 ff. of 16·1 × 9·5 c. and 17 ll., and is written in a small, neat Turkish *nasta'līq* with rubrications. **Or. 763,** undated, was bought of Géjou on May 13, 1907, contains 219 ff. of 18·8 × 12·2 c. and 15 ll., and is written in a good Turkish *naskh* with rubrications.

PART II

UNTITLED MANUSCRIPTS ARRANGED IN ORDER OF SUBJECTS ACCORDING TO THE SCHEME SET FORTH ON THE FOLLOWING PAGE

I. Jewish and Christian Theology.

II. Muḥammadan Theology and Law.

- i. Devotional Manuals.
- ii. Tradition.
- iii. Law.
- iv. Controversy.
- v. Heretical sects (Nuṣayrís, Druzes, Ḥurúfís, Bábís and Bahá'ís).
- vi. Mysticism.

III. Hinduism.

IV. History and Biography.

V. Letters and official documents.

VI. Science.

- i. Philosophy, Logic, Mathematics, Astronomy, Calendars.
- ii. Medicine and allied sciences.
- iii. Astrology, Geomancy and other Occult Sciences.
- iv. Philology and Calligraphy.

VII. Poetry, Ornate Prose and Anthologies.

VIII. Stories, Anecdotes, Proverbs, etc.

IX. Manuscripts of mixed contents, Miscellanea, etc.

I. JEWISH AND CHRISTIAN THEOLOGY

1387 (p) *Story of Judith in Persian* **Queens', No. 8**

A Persian version of the Story of Judith from the Apocrypha.

1388 (p) *Christian Apology* **Or. 429** (8)

A Persian work without title, composed by a Christian named Awánús (اوانوس), apparently for one of the Ṣafawí Sháhs, in A.D. 1690, on Christian doctrine and philosophy. For other copies of this work, see *B.M.P.C.*, pp. 5 and 1077. This MS., dated 1234/1818–19, comprises 94 ff. of 20·6 × 16·2 c. and 11 ll., and is written in a neat and legible *naskh* with rubrications. Bought of Hannan and Watson, August 29, 1903.

II. MUḤAMMADAN THEOLOGY AND LAW

i. *Devotional Manuals*

1389 (a) **Or. 413** (5)

A leather case of 13 × 10·5 c., fastened by a strap, containing two sheets of paper inscribed with Arabic prayers, verses of the *Qur'án*, and two talismanic figures, one containing the "Most Comely Names of God," written in a Maghribí hand, and apparently from West Africa. Bought of W. D. Webster, April, 1903; undated.

1390 (a, p) **Or. 416** (6)

Arabic prayers for use in the months of Rajab, Sha'bán and Ramaḍán, with interlinear Persian translation. Ff. 58 of 14·6 × 9·8 c. and 8 ll. text and 8 ll. interlinear translation, the Arabic in black in good *naskh* and the Persian in red in a smaller *ta'líq*. Bought of Hayder Kenn, July 27, 1903; undated.

1391 (a, p) **Or. 432** (6)

A book of Arabic prayers with Persian interlinear glosses, the text in fine *naskh*, 7 lines to the page, and the interlinear glosses in a smaller hand in red. Ff. 92 of 15·7 × 10 c., undated. Bought of Hannan and Watson, August 29, 1903.

1392 (a) **Or. 586 (8)**

A book of Arabic prayers. Ff. 25 of 19·8 × 11·8 c. and 10 ll.; good, large *naskh*, between gold lines, dated 1011/1602–3, or 1111/1699–1700. Bought of Géjou, July 14, 1905.

1393 (a) **Or. 776 (3)**

Portions of the *Qur'án*, including *súras* xxxvi and xlviii, and a number of prayers, spells and similar formulae. Ff. 151 of 9·3 × 6·4 c. and 6 or 7 ll.; undated. Belonged to Wm H. Morley in 1851. Presented by Khalíl Khálid, December 1, 1908.

1394 (a) **Or. 870 (5)**

Some 200 unnumbered detached leaves, hopelessly disarranged, of 11·8 × 9·6 c., containing prayers in Arabic, written in a Kufic-like Maghribí hand and undated.

1395 (a) **Or. 884 (8)**

Various devotional works and prayers, including the *Dalá-'ilu'l-Khayrát* and the *Burda*, *q.v.* Ff. 56 of 21·7 × 15·5 c. and 15 ll. Written in a large Maghribí hand, pointed, with crimson, red and blue initial words in the prayers, dated Ṣafar 24, 1300 (Jan. 4, 1883). Presented by Donald Mackenzie to the Archbishop of Canterbury on March 15, 1889, and given to the Library by A. C. Benson, Master of Magdalene College, in 1912.

1396 (a) **Or. 891 (5)**

An African prayer-book in an outer leather case of 12 × 7 c. secured by a leather thong. The leaves are detached and disarranged; they measure 9·6 × 6·5 c. and contain 3 to 5 lines each of coarse Maghribí writing. Presented by S. Gaselee, M.A., May 22, 1913.

1397 (a) **Or. 954 (5)**

Ff. 8 of 11·8 × 8·3 c. and 12 ll. inscribed in the Arabic character in an African hand with what appear to be prayers in some African language. Deposited by the Rev. J. M. Wilson, D.D., Worcester, December 6, 1916.

1398 (a) **Christ's, Dd.3.29**

Arabic prayers and extracts from the *Qur'án* in a Maghribí hand. Ff. 212 of 12 × 7·6 c. and 8 ll.; undated.

1399 (a, p) **Corpus, No. 183**[1]

Invocations of the Names of God arranged in groups of ten, each group being devoted to some special object, e.g.

ده نام بجهت نصرت و سعادت يافتن

The author or compiler seems to be called Muḥammad Sajjád, and the work appears to be entitled *Yak hazár u yak nám* ("a thousand and one Names"). Written in *ta'líq* with points on pages of 16 × 11 c.; undated.

1400 (t) **Trinity, R. 13. 23**

A Turkish devotional manual, fully described by Palmer, *Trin. Cat.*, pp. 52–55. Ff. 315; large, clear *naskh*, fully pointed.

1401 (a) **Trinity, R. 13. 53**

Extracts from the *Qur'án*, prayers and poems, fully described by Palmer, *Trin. Cat.*, p. 140. Ff. 84, written in a poor European hand.

1402 (a, t) **Trinity, R. 13. 61**

Devotional formulae in Arabic explained in Turkish. Ff. 24 in a poor Turkish hand. See Palmer's *Trin. Cat.*, p. 150.

1 40 (a, t) **Trinity, R. 13. 63**

Extracts from the *Qur'án* and prayers. Ff. 170, poorly written. See Palmer, *Trin. Cat.*, p. 151.

ii. *Tradition*

1404 (a) **Add. 3721 (9)**

Two untitled, anonymous and fragmentary works on the science of Tradition (*Ḥadíth*). The first (ff. 1–63), a text written in red with running commentary in black, begins, after a short doxology,

و بعدُ، فهذا مختصرٌ جامعٌ لمعرفة علم الحديث مرتّبٌ على مقدّمةٍ و مقاصد،

المقدّمة فى بيان اصوله و اصطلاحاته الخ

The second, which lacks 26 ff. at the beginning and an unknown number at the end, and is further marred by several dislocations and lacunae (after f. 142), is also a commentary on a text dealing with traditions of a more mystical character than the preceding. Ff. 175 of 20 × 14·75 c. and 21 ll.; clear, coarse *naskh* with rubrications. Bought of Naaman, November 23, 1900.

1405 (a) **Or. 48 (10)**

Fragments of an unidentified work on Tradition, in great confusion, without title or author's name. The catch-words are often missing, or when present do not correspond, so that the proper arrangement of the pages would be a matter of great difficulty. Ff. 110 of 24 × 17 c. and 26 ll., written in a coarse old *naskh* on brownish paper; date illegible. Bought of Géjou, Feb. 20, 1901.

1406 (a) **Or. 758 (11)**

Fragment of a work on Tradition containing two books dealing respectively with Patience and Thankfulness (الصبر و الشكر) and Hope and Fear (الخوف و الرّجا), the former occupying ff. 1–86 and the latter ff. 87–134. The MS., undated, was bought of Géjou on May 13, 1907, is written in a large, clear *naskh* with rubrications, the last leaf supplied in a modern hand, and comprises 134 ff. of 27 × 19 c. and 21 ll.

iii. *Law*

1407 (a) **Add. 3670 (10)**

The concluding volume of a work on Ḥanafí law, beginning with the section on Sales. Ff. 298 of 25·5 × 15·3 c. and 35 ll., dated 1082/1671–2.

1408 (a) **Add. 3717 (8)**

An acephalous manual of law, followed on ff. 63–72 by part of a treatise on *tajwíd* in 7 chapters. The volume begins abruptly on the conditions of the legal purity of water. It contains 72 ff. of 20·2 × 15 c. and 11–13 ll., is written in a poor, childish hand, undated, and was bought of Naaman on Nov. 23, 1900.

1409 (a) **Or. 49** (8)

A fragment (ff. 72–391) of a work on Jurisprudence by Muḥammad b. Yaḥya 'Umar. Ff. 320 of 19·5 × 15·8 c. and 17 ll., bought of Géjou on Feb. 20, 1901; transcribed in 662/1263–4.

1410 (a) **Or. 50** (11)

The first third of a work on Jurisprudence, down to the section dealing with fasting, by al-Kirmání. Ff. 120 of 26·5 × 17·9 c. and 29 ll.; bought of Naaman on March 4, 1901.

1411 (p) **Or. 69** (6)

Extracts from a Shí'ite legal work by Shaykh Muḥammad Ḥasan b. Shaykh Báqir-i-Najafí. Ff. 87 of 15·5 × 10·8 c. and 11 ll.; clear modern *naskh* with rubrications; undated; bought of Géjou, May 11, 1901.

1412 (a, m) **Or. 194** (11)

Five tracts on Jurisprudence, *Uṣúl*, etc., one by Abu'l-Layth Muḥammad b. Naṣr as-Samarqandí, with Malay interlinear glosses. Ff. 80 of 28·5 × 19·8 c. and 7 ll. of text, apart from the glosses; undated; bought of Quaritch, Sept. 8, 1902.

1413 (a) **Or. 448** (8)

Four Shí'ite treatises, the first (ff. 1–19) by Muḥammad Báqir b. Muḥammad Akmal; the second (ff. 21–36) entitled *Jam' bayna'l-Akhbár*; the third (ff. 37–99) untitled; the fourth (ff. 101–144) entitled *Al-Fawá'idu'l-Jadída* by al-Ustádhu'l-Bihbihání. Ff. 144 of 21·3 × 16 c. and 20 ll.; clear, modern *naskh*; copied in 1182/1768–9 by 'Alí Naqí al-Khurásání. Bought of Hannan and Watson, August 29, 1903.

1414 (a) **Or. 681** (11)

Part of an anonymous and acephalous work on Ḥanafí law, bought of Géjou on May 10, 1906. Ff. 170 of 27·5 × 16·5 c. and 15 ll.; dated 775/1373–4.

1415 (a) **Or. 712** (10)

Part iv of a work on Ḥanbalí law, extending from the Book of Sales to the Book of Clothes and Ornaments. Ff. 239 of

25·7 × 17·6 c. and 21 ll.; written in a fine old *naskh* dated 685/1286–7 by Abú Bakr al-Ḥanbalí al-Qádirí. Bought of Géjou, Dec. 1906.

1416 (a) **King's, No. 144**

A treatise on *Uṣúl* entitled *al-Ḥusámí.* See Palmer's *King's Cat.*, pp. 21 and 24. Ff. 224 of 26 × 15·5 c. and 5 ll.; large, clear, clumsy *naskh* with rubrications; transcribed in 991/1583 by Ḥusayn b. 'Abdu'r-Raḥmán al-Anṣárí.

1417 (a) **Trinity, R. 13. 33**

A treatise on Málikí law and practice by Abú Muḥammad 'Abdu'lláh b. Abí Zayd al-Málikí al-Qayruwání, followed by various prayers and poems, including the *Alfiyya* of Ibn Málik and the *Ajurrumiyya.* Ff. 173, written in a Maghribí hand. See Palmer's *Trin. Cat.*, pp. 77–81.

iv. *Controversy*

1418 (p) **Or. 22 (6)**

A refutation of various opinions of the philosophers, defective both at beginning and end, and lacking date, title and author's name. Ff. 109 of 14·3 × 10 c. and 20 ll.; small, neat *naskh* with rubrications. Bought of Naaman, Feb. 5, 1901.

1419 (a) كتاب فى العقائد (فى معرفة الصّانع) **Or. 28 (8)**

An anonymous Arabic work on Islamic doctrine. Ff. 101 of 20·5 × 15·6 c. and 15 ll.; large, clear, poor *naskh* with rubrications; copied in 1267/1850–1 by Khamís b. Muḥammad b. Idrís. Bought of Naaman, Feb. 5, 1901.

1420 (p) **Corpus, No. 116**[1]

A controversial treatise in vindication of the Shí'a doctrine written by an Egyptian Jewish convert named Yokhai (يوخاء بنى اسرائيل الّذى المصرى), who states that after his conversion to Islám he was puzzled by the doctrinal and ritual differences of the Four Orthodox Sects. Discussions with their representatives led to the vindication of the Shí'a or

Imámiyya doctrine, to which not only he but his antagonists are finally converted. The MS. is written in a cursive *nasta'líq* on 40 ff. of 21 × 19 c.; the pages are somewhat wormed, and some of them are misplaced.

1421 (a, p) حاشيهٔ مصنّف علی رضا **Corpus, No. 226**

A Persian commentary on an Arabic religious work composed by one 'Alí Riḍá "in the glorious times of Ibráhím Khán." It is labelled on the outside "*Kitáb dar madhhab-i-ṣaḥíḥ.* Sunní doctrine." Written in *nasta'líq* on leaves of 21 × 16 c. in 1245/1829–1830.

v. *Heretical Sects*

1422 (a) **Jesus, No. 17**

A "Manual of Nuṣayrí Shaykhs" bought in Sept. 1859 for £10 from a merchant of Latakia, and bequeathed to Jesus College by S. Lyde on March 1, 1860. It comprises 32 sections and 188 pp. The substance of the book is incorporated in Lyde's *Asian Mystery*, ch. ix, published in 1860 by Longmans and Green. (There is a copy of this work in the University Library with the class mark **7 . 32 . 33.**)

1423 (a) كتاب فی عقائد الدّروز **Or. 198** (8)

A collection of Druze tracts, bought of Géjou on Oct. 23, 1902. Ff. 102 of 20 × 13·6 c. and 15 ll.; large, clear *naskh* with rubrications.

1424 (a) **Or. 465** (9)

Another collection of Druze tracts, similar to the last, bought of Géjou on Jan. 29, 1904. Ff. 259 of 22·2 × 17·2 c. and 13 ll.; clear *naskh* with rubrications.

1425 (a) رسالة فی خواصّ المفردات العجيبة **Or. 42** (6)

A Ḥurúfí treatise on the peculiar virtues of the letters in five chapters, by Darwísh Bábá Uways. Ff. 35 of 14·3 × 9·9 c. and 11 ll. One of six MSS. bought of Naaman on Feb. 5, 1901.

1426 (p) **Or. 43** (6)

A collection of six Ḥurúfí tracts, *viz.* (1) the *Shiráb-náma* of Sayyid Isḥáq; (2) extracts from the *Jáwidán-i-Kabír* of Faḍlu'lláh, the founder of the Ḥurúfí sect; (3) the *Zubdatu'n-Naját* of Shaykh Abu'l-Ḥasan; (4) the *Taḥqíq-náma*; (5) the *Wiláyat-náma*; and (6) a commentary on the *Jáwidán-i-Kabír*. Ff. 112 of 14·9 × 9·9 c. and about 19 ll.; dated 1118/1706–7; poor *nasta'líq*. Bought of Naaman, Feb. 5, 1901.

1427 (p) شرح جاودان نامه **Or. 62** (9)

A commentary on Sayyid-i-Sharíf's *qaṣída* entitled *Jáwidán-náma* by the Bektáshí Darwísh Yúsuf b. Ḥaydar the Albanian of Áq-Ḥiṣár. Ff. 194 of 21 × 15·1 c. and 25 ll.; fair *naskh* with rubrications; dated 1240/1824–5. Bought of Naaman, May 3, 1901.

1428 (t) (۱) کنز الحقائق (۲) کشف نامه ' **Or. 530** (8)

A Ḥurúfí MS. of 86 ff. of 19·2 × 14 c. and 21 ll., written in good *naskh* with rubrications, and dated 1223/1808–9, containing (1) the *Kanzu'l-Ḥaqá'iq wa Kashfu'd-Daqá'iq* (ff. 1–40), originally written in Persian by Shaykh Muḥammad *'Aynu'l-Quḍát* al-Hamadání; and (2) the *Kashf-náma-i-Iláhí* (ff. 42–86). One of 11 MSS. bought of Géjou on Nov. 1, 1904.

1429 (t) **Or. 532** (6)

A collection of the following 11 Ḥurúfí and other tracts: (1) the *Ḥaqíqat-náma* of Shaykh Ṣáfí; (2) the *Pand-náma*; (3) the *Tuḥfa-i-Muḥammad*; (4) translation of the *Burda* or "Mantle-poem"; (5) the "Treatise of the Seven Circles"; (6) the *Taṣfiyatu's-Sulúk*; (7) the *Maqámát-i-Awliyá*; (8) the Discourses of Ḥájji Bektásh of Khurásán; (9) the *Maqámátu'l-Aqṭáb*; (10) the Circle of the *Rijálu'l-Ghayb*; (11) the *Asmá-i-Ḥusná*, or "Most Comely Names." Ff. 157 of 16·1 × 11 c. and 15 ll.; neat Turkish *naskh*; the colophons bear various dates from 944/1537–8 to 1173/1759–60. One of 11 MSS. bought of Géjou on Nov. 1, 1904.

1430 (a, t) (١) مرآة الطالبين، (٢) نقطة البيان، **Or. 544 (7)**

Two Ḥurúfí tracts, *viz.* (1) the *Mirátu'ṭ-Ṭálibín* by Zaynu'd-Dín of Khwáf, in Arabic; (2) the *Risála-i-Nuqṭatu'l-Bayán*, in Turkish, which fills the bulk of the volume. Ff. 36 of 19 × 10·6 c. and 15 ll.; fair *ta'líq* with rubrications; dated 1033/1623–4. One of eight MSS. bought of Géjou on Jan. 4, 1905.

1431 (a) **Add. 3704 (6)**

A Bábí book of the earliest period, apparently by Mírzá 'Alí Muḥammad the Báb himself, and resembling in style his *Commentary on the Súratu Yúsuf*, in which he speaks of himself as *Baqiyyatu'lláh Ṣaḥibu'z-Zamán*. The MS., defective at the beginning, comprises 71 ff. of 15 × 10 c. and 10 ll., and is written in a neat *naskh*. Bought of Naaman on Nov. 7, 1900.

1432 (a, p) **Add. 3705 (8)**

A commentary in Arabic and Persian on a *takhmís*, or "five-some," in praise of Yúsuf Maẓhar Pasha, composed in 1287/1870–1 by Rajab 'Alí b. Muḥammad Ḥusayn of Iṣfahán, presumably the Azalí-Bábí leader Mullá Rajab 'Alí, entitled *Janáb-i-Qahír*, who was assassinated at Baghdád by Bahá'ís. See E. G. Browne's *Traveller's Narrative*, vol. ii, pp. 356, 359, 363 and 371. The MS., bought of Naaman on Nov. 7, 1900, contains 63 + 5 ff. of 19 × 12·5 c. and 9 ll., with rubrications.

1433 (a, p) آثار . . بهاء الله **Or. 843 (10)**

A beautifully written and illuminated MS. containing selections from the writings of Mírzá Ḥusayn 'Alí *Bahá'u'lláh*, presented to the Library by M. Hippolyte Dreyfus in Nov. 1910, and entitled:

مجموعهٔ مبارکه محتوی بعضی از آثار مقدّسه ایست که از خزینهٔ
قلم حضرت بهآء الله . . . ظاهر و باهر و صادر گردید،

The MS., containing 128 written pp. of 24·7 × 15·8 c. and 17 ll., was copied by 'Alí Akbar of Mílán, gilded and illuminated by Mírzá Ḥasan, and bound by Muḥammad Ṣádiq al-Bahá'í. It was completed in Jumáda i, 1327/May–June, 1909.

1434 (a, p) **Or. 943 (8)**

A volume containing six Bábí and Azalí tracts in Arabic and Persian, *viz.* (i) Persian *A'lwáḥ* (ff. 4–30); (ii) *Wajdiyya* in Arabic (ff. 31–76); (iii) *Júdí wa'th-Thamar*, a commentary by Ṣubḥ-i-Azal on the *Súratu'l-Baqar* (ff. 79–253); (iv) *Rúḥ wa'l-Qamar*, also by Ṣubḥ-i-Azal (ff. 254–486); (v) *Ṣaḥífatu'l-Haramayn*, one of the earliest of the Báb's writings, composed on the Pilgrimage in 1261/1845, the year after his "Manifestation" (ff. 489–545); (vi) *Áthár-i-Azaliyya* (writings of Ṣubḥ-i-Azal) in Arabic (ff. 546–630). The volume was given by Ṣubḥ-i-Azal to Claude Delaval Cobham, Esq., then Commissioner of Larnaca, Cyprus, on Jan. 26, 1897, and later by him to Guy le Strange, Esq., who presented it to the Library in February, 1916. For particulars concerning most of the tracts enumerated above, see the Index to E. G. Browne's *Materials for the Study of the Bábí Religion* (Cambridge, 1918).

vi. *Mysticism*

1435 (a, p) **Add. 3713 (7)**

A collection of 27 Ṣúfí and other tracts, including (1) Sayings of 'Alí; (2) Explanation of "the Path," by Najmu'd-Dín Kubrá; (3) Prayers; (4) Letter to Khwája Muḥammad Pársá; (5) Proof of Being; (6) Praise of effort and blame of indolence; (7) Verses by Jámí; (8) *Lawá'iḥ* of Jámí; (9) Treatise on Rhyme, probably Jámí's; (10) Commentary on the *Tá'iyya* poem of Ibnu'l-Fáriḍ, etc. Ff. 228 of 17 × 12 c. and 15 ll. Bought of Naaman, Nov. 23, 1900.

1436 (p) **Or. 513 (6)**

A collection of seven Ṣúfí tracts and poems, *viz.* (1) the *'Urwatu'l-Wuthqá wa 'Aqá'id-i-Awliyá* (ff. 3–54); (2) a *tarjí'-band* of the poet Hátif (ff. 54–59); (3) the *Gulshan-i-Ráz* of Shaykh Maḥmúd-i-Shabistarí (ff. 61–96); (4) the *Ḥáqqu'l-Yaqín* of the same (ff. 100–119); (5) a tract by Sháh Ni'matu 'lláh (ff. 119–188); (6) the *Mirátu'l-Muḥaqqiqín* (ff. 192–205); (7) a *mathnawí* poem (ff. 206–230). The MS., bought of Hannan and Watson on Aug. 20, 1904, comprises 230 ff. of 15 × 10 c.

and 12 ll., is written in a modern Persian *ta'líq*, and is incomplete at the end. The date 1261/1845 occurs on f. 58ᵇ.

1437 (p) **Christ's, Dd. 3. 13**

Several mystical and devotional tracts, concluding with a short grammatical treatise. Ff. 42 of 22·4 × 12·5 c. and 17 ll.; poor Indian *ta'líq* with rubrications.

1438 (p) **Christ's, Dd. 3. 26**

Four Ṣúfí tracts, the *first* anonymous, mostly in verse; the *second*, entitled *Gulzár-i-Jalálí*, by Darwísh Táju'd-Dín Jalálí, on Union with God; the *third*, entitled *Anísu'l-Ghurabá*, by Ḥusayní; and the last a *mathnawí* poem by the same beginning:

باز طبعمرا هوای دیگرست

Ff. 113 of 19·4 × 12 c. and 13 ll.; undated.

III. Hindúism

(*The six following manuscripts, being written in the Nágarí character, are only included in this Hand-list to complete the tale of the Corpus MSS. The titles inscribed in them in the Roman character by a former owner are here reproduced, but no further attempt at description or identification has been made.*)

1439 (hindí) **Corpus, No. 32**

Stories and religious tracts in Hindí or Sanskrit.

1440 (hindí) **Corpus, No. 37**

1441 (hindí) **Corpus, No. 82**

"Couplets written by Dhoveender ile Shree Kuhi Dhoveender."

1442 (hindí) **Corpus, No. 93**

"Sool buchan Kul Pund Seeka."

1443 (hindí) **Corpus, No. 120**

"Kunam ka chowper."

1444 (hindí) **Corpus, No. 121**

"Rutle Ruhas Rus Kubit."

1445 (brij-bhaka) **Corpus, No. 143**

A MS. in the Arabic character and the Brij-bhaka language, described as "a Sráwuk religious work about the 24 Tírthankars of the Jains."

1446 (p) **King's, No. 14**

A collection of five Persian tracts on Hindú religion, etc., *viz.* (1) *Kayán top-hí* in verse; (2) *Rám Gítá*; (3) *Miṣbáḥu'l-Hudá*; (4) *Arjun Gítá*; (5) Discussion between Dárá Shukúh and Bábá Lál, all by Walí Rám except No. 4, which is by Abu'l-Faḍl. See Palmer's *King's Cat.*, pp. 16 and 25.

IV. History and Biography

1447 (a) **Or. 926 (7)**

Part of an unidentified Arabic chronicle, defective at beginning and end, and without indication of title or authorship, beginning with the year 94/712–3 and extending to the year 422/1031. Ff. 258 of 18·8 × 13·5 c. and 19 ll.; fine, large, clear *naskh*, apparently of the 14th century, with rubrications. Lynch Bequest, Jan. 1915.

1448 (a) **Or. 912 (8)**

A volume described in a note at the end as the *Kitábu Asmá'i'r-Rijál* of Ibnu'l-Athír. Ch. i, in 10 sections, is devoted to the Prophet Muḥammad; ch. ii to the other prophets; ch. iii to the "Ten harbingers of good tidings" (العشرة المبشّرة); and ch. iv to the Companions of the Prophet, arranged alphabetically. There is an extract from Ṭabarí's Chronicles on f. 1 and some traditions on ff. 308–312. The MS., copied in 1000/1592 by one Muḥammad-qulí, forms part of the Lynch Bequest. It comprises 314 ff. of 20·5 × 14·2 c. and 23 ll., and is written in a clear *naskh* with rubrications. The colophon, which contained the proper title of the book, is unhappily nearly obliterated.

1449 (a) **Or. 928 (11)**

A large, thick volume, defective at beginning and end, containing a very full history of Egypt and an account of the topography of Cairo. Mas'údí is amongst the authors quoted. Ff. 527 of 26·8 × 17 c. and 29 ll.; minute, clear *naskh*, undated. The first section deals with the Red Sea (*Baḥru'l-Qulzum*), and the next with the derivation and meaning of the name of Egypt (*Miṣr*). From the Lynch Bequest.

1450 (p) **Or. 196** (7)

A Persian versified account of the achievements of the Ottoman Sultan Báyazíd "the Thunderbolt," beginning:

بنام جهاندار جان آفرین، خداوندگار جهان آفرین،

Ff. 109 of 17 × 10·5 c. and 11 ll.; good *nasta'líq* with rubrications and some miniatures, dated 891/1486. Bought of Géjou on Oct. 23, 1902.

1451 (p) **Or. 427** (10)

An acephalous, incomplete, and unidentified history of the Emperor Akbar. The first section (f. 2^b) is headed:

ذکر بعضی بشارات غیبی و اشارات قدسی که پیش از سعادت ولادت حضرت شاهنشاهی ظهور یافته،

Begins with the birth of Akbar and extends to the birth of Sháh Murád on Muḥarram 3, 978 (June 7, 1570), in the 15th year of Akbar's reign. Ff. 348 of 26·6 × 16·5 c. and 22 ll., undated. Bought of Hannan and Watson on August 29, 1903.

1452 (p) **Or. 506** (12)

A popular history of the Imáms and their partisans (the *Shí'a*), without title or author's name, from the death of al-Ḥusayn at Karbalá to the overthrow of the Umayyads. Ff. 208 of 30 × 20 c. and 19 ll.; fair modern Persian *ta'líq* with rubrications, dated 1238/1822–3. One of 30 MSS. bought of Hannan and Watson, Aug. 20, 1904.

1453 (p) **Or. 508** (9)

Narratives of the martyrdom of the Imáms, divided into *Majális*, adapted for recitations in the month of Muḥarram. Ff. 212 of 21·6 × 17·3 c. and 13 ll.; large, clear Persian *naskh* with rubrications on blue paper; defective at beginning and end; undated, but quite modern. One of 30 MSS. bought of Hannan and Watson on Aug. 20, 1904.

1454 (t) **Or. 600 (9)**

A narrative of the events connected with the deposition of Sulṭán Salím III in 1221/1806–7, by Muṣṭafá Najíb. Ff. 52 of 23·6 × 14·2 c. and 23 ll.; good Turkish *naskh* with rubrications; dated Muḥarram 1264/Dec. 1847. Bought of Géjou, Oct. 30, 1905.

1455 (t) **Or. 674 (8)**

A Turkish historical manual of the most miscellaneous contents, beginning with the origin of the different races of mankind and the building of Constantinople, and ending with the Áq-Qoyúnlú dynasty in Persia. Ff. 103 of 19·5 × 13·4 c. and 25 ll.; clear Turkish *naskh* with rubrications; undated, but copied subsequently to 1142/1729–30. Bought of Géjou, Feb. 17, 1906.

1456 (t) **Or. 703 (8)**

Account of the war of Sulṭán Sulaymán "the Magnificent" with the Austrians, etc. Ff. 40 of 20·8 × 14 c. and 9 ll.; large, clear Turkish *naskh* with rubrications; dated 1182/1768-9. Bought of Géjou, Dec. 1906.

1457 (a, t) **Clare, Kk. 3. 11**

A collection of nine tracts, mostly historical, the first, described in a Latin note as "Annales Calipharum," containing a history of the Ottoman Sultans from 641/1243–4 to 1115/1703–4, by Ḥájji Muḥammad b. Mamí b. Muḥammad b. Ilyás al-Atnáwí. This is followed by: (2) the *Muḥallafát* of the Grand Wazír Sinán Páshá; (3) the Plague in the years 960–1109 (1553–1697) in Algiers; (4) List of mosques and churches; (5) Illumination of Algiers; (6) Rulers of Algiers 910–1101 (1504–1689); (7) Necrology of Sultans 951–1101 (1544–1689); (8) Necrology of Saints and Doctors in Algiers 875–1107 (1470–1695); (9) Chronological list of events from 996/1588 onwards. The MS. was presented to the College in 1796 by Henry Freeman, ex-Fellow.

1458 (p) **Corpus, No. 115²**

An anonymous and untitled *résumé* of Indian history, apparently identical with No. 332 of Blochet's *Catalogue des Manuscrits Persans de la Bibliothèque Nationale*. This part of the MS. occupies ff. 121–146.

1459 (p) **Corpus, No. 118**

A volume written in rather illegible *shikasta* on pages of 21 × 13 c. containing fragments of works on Indian history (Awrang-zíb, etc.) and some poetical extracts.

1460 (h) **Corpus, No. 152**

Biographies of eight notable persons of antiquity (perhaps from Plutarch's *Lives*) in Urdú. Lithographed, without place or date. Part iii only. Pp. 102 + 6.

1461 (h) **Corpus, No. 159**

Two Urdú *tadhkiras* of Indian poets.

1462 (p) **Trinity, R.13.97**

A treatise on the alleged Jewish origin of the Afgháns, by Sa'ádat Yár Khán, grandson of Ḥáfiẓ Raḥmat Khán. Ff. 18. See Palmer's *Trin. Cat.*, p. 157.

V. LETTERS, OFFICIAL PAPERS, ETC.

1463 (a) **Or. 234 (14)**

An Arabic proclamation issued by the Khalífa of the Mahdí of the Súdán commandeering ships for the war against the English, signed and sealed by about a score of the Darwísh Amírs, and dated 23 Sha'bán, 1309/March 23, 1892. The document was taken from the pocket of one of the Amírs slain at the Battle of Omdurman in 1898. Presented by Dr F. H. Guillemard in 1902.

1464 (m) **Or. 637–640**

Four Malay letters with Dutch translations, dated 1238–9/1826, in a box.

1465 (p) **Or. 653** (5)

A roll of Persian letters, written in an execrable Indian *ta'líq*, pasted together lengthwise to form a long strip 11 c. in width. They are quite modern, one being dated 1277/1860–1. Presented by Mr W. Aldis Wright, February 5, 1906.

1466 (t) **Or. 669** (9)

A note-book of 155 ff. of 24 × 13 c. and 11 ll. containing lists of *'ulamá* and their appointments and salaries throughout the Ottoman Empire, and described in a note in a different hand as سجّل طريق علميّه. The list begins with those who have held the high office of *Shaykhu'l-Islám*. The dates range from '48 to '67 (probably 1248–1267 = A.D. 1832–1851). Opposite many names stands the note فوت شد or رحمه الله, indicating that the person in question is dead. Bought of Géjou, February 17, 1906.

1467 (a) **Or. 687** (7)

Five sheets of about 17 × 11·7 c. on one side only of which are reported in Arabic, in a bad African hand, cases referred from Native Courts in Northern Nigeria to the Resident Magistrate. Given by H. R. Palmer of Ketsina to A. S. B. Miller, and by the latter, on Oct. 17, 1906, to the Library.

1468 (p) **Or. 869**

Rubbing of a Persian inscription dated 856/1452 recording the restoration of a mosque at Hangchow in China, presented by Mrs Agnes S. Lewis, who published a short account of it at the University Press, Cambridge, in 1911. In a box.

1469 (p) **Or. 875** (16)

Ten Persian letters of various sizes, written in an Indian hand on one side only of each sheet; undated; without indication of the writer or the person addressed. Some of them are ornamented and punctuated with gold. Presented by R. T. Wright, M.A., April 19, 1912.

1470 (a, p, t) **Add. 4166, 52–61**

A volume of papers forming part of the Sandars Bequest. In this volume the papers numbered 52 to 61 are Arabic, Persian and Turkish letters and *farmáns*. **SSS. 6. 2.**

1471 (p) **Corpus, No. 18²**

A collection of Persian letters, not identified, occupying ff. 52–81 of the MS. and written in *nasta'líq*.

1472 (p) **Corpus, No. 115¹**

A collection of Persian letters and essays in the form of letters in two *daftars*, apparently by a certain Mírzá Ibráhím Beg. Ff. 119 of 22 × 13 c., dated 1066/1655–6.

1473 (p) **Corpus, No. 130**

A collection of Persian letters and documents, defective at beginning, untitled and of unknown authorship. It includes letters addressed to the poet Jámí and a proclamation of victory (*Fatḥ-náma*) dated 822/1419. Written in fair *nasta'líq* on pages of 23 × 14 c.

1474 (p) **Or. 895 (19)**

"A statement of the number of crimes of an heinous nature committed in the district of Etawa in Bengal, between the years 1809 and 1814 inclusive, with details of matters relating to the same subject." Here follows a statement of the object of this compilation dated March 1, 1833, and signed by Thomas Pelly. Cf. Thos. Perry's note-books, bearing class-marks **Add. 5375–5380.** Ff. 85 of 48 × 32·4 c. and about 25 ll.; bad Indian *ta'líq*. Bought of David, Aug. 1, 1913.

1475 (t) **Or. 885**

A Turkish *farmán*, in box, dated Rabí' ii, 1257/June, 1841.

1476 (t) **Or. 886**

A Turkish *farmán*, in box, dated 1113/1701–2.

1477 (t) **Or. 949**

A Turkish *farmán* dated mid-Sha'bán, 1267/June, 1851, written in the *Díwání* hand on a sheet of 59·5 × 53 c. and 7 ll. In a box.

1478 (p, h) اخبارات **Corpus, No. 198**

Part of a kind of Court Gazette of the time of Awrang-zíb, compiled, according to an English note on the fly-leaf, by Buland 'Alí Munshí. Ff. 32 of 21 × 13 c., written in *nasta'líq* and *shikasta*, undated.

1479 (p) **Corpus, No. 238**

Statement of the revenues of the different *Ṣúbas* of India, said to be extracted from the *Á'ín-i-Akbarí* or "Institutes of Akbar." Written in *shikasta* on pages of 21 × 15 c., undated.

VI. Science

i. *Philosophy, Logic, Mathematics, Astronomy, Calendars*

1480 (a) **Or. 658 (8)**

Part of a work on Natural Philosophy, beginning:

المقالة الاولى من الطبيعيّات فى موضوع هذا العلم، نريد أن نحصر جوامع العلم الطبيعىّ الخ

preceded by letters to and from Avicenna. Ff. 119 of 19·4 × 12·5 c. and 21–28 ll.; dated 1057/1647–8; bought of Géjou, Feb. 12, 1906.

1481 (a, p) **Or. 442 (8)**

A volume of 78 ff. of 20·6 × 15·5 c. and 13–17 ll. written in various modern *nasta'líq* hands and containing: (1) A commentary on a treatise on Logic, both in Arabic, entitled, apparently, *Ghdyatu tahdhíbi'l-Kalám*, and addressed by the author to his son Ḥabíbu'lláh (ff. 1–40); (2) the next portion (ff. 41–52) has been torn away; (3) a Persian treatise on Logic (ff. 53–62); (4) an Arabic treatise on Grammar entitled *Fawá'idu'ṣ-Ṣamádiyya* (ff. 63–78); dated 1263/1847. Bought of Hannan and Watson, Aug. 29, 1903.

1482 (a) **Jesus, No. 14**

A treatise on Logic comprising 63 pp. and 198 paragraphs, incomplete at end. Copied by As'ad b. Jirjís Háshim, a student in the American College (? at Beyrout), and presented to the College by Samuel Lyde, Fellow, who died in A.D. 1860.

1483 (a) **King's, No. 250**

Three commentaries on tracts on Geometry and Astronomy, the first entitled *Ashkálu't-ta'sís*; the second by Maḥmúd b. Muḥammad b. 'Umar al-Jaghmíní as-Samarqandí; the third, incomplete at end, entitled *Tashríḥu'l-Aflák.* See Palmer's *King's Cat.*, pp. 9, 17 and 237.

1484 (p) **Or. 436$^{2-3}$ (8)**

The second and third portions of the MS. described under **No. 437** above (*s.v.* خلاصة الكتاب فى علم الحساب), containing respectively a short treatise on Surveying (مساحت) in four sections called *Rukn* (ff. 39–47), written in fair legible *ta'líq* with rubrications; and an anonymous Persian treatise on Geometry (ff. 49–59). The MS. is dated 1245/1829–1830, and was bought of Messrs Hannan and Watson on August 29, 1903.

1485 **Corpus, No. 39^5**

Tables of the cypher known as *Siyáq*. Ff. 15.

1486 (a) **Or. 782 (8)**

An acephalous, untitled and anonymous treatise on Astronomy, containing four chapters, each subdivided into a number of sections. Ff. 150 of 19·5 × 14 c. and 11 ll.; poor *naskh* with rubrications and numerous geometrical diagrams; dated 784/1382–3; bought of Géjou, Jan. 7, 1909.

1487 (p) **Or. 693 (8)**

A treatise on Astronomy, dedicated to Sháh 'Abbás, by Muẓaffar of Birjand, based on the *Bíst Báb* ("Twenty chapters") of Birjandí. Ff. 119 of 20·9 × 14 c. and 17 ll.; modern Persian *ta'líq* with rubrications; dated Shawwál, 1241/May, 1826; bought of Géjou, Dec. 1906.

1488 (p) **Or. 694 (8)**

An Introduction to Astronomy containing a Preface and two Discourses. Ff. 38 of 21·3 × 15·2 c. and 19 ll.; fair *nasta'líq*; rubrications and diagrams; dated 1052/1642–3; bought of Géjou, Dec. 1906.

1489 (p) **Or. 38 (7)**

A treatise on Astronomy in Persian of unknown title and authorship. Ff. 62 of 18·7 × 12·4 c. and 11 ll.; very poor *ta'líq* with illustrations; undated. Bought of Naaman, Feb. 5, 1901.

1490 (p) **Or. 457 (7)**

A volume of 85 ff. of 17·6 × 13 c. and 12 ll., written in fair *ta'líq* with rubrications and containing: (1) Mawláná 'Abdu'l-'Alí of Birjand's *Bíst Báb dar ma'rifat-i-Taqwím* (ff. 2–24); (2) an acephalous tract on the Calendar, Epochs, etc. (ff. 26–43); (3) the *Tansáq-náma-i-Ílkhání* of Naṣíru'd-Dín Ṭúsí, on precious stones, etc. (ff. 48–66). The dates of transcription lie between 839/1435–6 and 969/1561–2. Bought of Géjou, Nov. 27, 1903.

1491 (a) **Add. 3700 (8)**

A treatise on the Calendar (*Taqwím*), lucky and unlucky days, etc., in 10 sections, by Aḥmad b. Muḥammad al-Mahdí of Iṣfahán. Ff. 31 of 21·6 × 15·3 c. and 19 ll., fair *naskh* with rubrications, dated end of Rabí' i, 1126/April 15, 1714.

1492 (a, p) **King's, No. 203**

Two treatises on chronology and the Calendar, the first in Arabic, entitled *Aḥkámu sani'l-'álam* [? *-ám*] by Muḥiyyu'd-Dín Yaḥyá b. Muḥammad b. Abi'sh-Shukr al-Maghribí al-Andalusí; the second in Persian, on the computation of the Zoroastrian era known as Yazdijirdí. Transcribed in 1020/1611–12 by Muḥammad Sharíf b. Sulṭán Muḥammad of Multán. See Palmer's *King's Cat.*, pp. 4 and 18.

1493 (p) **Trinity, R.13.94**

A Persian Almanac for 1231/1816, presented by Mírzá Ibráhím, formerly Persian teacher at the old East India College of Haileybury, and author of the well-known Persian grammar. Ff. 21. See Palmer's *King's Cat.*, p. 156.

1494 (p) **Add. 3699 (7)**

Two treatises, the first (ff. 1–8) on the Calendar, by 'Abdu'l-Ghaffár Rúdmálí, comprising a Preface and two chapters; the second (ff. 9–53) on Anatomy, by Manṣúr b. Muḥammad b. Aḥmad, comprising a Preface, five Discourses, and a conclusion. Ff. 53 of 18 × 12·5 c. and 16 ll.; poor *ta'líq*, dated 1064/1653–4. Bought of Sethian, Nov. 5, 1900.

1495 (t) **Pembroke, No. 290[a]**

A Turkish Calendar (*Taqwím*) for the years 1086–7/1675-6, beginning with the month of Ázar (March) and ending with the month of February. Ff. 12 (1–2 and 11–12 blank) of 19·5 × 12·5 c.; written in a fine Turkish *naskh* with diagrams and tables outlined in red and gold. Begins:

هذا روزنامهٔ معه میقات لیل و نهار و سایر الاوقات المعلومه نقله شیخ وفا

ii. *Medicine and Allied Sciences*

1496 (p) **Add. 3671 (7)**

An anonymous, untitled and acephalous work on Pharmacology and Therapeutics in 24 chapters. Ff. 147 of 18·3 × 11·4 c. and 20 ll.; neat Persian *ta'líq* with rubrications; transcribed in Luristán in 1091/1680–1. Bought of Sethian, July 17, 1900.

1497 (p) **Add. 3693 (9)**

A Persian rhymed treatise on Medicine by Muḥammad Báqir of Tabríz entitled Kámil. Dated 1283/1866–7. Bought of Sethian, Nov. 1, 1900.

1498 (p) **Or. 682 (10)**

A Persian treatise on the theory and practice of Medicine (perhaps the *Tuḥfa-i-Khání*), composed at Shíráz in 902/1496–7 by Maḥmúd b. Muḥammad 'Abdu'lláh. See Adolf Fonahn, *Zur Quellenkunde der Persischen Medizin* (Leipzig, 1910), p. 133, No. 21, and Ethé's *Ind. Off. Pers. Cat.*, No. 2303. Ff. 220 of 26 × 19 c. and 21 ll.; good, clear *nasta'líq*; rubrications; undated. Bought of Géjou, May 10, 1906.

1499 (a) **Or. 595 (9)**

The second Discourse (*Maqála*) of an Arabic work on Medicine, beginning with Fevers (26 chapters). This is followed by the third Discourse on diseases of the different organs (108 chapters), and this in turn by the fourth Discourse on drugs (arranged alphabetically) and diet. Ff. 122 of 24 × 16 c. and 26 ll.; bad *nasta'líq* on coarse brown paper; dated

618/1221, but evidently of much later date. Bought of Géjou, Oct. 30, 1905.

1500 (a) **Or. 464 (7)**

An Arabic treatise on Falconry in 63 chapters, without title or author's name. Ff. 64 of 19 × 13·4 c. and 17 ll.; good *ta'líq* with rubrications; copied in 1003/1594–5 from a MS. dated 880/1475–6. Bought of Géjou, Jan. 29, 1904.

1501 (p) تحفة المأكولات و غيره **Christ's, Dd.3.2**

A volume containing the following Persian treatises: (1) *Tuḥfatu'l-Ma'kúlát* (ff. 5[b]–105[a]), a collection of culinary receipts; (2) selections from a book on sweetmeats entitled *Kanzu'l-Ḥaláwat* (ff. 106[b]–129); (3) another treatise on sweetmeats (ff. 130[b]–132[b]); (4) *Majmú'u'ṣ-Ṣanáyi'* (ff. 133[b]–235) in 96 chapters; (5) a treatise on scents (ff. 236[b]–258) in five *faṣls* and 15 *bábs*, by Muḥammad b. Muḥammad, known as Shamsu'd-Dín b. Ẓahír al-Khayrí; (6) a treatise on the purification of metals (ff. 260[b]–271[a]), being the 73rd *faṣl* of some much larger work; (7) a treatise on perfumes (ff. 274[b]–323[b]) entitled *Nuzhatu'l-Qulúb*; (8) a treatise on dyeing wool, silk, etc. (ff. 324[b]–343[a]), by Sayyid Yaḥyá (or Masíḥí) of Sabzawár. Ff. 344 of 24·9 × 13·5 c. and 12 ll.; bad Indian *ním-shikasta*.

iii. *Astrology, Geomancy and other Occult Sciences*

1502 (a, p) **Add. 3698 (4)**

A collection of prayers, magical formulæ, talismans, etc. Bought of Sethian, Nov. 5, 1900.

1503 (p) **Or. 431 (7)**

A treatise on Geomancy beginning:

...امّا بعد، چند احکامِ رمل بنده، درگاهِ الله ارسطو از کتب معتبر.. الخ

Ff. 148 of 18·8 × 10 c. and 15 ll.; written in fair *ta'líq* obliquely across the page; undated. Bought of Hannan and Watson, Aug. 29, 1903.

1504 (p) **Or. 901 (8)**

Five tracts in Persian on Geomancy and similar subjects, *viz.* (1) *Tuḥfatu'r-Raml*, by Khwája Náṣiru'd-Dín Aḥmad b. Ḥaydar of Shíráz (ff. 2^b–33^a) dated 965/1557–8, in four Discourses; (2) tables (ff. 34^b–36^a); (3) another treatise on Geomancy (ff. 42^b–46^a); (4) *az-Zubda fí 'ilmi'r-Raml* (ff. 49^b–64^a), a *mathnawí* poem; (5) a treatise on thought-reading (ff. 65^a–69^a), and some other shorter tracts. Ff. 71 of 19·8 × 13·7 c. and 15 ll.; good, clear *naskh* with rubrications. Bought of Naaman, August 1914.

1505 (p) **Corpus, No. 80**

A collection of works or extracts from works on Divination, especially Geomancy, *viz.* (1) an untitled treatise on Geomancy (ff. 1–98) by Núru'd-Dín Fatḥu'lláh, based on the work of Naṣíru'd-Dín Ṭúsí, the *Mafátíḥ* of Ibn Manṣúr, etc.; (2) extracts from another untitled treatise on Geomancy (ff. 98–148) by an author of whose name only the final syllable *-shah* is legible; (3) extracts from a work entitled *Hidáyatu'r-Raml* (ff. 149–268) on the same subject; (4) extracts from a similar work (ff. 272–307) entitled *Anwáru'r-Raml*: cf. Ethé's *Ind. Off. Pers. Cat.*, No. 2267; (5) fragment of a work on Divination (ff. 308–312), ending abruptly; (6) a treatise on the form of Divination known as *shugún* (ff. 314–349), translated from the Sanskrit. The MS., written in three different hands, *shikasta* and *ta'líq*, is undated, and contains 351 ff. of 21 × 15 c.

1506 (a) **Trinity, R. 13. 16**

A volume of 251 ff. containing 42 tracts on Astronomy, the Calendar, Geomancy, Magic, Medicine, etc., transcribed in 959–961/1552–1554 by Shamsu'd-Dín b. Muḥammad b. Ruzayq. See Palmer's *Trin. Cat.*, pp. 28–39.

iv. *Philology and Calligraphy*

1507 (a, lat.) **Or. 831 (15)**

Three large fragments of an Arabic-Latin Lexicon (originally bearing the class-marks # B. α. 20, 21 and 22) in Bedwell's writing, containing respectively lexicographical material for the letters ب—ح, د—ض, and ط—ك. The leaves, which are not numbered, measure 31 × 21 c. See the *Catalogue of Benefactors* (**Oo . 7 . 52**), p. 45.

1508 (a, p, h) **Corpus, No. 107[2]**

An Arabic-Persian-Hindustání glossary in *mathnawí* verse, without title or author's name. Ff. 23 of 21 × 15 c.; good *nasta'líq*.

1509 (p, h) **Jesus, No. 10**

A Persian and Hindustání glossary (chiefly paradigms of verbs), incomplete.

1510 (a, p) **Or. 220 (9)**

Three treatises on Prosody, *viz.* (1) one by Abú 'Abdi'lláh Muḥammad Abu'l-Jaysh al-Anṣárí al-Andalusí (ff. 1^b–24^b) with commentary; (2) text of the same (ff. 25^b–28^a) without commentary; (3) Persian treatise on Prosody (ff. 29^b–44^a). Ff. 44 of 23 × 15·5 c. and 21 ll.; good *naskh*; rubrications; undated. Bought of Naaman, Nov. 12, 1902.

1511 (a, p) **Or. 773 (8)**

A volume of 156 ff. of 21 × 14 c. containing a number of Arabic and Persian tracts, mostly on grammar, *viz.* (1) nine sections of a Persian mystical poem (ff. 1–5); (2) a glossary called *Tuḥfatu'n-Naṣá'iḥ* (ff. 6–13); (3) an Arabic grammar entitled *Mízán* (ff. 14–26); (4) *Kitábu'l-Ajnás* (ff. 27–31); (5) *Kitáb-i-'Iqd* (ff. 31–37); (6) second part of the above (ff. 37–48); (7) *Ṣarf-i-Mír* (ff. 48–75); (8) the *Amthila* of al-Jurjání (ff. 75–87); (9) *Mi'at 'Ámil* (ff. 87–89); (10) commentary on the preceding (ff. 89–95); (11) *Kitáb-i-Ḍaríri* (ff. 96–114); (12) *Kitáb-i-Sajáwandí* (ff. 114–126); (13) *Hidáyatu'n-Naḥw* (ff. 127–156).

1512 (a) **Trinity, R. 13. 64**

An Arabic spelling-book. Pp. 17. See Palmer's *Trin. Cat.*, p. 151.

1513 (p) **Corpus, No. 39[2]**

A short treatise on the conjugation of the Arabic verb, without indication of title or author's name. Ff. 16; large, clear *nasta'líq*, dated 1235/1819–1820.

1514 (p) **Corpus, No. 65[2]**

A short tract on Persian accidence, anonymous and untitled, wrongly described in a heading in a different hand as a "Commentary on the *Káfiya*." Ff. 8 of 26 × 16 c.; clear *nasta'líq*, dated 1258/1842.

1515 (p) **Corpus, No. 227**

A volume containing: (1) a collection of epistolary models entitled *Inshá-yi-Jámi'a*; (2) a rhymed vocabulary entitled *Niṣáb-i-muthallath*; (3) the *Niṣáb-i-Ṣibyán* of Abú Naṣr-i-Faráhí.

1516 (a, lat.) **Trinity, O.3.53**

Tables of Arabic verbs, with Latin equivalents, in a very bad European hand. See Palmer's *Trin. Cat.*, p. 180.

1517 (a, p) **Or. 498 (11)**

An album containing specimens of writing in Arabic and Persian in different hands, *naskh*, *ta'líq*, *shikasta*, etc.; 48 specimens mounted on coloured leaves of 27·5 × 17·8 c., the dates of such specimens as are dated varying between 1229/1814 and 1311/1893–4. One of 30 MSS. bought of Hannan and Watson, Aug. 20, 1904.

1518 (a) **Or. 887 (10)**

An Arabic copy-book comprising 16 ff. of 25·2 × 18·8 c. and 6 or 7 ll. The pages are for the most part ruled in 30 (5 × 6) squares divided and surrounded by gold lines. The isolated letters are first shown, then the same with vowel-points, then combinations of letters, and on the last three pages a few short prayers. Fair *naskh*, undated. Presented by R. F. Scott, M.A., Master of St John's College, Nov. 22, 1912.

1519 (p, t) **Or. 960 (12)**

An album measuring 31·5 × 21·5 c. containing specimens of Persian and Turkish calligraphy, *viz.* 8 pp. from a Turkish work on religious and ethical subjects, not continuous, written in fine *ta'líq* with rubrications, and six Persian letters, dated 1123/1711–12, 1169/1755–6, 1174/1760–1 and 1181/1767–8. The calligraphists represented include 'Abdu'l-Majíd of Iṣfahán. Bought of A. Muḥsin, May 15, 1917.

1520 (a) **Fitzwilliam, No. 201**

An album containing specimens of calligraphy.

VII. Poetry, Ornate Prose, and Anthologies.

1521 (a) **Or. 30 (8)**

A collection of Arabic poetry, without title, preface, or name of compiler. Ff. 127 of 20·5 × 13 c. and 18 ll.; fair *naskh*; rubrications; undated. Bought of Naaman on Feb. 5, 1901.

1522 (a) **Or. 35[1] (8)**

A few Arabic poems in the *zajal* style, full of word-plays and collocations of similar words with different meanings. Ff. 17 of 21 × 15·4 c. and 17 ll.; clear modern *naskh*, dated 1250/1834–5. Bought of Naaman, Feb. 5, 1901.

1523 (p) **Or. 428 (15)**

A large volume of 185 ff. of 38 × 22·3 c., for the most part written in a bad modern hand, containing: (1) the *Gulistán* (ff. 1–33) of Sa'dí; (2) the *Bustán* (ff. 34–63), and selections from the following amongst other Persian poets: Ibn Ḥusám, Adíb Ṣábir, Imámí, Ibn-i-Yamín, Farídu'd-Dín 'Aṭṭár, Niẓámí, etc. Undated; bought of Hannan and Watson, August 29, 1903.

1524 (p) **Or. 499 (11)**

A large anthology of Persian poetry. Amongst the poets represented are Kalím of Hamadán, Sarwar (or Surúr), Hilálí of Hamadán, Ṣabúḥ, Darwísh 'Abdu'l-Majíd, Muḥammad Ḥusayn Rafíq of Iṣfahán, Abu'l-Qásim of Tafrish, Hátif, etc. Ff. 232 of 28·5 × 18·5 c. ruled in four columns, each containing six *bayts* (*i.e.* 24 *bayts* to the page), written for the most part in a good bold *ta'líq*, undated. Bought of Hannan and Watson, August 20, 1904.

1525 (p) **Or. 524[1] (9)**

Poems of Imámu'd-Dín b. Shaykh Abu'l-Makárim, illustrating the various rhetorical devices, and preceded by a preface in ornate prose. Ff. 55 of 23·8 × 14·8 c. and 11 ll.; bad Indian *ta'líq* with rubrications; dated 1204/1789–1790. Bought of Luzac, August 27, 1904.

1526 (p) **Or. 685 (9)**

A collection of Ṣúfí poems and tracts, including: (1) a selection of 3333 *bayts* from the *Mathnawí* of Jalálu'd-Dín Rúmí, preceded by a prose preface, defective at the beginning (ff. 1–82); (2) selections from the *Manṭiqu't-Ṭayr* of Farídu'd-Dín 'Aṭṭár (ff. 83–99); (3) the *Muṣíbat-náma* of the same (ff. 100–113); (4) a poem beginning نمی دانم نمی دانم الهی (ff. 113–120); (5) selections from the *Bústán* of Sa'dí (ff. 120–128); (6) selections from the *Asrár-náma* of 'Aṭṭár (ff. 128–140); (7) the *Zádu'l-Musáfirín* of Ḥusayn Sádát (ff. 141–179); (8) the *Zubdatu'l-Ḥaqá'iq* of 'Azíz Muḥammad-i-Nasafí (ff. 180–217). Ff. 221 of 23 × 16·2 c. and 19 ll.; good and fairly old *nasta'líq*. Bought of Géjou, June 13, 1906.

1527 (h) **Corpus, No. 20[2]**

A narrative poem in Urdú *mathnawí* verse, beginning:

الهی دی مجهی توفیق تقریر، کرون تازه سا قصّه ایك تحریر،

Ff. 15; good *nasta'líq*; dated 1268/1851–2.

1528 (p) **Corpus, No. 50**

The *Sáqí-náma* and *Ghazaliyyát* of Ẓuhúrí, followed by the *mathnawí* of Maḥmúd and Ayáz. See articles **1155, 746** and **883** *supra*.

1529 (p, h) **Corpus, No. 53**

A *Bayáḍ*, or common-place book, containing selections of Persian and Hindustání poetry. Written chiefly in *shikasta* on pages of 16 × 9 c.; undated.

1530 (h) **Corpus, No. 66**

Selections of Hindustání poetry. See articles **1138, 1135, 1133, 1134, 1350, 882, 972, 1115, 49** and **970** *supra*.

1531 (p) **Corpus, No. 57**

A volume containing: (1) the *Inshá*, or epistolary models, of Bídil; (2) 34 pages of miscellaneous poetical selections; (3) the *Díwán* of Shawkat. See articles **105** and **567** *supra*.

1532 (p, t) **Corpus, No. 75[1]**

Miscellaneous extracts in prose and verse, comprising traditions, poetical selections, etc., and including 20 ff. of poetical extracts, chiefly Turkish. Amongst the Turkish poets represented are Janábí, 'Ulwí, Abu's-Su'úd, Nasímí, etc., and amongst the Persians Shams-i-Tabríz.

1533 (p, h) **Corpus, No. 107**

A volume containing: (1) the *Laylá and Majnún* of Hátifí; (2) a rhymed Persian-Hindustání glossary; (3) the *Laylá and Majnún* of Mír Tajallá; (4) the *Díwán* of Dard.

1534 (h) **Corpus, No. 140**

A *Bayáḍ*, or note-book, containing Hindustání verses for the Muḥarram celebrations. Written mostly in *shikasta* on leaves of 26 × 12 c.

1535 (h) **Corpus, No. 147**

A *Bayáḍ*, or note-book, containing selections of Hindí and Urdú poetry. Written in good *nasta'líq* on leaves of 22 × 13 c.

1536 (h) **Corpus, No. 150[2]**

A religious poem in *mathnawí* verse by Shaykh Jamálu'd-Dín. Written in A.D. 1851 on leaves of 22 × 13 c. in *nasta'líq*.

1537 (p, h) **Corpus, No. 154**

Miscellaneous fragments of Persian and Hindustání poetry, including extracts from Jámí's *Yúsuf u Zulaykhá*. Written in different hands on leaves of 22 × 15 c.

1538 (p) **Corpus, No. 158**

The *Díwán* of Anjab, followed by the *Díwán* of 'Ayán, both incomplete. Written in cursive *nasta'líq* and *ním-shikasta* on leaves of 21 × 12 c.

1539 (p) **Corpus, No. 172**

A *Bayáḍ*, or common-place book, containing selections from a number of Persian poets, including Ṣá'ib, Asír, Naṣír, Kamál, Ṭálib, Ḥáfiẓ, Sa'dí, Khusraw, Maẓhar, Náṣir 'Alí, Shams-i-Tabríz, etc. Written in various *nasta'líq* and *shikasta* hands during the reign of Sháh 'Álam on pages of 23 × 13 c.

1540 (p) **Corpus, No. 191**

A volume containing a selection of the *qaṣídas* of 'Iráqí and Anwarí, followed by an anthology of the "Persian Masters" (*Ústádán-i-ahl-i-Furs*).

1541 (p) **Corpus, No. 201**

A volume of poetical extracts. The binding is broken and most of the leaves are loose and hopelessly disarranged. Written in *nasta'líq* on pages of 26 × 16 c.

1542 (p) **Corpus, No. 204**

An oblong volume of recitations for the Muḥarram celebrations, dealing with the sufferings of the Imáms. Written in cursive *nasta'líq* on leaves of 8 × 16 c.

1543 (p) **Corpus, No. 230**

The romance of Bahrám Gúr in *mathnawí* verse. It is not clear whether this is Niẓámí's *Haft Paykar* or another poem on the same subject.

1544 (p, h) **Corpus, No. 233**

Another volume of recitations for the Muḥarram celebrations in Persian and Hindustání verse and prose. Ff. 72 of 29 × 16 c.; clear *nasta'líq*.

1545 (p, t) **Christ's, Dd. 3. 23**

Poems and maxims in Persian and Turkish, mostly the latter, including Ummí, Uṣúlí, Najátí, Nasímí, and the *Qiyáfat-náma* (or Physiognomy) of Ḥamdí. Ff. 182 of 20·1 × 18·7 c. and 17 ll.

1546 (p) **Jesus, No. 9**

A volume containing a selection of Persian poems, including a *Mukhammas*, or "Fivesome," of Kátibí, and Ẓuhúrí's *Sáqí-náma*, an account of Awrang-zíb, several *farmáns*, etc.

1547 (p) **King's, No. 65**

Three volumes of Persian selections, the first containing extracts from various poets of Akbar's time; the second elegies (*maráthí*), and the third prose selections. See Palmer's *King's Cat.*, pp. 6 and 20.

1548 (e. turkí) **Queens', No. 9**

An anonymous *Díwán* of poetry in Eastern Turkí, defective at the end.

1549 (p, t) **Trinity, R. 13. 47**

Poetical extracts in Persian and Turkish. Ff. 24. See Palmer's *Trin. Cat.*, pp. 124–9.

1550 (a) **Trinity, R. 13. 31**

A selection of *qaṣídas* and other poems in Arabic by Ibn Saráyá al-Ḥillí (d. 750/1349) and other poets. See Brockelmann, ii, pp. 159–160; Palmer's *Trin. Cat.*, pp. 65–9.

1551 (t) **Or. 671² (8)**

Fragment (ff. 22^b–36^a) of an anonymous Turkish work of unknown authorship on rhetoric. Written in an excellent modern *naskh*, 21 ll. to the page of 20·7 × 12 c., undated. Bought of Géjou, Feb. 17, 1906.

1552 (p) **Corpus, No. 48**

Fragment of an *Inshá*, or collection of epistolary models, beginning, after the Introduction, with a letter from Sháh 'Álam to one Tímúr Sháh, followed by the latter's reply. Incomplete at end; ff. 44 of 27·5 × 18·5 c.; written in an illegible *shikasta*.

1553 (p) **Corpus, No. 84**

Two *Inshás, viz.* that of Harkarn and that of Khalífa.

1554 (p) **Corpus, No. 155**

The prose writings of Ṭughrá followed by the *Fasána-i-'Ajá'ib.*

1555 (p) **Corpus, No. 192**

A volume containing: (1) the *Dastúru'ṣ-Ṣibyán*; (2) the *Inshá* of Fayḍ-bakhsh; (3) the *Inshá* of Muḥammad Fá'iq. An English note states that this book was written for Fayḍ-'Alí Khán when a child. He was afterwards Nawwáb of Jagpúr, and was hanged after the Mutiny in 1857 in the Chandni Chawk on account of the part he took against the English.

VIII. Stories, Anecdotes, Proverbs, etc.

1556 (a) **Or. 20 (8)**

A collection of anecdotes, poems, etc., defective at both beginning and end, without title or indication of authorship. Ff. 196 of 19·2 × 14·5 c. and 19 ll., excellent *naskh* with rubrications. Bought of Naaman, Feb. 5, 1901.

1557 (a) فى الحكايات الجليلة و النكت الظريفة **Or. 29 (8)**

A collection of stories without proper title or indication of authorship. Ff. 88 of 20·4 × 13 c. and 23 ll.; fair, legible *naskh* with rubrications; dated Rabí' i, 1117/June–July, 1705. Bought of Naaman, Feb. 5, 1901.

1558 (t) نوادر و بدايع و لطائف **Or. 680 (8)**

A volume containing 218 ff. of 18·9 × 12·7 c. and 20 ll., written for the most part in fair Turkish *nasta'líq*, but towards the end in a curious angular *naskh*. Contains: (1) the *Badá-yi'u'l-Áthár* or *Nawádir* of Janání (ff. 1–176), dated 1039/1629–30; (2) the *Laṭá'if*, or Witticisms, of the poet Baṣírí (ff. 177–189), dated 1037/1627–8; (3) the *Laṭá'if*, or Witticisms, of the poet Sham'í, dated Shawwál 997/Aug.–Sept., 1589. Bought of Géjou, May 10, 1906.

1559 (p) **Corpus, No. 23[3]**

A story (apparently that of *Wámiq and 'Adhrá*) in ornate prose, written in *nasta'líq*, undated, and incomplete at end. Ff. 56.

1560 (p) **Corpus, No. 116[2]**

The story of the wooing of Badí'u'l-Jamál, the daughter of the King of China, by 'Abdu'l-Ghaffúr, imperfect at the end. Written in *nasta'líq*, undated.

1561 (p) **Corpus, No. 132**

An anonymous and untitled collection of Persian stories.

1562 (p) **Corpus, No. 139**

A collection of historical anecdotes, possibly from 'Awfí's *Jawámi'u'l-Ḥikáyát.* Copied at Fayḍábád in 1221/1796–7 in a good, clear *nasta'líq* on pages of 32 × 24 c.

1563 (p) **Corpus, No. 181**

A volume containing (1) the *Jang-náma-i-Muḥammad*, and (2) the *Qiṣṣa-i-Mihr u Máh.*

IX. MSS. of Mixed Contents

1564 (a) **Add. 3732 (9)**

A volume of 78 ff. of 21 × 15 c. and 19 ll., written in fair *naskh* and dated 1194/1780, containing: (1) anonymous *qaṣídas* of a religious character (ff. 1–14); (2) a treatise on the different classes of traditions (ff. 16–40) by 'Alí b. Sulṭán Muḥammad al-Qárí; (3) a treatise on the abrogated and abrogating verses of the *Qur'án.* Bought of Sethian, Nov. 28, 1900.

1565 (m) شعير بيداسارى **Or. 871 (8)**

A Malay work entitled *Sha'ír Bídásárí,* copied at Singapore at a date unspecified. A note at the beginning states that it belonged formerly to Tankerville J. Chamberlain in 1871, and refers for a description of it to the *J.R.A.S.* (Straits Branch), No. 6, p. 261. Ff. 101 of 20·8 × 15·5 c. and 15 ll., written in clear but childish and unformed *naskh* with rubrications. Bought in London on June 8, 1911.

1566 (p, h) **Or. 936 (9)**

A volume of miscellaneous contents in Persian and Urdú; including amusing stories (*Laṭá'if-i-muḍḥik*) in Urdú (ff. 1–10);

some Persian verses; a number of Persian letters, including some written by Ṭáhir Waḥíd for Sháh 'Abbás to the ruler of the Deccan; and a list of the books seen in the mosque and other libraries at Sháh-Jahán-ábád by Mr Adam Durnford Gordon during a visit to that place. Average measurement of leaves, 22·8 × 14·5 c. Formerly belonged to the late Professor E. H. Palmer. Bought of Luzac, May 5, 1899.

1567 (a) **Or. 955 (11)**

Three separate African-Arabic documents in one envelope, *viz.*: (1) a complete tract on Prayer, Purification, Fasting, Repentance and other religious duties by the Imám Abú Zayd 'Abdu'r-Raḥmán b. Muḥammad b. 'Ámir al-Aḥḍarí. Ff. 8 of 22·5 × 16·5 c. and 21 ll.; (2) an Arabic *qaṣída* of 36 *bayts* by Shaykh Muḥammad 'Abdu'lláh b. Abí Zayd al-Qayruwání, with glosses in some non-Arabic African language. Ff. 2 of 23 × 17 c. and 13 ll.; (3) a long slip of paper of 45 × 17·4 c. and 21 ll. containing magical formulæ and a magic square. Deposited by the Rev. J. M. Wilson, D.D., Dec. 6, 1916.

1568 (a, p) **Christ's, S. 7. 5**

A volume from the library of the late Professor W. Robertson Smith containing two Arabic treatises by Abú 'Umar Yúsuf b....'Abdu'l-Barr, who died in 463/1071 at Xetiva in Spain (ff. 2–34 and 37–50), and a Persian commentary on some of the poems of Anwarí (ff. 51–106). For Ibn 'Abdu'l-Barr see Brockelmann, i, pp. 367–8, and Ibn Khallikán, No. 846.

(1) The first treatise, which appears to be an Introduction to the *Kitábu'l-Istí'áb* mentioned by Brockelmann (*loc. cit.*), is entitled:

كتاب الانباه فى ذكر اصول القبائل الرواه عن النّبىّ بما انضاف الى ذلك من علم اصول الانساب و هو كتاب المدخل لكتاب الاستيعاب فى معرفة الصّحابة تصنيف أبى عمر بن عبد البرّ رضى الله عنه ،

(2) The second treatise, not mentioned by Brockelmann, is entitled:

كتاب القصد و الأمم فى التعريف بأصول انساب العرب و العجم
و من اوّل من تكلّم بالعربيّة من الأُمم تأليف الحافظ أبى عمر
يوسف ...بن عبد البرّ النّمرى '

(3) The Persian commentary on verses of Anwarí is written in a good Persian *shikasta*, dated Rajab, 1271/March–April, 1855, by one Muḥammad Taqí. The MS. comprises 106 ff. of 21·6 by 15·4 c. and 16–19 ll.

1569 (p) **Corpus, No. 7**

A volume containing: (1) the *Karímá* or *Pand-náma* of Sa'dí; (2) the *Aḥmad-náma*, containing paradigms of Persian verbs in alphabetical order; (3) a short *mathnawí* poem; (4) a collection of letters. Written in clumsy *nasta'líq* on pages of 24 × 17 c. and dated 1259/1843–4.

1570 (p) **Corpus, No. 12**

A volume of miscellaneous contents written in different *nasta'líq* and *shikasta* hands on pages of 24 × 15 c. Most of the contents are described above under articles **307, 34, 306, 214, 1141, 313, 688, 682** and **831,** but the MS. also contains many miscellaneous notes, mostly medical prescriptions.

1571 (p) **Corpus, No. 17**

Another Persian miscellany, described above under articles **128, 218,** etc. Written in *ním-shikasta* on pages of 24 × 16 c.

1572 (h) **Corpus, No. 20**

An Urdú miscellany, described above under articles **1091, 1527** and **605.** Ff. 70 + 15 + 55 (= 140) of 24·5 × 16 c., written in fairly good *nasta'líq*.

1573 (p) **Corpus, No. 23**

Another Persian miscellany, described above under articles **1144** and **859.** Written in two different *nasta'líq* hands on pages of 23 × 15 c.

1574 (p) **Corpus, No. 31**

Another Persian miscellany, described above under articles **1347** and **112**. Written in *nasta'líq* and *ním-shikasta* on pages of 25·5 × 16 c.

1575 (p) **Corpus, No. 39**

Another Persian miscellany, described above under articles **111, 1513, 704, 971** and **1485**. Written in *nasta'líq* on pages of 24 × 16 c.

1576 (p) **Corpus, No. 51**

Another Persian miscellany, described above under articles **104, 615** and **1164**.

1577 (p) **Corpus, No. 54**

A volume containing: (1) the *Khuláṣatu's-Siyáq*; and (2) the *Inshá-yi-Mas'údí*. See above, articles **439** and **122**.

1578 (p) **Corpus, No. 65**

A volume containing: (1) the *Nahru'l-Faṣáḥat*; (2) a Persian grammar; (3) *Risála-i-Qáfiya*, a treatise on rhyme; and (4) the *Tawqí'át-i-Kisrá*. See articles **1343, 1514, 667** and **336** *supra*.

1579 (p) **Corpus, No. 67**

A volume containing: (1) the *Shajaratu'l-Amání*; (2) the *Nahru'l-Faṣáḥat*; (3) the *Chár Sharbat*; (4) the *Qánún-i-Mujaddad*; and (5) the *Farmán-i-Ja'farí*. See articles **797, 1344, 371, 913** and **892** *supra*.

1580 (p) **Corpus, No. 70**

A volume containing: (1) a commentary on the *Gulistán* of Sa'dí; (2) the letters (*Ruqa'át*) of Abu'l-Faḍl. See articles **1092** and **697** *supra*.

1581 (p, t) **Corpus, No. 75**

A volume containing: (1) miscellaneous Turkish writings; (2) a commentary on the *Burda*, or "Mantle-poem"; (3) a fragment of the *Lama'át* of 'Iráqí; (4) selections from the *Díwán* of Ṣá'ib. See articles **168, 1107, 569** and **1532** *supra*.

1582 (p) **Corpus, No. 98**

A volume containing: (1) the *Díbácha-i-Dil-gushá*; (2) the *Díbácha-i-Sa'ádat*; (3) the *Díbácha-i-Faraḥ-bakhsh*. See articles **494, 495** and **496** *supra*.

1583 (p) **Corpus, No. 102**

A volume of mixed contents, of which the component parts are described in articles **1365, 852, 681** and **975** *supra*. The leaves of each part are numbered separately.

1584 (p) **Corpus, No. 115**

A volume containing: (1) the *Inshá* of Ibráhím Beg; (2) a tract on Indian history; (3) the *Ẓafar-náma* of Buzurj-mihr; and (4) the *Ṣad Pand*, or "Hundred Counsels," ascribed to Luqmán. See articles **1472, 1458, 848** and **832** *supra*.

1585 (p) **Corpus, No. 116**

A volume of mixed contents, of which the component parts are described in articles **1420, 545** and **1560** *supra*.

1586 (p) **Corpus, No. 137**

A volume containing: (1) a fragment of the *Shajaratu'l-Amání*; and (2) the *Díwán* of 'Urfí.

1587 (h) **Corpus, No. 144**

A note-book of 11 × 21 c., written in *shikasta*, containing miscellaneous extracts, chiefly of Urdú verse.

1588 (h) **Corpus, No. 150**

A volume of miscellaneous contents, chiefly lithographed books. See articles **1150, 324** and **1536** *supra*.

1589 (p) **Corpus, No. 178**

A volume containing: (1) the *Gulshan-i-Shu'úr*; (2) the *Naw-báwa-i-Munír*; (3) the *Mátam-kada-i-Munír*. See articles **1099, 1334** and **1118** *supra*.

1590 (p) **Corpus, No. 189**

A volume of miscellaneous contents. See articles **895, 1292** and **1312** *supra*.

1591 (p) **Corpus, No. 205**

A volume containing: (1) the *Baḥru'l-Ansáb*; (2) the *Maṭáli'u'l-Anwár*. See articles **153** and **1204** *supra*.

1592 (p) **Corpus, No. 228**

A volume containing: (1) the Romance of Ḥátim-i-Ṭayy; (2) the *Manqúlu'l-Ḥikmat*; (3) a story in prose translated from the Hindí by Luṭfí; (4) a fragment of a *mathnawí* poem on the romance of *Laylá and Majnún*; (5) a tract on divination and on the legend of Khiḍr; (6) the *Ḥikáyatu'ṣ-Ṣáliḥín*.

1593 (a) **Fitzwilliam, No. 192**

در حدیث کوکب دری و چند رسالهٔ دیگر،

An acephalous MS. consisting of seven detached fragments with many dislocations, in various hand-writings, labelled as above, and undated. Ff. 177 (the last numbered 217) of 25 × 17·7 c. and 27 ll.

1594 (a) فوائد فی العلوم العربیّة، **Jesus, No. 16**

A collection of Arabic proverbs, verses, *Maqámát* and other pieces, including the oath of the Druzes, copied out for Samuel Lyde in A.D. 1853 by Yúnus b. al-Asír aṣ-Ṣaydáwí.

1595 (p) **Trinity, R. 13. 32**

A miscellany of some dozen religious, philosophical and historical tracts in Persian, including the *Maqṣad-i-Aqṣá*, the *Nasab-náma*, or genealogy, of Mawláná Jalálu'd-Dín Rúmí; the *Gulshan-i-Ráz*; with commentary on the same; the Testament (*Waṣiyyat*) of the Prophet; the *Manásiku'l-Ḥajj*; and the *Niẓámu't-Tawáríkh* of al-Bayḍáwí. See Palmer's *Trin. Cat.*, pp. 69–76.

1596 (a, p) **Trinity, R. 13. 45**

A collection of 34 short tracts in Arabic and Persian on various subjects. Ff. 275. See Palmer's *Trin. Cat.*, pp. 102–123.

PART III

CLASS-MARKS OF ALL MANUSCRIPTS DESCRIBED IN THIS HAND-LIST ARRANGED CONSECUTIVELY

In the following table, intended principally for the use of the Library officials, the class-marks of the manuscripts described are arranged consecutively, preceded by ordinal numbers. The number in brackets which follows each class-mark indicates the approximate height of the MS. in inches, the volumes being arranged on the shelves according to size. In assigning these numbers, the usual practice now is to give the round number of inches to which the height of the MS. most nearly approximates; e.g. *a volume* 9¼ *inches in height is marked* (9), *but one* 9¾ *inches in height* (10), *and so on. The italic letters following these numbers indicate the language or languages in which the MS. in question is written,* viz.—*a.* Arabic; *af.* Afghání; *e.* English; *h.* Hindustání (Urdú or Hindí); *l.* Latin; *m.* Malay; *p.* Persian; *panj.* Panjábí; *t.* Turkish, and *east. t.* Turkí.

In the middle column are noted the sources, where ascertainable, whence the MSS. were derived, together with the date of acquisition, to which is prefixed one of the three letters b. ("*bought from*"), g. ("*given by*"), l. ("*left or bequeathed by*").

The thick numbers in the last column indicate the article or articles under which each MS. is described, either in Part I (**Nos. 1–1386**) *or in Part II* (**Nos. 1387–1596**).

In this table the University Library MSS. (**Add. 3608–Or. 967**) *come first, and then the MSS. of the different College Libraries in order of antiquity,* viz.—Clare, Pembroke, Corpus Christi, King's, Queens', St Catharine's, Jesus, Christ's, St John's, Magdalene, Trinity, and Emmanuel, and the Fitzwilliam Museum.

UNIVERSITY LIBRARY

1.	**Add. 3608** (10) *a.*	Géjou, *b.* Dec. 1899.	**909**
2.	**Add. 3609** (8) *a.*	,, ,,	**1248**
3.	**Add. 3610** (8) *a.*	,, ,,	**1361**
4.	**Add. 3611** (10) *a.*	,, ,,	**55**
5.	**Add. 3612** (8) *p.*	,, ,,	**1046**
6.	**Add. 3613** (11) *p.*	,, ,,	**1047**
7.	**Add. 3614** (10) *p.*	,, ,,	**1048, 26, 1376**
8.	**Add. 3615** (9) *a*, *p.*	,, ,,	**1024, 731**
9.	**Add. 3616** (10) *p.*	,, ,,	**370, 1228, 744**
10.	**Add. 3617** (11) *a.*	Géjou, *b.* Feb. 14, 1900.	**9**
11.	**Add. 3618** (13) *a.*	,, ,,	**58**
12.	**Add. 3619** (10) *t.*	,, ,,	**500**
13.	**Add. 3620** (8) *a.*	,, ,,	**1182**
14.	**Add. 3621** (9) *a.*	,, ,,	**713**
15.	**Add. 3622** (10) *a.*	,, ,,	**1270**
16.	**Add. 3623** (7) *a.*	,, ,,	**287, 1188, 261, 1242, 434**
17.	**Add. 3624** (8) *a.*	,, ,,	**480**
18.	**Add. 3625** (9) *a.*	,, ,,	**872**
19.	**Add. 3626** (9) *a.*	,, ,,	**899**
20.	**Add. 3627** (8) *a.*	,, ,,	**814**
21.	**Add. 3628** (9) *a.*	,, ,,	**802**
22.	**Add. 3629** (9) *a.*	,, ,,	**982**
23.	**Add. 3630** (6) *a.*	,, ,,	**900**
24.	**Add. 3631** (7) *a.*	,, ,,	**59**
25.	**Add. 3632** (12) *p.*	J. J. Naaman, *b.* March 5, 1900.	**1056**
26.	**Add. 3634** (10) *a.*	Prof. W. Robertson Smith, *l.* 1894.	**321**
27.	**Add. 3635** (12) *p.*	J. J. Naaman, *b.* March 16, 1900.	**475**
28.	**Add. 3636** (7) *a.*	Géjou, *b.* April 3, 1900.	**380**
29*.	**Add. 3637** (8) *a.*	,, ,,	**911**
30.	**Add. 3638** (9) *p.*	,, ,,	**292**
31.	**Add. 3639** (11) *a.*	,, ,,	**1142**
32.	**Add. 3640** (11) *p.*	A. Reader, *b.* April 23, 1900.	**94**
33.	**Add. 3641** (8) *t.*	Dr Sethian, *b.* May 9, 1900.	**635**
34.	**Add. 3642** (8) *p.*	,, ,,	**521**
35.	**Add. 3643** (9) *p.*	,, ,,	**955**
36.	**Add. 3644** (8) *p.*	,, ,,	**27**

* Wrongly entered on p. 151 *supra* as **Add. 3639** (11) instead of **Add. 3637** (8).

37.	**Add. 3645** (8) *a.*	Dr Sethian, *b.* May 9, 1900.	**62**
38.	**Add. 3646** (8) *t.*	,, ,,	**641**
39.	**Add. 3647** (9) *a.*	,, ,,	**88**
40.	**Add. 3648** (8) *a.*	,, ,,	**325**
41.	**Add. 3649** (9) *t.*	,, ,,	**642**
42.	**Add. 3650** (12) *a.*	Dr Sethian, *b.* May 21, 1900	**1281**
43.	**Add. 3651** (10) *a.*	,, ,,	**1015**
44.	**Add. 3652** (8) *a.*	,, ,,	**898**
45.	**Add. 3653** (8) *a.*	,, ,,	**671, 995**
46.	**Add. 3654** (9) *t.*	,, ,,	**297**
47.	**Add. 3655** (10) *a.*	,, ,,	**873**
48.	**Add. 3656** (9) *a.*	,, ,,	**992**
49.	**Add. 3657** (10) *a, p.*	,, ,,	**750**
50.	**Add. 3658** (8) *p.*	,, ,,	**1166**
51.	**Add. 3663** (10) *p.*	J. J. Naaman, *b.* June 3, 1900.	**267, 751**
52.	**Add. 3664** (8) *a.*	Dr Sethian, *b.* July 17, 1900.	**277**
53.	**Add. 3665** (8) *a.*	,, ,,	**673**
54.	**Add. 3666** (8) *a.*	,, ,,	**1362**
55.	**Add. 3667** (8) *a.*	,, ,,	**203**
56.	**Add. 3668** (8) *a.*	,, ,,	**258**
57.	**Add. 3669** (6) *t.*	,, ,,	**472**
58.	**Add. 3670** (10) *a.*	,, ,,	**1407**
59.	**Add. 3671** (7) *p.*	,, ,,	**1496**
60.	**Add. 3672** (8) *p.*	,, ,,	**1083**
61.	**Add. 3673** (10) *a.*	,, ,,	**1160**
62.	**Add. 3674** (9) *p.*	J. J. Naaman, *b.* July 23, 1900.	**678**
63.	**Add. 3675** (9) *p.*	,, ,,	**679**
64.	**Add. 3676** (8) *p.*	,, ,,	**1297**
65.	**Add. 3677** (9) *p.*	,, ,,	**752**
66.	**Add. 3678** (8) *p.*	Breslauer & Meyer, *b.* Aug. 11, 1900.	**268, 753**
67.	**Add. 3679** (8) *p.*	J. J. Naaman, *b.* Aug. 16, 1900.	**631**
68.	**Add. 3685** (10) *p.*	J. J. Naaman, *b.* Sept. 29, 1900.	**1059**
69.	**Add. 3686** (8) *p.*	,, ,,	**129**
70.	**Add. 3687** (11) *a.*	Khayyâṭ (late Géjou), *b.* Oct. 20, 1907.	**457**
71.	**Add. 3688** (8) *a.*	Dr Sethian, *b.* Nov. 1, 1900.	**479**
72.	**Add. 3689** (10) *a.*	,, ,,	**817**
73.	**Add. 3690** (6) *a.*	,, ,,	**691**
74.	**Add. 3691** (10) *p.*	,, ,,	**1120**
75.	**Add. 3692** (13) *p.*	,, ,,	**53**
76.	**Add. 3693** (9) *p.*	,, ,,	**1267, 1497**
77.	**Add. 3694** (8) *t.*	,, ,,	**793**
78.	**Add. 3695** (9) *east. t.*	,, ,,	**1382**
79.	**Add. 3696** (10) *a.*	Dr Sethian, *b.* Nov. 5, 1900.	**160**
80.	**Add. 3697** (12) *a.*	,, ,,	**349**

81.	**Add. 3698** (4) *a, p.*	Dr Sethian, *b.* Nov. 5, 1900.		**1502**
82.	**Add. 3699** (7) *p.*	”	”	**1494**
83.	**Add. 3700** (8) *a.*	”	”	**659**
84.	**Add. 3701** (8) *a.*	J. J. Naaman, *b.* Nov. 7, 1900.		**159**
85.	**Add. 3702** (8) *a.*	”	”	**985**
86.	**Add. 3703** (8) *a.*	”	”	**1303**
87.	**Add. 3704** (6) *a.*	”	”	**1431**
88.	**Add. 3705** (8) *a, p.*	”	”	**1432**
89.	**Add. 3706** (7) *a, p.*	”	”	**582**
90.	**Add. 3707** (7) *p.*	”	”	**591**
91.	**Add. 3708** (8) *p.*	”	”	**578**
92.	**Add. 3709** (8) *p.*	”	”	**599**
93.	**Add. 3710** (8) *p.*	”	”	**628**
94.	**Add. 3711** (8) *t.*	”	”	**460**
95.	**Add. 3712** (12) *a.*	J. J. Naaman, *b.* Nov. 23, 1900.		**163**
96.	**Add. 3713** (7) *p, a.*	”	”	**1435**
97.	**Add. 3714** (8) *t.*	”	”	**463**
98.	**Add. 3715** (6) *t.*	”	”	**65**
99.	**Add. 3716** (8) *p.*	”	”	**390**
100.	**Add. 3717** (8) *a.*	”	”	**1408**
101.	**Add. 3718** (8) *a.*	”	”	**993**
102.	**Add. 3719** (9) *a.*	”	”	**343, 685**
103.	**Add. 3720** (7) *a.*	”	”	**881**
104.	**Add. 3721** (9) *a.*	”	”	**1404**
105.	**Add. 3722** (8) *a.*	”	”	**822, 20, 666**
106.	**Add. 3723** (8) *a.*	”	”	**1310**
107.	**Add. 3724** (8) *a.*	”	”	**886**
108.	**Add. 3725** (7) *a.*	”	”	**426, 362**
109.	**Add. 3726** (9) *a.*	”	”	**83**
110.	**Add. 3727** (8) *a.*	”	”	**1273**
111.	**Add. 3728** (9) *a.*	”	”	**1167**
112.	**Add. 3729** (8) *a.*	”	”	**828**
113.	**Add. 3730** (12) *a.*	Dr Sethian, *b.* Nov. 28, 1900.		**425**
114.	**Add. 3731** (9) *p.*	”	”	**956**
115.	**Add. 3732** (9) *a.*	”	”	**1564**
116.	**Add. 3733** (9) *p.*	”	”	**625**
117.	**Add. 3734** (9) *p.*	”	”	**124, 404, 423**
118.	**Add. 3735** (9) *a.*	”	”	**1025**
119.	**Add. 3736** (10) *p.*	”	”	**763**
120.	**Add. 3737** (7) *p.*	”	”	**672, 662, 1049**
121.	**Add. 3738** (7) *a.*	”	”	**989**
122.	**Add. 3739** (12) *p.*	”	”	**45**
123.	**Add. 3740** (12) *p.*	”	”	**722**
124.	**Add. 3741** (7) *a.*	”	”	**1200**

125.	**Add. 3742** (8) *a*, *p*.	Khayyát (Géjou), *b*. Dec. 2, 1900.	**1231**
126.	**Add. 3743** (11) *p*.	,, ,,	**285**
127.	**Add. 3744** (9) *a*.	,, ,,	**1282**
128.	**Add. 3746** (8) *a*.	J. J. Naaman, *b*. Dec. 8, 1900.	**1039**
129.	**Add. 3747** (7) *a*.	,, ,,	**1078**
130.	**Add. 3748** (8) *a*.	,, ,,	**950**
131.	**Add. 3749** (8) *a*.	,, ,,	**1274**
132.	**Add. 3750** (8) *a*.	,, ,,	**904**
133.	**Add. 3751** (7) *a*.	,, ,,	**1360**
134.	**Add. 3752** (11) *a*.	Géjou, *b*. Dec. 8, 1900.	**712**
135.	**Add. 3753** (10) *p*.	,, ,,	**1212**
136.	**Add. 3754** (9) *a*.	,, ,,	**303**
137.	**Add. 3755** (13) *m*.	R. J. Wilkinson, Esq., *g*. Nov. 1900.*	
138.	**Add. 3756** (13) *m*.	,, ,,	
139.	**Add. 3757** (13) *m*.	,, ,,	
140.	**Add. 3758** (13) *m*.	,, ,,	
141.	**Add. 3759** (13) *m*.	,, ,,	
142.	**Add. 3760** (13) *m*.	,, ,,	
143.	**Add. 3761** (13) *m*.	,, ,,	
144.	**Add. 3762** (13) *m*.	,, ,,	
145.	**Add. 3763** (13) *m*.	,, ,,	
146.	**Add. 3764** (13) *m*.	,, ,,	
147.	**Add. 3765** (13) *m*.	,, ,,	
148.	**Add. 3766** (13) *m*.	,, ,,	
149.	**Add. 3767** (13) *m*.	,, ,,	
150.	**Add. 3768** (13) *m*.	,, ,,	
151.	**Add. 3769** (13) *m*.	,, ,,	
152.	**Add. 3770** (12) *m*.	,, ,,	
153.	**Add. 3771** (12) *m*.	,, ,,	
154.	**Add. 3772** (12) *m*.	,, ,,	
155.	**Add. 3773** (13) *m*.	,, ,,	
156.	**Add. 3774** (12) *m*.	,, ,,	
157.	**Add. 3775** (12) *m*.	,, ,,	
158.	**Add. 3776** (12) *m*.	,, ,,	
159.	**Add. 3777** (12) *m*.	,, ,,	
160.	**Add. 3778** (12) *m*.	,, ,,	
161.	**Add. 3779** (11) *m*.	,, ,,	
162.	**Add. 3780** (11) *m*.	,, ,,	
163.	**Add. 3781** (11) *m*.	,, ,,	
164.	**Add. 3782** (11) *m*.	,, ,,	
165.	**Add. 3783** (11) *m*.	,, ,,	
166.	**Add. 3784** (10) *m*.	,, ,,	
167.	**Add. 3785** (10) *m*.	,, ,,	

* These Malay MSS. remain undescribed for lack of any available scholar competent and willing to deal with them.

168.	**Add. 3786** (9) *m.*	R. J. Wilkinson, Esq., *g.*	Nov. 1900.	
169.	**Add. 3787** (9) *m.*	,,	,,	
170.	**Add. 3788** (9) *m.*	,,	,,	
171.	**Add. 3789** (9) *m.*	,,	,,	
172.	**Add. 3790** (9) *m.*	,,	,,	
173.	**Add. 3791** (9) *m.*	,,	,,	
174.	**Add. 3792** (8) *m.*	,,	,,	
175.	**Add. 3793** (8) *m.*	,,	,,	
176.	**Add. 3794** (8) *m.*	,,	,,	
177.	**Add. 3795** (8) *m.*	,,	,,	
178.	**Add. 3796** (8) *m.*	,,	,,	
179.	**Add. 3797** (8) *m.*	,,	,,	
180.	**Add. 3798** (8) *m.*	,,	,,	
181.	**Add. 3799** (8) *m.*	,,	,,	
182.	**Add. 3800** (8) *m.*	,,	,,	
183.	**Add. 3801** (10) *m.*	,,	,,	
184.	**Add. 3802** (8) *m.*	,,	,,	
185.	**Add. 3803** (8) *m.*	,,	,,	
186.	**Add. 3804** (8) *m.*	,,	,,	
187.	**Add. 3805** (8) *m.*	,,	,,	
188.	**Add. 3806** (8) *m.*	,,	,,	
189.	**Add. 3807** (8) *m.*	,,	,,	
190.	**Add. 3808** (8) *m.*	,,	,,	
191.	**Add. 3809** (8) *m.*	,,	,,	
192.	**Add. 3810** (8) *m.*	,,	,,	
193.	**Add. 3811** (8) *m.*	,,	,,	
194.	**Add. 3812** (8) *m.*	,,	,,	
195.	**Add. 3813** (7) *m.*	,,	,,	
196.	**Add. 3814** (7) *m.*	,,	,,	
197.	**Add. 3815** (7) *m.*	,,	,,	
198.	**Add. 3816** (7) *m.*	,,	,,	
199.	**Add. 3817** }	Class-marks left for 2 additional MSS.		
200.	**Add. 3818** }	promised by R. J. Wilkinson, Esq.		
201.	**Add. 4166,** Nos. 52–61, *a*, *p*, *t*, 10 documents.	Sandars Bequest.		**1470**
202.	**Add. 4510** (**G**) *p.*	Cowell Bequest.		**649**
203.	**Or. 1** (8) *a.*	Géjou, *b.*	Jan. 28, 1901	**1283**
204.	**Or. 2** (9) *a.*	,,	,,	**994**
205.	**Or. 3** (8) *a.*	,,	,,	**1318**
206.	**Or. 4** (8) *a.*	,,	,,	} **1271**
207.	**Or. 5** (8) *a.*	,,	,,	}
208.	**Or. 6** (7) *a.*	,,	,,	**914**
209.	**Or. 7** (10) *a.*	,,	,,	**1199**
210.	**Or. 8** (8) *a.*	,,	,,	**1163**

211.	**Or. 9** (8) *a*.	Géjou, *b*. Jan. 28, 1901.	**901, 1016, 1026**
212.	**Or. 10** (8) *a*, *p*.	" "	**395**
213.	**Or. 12** (7) *a*.	J. J. Naaman, *b*. Feb. 5, 1901.	**864**
214.	**Or. 13** (6) *p*.	" "	**1110**
215.	**Or. 14** (9) *p*.	" "	**680**
216.	**Or. 15** (7) *a*.	" "	**318**
217.	**Or. 16** (6) *a*.	" "	**771**
218.	**Or. 17** (8) *a*.	" "	**412**
219.	**Or. 18** (8) *a*.	" "	**357**
220.	**Or. 19** (7) *a*.	" "	**176**
221.	**Or. 20** (8) *a*.	" "	**1556**
222.	**Or. 21** (9) *a*.	" "	**156, 1028**
223.	**Or. 22** (6) *p*.	" "	**1418**
224.	**Or. 23** (9) *a*.	" "	**73**
225.	**Or. 24** (8) *a*.	" "	**836**
226.	**Or. 25** (10) *a*.	" "	**61**
227.	**Or. 26** (8) *a*.	" "	**165, 823**
228.	**Or. 27** (10) *p*.	" "	**1052**
229.	**Or. 28** (8) *a*.	" "	**1419**
230.	**Or. 29** (8) *a*.	" "	**1557**
231.	**Or. 30** (8) *a*.	" "	**1521**
232.	**Or. 31** (8) *a*.	" "	**809**
233.	**Or. 32** (9) *a*.	" "	**1008**
234.	**Or. 33** (7) *a*.	" "	**885**
235.	**Or. 34** (8) *p*.	" "	**206**
236.	**Or. 35** (8) *a*.	" "	**1522, 661, 1233**
237.	**Or. 36** (8) *a*.	" "	**4**
238.	**Or. 37** (6) *a*.	" "	**490**
239.	**Or. 38** (7) *p*.	" "	**1489**
240.	**Or. 39** (9) *p*.	" "	**504**
241.	**Or. 40** (9) *t*.	" "	**574**
242.	**Or. 41** (10) *t*.	" "	**1366**
243.	**Or. 42** (6) *a*.	" "	**1425**
244.	**Or. 43** (6) *p*.	" "	**1426**
245.	**Or. 44** (7) *t*.	" "	**860**
246.	**Or. 45** (7) *t*.	" "	**759**
247.	**Or. 46** (13) *p*.	E. Parsons & Sons, *b*. Feb., 1901.	**720**
248.	**Or. 47** (9) *p*.	" "	**1050**
249.	**Or. 48** (10) *a*.	Géjou, *b*. Feb. 20, 1901.	**1405**
250.	**Or. 49** (8) *a*.	" "	**1409**
251.	**Or. 50** (11) *a*.	J. J. Naaman, *b*. March 4, 1901.	**1410**
252.	**Or. 51** (8) *a*.	" "	**692**
253.	**Or. 52** (8) *a*.	" "	**1013, 1042**
254.	**Or. 53** (10) *a*.	" "	**1353**

255.	**Or. 54** (10) *a.*	J. J. Naaman, *b.* March 4, 1901.	**1353**
256.	**Or. 55** (10) *a.*	" "	
257.	**Or. 56** (8) *a.*	" "	**368**
258.	**Or. 57** (8) *a.*	" "	**869**
259.	**Or. 58** (8) *t.*	" "	**1383**
260.	**Or. 59** (10) *t, p.*	" "	**1234**
261.	**Or. 60** (12) *p.*	J. J. Naaman, *b.* May 3, 1901.	**1**
262.	**Or. 61** (11) *p.*	" "	**553**
263.	**Or. 62** (9) *p.*	" "	**1427**
264.	**Or. 63** (9) *a.*	" "	**1305**
265.	**Or. 64** (7) *a.*	Géjou, *b.* May 11, 1901.	**1336**
266.	**Or. 65** (10) *a.*	" "	**1217**
267.	**Or. 66** (8) *a.*	" "	**1218**
268.	**Or. 67** (7) *a.*	" "	**876**
269.	**Or. 68** (7) *a.*	" "	**826**
270.	**Or. 69** (6) *p.*	" "	**1411**
271.	**Or. 163** (13) *a.*	J. J. Naaman, *b.* Dec. 6, 1901.	**1032**
272.	**Or. 164** (13) *a.*	" "	
273.	**Or. 165** (8) *a.*	" "	**338**
274.	**Or. 166** (8) *a.*	" "	**391**
275.	**Or. 167** (8) *p.*	" "	**965**
276.	**Or. 168** (6) *t.*	" "	**589**
277.	**Or. 169** (7) *t.*	" "	**617**
278.	**Or. 170** (7) *p.*	" "	**1255**
279.	**Or. 171** (8) *p.*	" "	**1226**
280.	**Or. 172** (8) *a.*	" "	**1041, 1029**
281.	**Or. 175** (8) *t.*	Géjou, *b.* Jan. 1, 1902.	**219**
282.	**Or. 176** (7) *a.*	" "	**1221**
283.	**Or. 177** (8) *t.*	" "	**461**
284.	**Or. 178** (8) *t.*	" "	**620**
285.	**Or. 179** (8) *t.*	" "	**1384**
286.	**Or. 180** (8) *t.*	" "	**1104**
287.	**Or. 181** (10) *t.*	" "	**541**
288.	**Or. 182** (10) *p.*	" "	**879**
289.	**Or. 183** (11) *p, a.*	" "	**1044**
290.	**Or. 184** (11) *a.*	" "	**421**
291.	**Or. 186** (7) *a.*	Géjou, *b.* Jan. 3, 1902.	**204**
292.	**Or. 187** (8) *a.*	Géjou, *b.* July 3, 1902.	**810**
293.	**Or. 188** (8) *p.*	" "	**556**
294.	**Or. 189** (10) *a.*	" "	**1143**
295.	**Or. 190** (7) *p.*	" "	**1262**
296.	**Or. 193** (13) *a, m.*	B. Quaritch, *b.* Sept. 8, 1902.	**760**
297.	**Or. 194** (11) *a, m.*	" "	**1412**
298.	**Or. 195** (7) *p.*	Géjou, *b.* Oct. 23, 1902.	**1263**

299.	**Or. 196** (7) *p*.	Géjou, *b*. Oct. 23, 1902.	**1450**
300.	**Or. 197** (8) *t*.	,, ,,	**416**
301.	**Or. 198** (8) *a*.	,, ,,	**1423**
302.	**Or. 199** (12) *a*.	,, ,,	**1208**
303.	**Or. 200** (8) *a*.	,, ,,	**46**
304.	**Or. 201** (10) *a*.	,, ,,	**811**
305.	**Or. 202** (8) *a*.	,, ,,	**1165**
306.	**Or. 203** (8) *a*.	,, ,,	**1241**
307.	**Or. 204** (9) *a*.	,, ,,	**1082**
308.	**Or. 205** (10) *a*.	,, ,,	**56, 1119**
309.	**Or. 206** (11) *a*.	J. J. Naaman, *b*. Nov. 12, 1902.	**757**
310.	**Or. 207** (8) *a*.	,, ,,	**162**
311.	**Or. 208** (8) *a*, *t*.	,, ,,	**164, 863, 157, 637, 990, 478, 988**
312.	**Or. 209** (9) *a*.	,, ,,	**875**
313.	**Or. 210** (9) *a*.	,, ,,	**143**
314.	**Or. 211a** (8) *t*.	,, ,,	**1257**
315.	**Or. 211b** (8) *p*.	,, ,,	**283, 658, 871**
316.	**Or. 212** (9) *a*.	,, ,,	**549**
317.	**Or. 213** (10) *a*.	,, ,,	**264**
318.	**Or. 214** (9) *a*.	,, ,,	**1040**
319.	**Or. 215** (9) *a*.	,, ,,	
320.	**Or. 216** (9) *t*.	,, ,,	**779**
321.	**Or. 217** (7) *a*, *p*.	,, ,,	**378**
322.	**Or. 218** (9) *t*.	,, ,,	**513**
323.	**Or. 219** (9) *t*.	,, ,,	**546**
324.	**Or. 220** (9) *a*, *p*.	,, ,,	**1510**
325.	**Or. 221** (11) *t*.	,, ,,	**1374**
326.	**Or. 222** (10) *t*.	,, ,,	**643**
327.	**Or. 223** (7) *t*.	,, ,,	**48**
328.	**Or. 224** (8) *t*.	,, ,,	**1045**
329.	**Or. 225** (12) *t*.	,, ,,	**749**
330.	**Or. 226** (10) *a*.	,, ,,	**947**
331.	**Or. 234** (14) *a*.	Dr F. H. H. Guillemard, *g*. 1902.	**1463**
332.	**Or. 235** (10) *p*.	Prof. E. B. Cowell, *l*. 1903.	**966**
333.	**Or. 236** (10) *p*.	,, ,, ,,	**954**
334.	**Or. 237** (10) *p*.	,, ,, ,,	**1373**
335.	**Or. 238** (10) *p*.	,, ,, ,,	**360**
336.	**Or. 239** (10) *p*.	,, ,, ,,	**850**
337.	**Or. 240** (12) *p*.	,, ,, ,,	**967**
338.	**Or. 241** (13) *p*.	,, ,, ,,	**1253**
339.	**Or. 242** (10) *p*.	,, ,, ,,	**432**
340.	**Or. 243** (11) *p*.	,, ,, ,,	**445**

341.	**Or. 244** (12) *p*.	Prof. E. B.	Cowell,	*l.* 1903.	**446**
342.	**Or. 245** (9) *p*.	,,	,,	,,	**447**
343.	**Or. 246** (10) *p*.	,,	,,	,,	**1064**
344.	**Or. 247** (6) *p*.	,,	,,	,,	**754**
345.	**Or. 248** (8) *p*.	,,	,,	,,	**1369**
346.	**Or. 249** (10) *p*.	,,	,,	,,	**527**
347.	**Or. 250** (12) *p*.	,,	,,	,,	**1060**
348.	**Or. 251** (9) *p*.	,,	,,	,,	**748**
349.	**Or. 252** (12) *p*.	,,	,,	,,	**333**
350.	**Or. 253** (13) *p*.	,,	,,	,,	**381**
351.	**Or. 254** (8) *p*.	,,	,,	,,	**392**
352.	**Or. 255** (9) *p*.	,,	,,	,,	**1061**
353.	**Or. 256** (9) *p*.	,,	,,	,,	**522, 1355**
354.	**Or. 257** (8) *p*.	,,	,,	,,	**702, 1370, 177, 1236**
355.	**Or. 258** (10) *p*.	,,	,,	,,	**1053**
356.	**Or. 259** (8) *p*.	,,	,,	,,	**441**
357.	**Or. 260** (7) *p*.	,,	,,	,,	**968**
358.	**Or. 261** (8) *p*.	,,	,,	,,	**528**
359.	**Or. 262** (8) *p*.	,,	,,	,,	**650**
360.	**Or. 263** (9) *p*.	,,	,,	,,	**231**
361.	**Or. 264** (8) *p*.	,,	,,	,,	**1264**
362.	**Or. 265** (9) *p*.	,,	,,	,,	**1289**
363.	**Or. 266** (10) *p*.	,,	,,	,,	**1298**
364.	**Or. 267** (10) *p*.	,,	,,	,,	} **1206**
365.	**Or. 268** (10) *p*.	,,	,,	,,	
366.	**Or. 269** (9) *p*.	,,	,,	,,	**37**
367.	**Or. 270** (9) *p*.	,,	,,	,,	**38**
368.	**Or. 271** (10) *p*.	,,	,,	,,	**1254**
369.	**Or. 272** (8) *p*.	,,	,,	,,	**393**
370.	**Or. 273** (8) *p*.	,,	,,	,,	**559**
371.	**Or. 274** (8) *p*, *skt.*	,,	,,	,,	**178, 1290**
372.	**Or. 275** (6) *p*.	,,	,,	,,	**594**
373.	**Or. 276** (6) *p*.	,,	,,	,,	**893**
374.	**Or. 277** (9) *p*.	,,	,,	,,	**278**
375.	**Or. 278** (8) *p*.	,,	,,	,,	**293**
376.	**Or. 279** (8) *p*.	,,	,,	,,	**1054**
377.	**Or. 280** (8) *p*.	,,	,,	,,	**1352**
378.	**Or. 281** (8) *p*.	,,	,,	,,	**1291**
379.	**Or. 282** (9) *p*.	,,	,,	,,	**603**
380.	**Or. 283** (10) *p*.	,,	,,	,,	**1055**
381.	**Or. 284** (11) *p*.	,,	,,	,,	**560**
382.	**Or. 285** (10) *p*.	,,	,,	,,	**1121**
383.	**Or. 286** (10) *p*.	,,	,,	,,	**1122**
384.	**Or. 287** (10) *p*.	,,	,,	,,	**1123**

385.	**Or. 288** (10) *p.*	Prof. E. B. Cowell, *l.* 1903.		**1124**
386.	**Or. 289** (9) *p.*	,, ,, ,,		**180**
387.	**Or. 290** (10) *p.*	,, ,, ,,		**181**
388.	**Or. 291** (9) *p.*	,, ,, ,,		**523**
389.	**Or. 292** (11) *p.*	,, ,, ,,		**1371**
390.	**Or. 293** (14) *p.*	,, ,, ,,		
391.	**Or. 294** (14) *p.*	,, ,, ,,		**236**
392.	**Or. 295** (14) *p.*	,, ,, ,,		
393.	**Or. 296** (8) *h.*	,, ,, ,,		**543**
394.	**Or. 297** (7) *p, engl.*	Duplicate class-mark assigned to **Add. 4510,** *q.v.*		**649**
395.	**Or. 298**	Unallotted class-mark.		
396.	**Or. 386** (11)		Trans. from the Persian.	
397.	**Or. 387** (8)			**529**
398.	**Or. 389** (7)		Trans. from the Persian.	
399.	**Or. 390** (11)	Cowell Note-books.	Trans. from Shams-i-Tabríz.	
400.	**Or. 391** (9)		Trans. fr. the *Makhzanu'l-Asrár.*	
401.	**Or. 392** (9)			
402.	**Or. 393** (9)		Trans. from Kháqání's *Tuḥfatu'l-'Iráqayn.*	
403.	**Or. 394** (9)			
404.	**Or. 410** (12) *a.*	Deputy Surgeon-Gen. A. M. Dallas, C.I.E., *g.* Feb. 27, 1903.		**935**
405.	**Or. 413** (5) *a.*	W. D. Webster, *b.* April, 1903.		**1389**
406.	**Or. 415** (10) *a.*	Géjou, *b.* June 3, 1903.		**1018**
407.	**Or. 416** (6) *a, p.*	Hayder Kenn, *b.* July 27, 1903.		**1390**
408.	**Or. 417** (10) *p.*	Géjou, *b.* Aug. 29, 1903.		**719**
409.	**Or. 418** (8) *a.*	,, ,,		**139**
410.	**Or. 419** (6) *a.*	,, ,,		**1176**
411.	**Or. 420** (13) *p.*	Hannan, Watson & Co., *b.* Aug. 29, 1903.		**785**
412.	**Or. 421** (9) *p.*	,, ,, ,,		**448**
413.	**Or. 422** (9) *p.*	,, ,, ,,		**1065**
414.	**Or. 423** (10) *p.*	,, ,, ,,		**1125**
415.	**Or. 424** (16) *p.*	,, ,, ,,		**1126**
416.	**Or. 425** (12) *p.*	,, ,, ,,		**767**
417.	**Or. 426** (10) *p.*	,, ,, ,,		**417**
418.	**Or. 427** (10) *p.*	,, ,, ,,		**1451**
419.	**Or. 428** (15) *p.*	,, ,, ,,		**1523**
420.	**Or. 429** (8) *p.*	,, ,, ,,		**1388**
421.	**Or. 430** (6) *p.*	,, ,, ,,		**265**
422.	**Or. 431** (7) *p.*	,, ,, ,,		**1503**
423.	**Or. 432** (6) *a, p.*	,, ,, ,,		**1391**
424.	**Or. 433** (9) *a, p.*	,, ,, ,,		**829**
425.	**Or. 434** (6) *p.*	,, ,, ,,		**1196**
426.	**Or. 435** (8) *a.*	,, ,, ,,		**805**

427.	**Or. 436** (8) *a*, *p*.	Hannan, Watson & Co., *b*. Aug. 29, 1903.	**437, 676, 1484, 677, 151, 654**
428.	**Or. 437** (12) *a*.	" " "	**718**
429.	**Or. 438** (12) *a*.	" " "	**1043**
430.	**Or. 439** (10) *a*.	" " "	**262**
431.	**Or. 440** (11) *a*.	" " "	**1175**
432.	**Or. 441** (8) *p*.	" " "	**664**
433.	**Or. 442** (8) *a*, *p*.	" " "	**1481**
434.	**Or. 443** (8) *a*.	" " "	**815**
435.	**Or. 444**[1,2] (9) *a*.	" " "	**910**
436.	**Or. 445** (9) *a*, *p*.	" " "	**322, 1269**
437.	**Or. 446** (11) *a*.	" " "	**90**
438.	**Or. 447** (10) *a*.	" " "	**43, 339**
439.	**Or. 448** (8) *a*.	" " "	**1413**
440.	**Or. 449** (8) *t*.	" " "	**1356**
441.	**Or. 450** (10) *a*.	" " "	**326**
442.	**Or. 451** (9) *a*.	" " "	**1169**
443.	**Or. 452** (6) *a*.	" " "	**669**
444.	**Or. 456** (12) *a*.	Géjou, *b*. Nov. 27, 1903.	**572**
445.	**Or. 457** (7) *a*, *p*.	" "	**1490**
446.	**Or. 458** (8) *t*.	J. J. Naaman, *b*. Nov. 27, 1903.	**547**
447.	**Or. 459** (9) *t*.	" "	**519**
448.	**Or. 460** (8) *t*.	" "	**645**
449.	**Or. 461** (10) *t*.	" "	**444**
450.	**Or. 463** (9) *a*.	Edward Van Dyck, Cairo, *g*. April 30, 1903.	**152**
451.	**Or. 464** (7) *a*.	Géjou, *b*. Jan. 29, 1904.	**1500**
452.	**Or. 465** (9) *a*.	" "	**1424**
453.	**Or. 466** (6) *p*.	" "	**1112, 524, 379**
454.	**Or. 467** (7) *p*.	" "	**1108**
455.	**Or. 468** (10) *p*.	" "	**1321**
456.	**Or. 469** (8) *t*.	" "	**1338, 1192, 912, 84, 79**
457.	**Or. 470** (8) *t*.	" "	**1300**
458.	**Or. 471** (8) *t*.	" "	**1147**
459.	**Or. 472** (10) *t*.	" "	**223**
460.	**Or. 473** (9) *t*.	" "	**1057**
461.	**Or. 474** (8) *t*.	" "	**1339**
462.	**Or. 475** (10) *p*.	Transferred from **Dd. 3. 8** (printed books).	**530**
463.	**Or. 476** (5″ × 8″) *a*.	Géjou, *b*. Aug. 18, 1904.	**936**
464.	**Or. 477** (8) *a*.	" "	**320**
465.	**Or. 478** (7) *a*.	" "	**865**
466.	**Or. 479** (8) *a*.	" "	**1272**
467.	**Or. 480** (10) *a*.	" "	**714**

468.	**Or. 481** (7) *a.*	Géjou, *b.* Aug. 18, 1904.	**52**
469.	**Or. 482** (8) *a.*	,, ,,	**315**
470.	**Or. 483** (8) *a.*	,, ,,	**1161**
471.	**Or. 484** (6) *a.*	,, ,,	**583**
472.	**Or. 485** (12) *p.*	,, ,,	**254**
473.	**Or. 486** (10) *p.*	,, ,,	**854**
474.	**Or. 487** (7) *p.*	,, ,,	**1381**
475.	**Or. 488** (9) *t.*	,, ,,	**574**
476.	**Or. 489** (8) *t.*	,, ,,	**473**
477.	**Or. 490** (8) *t.*	,, ,,	**31**
478.	**Or. 491** (10) *t.*	,, ,,	**330**
479.	**Or. 492** (10) *a.*	J. J. Naaman, *b.* Aug. 20, 1904.	**257**
480.	**Or. 493** (11) *a.*	,, ,,	**1247**
481.	**Or. 494** (9) *a.*	,, ,,	**1205, 1225**
482.	**Or. 495** (9) *a.*	,, ,,	**317**
483.	**Or. 496** (8) *a.*	,, ,,	**1195**
484.	**Or. 497** (9) *a.*	,, ,,	**584**
485.	**Or. 498** (11) *a, p.*	,, ,,	**1517**
486.	**Or. 499** (11) *p.*	,, ,,	**1524**
487.	**Or. 500** (10) *p.*	,, ,,	**1073**
488.	**Or. 501** (8) *a.*	,, ,,	**1216**
489.	**Or. 502** (8) *p.*	,, ,,	**1066**
490.	**Or. 503** (8) *p.*	,, ,,	**316**
491.	**Or. 504** (8) *p.*	,, ,,	**1237**
492.	**Or. 505** (8) *p.*	,, ,,	**464**
493.	**Or. 506** (12) *p.*	,, ,,	**1452**
494.	**Or. 507** (8) *p.*	,, ,,	**396**
495.	**Or. 508** (9) *p.*	,, ,,	**1453**
496.	**Or. 509** (6) *p.*	,, ,,	**1280**
497.	**Or. 510** (11) *p.*	,, ,,	**137, 397**
498.	**Or. 511** (9) *p.*	,, ,,	**7**
499.	**Or. 512** (9) *p.*	,, ,,	**458**
500.	**Or. 513** (6) *p.*	,, ,,	**1436**
501.	**Or. 514** (9) *p.*	,, ,,	**309**
502.	**Or. 515** (9) *p.*	Hannan, Watson & Co., *b.* Aug. 20, 1904.	**33**
503.	**Or. 516** (8) *a, p.*	,, ,, ,,	**841**
504.	**Or. 517** (7) *p.*	,, ,, ,,	**1239**
505.	**Or. 518** (8) *p.*	,, ,, ,,	**294**
506.	**Or. 519** (9) *p.*	,, ,, ,,	**1213**
507.	**Or. 520** (10) *p.*	,, ,, ,,	**382**
508.	**Or. 521** (8) *p.*	,, ,, ,,	**1193**
509.	**Or. 522** (8) *p.*	,, ,, ,,	**758**
510.	**Or. 523** (8) *a.*	Luzac & Co., *b.* Aug. 27, 1904.	**241**
511.	**Or. 524** (9) *p.*	,, ,,	**538, 1525**

512.	**Or. 525** (9) *p.*	Luzac & Co., *b.* Aug. 27, 1904.	**878**
513.	**Or. 526** (9) *hind.*	,, ,,	**465**
514.	**Or. 527** (6) *p.*	Géjou, *b.* Nov. 1, 1904.	**550**
515.	**Or. 528** (9) *a.*	,, ,,	**807**
516.	**Or. 529** (8) *a.*	,, ,,	**481**
517.	**Or. 530** (8) *t.*	,, ,,	**1428**
518.	**Or. 531** (6) *t.*	,, ,,	**861**
519.	**Or. 532** (6) *t.*	,, ,,	**1429**
520.	**Or. 533** (10) *a, p, t.*	,, ,,	**201**
521.	**Or. 534** (6) *t.*	,, ,,	**1385**
522.	**Or. 535** (8) *t, p.*	,, ,,	**1074**
523.	**Or. 536** (8) *t.*	,, ,,	**1249**
524.	**Or. 537** (12) *t.*	,, ,,	**917**
525.	**Or. 538** (9) *p.*	George Grahame, Esq., Shíráz, *b.* Nov. 9, 1904.	**855**
526.	**Or. 539** (7) *a.*	Géjou, *b.* Jan. 4, 1905.	**1284**
527.	**Or. 540** (9) *a.*	,, ,,	**782**
528.	**Or. 541** (8) *a.*	,, ,,	**801**
529.	**Or. 542** (6) *p.*	,, ,,	**389, 358**
530.	**Or. 543** (9) *p.*	,, ,,	**562**
531.	**Or. 544** (7) *a, t.*	,, ,,	**1430**
532.	**Or. 545** (6) *t.*	,, ,,	**1301**
533.	**Or. 546** (7) *t.*	,, ,,	**311**
534.	**Or. 559** (8) *a.*	Sandars Collection.	**491**
535.	**Or. 560** (9) *a.*	Khalíl Khálid Bey, M.A., *g.* March 16, 1905.	**424**
536.	**Or. 561** (8) *a.*	,, ,, ,,	**651**
537.	**Or. 563** (8) *p.*	Géjou, *b.* July 14, 1905.	**1071**
538.	**Or. 564** (9) *p.*	,, ,,	**449**
539.	**Or. 565** (8) *p.*	,, ,,	**611, 1109**
540.	**Or. 566** (11) *p.*	,, ,,	**738**
541.	**Or. 567** (9) *t.*	,, ,,	**619**
542.	**Or. 568** (7) *t.*	,, ,,	**1319**
543.	**Or. 569** (9) *t.*	,, ,,	**175**
544.	**Or. 570** (9) *t.*	,, ,,	**1349**
545.	**Or. 571** (8) *t.*	,, ,,	**597**
546.	**Or. 572** (6) *t.*	,, ,,	**400**
547.	**Or. 573** (9) *t.*	,, ,,	**761**
548.	**Or. 574** (8) *t.*	,, ,,	**1317**
549.	**Or. 575** (6) *t.*	,, ,,	**762**
550.	**Or. 576** (10) *a.*	,, ,,	**1168**
551.	**Or. 577** (12) *a.*	,, ,,	**857**
552.	**Or. 578** (8) *a.*	,, ,,	**369**
553.	**Or. 579** (6) *a.*	,, ,,	**781**
554.	**Or. 580** (5) *a.*	,, ,,	**986**
555.	**Or. 581** (5) *a.*	,, ,,	**830**
556.	**Or. 582** (7) *a.*	,, ,,	**1022**

557.	**Or. 583** (7) *a.*	Géjou, *b.* July 14, 1905.	**71**
558.	**Or. 584** (8) *a.*	" "	**813**
559.	**Or. 585** (8) *a.*	" "	**161**
560.	**Or. 586** (8) *a.*	" "	**1392**
561.	**Or. 589** (9) *p.*	Géjou, *b.* Oct. 30, 1905.	**566**
562.	**Or. 590** (7) *a.*	" "	**327**
563.	**Or. 591** (7) *a.*	" "	**1368**
564.	**Or. 592** (8) *a.*	" "	**1017**
565.	**Or. 593** (7) *a.*	" "	**1243**
566.	**Or. 594** (8) *a.*	" "	**413**
567.	**Or. 595** (9) *a.*	" "	**1499**
568.	**Or. 596** (8) *p, t.*	" "	**1106**
569.	**Or. 597** (7) *t.*	" "	**298**
570.	**Or. 598** (7) *t.*	" "	**271**
571.	**Or. 599** (8) *t.*	" "	**1181**
572.	**Or. 600** (9) *t.*	" "	**1454**
573.	**Or. 601** (8) *t.*	" "	**489**
574.	**Or. 602** (9) *t.*	" "	**1325**
575.	**Or. 603** (7) *t.*	" "	**593**
576.	**Or. 604** (8) *t.*	" "	**1019**
577.	**Or. 605** (6) *t.*	" "	**948** and p. 71, ll. 3–5
578.	**Or. 606** (9) *af.*	Prof. A. A. Bevan, *g.* Oct. 5, 1905.	**1173**
579.	**Or. 607** (8) *a.*	Bought from Khalíl Khálid Bey, who obtained them in Constantine (Algeria), in April, 1905.	**821**
580.	**Or. 608** (8) *a.*		**1027**
581.	**Or. 636** (8) *a.*	H. H. Peach, *b.* Jan., 1905.	**937**
582.	**Or. 637** (16 × 10) *m.*	B. Jolley & Sons, *b.* June 3, 1905.*	
583.	**Or. 638** (19 × 15) *m.*	" "	
584.	**Or. 639** (22 × 17) *m.*	" "	
585.	**Or. 640** (21 × 17) *m.*	" "	
586.	**Or. 642** (10) *a, m.*	" "	**737**
587.	**Or. 643**[1] (8) *a.*	Dr W. Wright, *g.* Jan. 31, 1882.	**91**
588.	**Or. 647** (11) *p.*	B. Quaritch from the O'Kinealy sale, *b.* Jan. 15, 1906.	**1306**
589.	**Or. 648** (11) *p.*	" " "	**272**
590.	**Or. 649** (9) *p.*	" " "	**951**
591.	**Or. 650** (8) *p.*	" " "	**501**
592.	**Or. 651** (8) *p.*	" " "	**1210, 209, 708**
593.	**Or. 652** (8) *a.*	Mr Aldis Wright, *g.* Feb. 5, 1906.	**938**
594.	**Or. 653** (5) *p.*	" "	**1465**
595.	**Or. 654** (12) *a.*	Géjou, *b.* Feb. 12, 1906.	**24**
596.	**Or. 655** (7) *a.*	" "	**477**
597.	**Or. 656** (9) *a.*	" "	**1201**

* See the footnote on p. 274 *supra*.

598.	**Or. 657** (6) *a.*	Géjou, *b.* Feb. 12, 1906.	**663, 656**
599.	**Or. 658** (8) *a.*	,, ,,	**1480**
600.	**Or. 659** (10) *a.*	,, ,,	**1222**
601.	**Or. 660** (8) *a.*	,, ,,	**838**
602.	**Or. 661** (9) *t.*	,, ,,	**227**
603.	**Or. 662** (8) *t.*	,, ,,	**284**
604.	**Or. 663** (7) *t.*	Géjou, *b.* Feb. 17, 1906.	**430**
605.	**Or. 664** (8) *p.*	,, ,,	**592**
606.	**Or. 665** (10) *a.*	,, ,,	} **889**
607.	**Or. 666** (10) *a.*	,, ,,	
608.	**Or. 667** (12) *a.*	,, ,,	**806**
609.	**Or. 668** (8) *t.*	,, ,,	**474**
610.	**Or. 669** (9) *t.*	,, ,,	**1466**
611.	**Or. 670** (9) *t.*	,, ,,	**398**
612.	**Or. 671** (8) *t.*	,, ,,	**1293, 1551**
613.	**Or. 672** (12) *t.*	,, ,,	**72**
614.	**Or. 673** (13) *t.*	,, ,,	**775**
615.	**Or. 674** (8) *t.*	,, ,,	**1455**
616.	**Or. 675** (8) *a.*	,, ,,	**668**
617.	**Or. 676** (9) *t.*	,, ,,	**984**
618.	**Or. 677** (9) *t.*	,, ,,	**576**
619.	**Or. 680** (8) *t.*	Géjou, *b.* May 10, 1906.	**1558**
620.	**Or. 681** (11) *a.*	,, ,,	**1414**
621.	**Or. 682** (10) *p.*	,, ,,	**1498**
622.	**Or. 683** (7) *p.*	,, ,,	**903**
623.	**Or. 684** (9) *p.*	Géjou, *b.* June 13, 1906.	**1259**
624.	**Or. 685** (9) *p.*	,, ,,	**1127, 1265, 1198, 182, 50, 732, 734, 1526**
625.	**Or. 687**$^{1-5}$ (7) *a.*	Mr A. S. B. Miller, *g.* Oct. 17, 1906. From H. R. Palmer, B.A., of Ketsīna.	**1467**
626.	**Or. 691** (8) *p.*	Géjou, *b.* Dec., 1906.	**567**
627.	**Or. 692** (7) *t, p.*	,, ,,	**215**
628.	**Or. 693** (8) *p.*	,, ,,	**1487**
629.	**Or. 694** (8) *p.*	,, ,,	**1488**
630.	**Or. 695** (8) *p.*	,, ,,	**1020**
631.	**Or. 696** (8) *p.*	,, ,,	**193**
632.	**Or. 697** (8) *p.*	,, ,,	**1235**
633.	**Or. 698** (8) *t.*	,, ,,	**618**
634.	**Or. 699** (8) *t.*	,, ,,	**401**
635.	**Or. 700** (8) *t.*	,, ,,	**462**
636.	**Or. 701** (8) *t.*	,, ,,	**11**
637.	**Or. 702** (8) *t.*	,, ,,	**862**
638.	**Or. 703** (8) *t.*	,, ,,	**1456**

639.	**Or. 704** (12) *t.*	Géjou, *b.* Dec., 1906.	**8**
640.	**Or. 705** (10) *a.*	,, ,,	**1223**
641.	**Or. 706** (8) *a.*	,, ,,	**710**
642.	**Or. 707** (8) *a.*	,, ,,	**665**
643.	**Or. 708** (8) *a.*	,, ,,	**301**
644.	**Or. 709** (7) *a.*	,, ,,	**435**
645.	**Or. 710** (7) *a.*	,, ,,	**1162**
646.	**Or. 711** (8) *a.*	,, ,,	**440**
647.	**Or. 712** (10) *a.*	,, ,,	**1415**
648.	**Or. 734** (14) *a.*	Géjou, *b.* March 27, 1907.	**51** (648–651)
649.	**Or. 735** (10) *a.*	,, ,,	
650.	**Or. 736** (10) *a.*	,, ,,	
651.	**Or. 737** (13) *a.*	,, ,,	
652.	**Or. 738** (9) *a.*	,, ,,	**652**
653.	**Or. 739** (10) *a.*	,, ,,	**323**
654.	**Or. 740** (10) *a.*	,, ,,	**1036**
655.	**Or. 741** (9) *p.*	,, ,,	**1085, 1380**
656.	**Or. 742** (7) *a.*	,, ,,	**302**
657.	**Or. 743** (8) *t.*	,, ,,	**121**
658.	**Or. 744** (6) *t.*	,, ,,	**1302**
659.	**Or. 745** (8) *a.*	,, ,,	**179**
660.	**Or. 746** (10) *a.*	,, ,,	**54**
661.	**Or. 747** (8) *t.*	,, ,,	**1159**
662.	**Or. 748** (6) *t.*	,, ,,	**891**
663.	**Or. 749** (7) *t.*	,, ,,	**468**
664.	**Or. 750** (7) *p*, *a.*	,, ,,	**1086**
665.	**Or. 751** (8) *p*, *a.*	,, ,,	**1078**
666.	**Or. 752** (8) *p*, *t.*	,, ,,	**1088**
667.	**Or. 757** (9) *p.*	Géjou, *b.* May 13, 1907.	**505**
668.	**Or. 758** (11) *a.*	,, ,,	**1406**
669.	**Or. 759** (8) *a.*	,, ,,	**25**
670.	**Or. 760** (8) *p.*	,, ,,	**595**
671.	**Or. 761** (8) *p.*	,, ,,	**1140**
672.	**Or. 762** (8) *t.*	,, ,,	**1058**
673.	**Or. 763** (7) *t.*	,, ,,	**1386**
674.	**Or. 767** (7) *t.*	Géjou, *b.* Feb. 20, 1908.	**32**
675.	**Or. 768** (8) *t.*	,, ,,	**577**
676.	**Or. 769** (7) *t.*	,, ,,	**794**
677.	**Or. 770** (10) *a.*	,, ,,	**939**
678.	**Or. 771** (13) *a.*	Bought in 1878 of Prof. E. H. Palmer & the representatives of the late C. F. Tyrwhitt Drake.	**940**
679.	**Or. 772** (7) *a.*	Two fragmentary leaves of a Kúfic *Qur'án.*	
680.	**Or. 773** (8) *a*, *p.*	No record of acquisition.	**1511**

681.	**Or. 776** (3) *a.*	Khalíl Khálid Bey, *g.* Jan. 7, 1909.	**1393**
682.	**Or. 777** (7) *t.*	Géjou, *b.* Jan. 7, 1909.	**1105**
683.	**Or. 778** (8) *t.*	" "	**402**
684.	**Or. 779** (8) *p.*	" "	**1250**
685.	**Or. 780** (8) *p.*	" "	**604**
686.	**Or. 781** (10) *p.*	" "	**607**
687.	**Or. 782** (8) *a.*	" "	**1486**
688.	**Or. 805** (9) *p.*	C. Marling, Esq., C.M.G., *g.* through Prof. E. G. Browne.	**450**
689.	**Or. 806** (12) *p.*	G. David, *b.* May 19, 1909.	**561**
690.	**Or. 807** (10) *p.*	" "	**554**
691.	**Or. 808** (11) *p.*	" "	**721**
692.	**Or. 828** (8) *a.*	J. J. Naaman, *b.* Aug. 12, 1910.	**345**
693.	**Or. 831** (15) *a, lat.*	" "	**1507**
694.	**Or. 832** (13) *m.*	R. J. Wilkinson, *g.* Nov. 22, 1910.*	
695.	**Or. 833** (13) *m.*	" "	
696.	**Or. 834** (13) *m.*	" "	
697.	**Or. 835** (13) *m.*	" "	
698.	**Or. 837** (11) ? *panj.*	G. David, *b.* July 14, 1910.	
699.	**Or. 839** (6) *a.*	J. J. Naaman, *b.* Feb. 8, 1911.	**1179**
700.	**Or. 840** (6) *a.*	" "	**1375**
701.	**Or. 841** (6) *a.*	" "	**142**
702.	**Or. 842** (8) *a.*	" "	**843**
703.	**Or. 843** (10) *a, p.*	M. Hippolyte Dreyfus, *g.* Nov., 1910.	**1433**
704.	**Or. 846** (12) *m.*	G. David, *b.* Dec. 10, 1910.*	
705.	**Or. 847** (12) *m.*	" "	
706.	**Or. 848** (11) *m.*	" "	
707.	**Or. 849** (10) *m.*	" "	
708.	**Or. 850** (8) *m.*	" "	
709.	**Or. 851** (8) *m.*	" "	
710.	**Or. 852** (8) *m.*	" "	
711.	**Or. 853** (8) *m.*	" "	
712.	**Or. 854** (8) *m.*	" "	
713.	**Or. 855** (8) *m.*	" "	
714.	**Or. 856** (8) *m.*	" "	
715.	**Or. 857** (8) *m.*	" "	
716.	**Or. 858** (8) *m.*	" "	
717.	**Or. 859** (8) *m.*	" "	
718.	**Or. 862** (12) *p.*	Luzac & Co., *b.* May, 1911.	**745**
719.	**Or. 863** (10) *p.*	" "	**1154**
720.	**Or. 864** (8) *a.*	"Found in W. Robertson Smith's rooms and believed to have been his and sent to the Univ. Library accordingly by the Master of Christ's Coll., 1895."	**172**

* See the foot-note on p. 274 *supra*.

721. **Or. 865** (8) *a*. "Found in W. Robertson Smith's rooms etc." **907**
722. **Or. 866** (9) *a*. „ „ „ **155**
723. **Or. 867** (9) *a*. „ „ „ **1030**
724. **Or. 868** (9) *a*. „ „ „ **835**
725. **Or. 869** (in box) *p*. Mrs Lewis, *g*. April 1, 1911. **1468**
726. **Or. 870** (5) *a*. Bernard Halliday, *b*. Dec. 19, 1911. **1394**
727. **Or. 871** (8) *m*. Bought by E. Burrell, June 8, 1911. **1565**
728. **Or. 875** (16) *p*. R. T. Wright, *g*. April 19, 1912. **1469**
729. **Or. 877** (11) *p*. „ „ **28**
730. **Or. 878** (7) *a*. „ „ **1184**
731. **Or. 880** (13) *h*. G. David, *b*. July 3, 1912. **846**
732. **Or. 881** (16) *h*. „ „ **150**
733. **Or. 882** (5) *a*. Lady Scott, *g*. July 3, 1912. **922**
734. **Or. 884** (8) *a*. A. C. Benson, M.A., Magd. Coll., *g*. Oct. 25, 1912. **1395**
735. **Or. 885** (29×17) *t*. No record of acquisition. **1475**
736. **Or. 886** (17×12) *t*. No record of acquisition. **1476**
737. **Or. 887** (10) *a*. R. F. Scott, M.A., Master of St John's Coll., *g*. Nov. 22, 1912. **1518**
738. **Or. 889** (9) *a*. G. David, *b*. Nov. 22, 1912. **991**
739. **Or. 890** (9) *a*. „ „ **1189**
740. **Or. 891** (5) *a*. S. Gaselee, Esq., M.A., *g*. May 22, 1913. **1396**
741. **Or. 895** (19) *p*. G. David, *b*. Aug. 1, 1913. **1474**
742. **Or. 899** (8) *p*, *h*. G. David, *b*. Feb. 20, 1914. **756**
743. **Or. 900** (8) *p*. „ „ **131**
744. **Or. 901** (8) *p*. J. J. Naaman, *b*. Aug., 1914. **1504**
745. **Or. 902** (6) *a*. „ „ **853**
746. **Or. 907** (13) *a*. Bequest of H. F. B. Lynch, Esq., M.P., Jan., 1915. **1007**
747. **Or. 908** (12) *a*. „ „ „ **1178**
748. **Or. 909** (12) *a*. „ „ „ **1183**
749. **Or. 910** (10) *a*. „ „ „ **1256**
750. **Or. 911** (11) *p*. „ „ „ **856**
751. **Or. 912** (8) *a*. „ „ „ **1448**
752. **Or. 913** (8) *a*. „ „ „ **348**
753. **Or. 914** (12) *p*. „ „ „ **1146**
754. **Or. 915** (12) *p*. „ „ „ **1307**
755. **Or. 916** (13) *a*. „ „ „ **923**
756. **Or. 917** (15) *p*. „ „ „ **383**
757. **Or. 918** (9) *a*. „ „ „ **138**
758. **Or. 919** (8) *a*. „ „ „ **1232**
759. **Or. 920** (8) *a*. „ „ „ **1006**
760. **Or. 921** (8) *a*. „ „ „ **987**
761. **Or. 922** (8) *a*. „ „ „ **1177**
762. **Or. 923** (9) *p*. „ „ „ **216**

763. **Or. 924** (8) *p*. Bequest of H. F. B. Lynch, Esq., M.P., Jan., 1915. **531**

764. **Or. 925** (7) *t*. „ „ „ **136**

765. **Or. 926** (7) *a*. „ „ „ **1447**

766. **Or. 927** (12) *a*. „ „ „ **1010**

767. **Or. 928** (11) *a*. „ „ „ **1449**

768. **Or. 929** (10) *a, greek, hebrew, syriac*. „ „ **1185**

769. **Or. 934** (12) *a*. Mrs William Wright, *g*. Date not recorded. **1003**

770. **Or. 935** (8) *a*. „ „ **1238**

771. **Or. 936** (9) *hind*. Luzac & Co., *b*. May 5, 1899. **1566**

772. **Or. 938** (10) *p*. G. David, *b*. Nov. 5, 1915. **1128**

773. **Or. 939** (8) *p*. „ „ **1089**

774. **Or. 940** (9) *a*. S. Gaselee, Esq., M.A., *g*. Feb., 1916. **1149**

775. **Or. 941** (11) *p*. Guy le Strange, Esq., M.A., *g*. Mar. 1, 1916. **1067**

776. **Or. 942** (8) *p*. „ „ **183**

777. **Or. 943** (8) *p, a*. „ „ **1434**

778. **Or. 944** (9) *p*. „ „ **246**

779. **Or. 945** (10) *p*. „ „ **1308**

780. **Or. 946** (9) *p*. „ „ **1309**

781. **Or. 947** (11) *p*. „ „ **839**

782. **Or. 949** (23×21) *t*. Rev. Dr C. H. W. Johns, D.D., St Cath. Coll., *g*. Jan. 18, 1916. **1477**

783. **Or. 950** (7) *a, english*. Prof. E. G. Browne, *g*. April 27, 1916 (*Adversaria*).*

784. **Or. 951** (10) *a*. „ „

785. **Or. 954** (5) *a*. Deposited by the Rev. J. M. Wilson, D.D., Worcester, Dec. 6, 1917. **1397**

786. **Or. 955**^{1,2,3} (11) *a*. „ „ „ **1567**

787. **Or. 959** (7) *t*. 2nd Lieut. R. H. Aldis, *g*. 1917. **1153**

788. **Or. 960** (12) *p, t*. Mírzá Muḥsin, *b*. May 15, 1917. **1519**

789. **Or. 961** (12) *p*. Sir E. Denison Ross, *b*. Nov. 28, 1917. **237**

790. **Or. 962** (6) *a*. J. Whitaker, Cambridge, *b*. Nov. 30, 1917. **1299**

791. **Or. 963** (10) *a, p*. „ „ **1278**

792. **Or. 964** (12) *p*. „ „ **451**

793. **Or. 966** (9) *english*. Guy le Strange, Esq., M.A., *g*. April, 1918. **384**

794. **Or. 967** (13) *english*. „ „ **247**

The existence of eighteen more Oriental MSS. bearing the class-marks **Or. 968—Or. 985** only became known to me when this sheet was in the Press. Eight of these MSS. (**Or. 968, 971, 972, 974, 976, 980, 983** and **984**) are in the Arabic character, but none of them are valuable or interesting. They will be briefly described at the end of this section, immediately before the Index.

* An interleaved copy of the *Díwán* of Bahá'u'd-Dín Zuhayr, lithographed in 1278/1861–2, with the late Professor E. H. Palmer's autograph copy of his English versified translation, and his Arabic notes on the text.

THE COLLEGE LIBRARIES

Only the twelve following Colleges, so far as I have been able to ascertain, include in their libraries Oriental manuscripts written in the Arabic character*:

Clare, 3 MSS.
Pembroke, 3 MSS.
Corpus Christi, 254 MSS.
King's, 257 MSS.
Queens', 13 MSS.
St Catharine's, 4 MSS.
Jesus, 17 MSS.
Christ's, 58 MSS.
St John's, 39 MSS.
Magdalene, 1 MS.
Trinity, 89 MSS.
Emmanuel, 23 MSS.
Fitzwilliam Museum, 12 MSS.

The following table indicates the class-marks of these MSS.; their donors, when known; and the articles in this *Hand-List* under which each is described. In some cases supplementary notes, taken on a later examination, after the *Hand-List* had gone to press, are incorporated here. Where a College Library (e.g. **Corpus Christi**) contains amongst its Oriental MSS. a few in the Dêvanâgarî or other non-Arabian character, mention is sometimes made of these for the sake of completeness, without any attempt at accurate description.

CLARE.

795.	**C.7.12** (*a*)	*Qur'án.*	**924**
796.	**Kk.3.10** (*t*)	*Jarráḥ-náma.*	**356**
797.	**Kk.3.11** (*a*, *t*)	Ottoman history. Henry Freeman, *g.* 1796.	**1457**

PEMBROKE.

798.	**289** (*a*)	*Qur'án.*	**945**
799.	**290** (*a*)	*Qur'án.* Christopher Wren, *g.* 1626.	**946**
800.	**290**[a] (*t*)	Calendar for 1086–7/1675–6.	**1495**

CORPUS CHRISTI.

All the Oriental MSS. in this library, with two exceptions (**No. 153** and **Parker 401**), appear to have been collected in India, for the most part in Lucknow, in 1863–4, by Colonel

* Slight discrepancies between the number of MSS. given in this summary and in the fuller lists which follow arise from the fact that in some libraries two volumes have only one class-mark, while in others each has a separate one.

Honnor of the 1st Bombay Grenadiers, and subsequently to have passed into the possession of Francis Hodder, Esq., of Cork. In February, 1883, fifty-eight of them were presented to the College (possibly at the suggestion of the Rev. S. S. Lewis, at that time Fellow and Librarian) by Dr R. Caulfield, LL.D., Librarian of Queen's College, Cork. A notice of this first gift appeared in the *Athenaeum* of May 5, 1883, but how the MSS. came into the possession of Dr Caulfield, or whether he merely acted as an intermediary in the transaction is not clear. In July of the following year (1884) there was a second donation of nearly two hundred MSS., which appear to have been presented directly by Mr Hodder. The collection contains few MSS. of value, and a good deal of quite worthless material. It includes some lithographed books and a few Hindí and other MSS. in the Dêvanâgarî character. These, though they have really no place in this *Hand-List*, are mentioned below for the sake of convenience and completeness. The numbers now borne by these books were assigned to them arbitrarily by myself according to their position on the shelves.

801.	**1** (*p*)	*Díwán* of 'Urfí.	**579**
802.	**2** (*p*)	Story of Badr-i-Munír.	**960**
803.	**3** (*p*)	The *Nigáristán* of Ghaffarí.	**1327**
804.	**4** (*p*)	Letters of Ṭáhir Waḥíd, followed by a medical work entitled *Tuḥfatu'l-Fawá'id.*	**703**
805.	**5** (*p*)	*Dastúr-i-Shagarf.*	**483**
806.	**6** (*p*)	A legal note-book.	**281**
807.	**7** (*p*)	Tracts in prose and verse.	**1569**
808.	**8** (*p*)	*Bahár-i-Dánish.*	**191**
809.	**9** (*p*)	*Inshá-yi-Badáyi'.*	**102**
810.	**10** (*p*)	Story of *Máh u Mushtarí.*	**978**
811.	**11** (*h*)	*Qiṣṣa-i-Chár Darwish.*	**961**
812.	**12** (*p*)	Ten tracts.	**307, 34, 306, 214, 1141, 313, 688, 682, 831, 1570**
813.	**13** (*p*)	*Báz-náma.*	**149**
814.	**14** (*p*)	*Qiránu's-Sa'dayn.*	**920**
815.	**15** (*p*)	*Alfáẓ-i-Adwiya.* See Fonahn, p. 88, No. 231.	**86**
816.	**16** (*h*)	*Qiṣṣa-i-Úzsháh.*	**959**
817.	**17** (*p*)	*Muhadhdhibu'l-Akhláq* and other tracts.	**1288, 128, 405, 218, 1571**

818.	**18** (*p*)	*Tawqí'át-i-Kisrá.*	**335, 1471**
819.	**19** (*h*)	Story of Prince Bí-Naẓír.	**466**
820.	**20** (*h*)	Translation of *Gulistán* and various poems.	**1091, 1527, 605, 1572**
821.	**21** (*h*)	*Káristán.*	**999**
822.	**22** (*p*)	*Díwán* of Ghaní.	**585**
823.	**23** (*p*)	Treatises on Rhetoric and Prosody, etc.	**1144, 859, 1559, 1573**
824.	**24** (*p*)	*Díwán* of Sa'dí.	**551**
825.	**25** (*p*)	*Díwán* of Ḥáfiẓ.	**534**
826.	**26** (*p*, *h*)	Story of the Rose of Bakáwalí.	**977**
827.	**27** (*brij-bhaka*)	Translation of *Bhágavad-Gítá.*	**196**
828.	**28** (*p*)	Treatise on Rhetoric.	**1145**
829.	**29** (*p*)	Treatise on Therapeutics.	**808**
830.	**30** (*p*)	*Díwán* of Hilálí.	**632**
831.	**31** (*p*)	Story of Sháhid and 'Azíz, etc.	**1347, 112, 1574**
832.	**32** (*hindí*)	Tracts in the Dêvanâgarî script.	**1439**
833.	**33** (*p*)	*Qarábádín-i-Qádirí* (lith. 1271/1854–5). See Fonahn, p. 102, No. 266.	**918**
834.	**34** (*p*)	*Díwán* of Wáqif.	**626**
835.	**35** (*h*)	*Díwán* of Riḍá.	**548**
836.	**36** (*p*)	*Majmú'-i-Khání.*	**1148**
837.	**37** (*hindí*)	Tracts in the Dêvanâgarî script.	**1440**
838.	**38** (*p*, *h*)	Poem by Mír Ḥusayn, followed by medical receipts.	**1137**
839.	**39** (*p*)	Epistolary models and other tracts.	**111, 1513, 704, 971, 1485, 1575**
840.	**40** (*h*)	Legal decisions, followed by the *Díwán* of Walí.	**908, 629**
841.	**41** (*p*)	*Chahár Chiman.*	**377**
842.	**42** (*a*)	A medical tract.	**916, 280**
843.	**43** (*h*)	*Díwán* of Ḥasrat.	**540**
844.	**44** (*p*)	*Naw-Bahár-i-'Ishrát.*	**1335**
845.	**45** (*p*)	*Díwán* of Ghaní.	**586**
846.	**46** (*p*)	*Inshá-yi-Abu'l-Faḍl.*	**96**
847.	**47** (*h*)	*Díwán* of Naṣír of Dihlí.	**622**
848.	**48** (*p*)	Epistolary models.	**1552**
849.	**49** (*p*)	Epistolary models entitled *'Ináyat-náma* or *Majma'u'l-Jawáhir.*	**874**
850.	**50** (*p*)	Collected works of Ẓuhúrí.	**1155, 746, 883**
851.	**51** (*p*)	*Inshá-yi-Bí-dil* and *Díwán* of Náṣir 'Alí.	**104, 615, 1164, 1576**
852.	**52** (*p*)	*Ḥamla-i-Ḥaydarí.*	**418**
853.	**53** (*p*, *h*)	Common-place book of verses, etc.	**1529**

854.	**54** (*p*)	Tracts on arithmetic and letter-writing.	**439, 122, 1577**
855.	**55** (*h*)	Story of Máh-paykar and Sím-tan in verse.	**1136**
856.	**56** (*p*)	*Kusháyish-náma.*	**1038**
857.	**57** (*p*)	*Inshá-yi-Bí-dil*, followed by the *Díwán-i-Shawkat.*	**105, 564, 1531**
858.	**58** (*p*)	*'Iyár-i-Dánish.*	**877**
859.	**59** (*h*)	*Díwán* of Maṣḥafí.	**608**
860.	**60** (*p*)	*Mízánu'ṭ-Ṭibb.* See Fonahn, p. 27, No. 26.	**1294**
861.	**61** (*p*)	*Jámi'u'l-Qawánín.*	**353**
862.	**62** (*p*)	*Akbar-náma* (Pt. i).	**97**
863.	**63** (*h*)	Martyrdom of the Imáms.	**331**
864.	**64** (*h*)	*Laylá wa Majnún* of Hawas.	**1114**
865.	**65** (*p*)	Tracts by Jámí, Qatíl, etc.	**1343, 1514, 667, 336, 1578**
866.	**66** (*h*)	Poetical selections.	**1138, 1135, 1133, 1134, 1350, 882, 972, 1115, 49, 970, 1530**
867.	**67** (*p*)	Tracts by Qatíl, etc.	**797, 1344, 371, 913, 892, 1579**
868.	**68** (*p*)	The *Ṭúṭí-náma* of Nakhshabí.	**845**
869.	**69** (*p*)	Translation of the *Baitál Pachísí.*	**207**
870.	**70** (*p*)	Commentary on the *Gulistán*, etc.	**1092, 697, 1580**
871.	**71** (*h*)	*Díwán* of Átash.	**498**
872.	**72** (*p*)	*Inshá-yi-Harkarn.*	**126**
873.	**73** (*p*)	Poem by Ghanímat entitled *Nírang-i-'Ishq.*	**1348**
874.	**74** (*p*)	Story of *Mihr u Máh.*	**979**
875.	**75** (*p, t*)	*Lama'át* of 'Iráqí and poems.	**168, 1107, 569, 1532, 1581**
876.	**76** (*p*)	*Díwán* of Ḥáfiẓ.	**535**
877.	**77** (*a, p*)	Risála-i-Muḥammad Záhid.	**674**
878.	**78** (*p*)	*Díwán* of Qatíl.	**598**
879.	**79** (*p*)	*Díwán* of Naẓírí.	**623**
880.	**80** (*p*)	Tracts on Geomancy.	**1505**
881.	**81** (*p*)	Jámí's *Yúsuf u Zulaykhá.*	**1379**
882.	**82** (*hindí*)	Book in the Dêvanâgarî script.	**1441**
883.	**83** (*p*)	*Munsha'át-i-Brahman.*	**1258**
884.	**84** (*p*)	*Inshá-yi-Harkarn*, etc.	**127, 110, 1553**
885.	**85** (*p*)	*Riyáḍu'l-Adwiya.* See Fonahn, p. 109, No. 302.	**726**
886.	**86** (*p*)	*Bahár-i-Sukhun.*	**194**
887.	**87** (*p*)	Fayḍí's *Nal u Daman.*	**1330**
888.	**88** (*p*)	*Durr-i-Majális.*	**476**
889.	**89** (*p*)	Story of Mas'úd Sháh and 'Azíz Sháh.	**973**
890.	**90** (*p*)	*Qarábádín* of Shifá'í. See Fonahn, pp. 81–4, No. 227.	**919**

891.	**91** (*p*)	*Mushábahát-i-Rabí'í.*	**1190**
892.	**92** (*p*)	*Díwán* of Asír.	**502**
893.	**93** (*hindí*)	Book in the Dêvanâgarî script.	**1442**
894.	**94** (*p*)	*Chahár Chiman.*	**376**
895.	**95** (*p*)	*Inshá-yi-Mádhúrám.*	**118**
896.	**96** (*p*)	*Mufarriḥu'l-Qulúb.*	**1229**
897.	**97** (*p*)	*Qiránu's-Sa'dayn.*	**921**
898.	**98** (*p*)	*Díbácha-i-Dilgushá*, etc.	**494, 495, 496, 1582**
899.	**99** (*h*)	*Pand-náma* of Ḥájji Walí.	**220**
900.	**100** (*p*)	*Maḥshar-náma.*	**1152**
901.	**101** (*p*)	*Risála dar Aḥkám-i-Tijárat.*	**653**
902.	**102** (*p*)	*Waqáyi'-i-Badáyi'-i-Aḥwál*, etc.	**1365, 852, 681, 975, 1583**
903.	**103** (*p*)	Book of prayers by Imám Badru'd-Dín entitled *Maliku'l-Wá'izín.*	
904.	**104** (*p*)	Zulálí's poem *Maḥmúd u Ayáz.*	**1156**
905.	**105** (*p*)	*Káristán.*	**1000**
906.	**106** (*p*)	Verse translation of *Singhásan Battísí.*	**773**
907.	**107** (*p*)	Poems by Hátifí, Tajallá and Mír Dard.	**1113, 1508, 1116, 544, 1533**
908.	**108** (*p*)	*Ta'ríkh-i-Dilgushá.*	**235**
909.	**109** (*p*)	*Díwán* of Kalím.	**600**
910.	**110** (*p*)	*Inshá-yi-Abu'l-Faḍl.*	**98**
911.	**111** (*p*)	*Laylá wa Majnún* of Amír Khusraw.	**1111**
912.	**112** (*p*)	*Dastúru'l-'Amal.*	**485**
913.	**113** (*p*)	*Díwán* of Anwarí.	**509**
914.	**114** (*p*)	*Díwán* of Brahman.	**517**
915.	**115** (*p*)	*Khayálát-i-Khusrawí*, etc.	**1472, 1458, 848, 832, 1584**
916.	**116** (*p, h*)	Proverbs, poems, etc.	**1420, 545, 1560, 1585**
917.	**117** (*p*)	*Míná Bázár.*	**1295**
918.	**118** (*p*)	Historical fragments relating to India.	**1459**
919.	**119** (*p*)	Fragmentary commentary on the *Bústán.*	**184**
920.	**120** (*hindí*)	Book in the Dêvanâgarî script.	**1443**
921.	**121** (*hindí*)	" " "	**1444**
922.	**122** (*p*)	Letters of Bí-dil.	**700**
923.	**123** (*a*)	A fine old copy of *Kalíla wa Dimna* (xiv cent.).	**1076**
924.	**124*** (*p*)	*Díwán* of Ṣá'ib.	**570**
925.	**125** (*h*)	*Laylá wa Majnún* of Naẓír and other poems.	**1117**
926.	**126** (*p*)	*Riyáḍu'l-Awliyá*, etc.	**21, 728**
927.	**127** (*p*)	*Inshá-yi-Mádhúrám.*	**119**

* Wrongly numbered **129** twice on p. 94.

928. **128** (*h*) *Qiṣṣa-i-Chár Darwísh.* **1337, 962**
929. **129** (*h*) Poems of Shaykh Imám-bakhsh called Násikh. **613, 621**
930. **130** (*p*) *Ṣadru'l-Kuttáb.* **834, 1473**
931. **131** (*p*) Fragments of the *Anwár-i-Suhaylí* and other stories. **132**
932. **132** (*p*) Ditto, the two in one bundle. **1561**
933. **133** (*hindí*) A poem in some Indian language, not Urdú. **222**
934. **134** (*p*) Acephalous *Anwár-i-Suhaylí.* **133**
935. **135** (*p*) Mír Ḥaydar's *Shujá'-i-Ḥaydarí.* **796**
936. **136** (*p*) *Inshá-yi-Abu'l-Faḍl*, vol. ii. **99**
937. **137** (*p*) *Qaṣá'id-i-'Urfí*, etc. **798, 530, 1586**
938. **138** (*h*) Shí'a controversial poem (*Barq-i-Lámi'*). **170**
939. **139** (*p*) Historical anecdotes about Persian kings. **1562**
940. **140** (*h*) Poems for recitation in Muḥarram. **1534**
941. **141** (*a*) *Ṣaḥífa-i-Sajjádiyya.* **827**
942. **142** (*p*) *Jámi'u'l-Qawánín.* **354**
943. **143** (*brij-bháshá*) A Jain work. **1445**
944. **144** (*h*) A note-book of selections in prose and verse. **1587**
945. **145** (*p*) *Fawá'idu'l-Mubtadí.* **905**
946. **146** (*h*) Translation of the *Padmávat.* **211**
947. **147** (*h*) Poetical selections. **1535**
948. **148** (*h*) Abridged translation of the *Sháh-náma* **789**
949. **149** (*p*) *Qaṣídas* of 'Urfí and Ahlí. **953**
950. **150** (*h*) Three lithographed and printed tracts. **1150*, 1536, 324**
951. **151** (*h*) *Qiṣṣa-i-Chár Darwísh.* **963**
952. **152** (*h*) Biographies of ancient men of note (Part iii, lithographed). **1460**
953. **153** (*p*) *Gulistán* and *Bústán*, presented by the Rev. Dr E. H. Perowne, Master, in 1884. **185**
954. **154** (*p*) Poetical extracts. **1537**
955. **155** (*p, h*) Letters of Ẓuhúrí and *Fasána-i-'Ajá'ib.* **1260, 896, 1554**
956. **156** (*p*) *Nuzhatu'l-Arwáḥ.* **1304**
957. **157** (*p*) *Díwán* of Náṣir 'Alí. **616**
958. **158** (*p*) *Díwáns* of Anjab and 'Ayán. **1538**
959. **159** (*h*) Translation of the *Gulzár-i-Ibráhím.* **1084, 304, 1461**
960. **160** (*p*) Glossary to the Letters of Bí-dil. **701**
961. **161** (*p*) Niẓámí's *Makhzanu'l-Asrár.* **1171**
962. **162** (*p*) *Díwán* of Shawkat. **565**
963. **163** (*p*) Letters of Qatíl. **707**
964. **164** (*p*) *Inshá-yi-Fá'iq*, lithographed. **116**
965. **165** (*p*) *Tawáríkh-i-Bulandshahr*, lithographed. **332**
966. **166** (*p*) *Maḥmúd-náma*, lithographed. **1157**
967. **167** (*p*) *Inshá-yi-Abu'l-Faḍl* (Book i). **100**

* Wrongly numbered **151**[1] on p. 189, instead of **150**[1].

968.	**168** (*p*)	*Dastúru'l-Mubtadí.*	**487**
969.	**169** (*p*)	Complete poetical works of Ghaní.	**1072**
970.	**170** (*p*)	Another very bad copy of the above.	**587**
971.	**171** (*p*)	*Díwán* of Maẓhar.	**609**
972.	**172** (*p*)	Anthology of Persian verse.	**1539**
973.	**173** (*p*)	*Gulistán.*	**1093**
974.	**174** (*p*)	*Nahru'l-Faṣáḥat.*	**1345**
975.	**175** (*h*)	*Díwán* of Taqí Maḥmúd "Gúyá," lithographed.	**606**
976.	**176** (*p*)	Fragment of a translation of the *Alf Layla.*	**85**
977.	**177** (*p*)	*Zubdatu'r-Ramal.*	**735**
978.	**178** (*p*)	*Gulistán-i-Shu'úr*, *Mátam-kada*, etc.	**1099, 1334, 1118, 1589**
979.	**179** (*p*)	*Díwán* of Qáni'.	**596**
980.	**180** (*p*)	History of Aḥmad Sháh Durrání.	**228**
981.	**181** (*p*)	*Jang-náma-i-Rasúl* and *Qiṣṣa-i-Mihr u Máh.*	**367, 980**
982.	**182** (*p*)	*Qiṣṣa-i-Mihr u Máh.*	**981**
983.	**183** (*a*)	Tracts on the virtues of the Divine Names, etc.	**1399, 482**
984.	**184** (*p*)	*Tawqí'át-i-Kisrá.*	**337**
985.	**185** (*h*)	Works of the poet Mír Abu'l-Qásim Nithár.	**1075**
986.	**186** (*p*)	Fayḍí's *Nal u Daman.*	**1331**
987.	**187** (*p*)	Amír Khusraw's *Á'ína-i-Sikandarí.*	**147**
988.	**188** (*p*)	*Risála-i-Ṭughrá.*	**660**
989.	**189** (*p*)	Lexicographical and grammatical tracts.	**895, 1292, 1312, 1590**
990.	**190** (*p*)	Five tracts, four in manuscript and one lithographed.	**705, 372, 1296, 1158**
991.	**191** (*p*)	Anthology of Persian verse.	**952, 290, 1540**
992.	**192** (*p*)	Epistolary models, etc.	**484, 115, 117, 1555**
993.	**193** (*p*)	*Riyáḍ-i-'Álamgírí.*	**729**
994.	**194** (*p*)	*Dah Majlis.*	**492**
995.	**195** (*p*)	*Sab'u Samáwát.*	**755**
996.	**196** (*p*)	*Miṣbáḥu'l-Mubtadí.*	**1197**
997.	**197** (*p*)	*Inshá-yi-Abu'l-Faḍl.*	**698**
998.	**198** (*p*)	Court Gazette of Awrangzíb's reign.	**1478**
999.	**199** (*p*)	*Kanzu'd-Daqá'iq.*	**1079**
1000.	**200** (*p*)	*Maṣábíḥu'l-Qulúb.*	**1194**
1001.	**201** (*p*)	Persian Anthology.	**1541**
1002.	**202** (*p*)	*Sháh-náma*, Part ii.	**786**
1003.	**203** (*p*)	Another fragment of the *Sháh-náma.*	**787**
1004.	**204** (*p*)	A note-book containing poetical extracts.	**1542**
1005.	**205** (*p*)	*Baḥru'l-Ansáb* and *Maṭáli'u'l-Anwár.*	**153, 1204, 1591**
1006.	**206** (*p*)	*Akbar-náma.*	**81**
1007.	**207** (*p*)	*Iqbál-náma.*	**76**

1008.	**208** (*p*)	Extract from *Nafá'isu'l-Funún.*	**1320**
1009.	**209** (*p*)	Niẓámí's *Khusraw wa Shírín.*	**428**
1010.	**210** (*p*)	*Zíj-i-Ulugh Beg.*	**739**
1011.	**211** (*p*)	*Díwán* of Wáqif.	**627**
1012.	**212** (*p*)	Niẓámí's *Sikandar-náma.*	**765**
1013.	**213** (*p*)	Commentary on the above.	**766**
1014.	**214** (*p*)	Glossary to *Bahár-i-Dánish* and Abu'l-Faḍl.	**894**
1015.	**215** (*p*)	*Díwán* of Badr-i-Chách.	**515**
1016.	**216** (*p*)	Treatise on Archery.	**1063**
1017.	**217** (*p*)	*Qiṣaṣu'l-Anbiyá.*	**957**
1018.	**218** (*p*)	Account of the Táj Maḥall, etc.	**431**
1019.	**219** (*p*)	*Ghunyatu'l-Munya*, on Indian music.	**884**
1020.	**220** (*p*)	*Zubdatu't-Tawáríkh.*	**733**
1021.	**221** (*p*)	*Mathnawí*, acephalous, dated 1041/1631–2.	**1129**
1022.	**222** (*p*)	Another *Mathnawí*, defective at end.	**1130**
1023.	**223** (*p*)	*Mathnawí*, Bk. i, dated 1135/1722.	**1131**
1024.	**224** (*p*)	*Qiṣṣa-i-'Azíz Sháh wa Mas'úd Sháh.*	**974**
1025.	**225** (*p*)	*Díwán* of Tháqib.	**520**
1026.	**226** (*a*, *p*)	A work on Sunní doctrine, with commentary.	**1421**
1027.	**227** (*p*)	The *Niṣáb*, etc.	**107, 1315, 1314, 1515**
1028.	**228** (*p*)	Seven tracts, mostly stories.	**467, 1268, 407, 1592**
1029.	**229** (*p*)	The *Haft Paykar* of Niẓámí.	**1372**
1030.	**230** (*p*)	Another poem ascribed to Niẓámí.	**1543**
1031.	**231** (*p*)	'Aṭṭár's *Manṭiqu't-Ṭayr.*	**1266**
1032.	**232** (*p*)	Selections from works of Bí-dil.	**1326**
1033.	**233** (*p*, *h*)	*Dah Majlis*, poems for Muḥarram.	**1544**
1034.	**234** (*p*)	Niẓámí's *Makhzanu'l-Asrár.*	**1172**
1035.	**235** (*p*)	Jámí's *Futúḥu'l-Ḥaramayn.*	**888**
1036.	**236** (*p*)	Letters of Naṣíru'd-Dín Hamadání.	**709**
1037.	**237** (*p*)	Jámí's *Tuḥfatu'l-Aḥrár.*	**270**
1038.	**238** (*p*)	An extract from the *Á'ín-i-Akbarí.*	**1479**
1039.	**239** (*p*)	Niẓámí's *Khusraw wa Shírín.*	**429**
1040.	**240** (*p*)	Jámí's *Shawáhidu'n-Nubuwwa.*	**820**
1041.	**241** (*p*)	The *Bustán* of Sa'dí.	*
1042.	**242** (*p*)	An untitled *Mathnawí* by Ghanímat.	*
1043.	**243** (*p*)	*Qiṣṣa-i-Mihr u Máh.*	*
1044.	**244** (*h*)	Translation of Majlisí's *Qiṣaṣu'l-Anbiyá.*	*
1045.	**245** (*h*)	*Kulliyyát* of Sawdá.	*

* These 13 MSS. (Nos. 241–253) were discovered too late for inclusion in the body of the *Hand-List.* None of them appear to be of any great importance. There are a few more fragments in the Dêvanâgarî character which I have not numbered or catalogued.

1046. **246** (*h*) *Tawárikh-i-Sulaymání.* *
1047. **247** (*h*) The *Bhágavat* transcribed in Persian characters. *
1048. **248** (*h*) A *mathnawí* poem by Surúr. *
1049. **249** (*h*) A poem on Yúsuf and Zulaykhá. *
1050. **250** (*h*) Ballads collected in Lahore in 1864. *
1051. **251** (*p*) Persian and other fragments in verse and prose. *
1052. **252** (*p*, *h*) Twelve fragments, one Persian (No. 9). *
1053. **253** (*p*, *h*) Four or five Persian and Urdú fragments. *
1054. **Parker 401** (*a*) *Ṭawáli'u'l-Anwár.* (This seems to be the only Arabic MS. possessed by the Library before 1883.) **844**

KING'S.

The Oriental manuscripts in King's College Library formed part of the collection made in India in the latter part of the eighteenth century by Edward Ephraim Pote and by him presented in 1788 in equal moities to the libraries of Eton College and King's College. A list of the MSS. in the latter library, to which is prefixed some account of the donor and his bequest by Henry Bradshaw dated 12th November, 1866, was published by the late E. H. Palmer (subsequently, until 1882, Lord Almoner's Professor of Arabic) in the *Journal of the Royal Asiatic Society* for June, 1867 (pp. 27), while a list of those in the library of Eton College was published by the Rev. Professor D. S. Margoliouth, Laudian Professor of Arabic in the University of Oxford, in 1904†. Professor Palmer's list of the King's MSS., which is arranged alphabetically under the different languages (I, Persian; II, Arabic; III, Persian Versions of Hindú Works; IV, Hindí and Hindú'í in the Persian character; and Urdú), is marred by some omissions (16 MSS. at least), and has been checked and revised by myself and by the late Mr Ballard of Clare College, whose untimely death was a great loss to Oriental studies. The MSS., in the order of the numbers which they bear, are as follows:

† Printed as a pamphlet at the Clarendon Press, Oxford, under the title *Catalogue of the Oriental Manuscripts in the Library of Eton College*, compiled by D. S. Margoliouth, D.Litt., Oxford, 1904. (35 pp.)

1055.	**1** (*p*)	*Irshádu's-Sálikín.* (Palmer, p. 4).	**44**
1056.	**2** (*a*)	*Rasá'ilu Ikhwánu'ṣ-Ṣafá.* (P., p. 19).	**689**
1057.	**3** (*p*)	*Inshá-yi-Abu'l-Faḍl.* (P., p. 5).	**101**
1058.	**4** (*p*)	*Aḥwál-i-Rája-há-yi-Jaypúr.* (P., p. 3).	**17**
1059.	**5** (*p*)	*Á'ín-i-Akbarí.* (P., p. 5).	**144**
1060.	**6** (*p*)	*Akhbár-i-Jahángírí.* (P., p. 3).	**23**
1061.	**7** (*p*)	*Akhláq-i-Pádisháhí.* (P., p. 4).	**30**
1062.	**8** (*a*)	Three works by Mír Dámád, one of which, however, appears to be missing. (P., pp. 20, 24 and 25).	**1151**
1063.	**9** (*a*)	*A'ráḍ wa Jawáhir.* (P., p. 20).	**1275**
1064.	**10** (*a*)	*Anwár*, a commentary on the *Miṣbáḥ.* (P., p. 20, wrongly numbered **70**).	**1023**
1065.	**11** (*a*)	The *Átháru'l-Bilád* of al-Qazwíní. (P., p. 19).	**2**
1066.	**12** (*p*)	*I'jáz-i-Khusrawí.* (P., p. 4).	**69**
1067.	**13** (*a*)	The Spherics of Theodosius, translated by Qusṭá ibn Lúqá. (P., p. 20).	**1009**
1068.	**14** (*p*)	Five Persian tracts on Hindúism. (P., pp. 16, 25, 26 *bis*).	**1446, 776**
1069.	**15** (*p*)	*Akhláq-i-Muḥsiní.* (P., p. 4).	**35**
1070.	**16** (*p*)	*Aḥkámu'd-Dín.* (P., p. 19).	**386**
1071.	**17** (*p*)	*Inshá-yi-Munír.* (P., p. 5).	**1333**
1072.	**18** (*p*)	*Akhbáru'l-Akhyár.* (P., p. 3).	**22**
1073.	**19** (*p*)	*Akhláq-i-Náṣirí.* (P., p. 4).	**40**
1074.	**20** (*p*)	*Aḥwál-i-Bíbí Julyáná.* (P., p. 3).	**16**
1075.	**21** (*p*)	*Anwár-i-Suhaylí.* (P., p. 5).	**134**
1076.	**22** (*p*)	*Inshá-yi-Ṭughrá.* (P., p. 5).	**113**
1077.	**23** (*a*)	The *Iḥyá'u 'Ulúmi'd-Dín* of al-Ghazzálí. (P., p. 19).	**19**
1078.	**24** (*a*)	*Ádábu'l-Muta'allimín.* (P., p. 19).	**6**
1079.	**25** (*p*)	*Ikhtiyárát-i-Badí'í.* (P., p. 4).	**29**
1080.	**26** (*p*)	*Intikhábát az Rawḍatu'ṣ-Ṣafá.* (P., p. 4).	**723**
1081.	**27** (*p*)	*Inshá-yi-Míram wa 'Abdu'lláh.* (P., p. 5).	**123, 103, 108**
1082.	**28** (*p*)	*Inshá-yi-Jámí.* (P., p. 5).	**109**
1083.	**29** (*p*)	*Alfáẓ-i-Adwiya.* (P., p. 4).	**87**
1084.	**30** (*a*)	*Aḥkámu'n-Nujúm.* (P., p. 19).	**14**
1085.	**31** (*p*)	*Akbar-náma*, vol. i. (P., p. 4).	**82**
1086.	**32** (*p*)	*Inshá-yi-'Abdu'l-Ḥayy.* (P., p. 5).	**114**
1087.	**33** (*p*)	*Iqbál-náma.* (P., p. 4).	**77**
1088.	**34** (*a*)	*Al-Ufuqu'l-Mubín* by Mír Dámád. (P., p. 20).	**74**
1089.	**35** (*p*)	*Asráru'l-Awliyá.* (P., p. 4).	**47**
1090.	**36** (*p*)	*Inshá-yi-Madhurám.* (P., p. 5).	**120**
1091.	**37** (*p*)	*Á'ína-i-Sháhí.* (P., p. 5, wrongly numbered **42**).	**148, 840**
1092.	**38** (*a*)	*Al-Ádábu'l-Báqiya*, by 'Abdu'l-Báqí, followed by glosses (*Ḥawáshí*) on the same. (P., p. 19).	**3**

1093.	**39** (*a*)	*A'lámu'l-Akhyár.* (P., p. 20).	**70**
1094.	**40** (*p*)	*Abwábu'l-Jinán.* (P., p. 3).	**10**
1095.	**41** (*a*)	*Ashrafu'l-Wasá'il ila fahmi'sh-Shamá'il.* (P., p. 19).	**64**
1096.	**42** (*p*)	*Á'ína-i-Bakht.* (P., p. 5).	**145**
1097.	**43** (*p*)	*Inshá-yi-Khán-zád Khán.* (P., p. 5).	
1098.	**44** (*p*)	*Inshá-yi-Mírzá Bí-dil.* (P., p. 5).	**106**
1099.	**45** (*p*)	*Ádáb-i-'Álamgírí.* (P., p. 4).	**5**
1100.	**46** (*a*)	*Aṭbáqu'dh-Dhahab.* (P., p. 19).	**66, 67, 1332**
1101.	**47** (*p*)	*Bahádur Sháh-náma.* (P., p. 6).	**189**
1102.	**48** (*p*)	*Bahár-i-Dánish.* (P., p. 6).	**192**
1103.	**49** (*p*)	*Bahár-i-Sukhun.* (P., p. 6).	**195**
1104.	**50** (*p*)	Persian translation of the *Bíchganit*, part of the *Lílávatí*, a Sanskrit work on Arithmetic. (P., pp. 9 and 25).	**208**
1105.	**51** (*a*)	*Baḥru'l-Jawáhir.* (P., p. 20).	**154**
1106.	**52** (*h*)	*Bhágavat Dayá Rám.* (P., p. 26).	**197**
1107.	**53** (*h*)	*Prábodh Náṭak*, by Nandadás. (P., p. 26).	**213**
1108.	**54** (*h*)	*Bhágavat Ṭoralmal* (or *Ṭoḍramal*). (P., p. 26).	**198**
1109.	**55** (*h*)	*Padmáwat Bhákhá* in Brij Bháshá dialect. (P., p. 26).	**212**
1110.	**56** (*p*)	*Barzú'í-náma.* (P., p. 5).	**171**
1111.	**57** (*h*)	*Bhágavat Bhúpatí.* (P., p. 26).	**199**
1112.	**58** (*p*)	*Bahjatu'l-Mabáhij.* (P., p. 6).	**202**
1113.	**59** (*a*)	*Bustánu'l-'Árifín.* (P., p. 20).	**174**
1114.	**60** (*h*)	(i) *Poṭhi Bhávatí*; (ii) *Poṭhi Chitrávatí*; (iii) *Sat Sayá*; (iv) *Fáḍil 'Alí Prakásh.* (P., p. 26).	**221**
1115.	**61** (*p*)	*Badáyi'u'l-'Uqúl.* (P., p. 25).	**158**
1116.	**62** (*p*)	*Bhágavat*, Persian translation in two volumes. (P., p. 25).	**200**
1117.	**63** (*a*)	*Badwu'l-Khalq.* (Palmer omits this MS.)	**1012**
1118.	**64** (*p*)	*Burhán-i-Ma'áthir.* (P., p. 6).	**173**
1119.	**65** (*p*)	*Bayáḍ* (note-book) containing selections in verse and prose. (P., p. 6).	**1547**
1120.	**66** (*p*)	*Bekat-i-Chintámani.* (P., p. 25).	**210**
1121.	**67** (*p*)	*Ta'ríkh-i-Maḥmúd Sháhí.* (P., p. 8).	**249**
1122.	**68** (*p*)	*Táju'l-Ma'áthir.* (P., p. 6).	**224**
1123.	**69** (*a*)	*Talwíḥu't-Tawḍíḥ.* (P. om.).	**329**
1124.	**70** (*a*)	*Anwáru't-Tanzíl.* (P., p. 20).	**130, 1034**
1125.	**71** (*p*)	*Ta'ríkh-i-Dilgushá.* (P., p. 7).	**234**
1126.	**72** (*a*)	*Ta'ríkhu'l-Yaman*, vol. ii. (P. om.).	**868**
1127.	**73** (*p*)	*Ta'ríkh-i-'Álí fí silki'l-La'álí.* (P., p. 7).	**242**
1128.	**74** (*p*)	*Tadhkira-i-Shaykh 'Alí Ḥazín.* (P., p. 9).	**300**

1129. **75** (*p*) *Tadhkiratu'l-Awliyá.* (P., p. 9). **291**
1130. **76** (*p*) *Ta'ríkh-i-Siyar.* (P., p. 7). **1211**
1131. **77** (*p*) *Ta'ríkh-i-Badá'úní.* (P., p. 7). **1252**
1132. **78** (*a*) *Ta'ríkh Khamís.* (P. om.). **233**
1133. **79** (*p*) *Ta'ríkh-i-Músá.* (P., p. 7). **250**
1134. **80** (*p*) *Ta'ríkh-i-Shír Sháh.* (P., p. 7). **240**
1135. **81**[1] (*p*) *Ta'ríkh-i-Kashmír*, prose, copied in 1027/1618. (P., p. 8). **245**
1136. **81**[2] (*p*) *Ta'ríkh-i-Kashmír*, verse. (P., p. 18).
1137. **82** (*p*) *Tuḥfatu'l-Mú'minín.* (P., p. 8). **286**
1138. **83** (*a*) *Tadhhíbu't-Tahdhíb.* (P. om.). **305**
1139. **84** (*p*) *Ta'ríkh-i-Humáyúní.* (P., p. 8). **256**
1140. **85** (*p*) *Tímúr-náma* by Hátifí. (P., p. 10). **344**
1141. **86** (*a*) Vol. ii. of the *Kashsháf* of Zamakhsharí. (P. om.). **1033**
1142. **87** (*p*) The *Ṣafwatu'ṣ-Ṣafá*, containing the older recension of this rare biography of Shaykh Ṣafiyyu'd-Dín Isḥáq, the ancestor of the Ṣafawí Kings of Persia. **837**
1143. **88** (*p*) *Túzuk-i-Jahángírí*, in 3 vols. The first two, in different handwritings, identical, but the second carried about eight years further; the third, according to Mr Ballard, containing the genuine memoirs. (P., pp. 9, 10 and 18). **333**
1144. **89** (*p*) *Ta'ríkh-i-Quṭb-sháhí.* (P., p. 7). **244**
1145. **90** (*p*) Persian translation of the *Nahju'l-Balágha.* **1341**
1146. **91** (*a*) *Tafsír-i-Awrangzíb.* **319**
1147. **92** (*p*) *Tadhkiratu'sh-Shu'ará.* (P., p. 9). **296**
1148. **93** (*p*) *Túzuk-i-Tímúrí.* Two copies, not vols. (P., p. 10). **1245, 1246**
1149. **94** (*p*) *Ta'ríkh-i-shahádat-i-Farrukh-Siyar wa julús-i-Muḥammad Sháh.* (P., p. 7). **239**
1150. **95** (*p*) *Ta'ríkh-i-Waṣṣáf.* (P., p. 8). **255**
1151. **96** (*p*) *Túzuk-i-Báburí.* (P., p. 10). **1351**
1152. **97** (*p*) *Ta'ríkhu'l-Ḥukamá.* (P., p. 6). **232**
1153. **98** (*a*) *Kitábu'ḍ-Ḍu'afá wa'l-Wá'iẓín.* (P., p. 24). **1021**
1154. **99** (*a*) Samhúdí's History of Madína entitled *Wafá'u'l-Wafá.* **1358**
1155. **100** (*a*) A commentary on the *Ṣaḥíḥ* of al-Bukhárí, entitled *Taysír*, 2 vols. (P., p. 17). **341**
1156. **101** (*p*) *Ta'ríkh-i-Nádir Sháh.* (P., p. 8). **253**
1157. **102** (*p*) *Ta'ríkh-i-Firishta*, 2 vols. (P., p. 8). **1103**
1158. **103** (*p*) *Tadhkiratu'l-Abrár wa'l-Ashrár.* (P., p. 8). **289**
1159. **104** (*p*) *Tímúr-náma.* (P., p. 10). **387**

1160. **105** (*p*) *Ta'ríkh-i-A'tham-i-Kúfí.* (P., p. 5). **890**

1161. **106** (*p*) *Tadhkiratu'sh-Shu'ará* of Dawlatsháh. (P., p. 9). **295**

1162. **107** (*p*) *Qánúncha*, an abridgement of the *Qánún* of Avicenna. **915**

1163. **108** (*p*) *Ta'ríkh-i-Banákatí*, properly entitled *Rawḍatu Úli l-Albáb.* (P., pp. 7 and 15). **716**

1164. **109** (*p*) *Ta'ríkh-i-Saláṭín-i-Dihlí.* (P., p. 7). **1180**

1165. **110** (*p*) Persian translation of Ibn Khallikán's *Wafayátu'l-A'yán.* (P., pp. 7 and 9). **1359**

1166. **111** (*p*) *Ta'ríkh-i-Alláh-virdí Khán.* (P., p. 7). **251**

1167. **112** (*p*) *Ta'ríkh-i-Alfí*, 2 vols. (P., p. 6). **229**

1168. **113** (*p*) *Mawáhib-i-'Aliyya*, Ḥusayn Wá'iẓ-i-Káshifí's well-known commentary on the *Qur'án.* **1279**

1169. **114** (*p*) *Ta'ríkh-i-Guzída.* (P., p. 8). **248**

1170. **115** (*p*) Kháqání's *Tuḥfatu'l-'Iráqayn.* (P., p. 8). **279**

1171. **116** (*p*) *Al-Mu'jam fí Ta'ríkhi Mulúki'l-'Ajam.* (P., p. 6). **1214**

1172. **117** (*a*) Euclid in Arabic. (P. om.). **1011**

1173. **118** (*p*) Jámí's *Nafaḥátu'l-Uns.* (P., p. 18). **1322**

1174. **119** (*p*) *Tuḥfatu'l-Hind.* (P., p. 8). **288**

1175. **120** (*p*) *Nírang-i-'Ishq* and other poems by Ghanímat. (P., pp. 18 and 19). **1346**

1176. **121** (*p*) The *Mathnawí* of Jalálu'd-Dín Rúmí. (P., p. 18). **1132**

1177. **122** (*p*) Poems of Ṭughrá. (P., p. 18). **747**

1178. **123** (*t*) A *mathnawí* poem in Turkish. (P., p. 18). **408**

1179. **124** (*p*) Vol. iv (containing the *mathnawí* poems) of Shaykh 'Alí Ḥazín's works. (P., p. 124). **1139**

1180. **125** (*p*) *Siráju'l-Lughát*, a Persian dictionary. (P., pp. 11 and 16) **375**

1181. **126** (*a*) *Jawámi'u'l-Kalim.* (P. om.). **359**

1182. **127** (*p*) *Jámi'-i-'Abbásí.* (P., p. 10, wrongly numbered **129**). **351**

1183. **128** (*p*) *Jog Báshisht.* (P., p. 25). **363**

1184. **129** (*p*) Awḥadi's *Jám-i-Jam.* (P., p. 10). **346**

1185. **130** (*p*) *Jawáhiru'ṣ-Ṣanáyi'.* (P., p. 10). **361**

1186. **131** (*p*) *Chahár 'Unṣur*, by Mírzá Bí-dil. (P., p. 11). **374**

1187. **132** (*p*) *Jawhar-i-Ṣamṣám.* (P., p. 11). **364**

1188. **133** (*a*) Járbardí's commentary on the *Káfiya.* (P., p. 23). **783**

1189. **134** (*a*) *Jadhbu'l-Qulúb ila Diyári'l-Maḥbúb.* **355**

1190. **135** (*p*) Seventy verses from the *Sháh-náma*, with two miniatures. (P., p. 10). **788**

1191. **136** (*a*) The *Ḥayátu'l-Ḥayawán* of ad-Damírí, in two vols. (P., p. 21). } **422**

1192. **137** (*p*) A Persian version of the above. (P., p. 11). }

1193. **138** (*p*) The *Ḥabíbu's-Siyar* of Khwándamír. (P., p. 11). **385**

1194. **139** (*p*) *Ḥamla-i-Ḥaydarí.* (P., p. 10). **419**

1195.	**140** (*a*)	Glosses by at-Taftázání on the *Kashsháf* of az-Zamakhsharí. (P., p. 21).	**1035**
1196.	**141** (*a*)	Glosses by 'Abdu'l-Ghafúr on Jámí's commentary on the *Káfiya* of Ibnu'l-Ḥájib. (P., p. 21).	**803**
1197.	**142** (*a*)	Glosses by Mullá Mírzá Ján on the *Ḥikmatu'l-'Ayn*. (P., p. 21).	**411**
1198.	**143** (*a*)	Glosses by Ḥáfiẓ Sulṭán Muḥammad on Jámí's commentary on the *Káfiya*. (P., p. 21, wrongly numbered **140**).	**804**
1199.	**144** (*a*)	A treatise on the principles of Jurisprudence (*Uṣúlu'l-fiqh*) by one Ḥusámu'd-Dín, probably ar-Ruháwí, a jurisconsult who flourished in the latter part of the eighth century of the *hijra*. See Brockelmann, ii, 81. (P., pp. 21 and 24).	**1416**
1200.	**145** (*a*)	*Ḥalbatu'l-Kumayt*. (P., p. 21).	**414**
1201.	**146** (*a*)	Glosses by al-Ḥalabí on the *Muṭawwal* of Sa'du'd-Dín at-Taftázání. (P., p. 21).	**328**
1202.	**147** (*a*)	Glosses by Khayálí on Járbardí's commentary on the *Kashsháf* of az-Zamakhsharí. (P., p. 21).	**1037**
1203.	**148** (*p*)	Glosses by al-Jurjání on a commentary on the *Maṭáli'u'l-Anwár*. (P., p. 11).	**1202**
1204.	**149** (*p*)	*Ḥujjatu'l-Hind*, a Persian version of the Indian story of Nala and Damayanti (*Nal u Daman*). (P., p. 11).	**388**
1205.	**150** (*p*)	Superglosses of Mír Akmal on the glosses of Khayálí mentioned above (**147**). (P., p. 11).	**866**
1206.	**151** (*p*)	The *Ḥadíqatu'l-Ḥaqíqat* of Saná'í.	**394**
1207.	**152** (*p*)	The *Panj Ganj* or *Khamsa* of Niẓámí of Ganja. (P., p. 12).	**453**
1208.	**153** (*p*)	The *Khamsa* of Amír Khusraw of Dihlí. (P., p. 12).	**442**
1209.	**154** (*p*)	An abstract (*Khuláṣa*) of the *Khamsa* of Niẓámí above mentioned. (P., p. 12).	**454**
1210.	**155** (*p*)	*Khuláṣatu'l-Akhbár*, a general history. (P., p. 12).	**433**
1211.	**156** (*p*)	*Khuláṣatu't-Tawáríkh*. (P., p. 11).	**436**
1212.	**157** (*p*)	*Khwán-i-Ni'mat*, a cookery-book. (P., p. 11).	**459**
1213.	**158** (*p*)	*Khazá'inu'l-Futúḥ*, a work on prosody by Amír Khusraw of Dihlí. (P., p. 11).	**427**
1214.	**159** (*p*)	The *Díwán* of Ḥáfiẓ of Shíráz. (P., p. 13).	**536**
1215.	**160** (*p*)	The poetical works of 'Urfí of Shíráz. (P., p. 13).	**581**
1216.	**161** (*p*)	The *Díwán* of Sháhí. (P., p. 13).	**557**
1217.	**162** (*p*)	The *Dastúru'l-'Amal* of Rájá Ṭoralmál. (P., p. 12).	**486**
1218.	**163** (*p*)	The *Díwán* of Salím, one of Sháh Jahán's poets. (P., p. 13).	**552**
1219.	**164** (*h*)	The *Díwán* of Walí. (P., p. 27).	**630**

1220. **165** (*p*) The *Díwán* of Naẓírí. (P., p. 13). **624**

1221. **166** (*p*) The *Díwán* of Maẓhar. (P., p. 13). **610**

1222. **167** (*p*) The poetical works of Kháqání. (P., p. 13). **542**

1223. **168** (*p*, *h*) The *Díwáns* of Yaqín, Sawdá and Na'ím. (P., p. 14, l. 1, where **161** is a mistake for **168**, and p. 27). **636**

1224. **169** (*p*) The *Díwán* of Muḥammad-bakhsh. (P., p. 13). **499**

1225. **170** (*p*) Selections from the *Díwán* of Ṣá'ib. (P., p. 13). **571**

1226. **171** (*p*) The *Díwán* of Kamálu'd-Dín Isma'íl of Iṣfahán. (P., p. 13). **602**

1227. **172** (*p*) The *Díwán* of Ṭálib of Ámul. (P., p. 13). **573**

1228. **173** (*p*) The *Díwán* of Jalál-i-Asír. (P., p. 12). **503**

1229. **174** (*h*) The *Díwán* of Mír Taqí. (P., p. 27, wrongly numbered **274**). **612**

1230. **175** (*p*) The poetical works of Anwarí. (P., p. 12). **510**

1231. **176** (*p*) The poetical works of Shafí'í and Awḥadí. (P., pp. 13 and 17). **558**

1232. **177** (*p*) The *Díwán* of Ghaní. (P., p. 13). **588**

1233. **178** (*p*) The *Díwán* of Mu'izz-i-Fiṭrat. (P., p. 13). **590**

1234. **179** (*p*) The *Díwán* of Áhí. (P., p. 12). **512**

1235. **180** (*h*) The *Díwán* of Abrú. (P., p. 27, wrongly numbered **80**). **497**

1236. **181** (*p*) The *Díwán* of Yúsuf Beg Shámlú. (P., p. 14). **634**

1237. **182** (*p*) *Dánish-árá*. (P., p. 12). **469**

1238. **183** (*a*) Glosses by one Dáwud on the *Shamsiyya*. (P., p. 22). **816**

1239. **184** (*p*) *Durratu't-Táj*. (P., p. 12). **471**

1240. **185** (*p*) *Dah Majlis*, an account of the Twelve Imáms. (P., p. 12). **493**

1241. **186** (*p*) The *Díwán* of Hilálí. (P., p. 14). **633**

1242. **187** (*p*) *Dánish-náma-i-Jahán*. (P., p. 12). **470**

1243. **188** (*p*) The *Díwán* of Shaykh 'Alí Ḥazín. (P., p. 13). **539**

1244. **189** (*p*) The *Dhakhíratu'l-Mulúk*. (P., p. 14). **640**

1245. **190** (*a*) The *Dhakhíratu'l-Fiqh*. (P., p. 22). **639**

1246. **191** (*p*) The *Rawḍatu'ṣ-Ṣafá* of Mírkhwánd. (P., p. 15). **724**

1247. **192** (*p*) The *Rawḍatu'l-Aḥbáb*, an account of the Prophet and his Companions. (P., p. 15). **715**

1248. **193** (*a*) An astronomical treatise by Abú Ma'shar al-Balkhí. (P., p. 22, wrongly numbered **203**). **12**

1249. **194** (*p*) *Ruqa'át* (Letters) of 'Ináyat Khán. (P., p. 15, wrongly numbered **190**). **706**

1250. **195** (*p*) Persian translation of the *Rág Darpan*, an Indian treatise on Music. (P., p. 14). **646**

1251. **196** (*h*) Vol. i of the *Ramáyana* of Tulsí Dás. (P., p. 26). **647**

1253. **197** (*p*) Persian prose rendering of the *Ramáyana*. (P., p. 14). **648**

1254. **198** (*p*) Persian version of the chronicle entitled *Rájáwalí*. (P., p. 14, wrongly numbered **195**). **644**

1255. **199** (*p*) Treatise on the virtues of different animals, by Shaykh 'Alí Ḥazín. (P., p. 14). **299**

1256. **200** (*p*) Persian translation of an Arabic astronomical treatise entitled *Risála-i-Mu'ína*. (P., p. 15 *bis*). **686**

1257. **201** (*p*) *Risála-i-Khams* (five treatises of Sa'dí). (P., p. 14). **1068**

1258. **202** (*p*) Ruqa'át-i-Amánu'lláh Ḥusayní. (P., pp. 5 and 15). **699**

1259. **203** (*a, p*) Treatise on Astrology in Arabic by Yaḥyá ibn 'Alí al-Maghribí, followed by a Persian tract on the calendar. (P., pp. 4, 18 and 19). **13, 655, 670, 1492**

1260. **204** (*p*) *Risála-i-Muḥammad Sháh*. (P., p. 14). **675**

1261. **205** (*p*) *Raqá'im-i-Kará'im*, the Letters of 'Álamgír. (P., p. 15). **694**

1262. **206** (*p*) An astronomical treatise by Mullá 'Alí Qúshjí. (P., p. 15). **687**

1263. **207** (*p*) Sayfí's Treatise on Prosody. (P., p. 14). **858**

1264. **208** (*p*) *Ruqa'át-i-Ibráhím*. (P., p. 15). **695**

1265. **209** (*p*) *Riyáḍu'l-Inshá*. (P., p. 18). **727**

1266. **210** (*p*) *Rawḍatu'l-Anwár*, a poem by 'Urfí of Shíráz. (P., p. 15). **717**

1267. **211** (*p*) *Kanzu't-Tuḥaf*, a treatise on Music ascribed to Naṣíru'd-Dín Ṭúsí. (P., p. 14). **1077**

1268. **212** (*p*) *Zíj-i-Muḥammad Sháhí*. (P., p. 15). **742**

1269. **213** (*p*) The very rare and important historical and chronological work of Gardízí entitled *Zaynu'l-Akhbár*. The only other known MS. is in the Bodleian. See Ethé's *Persian Catalogue* of that Library, No. **15**. (P., pp. 7 and 16; on p. 7 the number is wrongly given as **313**). **743**

1270. **214** (*p*) *Zíj-i-Ulugh Beg*. (P., p. 16). **740**

1271. **215** (*p*) *Zubdatu'l-Lughát*, an Arabic-Persian lexicon. (P., p. 15). **736**

1272. **216** (*p*) *Zádu'l-Musáfirín*, a rare and important religious-philosophical work by Náṣir-i-Khusraw. (P., p. 15). **730**

1273.	**217** (*p*)	*Sirr-i-Akbar*, a Persian translation of the Upan.-shads. (P., p. 16).	
1274.	**218** (*h*)	A collection of Indian songs entitled *Sahasr-ras*, the "Thousand Delights." (P., p. 26).	**777**
1275.	**219** (*p*)	The *Siyásat-náma* of the *Nizámu'l-Mulk*. (P., p. 16).	**778**
1276.	**220** (*a*)	*Sa'diyya*, a commentary on the Arabic Grammar of az-Zanjání entitled *at-Taṣríf*. (P., p. 22).	**800**
1277.	**221** (*p*)	Persian translation of the *Singhásan Batísí*. (P., p. 25).	**774**
1278.	**222** (*a*)	*Samaru'l-Falásifa*. (P., p. 22).	**770**
1279.	**223** (*p*)	*Siráju'l-Istikhráj*. (P., p. 16).	
1280.	**224** (*h*)	*Sundar Singár*. (P., p. 26).	**772**
1281.	**225** (*a*)	Commentary on the *'Uyúnu'l-Ḥikmat*. (P., p. 23).	**880**
1282.	**226** (*p*)	Persian commentary on the well-known legal work entitled *Wiqáya*. (P., p. 17).	**1364**
1283.	**227** (*a*)	Commentary on the *Ashbáh wa Naẓá'ir*. (P., p. 22).	**60**
1284.	**228** (*a*)	Commentary on the *Qánún*. (P., p. 24).	**273**
1285.	**229** (*a*)	Commentary on a religious work entitled *al-Ḥiṣnu'l-haṣín*. (P., p. 23).	**406**
1286.	**230** (*a*)	The Commentary of Jámí on the *Káfiya* of Ibnu'l-Ḥájib. (P., p. 24).	**906**
1287.	**231** (*a*)	Commentary on the *Ishárát* of Naṣíru'd-Dín-i-Ṭúsí. (P., p. 23).	**57**
1288.	**232** (*a*)	Commentary on the *Arjúza* of Abú 'Sa'íd Muḥammad ibn Aḥmad ibn Rashíd. (P., p. 22).	**42**
1289.	**233** (*p*)	Commentary on the *Zíj* of Ulugh Beg by al-Birjandí. (P., p. 17).	**741**
1290.	**234** (*a*)	Commentary on the *Tajríd* of Mullá 'Alí Qúshjí. (P., p. 23).	**263**
1291.	**235** (*a*)	Commentary on the *Mawáqif* by as-Sayyid ash-Sharíf al-Jurjání. (P., p. 24).	**1276**
1292.	**236** (*a*)	Commentary on the *Ḥikmatu'l-'Ayn*. (P., p. 23).	**410**
1293.	**237** (*a*)	Commentary of al-Kázarúní on the *Mújizu'l-Qánún*. (P., p. 23).	**1285**
1294.	**238** (*p*)	*Sháh-náma-i-Sháh Isma'íl*. (P., p. 16).	**790**
1295.	**239** (*a*)	Commentary on the *Ṣad Kalima*, or Hundred Sayings, of Ptolemy. (P., p. 23).	**833**
1296.	**240** (*a*)	Commentary on the *Taṣríf* of az-Zanjání. (P., p. 23).	
1297.	**241** (*p*)	Commentary on the *Mathnawí*. (P., p. 17).	**1240**
1298.	**242** (*a*)	Commentary on the *Muṭawwal* of at-Taftázání. (P., p. 22).	**1209**
1299.	**243** (*a*)	Commentary on the *Irshádu'n-Naḥw*. (P., p. 22).	**1170**
1300.	**244** (*a*)	Commentary on the *Wiqáya*. (P., p. 24).	**1363**
1301.	**245** (*p*)	Commentary on the *Hidáya*. (P., p. 17).	**1367**
1302.	**246** (*a*)	Commentary on the *Nahju'l-Balágha*. (P., p. 24).	**1342**
1303.	**247** (*p*)	Commentary on the *Maṭáli'u'l-Anwár*. (P., p. 17).	**1203**

1304. **248** (*a*) Commentary on the *Qánún* of Avicenna in three volumes. (P., pp. 23–4). **1286**

1305. **249** (*a*) Commentary on the *Sullamu'l-'Ulúm* entitled *Mi'ráju'l-'Ulúm*. (P., pp. 22, 23, 25). **768**

1306. **250** (*a, p*) Three works on astronomy and geometry, the *Tashríḥu'l-Aflák*, a commentary on the *Mulakhkhaṣ* of al-Jaghmíní, and a commentary on the *Ashkálu't-Ta'sís*. (P., pp. 9, 17, 23). **1483**

1307. **251** (*p*) Commentary on the *Tahdhíbu'l-Manṭiq*. (P., p. 17). **340**

1308. **252** (*p*) *Sháh-Jahán-náma*. (P., p. 16). **791**

1309. **253** (*p*) The same in verse by Abú Ṭálib Kalím. (P., p. 16). **792**

1310. **254** (*p*) The *Shawáhidu'n-Nubuwwat* of Jámí. (P., p. 24). **819**

1311. **255** (*a*) The *Shawáhidu'r-Rubúbiyyat* of Mullá Ṣadrá. (P., p. 24). **818**

1312. **256** (*p*) The *Shabistán-i-Khayál*. (P., p. 16). **795**

1313. **257** (*p*) The *Khusraw wa Shírín* of Niẓámí of Ganja. (P., p. 17). **455**

QUEENS'.

1314. **1** (*p*) Xavier's *Á'ína-i-Ḥaqq-numá*. **146**

1315. **2** (*p*) *Anwár-i-Suhaylí*, dated 972/1564–5. **135**

1316. **3** (*p*) The *Gulistán* of Sa'dí. } **1095**

1317. **4** (*p*) Another copy of the same. }

1318. **5** (*p*) The *Akhláq-i-Náṣirí*, a good copy made in 1020/1611–12 by Shaykh 'Alí Láhijání. **41**

1319. **6** (*p*) The *Jám-i-Gítí-numá*. **347**

1320. **7** (*p*) The *Akhláq-i-Muḥsiní*, copied in a beautiful and minute writing in 966/1558–9. **36**

1321. **8** (*p*) Persian version of the Story of Judith, from the Apocrypha. **1387**

1322. **9** (*E. Turkí*) Anonymous *Díwán*, defective at end. **1548**

1323. **10** (*t*) The *Taḍarru'-náma* of Sinán Páshá. **312**

1324. **11** (*t*) The *Tuḥfa-i-Sháhidí*. **274**

1325. **12** (*t*) *Aḥwál-i-Qiyámat*, on the Resurrection. **18**

1326. **13** (*t*) *Ta'bír-náma-i-Rúyá*, a book on the Interpretation of Dreams in 53 chapters. **314**

ST CATHARINE'S.

This library appears to possess only two Arabic and two Persian MSS. which Mr H. Loewe kindly examined for me. They are:

1327. **1** (*a*) *Qur'án*.

1328. **2** (*a*) *Prayers*.

1329. **3** (*p*) *Díwán* of Ḥáfiẓ.

1330. **4** (*p*) *Díwán* of Ṣá'ib.

JESUS. (No proper class-marks.)

1331. **1** (*p*) Gospel of St Matthew in Persian, good Indian *ta'líq*, undated, two verses missing at the end. **93**

1332. **2** (*p*) *Tuḥfatu'l-Aḥbáb*, "an essay in Ethics...in the Persian language" in 20 chapters, followed by verses by various poets, including Mír Naját, Mu'izz of Mashhad, Mírzá Amín Munshí, Ṭálib, Ṣafí-qulí Beg, Ṭálib-i-Kalím, Wá'iẓ, Shawkat, Mahdí, Humáyún, Adham, Mír Ṣaydí, Shápúr, 'Arshí of Yazd, Nawá'í, 'Urfí, Áqá Ḥusayn, Qudsí, Iḥsán, Mírzá Raḍí, and Dánish. Small, neat MS. of 13·5 × 8·8 c. **266**

1333. **3** (*p*) The *Jámi'-i-'Abbásí*, written in bad modern Indian *ta'líq*. **352**

1334. **4** (*p*) The *Díwán* of Badr-i-Chách. Fair Indian *ta'líq*, dated Muḥarram, 1049/May, 1639. Presented by G. Lewis. **516**

1335. **5** (*p*) *Díwán* of Ḥáfiẓ, written in good *ta'líq* and dated Rajab 26, 1099/May 27, 1688. **533**

1336. **6** (*p*) The *Kulliyyát* of Kháqání, a fine and copious MS. containing 447 ff. of 16·7 × 8·7 c., undated, but probably ninth or 10th century of the *hijra*. Presented by Captain Edward Thurlow Hibgame, through his cousin Edward Hibgame, Fellow of Jesus. **1062**

1337. **7** (*p*) The *Gulistán* of Sa'dí, dated 1096/1685, good hand. **1094**

1338. **8** (*p*) *Mufarriḥu'l-Qulúb*, Indian *ta'líq*, older than 1120/1708–9. **1230**

1339. **9** (*p*) A miscellany containing poems (including the *Mukhammas* of Kátibí, extracts from Ẓuhúrí's *Sáqí-náma*, etc.), *farmáns*, and an account of the Emperor Awrang-zíb. Dated 7 Dhu'l-Ḥijja, 1118/March 12, 1707. **1546**

1340. **10** (*p*, *h*) A Persian-Hindustání glossary, incomplete. **1509**

1341. **11** (*a*) The 27th *Juz'* of the *Qur'án*, dated 22 Ṣafar, 1047/Feb. 15, 1637, and presented to the library in 1700. **943**

1342. **12** (*a*) Contains two treatises (i) *al-Káfí fí 'ilmi'l-'arúḍ wa'l-qawáfí*, by Abu'l-'Abbás Aḥmad al-Finá'í (d. 729/1328–9), and (ii) *aṣ-Ṣáfiya fí sharḥi'sh-Sháfiya*, by Yúsuf ibn 'Abdu'l-Malik. This and the following five Arabic **1001, 824**

MSS. were presented by the Rev. Samuel Lyde, Fellow of the College, who died at Alexandria on April 1, 1860. He was the author of a work entitled *The Ansyreeh and Ismaeleeh*, and another entitled *The Asian Mystery, illustrated in the history, religion and present state of the Ansaireeh, or Nusairis, of Syria* (London, Longmans and Green, 1860). There is a copy of the latter in the Cambridge University Library, bearing the class-mark **7 . 32 . 33.**

1343. **13** (*a*) Contains two treatises (i) the *Sháfiya*, a well-known treatise on Arabic grammar, transcribed in 1270/1853–4; and (ii) the *Fiqhu'l-Lugha wa Sirru'l-'Arabiyya* of Abú Manṣúr ath-Tha'álibí. **780, 902**

1344. **14** (*a*) A treatise on Logic in 198 paragraphs (63 pages), copied by As'ad ibn Jirjís Háshim, student at the American College (? of Beyrout), incomplete at end. **1482**

1345. **15** (*a*) The *Ísághújí*, composed by al-Khúrí Buṭrus ibn Buṭrus ibn Isḥáq aṭ-Ṭúlání, Maronite Bishop of Aleppo, about A.D. 1703. See Rieu's *Arabic Supplement*, No. 44. **140**

1346. **16** (*a*) A miscellany compiled and transcribed for the Rev. Samuel Lyde in A.D. 1853 by Yúnus ibnu'l-Asír aṣ-Ṣaydáwí, containing proverbs, verses, *dawrs*, *maqámát*, and the Oath of the Druzes, and entitled: **1594**

فوائد فى العلوم العربيّة و بعض اشعار و امثال

1347. **17** (*a*) "Manual of [Nuṣayrí] Shaykhs." The substance of this book is contained in Mr Lyde's *Asian Mystery*, ch. ix. It contains 188 pp. and comprises 32 pieces (enumerated in English on blank pages at the end). The volume was bought for £10 in September, 1859, from a merchant at Latakia, into whose hands it fell in the time of Ibráhím Pasha. It was copied in A.D. 1824, and bequeathed to Jesus College by Lyde on March 1, 1860. **1422**

Christ's College.

1348. **Dd.3.1** (formerly **18.3.1**) (*p*) The *Makhzan-i-Afghání* of Khwája Ni'matu'lláh, composed about 1020/1611–12. Ff. 430; large, clear Indian *ta'líq*; transcribed in 1181/1767–8 near Oude. 1174

1349. **Dd.3.2** (formerly **13.3.2**) (*p*) A cookery-book entitled *Tuḥfatu'l-Ma'kúlát*. Bad Indian *ta'líq*, undated. 1501, 283*

1350. **Dd.3.3** (formerly **13.3.3**) (*p*) The *Ta'ríkh-i-Jahán-gushá-yi-Nádirí* of Muḥammad Mahdí-i-Astarábádí, written in a good, clear Persian *ta'líq* in 1188/1774 in Calcutta. Ff. 177. 252

1351. **Dd.3.4** (formerly **13.3.4**) (*p*) A fine copy of the *Díwán* of Kamálu'd-Dín Isma'íl, good *ta'líq* with a beautiful *'unwán*. Ff. 347. 601

1352. **Dd.3.5** (formerly **13.3.8**) (*p*) The *Maṭla'u's-Sa'dayn*, written in a good, neat *ta'líq*, and dated the end of 989/Jan. 1582. Ff. 532. 1207

1353. **Dd.3.6** (formerly **13.3.9**) (*p*) The *Díwán* of Anwarí, dated 1030/1621. Ff. 328. 508

1354. **Dd.3.7** (formerly **13.3.11**) (*p*) *Ta'ríkh-i-Áshám*, a history of Assam, covering the years 1068–1073 (1657–1662). Ff. 121. 225, 887

1355. **Dd.3.8** (formerly **13.3.12**) (*p*) Fayḍí's *Nal u Daman*, a fine and beautifully written MS. 1329

1356. **Dd.3.10** (formerly **13.3.15**) (*p*) The *Díwán* of Ṣá'ib, slightly defective, good *ta'líq*. Ff. 153. 568

1357. **Dd.3.11** (formerly **13.3.16**) (*p*) The *Díwán* of Ḥáfiẓ, dated 977/1569, fine *ta'líq*, illuminated; copyist, Maqsúd 'Alí. Ff. 188. 532

1358. **Dd.3.12** (formerly **13.3.17**) (*p*) Amír Khusraw's *Dúl Rání wa Khiḍr Khán*; good *ta'líq*; ff. 155. Presented by Archibald Swinton. 969

1359. **Dd.3.13** (formerly **13.3.18**) (*p*) A collection of tracts, mostly Ṣúfí. 1437

1360. **Dd.3.14** (formerly **13.3.19**) (*p*) The *Inshá*, or Epistolary Models, of Abu'l-Faḍl; good *ta'líq*, incomplete at end. Ff. 136. 95

1361. **Dd.3.15** (formerly **13.3.20**) (*p*) Another history of Assam by Shihábu'd-Dín Aḥmad. Ff. 99. 125, 226

1362. **Dd.3.16** (formerly **13.3.21**) (*p*) An arithmetical treatise entitled *Khuláṣatu'l-Ḥisáb*, copied at 'Aẓímábád in 1124/1712. 438

1363. **Dd. 3. 17** (formerly **13. 3. 22**). Part i of the *Jahángír-náma*, entitled in the colophon *Iqbál-náma*. Good *ta'líq*, dated 1219/1804–5. Ff. 163. **365, 75**

1364. **Dd. 3. 18** (formerly **13. 3. 23**) (*p*) Book x of the *Dhakhíra-i-Khwárazm-sháhí*, containing the *Qarábádhín*, or Materia Medica, in 38 chapters. Ff. 56. **638**

1365. **Dd. 3. 19** (formerly **13. 3. 24**) (*p*) *Bústán-i-Khayál*, an anthology, preceded by a prose preface. Copied by Bektásh-qulí Abdál-i-Rúmí. Ff. 73. **188**

1366. **Dd. 3. 20** (formerly **13. 3. 25**) (*p*) *Tuzúkát-i-Tímúrí*, written in fair *ta'líq* with some quaint illustrations, undated. Ff. 113. **308**

1367. **Dd. 3. 21** (formerly **13. 3. 26**) (*a, p*) Contains (i) an Arabic devotional tract; (ii) a Persian translation of and commentary on the *Burda*; (iii) more short Arabic tracts, one dated 1134/1721–2. Ff. 55. **167**

1368. **Dd. 3. 22** (formerly **13. 3. 27**) (*h*) The *Díwán* of Sawdá (Mírzá Rafí'), dated 1194/1780. Ff. 63. **555**

1369. **Dd. 3. 23** (formerly **13. 3. 28**) (*p, t*) A large selection of Turkish and some Persian poems, including the *Pand-náma* of 'Aṭṭár, dated 975/1567–8. Ff. 182. **1545, 217**

1370. **Dd. 3. 24** (formerly **13. 3. 29**). The *Káfiya* with interlinear glosses. **1002**

1371. **Dd. 3. 25** (formerly **13. 3. 30**) (*p*) The *Káristán* of Munír. Ff. 172. **998**

1372. **Dd. 3. 26** (formerly **13. 3. 32**) (*p*) Ṣúfí tracts and poems, including (i) *Anísu'l-Ghurabá*; (ii) *Gulzár-i-Jalálí*; and (iii) a *mathnawí* poem by Ḥusayní, described in an English note as *Qiṣṣa-i-Shaykh 'Allám*. Ff. 113. **1438**

1373. **Dd. 3. 27** (formerly **13. 3. 33**) (*p*) The Story of Kámrúp. Ff. 181. **976**

1374. **Dd. 3. 28** (formerly **13. 3. 34**) (*p*) The *Díwán* of 'Alí or Náṣir 'Alí. Ff. 96. Presented by Archibald Swinton ("brother of Lord Swinton, one of the Judges of the Court of Session in Scotland, died at Bath, March 6, 1804"). **614**

1375. **Dd. 3. 29** (formerly **13. 3. 35**) (*a*) A small volume of ff. 212 containing extracts from the *Qur'án* and prayers in a Maghribí hand, vocalized in red. **1398, 941**

1376. **Dd. 4. 1** (formerly **13. 4. 8**) (*p*) The *Chár 'Unṣur* of Mírzá Bí-dil, written in a neat, clear Persian *ta'líq* with rubrications, within gilt borders, dated 1119/1707–8. Ff. 268 of 29·8 × 14·5 c. Bears the seal of Archibald Swinton, and was given to the College by John Hutton. **373**

1377. **Dd. 4. 2** (formerly **13. 4. 9**) (*p*) The *Akhláq-i-Náṣirí*. Ff. 160 of 27·8 × 17·6 c.; clear *ta'líq*. From Archibald Swinton's collection, presented by John Hutton. **39**

1378. **Dd. 4. 3** (formerly **13. 4. 10**) (*a*) The *Kanzu'd-Daqá'iq* of Abu'l-Barakát 'Abdu'lláh b. Aḥmad b. Maḥmúd an-Nasafí. Ff. 145 of 26·3 × 17 c. and 13 ll.; transcribed in Damascus in 904/1498–9; clear *naskh*. Presented by John Hutton. **1080**

1379. **Dd. 4. 4** (formerly **13. 4. 11**) (*p*) The *Ẓafar-náma* of Sharafu'd-Dín 'Alí Yazdí, copied in large, clear Indian *ta'líq* in 1181/1767–8 by Muḥammad 'Ábid. Ff. 489 of 28 × 18·6 c. **847**

1380. **Dd. 4. 5** (formerly **13. 4. 13**) (*a, p*) The *Niṣábu'ṣ-Ṣibyán* of Abú Naṣr-i-Faráhí. Ff. 33 of 27·5 × 16·8 c.; transcribed in 1184/1770–1 in Ḥaydarábád by 'Izzat 'Alí. Presented by John Hutton. **1313**

1381. **Dd. 4. 6** (formerly **13. 4. 16**) (*p*) The third volume of a historical work entitled *Miftáḥu'l-Qulúb*, containing accounts of Chingíz Khán, the Íl-Kháns, Ottoman Turks, Qará-qoyunlús, etc. Ff. 564 of 26·7 × 15·7 c. Presented by John Hutton. **1227**

1382. **Dd. 4. 7** (formerly **13. 4. 17**) (*p*) The *Ta'ríkh-i-Rashídí* of Mírzá Ḥaydar Dughlát, composed in 951/1544–5. Ff. 393 of 25·3 × 16 c. Presented by John Hutton. **238**

1383. **Dd. 4. 8** (formerly **13. 4. 18**) (*p*) The *Tuḥfatu'l-Aḥrár* and *Sibḥatu'l-Abrár* of Jámí, transcribed before 1166/1752–3 in fine Persian *ta'líq*; rubrications; gold and coloured borders and *'unwán*. Bears the seal of Edward Galley. Presented by John Hutton. Ff. 180. **269**

1384. **Dd. 4. 9** (formerly **13. 4. 19**) (*p*) The poems of Anwarí, followed by commentary on the same. Ff. 376 of 25·1 × 15·3 c. From Archibald Swinton's collection, presented by John Hutton. **507**

1385. **Dd. 4. 10** (formerly **13. 4. 20**) (*p*) The *Ta'ríkh-i-Quṭbsháhí*, dedicated to Abu'l-Muẓaffar Muḥammad-qulí Quṭb-sháh, containing an Introduction, 4 Discourses (*Maqála*) and a Conclusion. Ff. 222 of 24·8 × 15 c. **243**

1386. **Dd.4.12*** (formerly **13.4.22**) (*p*) The *Ruqa'át*, or 696
Letters, of Shaykh Abu'l-Faḍl-i-'Allámí. Ff. 148 of 28·5 × 15 c., poor Indian *ta'líq*. Presented by John Hutton.

1387. **Dd.4.13** (formerly **13.4.23**) (*p*) The *Khamsa* of Niẓámí 452
of Ganja. Ff. 352 of 26 × 15·8 c.; neat Persian *nasta'líq*, undated. Presented by John Hutton.

1388. **Dd.4.14** (formerly **13.4.24**) (*p*) The *Gulistán* of Sa'dí. 1090
Ff. 87 of 28·2 × 20 c.; clear Indian *ta'líq*; undated. Presented by John Hutton.

1389. **Dd.4.15** (formerly **13.4.25**) (*p*) The *Bahár-i-Dánish* of 190
'Ináyatu'lláh, with preface by Muḥammad Ṣáliḥ, the author's pupil. Ff. 326 of 28·5 × 19·5 c. Presented by John Hutton.

1390. **Dd.5.1** (formerly **13.4.27**) (*p*) The *Ta'ríkh-i-Firishta* or 1100
Gulshan-i-Ibráhímí, with full table of contents prefixed. Ff. 274 of 28·6 × 21·3 c.; undated. Presented by John Hutton.

1391. **Dd.5.2** (formerly **13.4.30**) (*p*) Another copy of the last- 1101
mentioned work, copied at Ḥaydarábád in beautiful *naskh*. Ff. 450 of 29·2 × 18·5 c. Presented by John Hutton.

1392. **Dd.5.3** (formerly **13.4.31**) (*p*) *Munshá'át-i-'Álamgírí*. 1261
Ff. 424 of 28·9 × 17 c.; Indian *ta'líq* with rubrications. Presented by John Hutton.

1393. **Dd.5.4** (formerly **13.4.33**) (*p*) Another copy of the 1102
Ta'ríkh-i-Firishta. Ff. 308 of 32 × 21·6 c.; Indian *ta'líq*, undated. Presented by John Hutton.

1394. **Dd.5.5** (formerly **13.4.34**) (*p*) The *Akbar-náma*. Ff. 80
331 of 33·8 × 21·6 c.; written in good Indian *ta'líq* before 1164/1750–1. Presented by John Hutton.

1395. **Dd.5.6** (formerly **13.4.36**) (*p*) Vol. ii of the *'Álam-ará-* 849
yi-'Abbásí, containing the reign of Sháh 'Abbás the Great. Ff. 575 of 34·7 × 20·7 c. Presented by John Hutton.

1396. **Dd.5.7** and **Dd.5.8** (*a*) The *Ḥayátu'l-Ḥaywáni'l-Kubrá* 420
of ad-Damírí, in two vols. Ff. 300 and 243 respectively of 29 × 18·8 c., written in coarse, clear *naskh*. A colophon at the end of vol. ii says that the author completed the rough draft in Rajab, 773 (Jan. 1372). Presented by John Hutton.

* **Dd.4.11** (formerly **13.4.21**) is a Chinese medical work, lithographed.

1397. **Dd.5.9** (*h*) *Rashk-i-Pariyán* (the "Envy of the Fairies"), "a Gentoo tale in the Hindústání language adorned with paintings," and dated 15 Ṣafar, 1077/Aug. 17, 1666. Ff. 79 of 27×18·6 c. Presented by John Hutton. **693**

1398. **Dd.5.10** (*a*) The *Díwán* of Jarír b. 'Aṭiyya at-Tamímí, copied for Professor Ed. Sachau in March—April 1895 by Aḥmad b. Muḥammad 'Abdu'r-Raḥmán from the Cairo Codex, and completed on the 5th Dhu'l-Ḥijja, 1312 (May 30, 1895). Ff. 525 of 26×18 c.; large, coarse *naskh* with rubrications; Sachau's autograph on the back. **526**

1399. **Dd.5.11** (*a*) The *Díwán* of Jarír, copied in Dublin by Dr W. Wright from the St Petersburg MS. and completed on March 19, 1859; collated at Cambridge in April, 1884; together with other materials for an edition. Pp. 211 of 21·1×16·8 c. and 19 ll. **525**

1400. **Dd.5.12** (*p*) The *Sikandar-náma* of Niẓámí of Ganja. In 1803 was in the possession of H. George Keene of Sidney Sussex College; presented by W. H. Lowe. Ff. 209 of 22·8×13 c.; clear, neat *ta'líq*; many marginal glosses. **764**

1401. **Dd.5.13** (*a, samar*). *Kitábu't-Tarjumán*, Jewish prayers in Samaritan and Arabic. Ff. 99 of 22·8×17 c. **1014**

1402. **Dd.5.14** (*t*) The Turkish *Díwán* of Báqí, copied in Constantinople in 1037/1627–8; clear *ta'líq*. Ff. 107 of 18·2×12·3 c. Presented by W. H. Lowe, Dec. 9, 1898. **514**

1403. **? Dd.5.15** (*a*) The *Naqá'iḍ* of Jarír and Farazdaq, with the commentary of as-Sukkarí, copied by Dr William Wright from the Bodleian MS. **Pococke 390,** revised and compared with the original MS. at intervals ending on Jan. 6, 1882. Ff. 399 of 21×16·7 c. Presented by Professor A. A. Bevan. **1323**

1404. **? Dd.5.16** (*a*) Another copy of the *Naqá'iḍ* made by Dr W. Wright from the Strassburg MS. (**Spitta'sche Sammlung, No. 36**) and completed in Cambridge on Oct. 6, 1886. Ff. 225 of 27×21·8 c. **1324**

1405. **S.7.5** (*a, p*) A volume presented by the late Professor W. Robertson Smith, containing (i) the *Kitábu'l-Inbáh*, an introduction to the *Kitábu'l-Istí'áb fí ma'rifati'ṣ-Ṣiḥába* of Ibn 'Abdu'l-Barr (ff. 2–34); (ii) another Arabic treatise on the genealogies of the Arabs and Persians entitled *Kitábu'l-Qaṣd* **1568** *wa'l-Umam*, by the same author (ff. 37–50); (iii) a Persian commentary on some of Anwarí's verses (ff. 51–106), dated Rajab, 1271/March—April, 1855. Ff. 106 of 21·6 × 15·4 c.

ST JOHN'S COLLEGE.

Short descriptions of some of these MSS. (viz. **K. 1**—**K. 14** and **S. 13**) are given in the Rev. Morgan Cowie's *Descriptive Catalogue of the MSS. and scarce books in St John's College Library* (1842), pp. 99-101 and 137. The full list is as follows:

1406. **K. 1** (*a*) A plainly written *Qur'án*, presented to the College in 1639 by Theodore Holdich. 20·7 × 15·3 c.

1407. **K. 2** (*syr*) *Historia ecclesiastica a Georgio Elmacino historiæ Saracenicæ authore conscripta*, in Syriac. 20·7 × 14 c.

1408. **K. 3** (*t, p*) Presented to the library in 1691 by "Christianus Ranius N. G. Berlinensis." Contains (i) Turkish poems by Mawláná Aḥmad; (ii) Epistolary models in Turkish and Persian, followed by a *Fatḥ-náma*, or proclamation of Victory, and other official documents, and some *hazaliyyát* or *facetiæ*. 14·7 × 11·3 c.

1409. **K. 4** (*a*) An unidentified acephalous MS. containing traditions and historical matter about the early Caliphs, etc. Clear *naskh*, pointed, with rubrications, dated 9 Rabí'i, 863/Jan. 14, 1459. 17·8 × 13·5 c.

1410. **K. 5** (*a*) The Psalms of David, followed by *at-Tasábíḥu'l-'ashara*; good, clear modern *naskh* with rubrications; 20·8 × 14·5 c.

1411. **K. 6** (*a, t*) An account of Sayyid Aḥmad ibn Abi'l-Ḥasan ar-Rufá'í, entitled *Ummu'l-Baráhín*, the preface in Arabic, the remainder in Turkish. Good *naskh*, punctuated, within gold margins: 19 × 13·3 c.

1412. **K. 7** (*heb*) "*Hoc manuscriptum Rabbinicum in Archivis Collegii D. Johannis Evangelistæ Cantabrigiæ dedit vir clarissimus, Linguarum Orientalium peritissimus, Edmundus Castellus, S.T.D., ac in Academiâ Cantabrigiensi Linguæ Arabicæ Publicus Professor.*" 19·5 × 15·0 c.

1413. **K. 8** (*a*) Part of the *Síratu 'Antara*, ending abruptly, without colophon. Clear *naskh* with rubrications. 20·3 × 15 c.

1414. **K. 9** (*a*) Another portion of the same romance, defective at both ends, coarse, bad *naskh* with red punctuation. 18·0 × 12·9 c.

1415. **K. 10** (*a*) Another portion of the same, also defective, poor but clear *naskh* with rubrications. 15·4 × 10·2 c.

1416. **K. 11** (*a*) Another (the fifth) portion of the same.

1417. **K. 12** (*a*) Another portion of the same. This and the two MSS. previously mentioned are of uniform size.

1418. **K. 13** (*a*) Another portion of the same (the seventh volume), ending abruptly; 20·3 × 15 c.

1419. **K. 14** (*a*) Another portion of the same, ending abruptly; 21·8 × 15·3 c.

1420. **S. 13** (*a*) Extracts from the *Qur'án* (*Súras* xxxvi–cxiv), presented by William Wotton in 1686. Pp. 16.

(The above fifteen MSS. only are included in the Rev. Morgan Cowie's *Catalogue*, but not the following, to the first fifteen of which, in the absence of proper class-marks, I have assigned the numbers **16–30.**)

1421. **16** (*a*) A well-written *Qur'án*; gold borders and punctuation; 16·4 × 10·6 c. Presented by Professor John Palmer (d. April 9, 1840).

1422. **17** (*p*) The *Díwán* of 'Urfí, good *ta'líq*, dated 1024/1615, concluding with 'Urfí's dying behests. From Archibald Swinton's library, presented by Nathaniel Atcheson, Sept. 30, 1816; 19·3 × 10·3 c.

1423. **18** (*p*) The *Díwán* of Ḥáfiẓ, fair *ta'líq*, dated 27 Sha'bán, 1171/6 May, 1758; 21·7 × 14 c. Also presented by N. Atcheson.

1424. **19** (*p*) The *Díwán* of Amír Sháhí, transcribed in a beautiful *ta'líq* by Muḥammad Qásim b. Ḥájji Ḥusayn b. Ḥájji Akhí b. Shaykh 'Aṭṭár of Qazwín in Sha'bán, 908/Jan. 1503 or Sha'bán, 980/Dec. 1572; 23·8 × 16·1 c.

1425. **20** (*p*) The *Ṭúṭí-náma* by Ḍiyá'u'd-Dín Nakhshabí, poor *ta'líq*; 23·2 × 16·2 c. Presented by N. Atcheson, Dec. 27, 1819.

1426. **21** (*p*) Another copy of the same, transcribed at Iláh-ábád in 1119/1707–8, 24·5 × 17 c. Presented with the preceding MS., and containing a letter from N. Atcheson to the Rev. D. Wood.

1427. **22** (*p*) The *Kulliyyát*, or complete works of Sa'dí; clear Indian *ta'líq* with rubrications; 12 lines in body and 22 in margin of page of 28·3 × 17·8 c. Presented by N. Atcheson, Sept. 30, 1816.

1428. **23** (*h*) An account in Urdú of the pseudo-Mahdí Sayyid Muḥammad b. 'Abdu'lláh b. 'Uthmán b. Khiḍr, who traces his genealogy to the Imám Ja'far aṣ-Ṣádiq. He seems to have been born in 847/1443–4, and to have declared himself in 905/1499–1500 in Jawnpúr. Copied by Muḥammad Ya'qúb for Khwája Bahá'u'd-Dín; 22·7 × 15 c. The MS. was obtained by Captain Francis Ingram of the 46th Regiment, who died eight years after his arrival in India in the Madras Presidency at the age of 24 in 1832. These particulars are from a note of the donor, the Rev. D. S. Ingram, Great Oakley Rectory, Harwich, dated March 3, 1891, pasted inside the cover. The following is Captain Francis Ingram's note. "This is the account of Seyd Mahommed of Jaunpoor, the founder of the sect of Mehdevee Putans: it is a work which it is not easy to procure."

1429. **24** (*a*, *it*) An Arabic-Italian vocabulary, very neatly written in two columns on 654 pp., arranged from right to left according to the Arabic alphabetical order. Presented by Professor John Palmer (d. April 9, 1840).

1430. **25** (*p*) The *Díwán* of Naṣíbí, a poet of the time of Awrang-zíb, to whose praises the prose preface is devoted. The poet's proper name appears to be Alláh-yár ibn Ḥájji Muḥammad-yár Úzbek of Balkh. The poetry is of a religious character, consisting of *Tawḥíds* in imitation of Anwarí, Athíru'd-Dín Akhsíkatí, Kamálu'd-Dín Isma'íl, 'Aṭṭár, Abu'l-Faraj-i-Rúní, etc. Presented by the above-mentioned Rev. Delaval Shafto Ingram, M.A., in 1890.

1431. **26** (*p*) Vol. ii of a System of Muḥammadan Law compiled for Shír 'Alí, Amír of Afghánistán, in 1287/1870–1, and entitled *Qánún-i-Amírí*. Pp. 479, written in clear *ta'líq* with titles in blue and red, with full table of contents prefixed. "Bought at the prize-sale of property taken from the 'Kotwali' at Cabul; Cabul, Nov. 1879, by Granville Egerton, 2nd Lieut., 72nd Highlanders." "Presented to the Library of St John's College, Cambridge, by Major-General Granville Egerton, C.B., Nov. 1919." Pasted inside the cover is a letter from R. Murdoch Smith, dated Feb. 18, 1893, containing a brief description of the MS.

1432. **27** and **28** (*a*) A transcription into the Roman character of a large portion of the *Alf Layla wa Layla*, or "Thousand and one Nights," with English notes, written when of an obscene nature in the Arabic character, and presented to the College by the daughters of the late Henry Hilary, Scholar of the College from 1867–1870, in July, 1918. Vol. i, containing Nights i–ccxix, comprises 232 ff., and vol. ii, 163 ff.

1433. **29** (*a*, *p*) The original testimonial given to the late Professor Edward Henry Palmer by a number of learned Indian Muslims in 1867, bearing witness to his remarkable knowledge of Arabic, Persian and Hindustání. The document, written on a long scroll, is partly in Arabic and partly in Persian, the seals and signatures of the signatories being affixed at the side. An English translation of it will be found in Walter Besant's *Life of Palmer*, pp. 53–61. It is dated the 8th of Dhu'l-Ḥijja, 1283/April 13, 1867.

1434. **30** (*p*) A fine MS. of the *Khamsa* of Niẓámí, dated Ṣafar 947/June 1540, 786 pp., good *ta'líq*, 4 columns of 19 ll. each to the page, with 30 miniature paintings, of which a list is given in English inside the cover. Green binding, ornamented with figures in gold, in what the donor calls "ye true tawdry Mahometan taste." Bequeathed to the College on Dec. 13, 1770 by James Bate (Bishop of Ely, Fellow from March 28, 1726 until May 31, 1733). The MS. was "part of the loot taken from Bannárez [Benares] after the battle of Buxar, where Lord Clive defeated the Indians," and was afterwards bought by Mr Bate's son for ten guineas. Inside the cover is pasted a long Latin letter descriptive of the MS. from Sir William Jones, written in London in April, 1771 to "Dno Bate, S.P.D." and beginning "*Liber iste Persicus, quem possides, Domine, gemmâ quâvis est pretiosior.*" **456**

1435. **N. 10** (*a*) "Arabic Horarium of the Arabo-Greek Church," bought by George P. Badger on August 6, 1835, at the Convent of Már Hanná in the Lebanon.

1436. **N. 12** (*t*) MS. copy of "two humorous Turkish poems in the *ḥarem* dialect of women," by Wáṣif-i-Andarúní, with English verse translation by the late Sir James Redhouse, who published them anonymously in 1881. See E. J. W. Gibb's *History of Ottoman Poetry*, vol. iv, p. 285 *ad calc.* This copy, whether the original MS. or not, is in Redhouse's own hand.

1437. **H. 25** "English-Gentue Dialogues," followed by "the Alphabet, which contains 63 letters, and the manner of joining." The language here denoted by the term "Gentoo" or "Gentue" appears to be Canarese, Telugu, or Singhalese.

1438. [**No class-mark.**] "African *Qur'án* from Kano in the Haussa country, obtained by F. Westin, while resident on the upper Niger in 1882." Presented by Frederick W. Bond, January 20, 1885.

1439. [**No class-mark.**] An Arabic *ḥamá'il*, or talisman for wearing as a belt, containing the names of the Twelve Imáms, purchased from a "Mogul" from Kábul in Sept. 1825, and presented to the College by R. Hawes, B.D., in Oct. 1865.

1440. A roll in Aethiopic or Amharic.

1441. Papers of the late Professor John Palmer, B.D., from 1804 to 1819 Sir Thomas Adams's Professor of Arabic.

1442. The original MS. of a translation into Arabic verse of Moore's "Peri and Paradise" from "Lalla Rookh" begun by the late Professor E. H. Palmer. See Walter Besant's *Life of Palmer* (London, 1883), pp. 39 and 62, where it is spoken of as existing in 1863, when Palmer was only 23 years of age.

1443. A decorative scroll in Arabic, written by Professor E. H. Palmer.

1444. Palmer's note-books of his travels in Sinai with many sketches of ancient monuments and copies of inscriptions.

MAGDALENE COLLEGE.

1445. "**Pepys' MS. 1281** has in it a note by W. H. Mill that it is the *Díwán of Anwarí*. This is the only Oriental MS. in either of the College libraries. S. Gaselee, 30 April, 1912." **511**

TRINITY COLLEGE.

This collection comprises 89 MSS. in the Arabic character, and one or two Hebrew, Greek and Chinese books. A catalogue of these by the late Professor E. H. Palmer was published by Deighton & Bell of Cambridge in 1870, including in an Appendix the Hebrew and Samaritan MSS. described by Dr William Aldis Wright and Dr Schiller-Szinessy. This volume contains vii + 235 pp. The Hebrew and Samaritan MSS. are **R.4.53, R.8.1—R.8.6, R.8.10, R.8.11, R.8.13, R.8.14, R.8.18—R.8.24, R.8.26,**

R. 8. 27, R. 8. 35, R. 9. 14, R. 14. 51, R. 14. 61, R. 14. 62, R. 15. 53—R. 15. 57 (*Catalogue*, pp. 206–235). **R. 13. 51** is also Hebrew; **R. 13. 56** is Greek music; **R. 13. 93** and **R. 13. 95** are Chinese. In the following list of the remainder, I have thought it sufficient to indicate after the class-mark of each the page of Palmer's *Catalogue* and the number or numbers in this *Hand-List* where the description will be found.

1446.	**R. 8. 7** (*a*)	Palmer, p.	1	*Hand-List*, No.	**928**	
1447.	**R. 8. 12** (*a*)	„	2	„	**929**	
1448.	**R. 8. 17** (*a*)	„	2–3	„	**409**	
1449.	**R. 8. 25** (*p*)	„	3–4	„	**187**	bound together
1450.	**R. 8. 28** (*t*)	„	4	„	**711**	
1451.	**R. 10. 2** (*p*)	„	5–6	„	**851**	
1452.	**R. 10. 3** (*p*)	„	6–7	„	**563**	
1453.	**R. 13. 1** (*t*)	„	7–9	„	**1251**	
1454.	**R. 13. 2** (*p*)	„	9–10	„	**958**	
1455.	**R. 13. 3** (*p*)	„	11–13	„	**964**	
1456.	**R. 13. 4** (*a*)	„	13–14	„	**930**	
1457.	**R. 13. 5** (*a*)	„	14–15	„	**842**	
1458.	**R. 13. 6** (*a*)	„	15–16	„	**1224**	
1459.	**R. 13. 7** (*a*)	„	16–17	„	**931**	
1460.	**R. 13. 8** (*p*)	„	17–20	„	**443**	
1461.	**R. 13. 9** (*p*)	„	21	„	**15**	
1462.	**R. 13. 10** (*a*)	„	22	„	**260**	
1463.	**R. 13. 11** (*t*)	„	23	„	**350**	
1464.	**R. 13. 12** (*a*)	„	23–24	„	**1186**	
1465.	**R. 13. 13** (*a*)	„	24–26	„	**1218**	
1466.	**R. 13. 14** (*a, lat*)	„	26	„	**68**	bound together
1467.	**R. 13. 15** (*a, heb*)	„	27	„	—	
1468.	**R. 13. 16** (*a*)	„	28–39	„	**1506**	
1469.	**R. 13. 17** (*p, t*)	„	39–43	„	**784, 1354**	
1470.	**R. 13. 18*** (*a*)	„	43–44	„	**1287**	
1471.	**R. 13. 19** (*a*)	„	44–48	„	**205**	
1472.	**R. 13. 20** (*a*)	„	48–50	„	**690**	
1473.	**R. 13. 21** (*a*)	„	50–52	„	**1244**	
1474.	**R. 13. 22** (*a*)	„	52	„	**944**	
1475.	**R. 13. 23** (*t*)	„	52–55	„	**1400**	
1476.	**R. 13. 24** (*a*)	„	55–57	„	**518**	
1477.	**R. 13. 25** (*a*)	„	57–59	„	**166**	
1478.	**R. 13. 26** (*t*)	„	59	„	**259**	

* Wrongly entered on p. 212 as **R. 13. 8.**

1479.	**R.13.27** (*p*)	Palmer, p. 60	*Hand-List*, No. **537**
1480.	**R.13.28** (*t*)	„ 60–61	„ **275**
1481.	**R.13.29** (*p*)	„ 61–62	„ **276**
1482.	{**R.13.30** (*a*)	„ 62–65	„ **1316**
1483.	{**R.13.31** (*a*)	„ 65–69	„ **1550**
1484.	**R.13.32** (*p*, *t*)	„ 69–76	„ **1595**
1485.	**R.13.33** (*a*)	„ 77–81	„ **1417**
1486.	**R.13.34** (*t*)	„ 81–82	„ **949**
1487.	**R.13.35** (*a*, *lat*)	„ 82–83	„ **657**
1488.	**R.13.36** (*p*)	„ 83–84	„ **1096**
1489.	**R.13.37** (*a*)	„ 84–85	„ **1031**
1490.	**R.13.38** (*a*)	„ 85–86	„ **799**
1491.	**R.13.39** (*a*)	„ 86–87	„ **78**
1492.	**R.13.40** (*t*)	„ 87–88	„ **1220**
1493.	**R.13.41** (*a*)	„ 88–91	„ **63, 399, 342**
1494.	**R.13.42** (*a*)	„ 91–92	„ **897**
1495.	**R.13.43** (*a*)	„ 93–101	„ **1191, 870, 310**
1496.	**R.13.44** (*a*)	„ 101–102	„ **725**
1497.	**R.13.45** (*a*, *p*)	„ 102–123	„ **1596**
1498.	**R.13.46** (*a*)	„ 124	„ **867**
1499.	**R.13.47** (*p*, *t*)	„ 124–129	„ **1549**
1500.	**R.13.48** (*a*)	„ 129–130	„ **141**
1501.	[**R.13.49** (*karshúní*)	„ 130–137	„ —]
1502.	**R.13.50** (*a*, *p*)	„ 138	„ **825**
1503.	[**R.13.51** (*heb*)	„ —	„ —]
1504.	**R.13.52** (*a*)	„ 139	„ **83**
1505.	**R.13.53** (*a*)	„ 140	„ **1401**
1506.	**R.13.54** (*a*)	„ 141–144	„ **812**
1507.	**R.13.55** (*a*)	„ 144–146	„ **769**
1508.	[**R.13.56** (*gr*)	„ —	„ —]
1509.	**R.13.57** (*a*)	„ 146–147	„ **1187**
1510.	[**R.13.58** (*karshúní*)	„ 147–148	„ —]
1511.	**R.13.59** (*a*, *t*)	„ 148–149	„ **1357**
1512.	**R.13.60** (*a*)	„ 149	„ **415**
1513.	**R.13.61** (*t*)	„ 150	„ **1402**
1514.	**R.13.62** (*a*, *p*)	„ 150–151	„ **282**
1515.	**R.13.63** (*a*, *t*)	„ 151	„ **1403**
1516.	**R.13.64** (*a*)	„ 151	„ **1512**
1517.	**R.13.65** (*a*, *t*)	„ 152	„ **683**
1518.	**R.13.66** (*a*)	„ 152–153	„ **230**
1519.	**R.13.67** (*p*)	„ 153–154	„ **366**
1520.	**R.13.68** (*p*)	„ 154–155	„ **488**
1521.	**R.13.69** (*p*)	„ 155–156	„ **684**
1522.	**R.13.94** (*p*)	„ 156	„ **1493**

1523.	**R.13.97** (*p*)	Palmer, p. 157	*Hand-List*, No.	**1462**
1524.	**R.13.101** (*p*)	„ 158–170	„	**1069**
1525.	**R.13.104** (*p*)	„ 170	„	**1377**
1526.	**R.13.105** (*p*)	„ 171–172	„	**1378**
1527.	**R.13.106** (*p*)	„ 172	„	**1328**
1528.	**R.13.107** (*p*)	„ 173	„	**1097**
1529.	**R.13.108** (*p*)	„ 174	„	**1098**
1530.	**R.14.59** (*a*)	„ 174	„	**932**
1531.	**R.14.60** (*a*)	„ 174	„	**933**
1532.	**R.15.50** (*a*)	„ 175–176	„	**934**
1533.	**R.15.51** (*a*)	„ 176	„	**983**
1534.	**R.15.52** (*p*)	„ 176–180	„	**1070**
1535.	**O.3.53** (*a, lat*)	„ 180	„	**1516**
1536.	**O.5.15** (*a*)	„ 180	„	**1004**

EMMANUEL COLLEGE.

1537. **3.2.1** (*p*) The Four Gospels in Persian with rubrications. Presented by Richard Kidder, 1681. **92**

1538. **3.2.2** (*a*) The *Nuzhatu'l-Majális* of aṣ-Ṣaffúrí, composed in Mecca in 884/1479. See Brockelmann, ii, p. 178. This MS. was completed at the end of Jumáda ii, 1059/July 10, 1649. **1311**

1539. **3.2.3** (*a*) The *Kanzu'd-Daqá'iq* of Abu'l-Barakát an-Nasafí. Transcribed by Yúsuf b. Ni'matu'lláh b. Shukru'lláh and completed at the end of Ṣafar, 1051/June 9, 1641. **1081**

1540. **3.2.4** (*p*) Recorded as a copy of Áhí's *Ḥusn u Dil*, but apparently missing. **403**

1541. **3.2.5** (*p*) A MS. of the *Búståán* of Sa'dí, dated Sha'bán 1026/August 1617, presented to the College by Thomas Leigh in 1667. **186**

1542. **3.2.6** (*avestan*) Part of the *Yasna*, wanting the last quarter and ending with ch. iv, 2 of Westergaard's edition; undated, but probably transcribed in the middle of the 17th Christian century. Though not old, it is accurately written from a good MS. It agrees with the best MSS., but not entirely with any, though most closely with the Copenhagen MS. known as **K. 11.** It is important for critical purposes, and the orthography is very consistent. (The above information is from an unsigned German note contained in the MS.) Pp. 192. In English it is thus quaintly described: "This Booke is called Ejessney written in the language Jenwista and containes ye Religion of ye Antient Parsyes."

1543. **3 . 2 . 7** (*a*, *p*) A volume of miscellaneous contents, including the *Burda* of al-Búṣírí, with Arabic paraphrase and Persian verse translation, part of an Arabic devotional work and some prayers. **169**

1544. **3 . 2 . 8** (*a*, *p*) A work on Astrology, etc., in a Maghribí hand, with a few ill-spelt Persian quatrains at the end.

1545. **3 . 2 . 9** (*a*, *p*) A collection of 15 tracts on Ṣúfíism and other subjects, mostly in Persian but some in Arabic. Copied in 815/1412–3.

1546. **3 . 2 . 10** (? *malay*) A book in what appears to be Malay, presented by Sir William Mainstone.

1547. **3 . 2 . 11** (*a*) Printed texts of the *Ajrúmiyya* and the *Káfiya*, without indication of date or place, presented by Thomas Leigh in 1667.

1548. **3 . 2 . 12** (*arm*) *Liber precum Armenicarum*, printed, pp. 66.

1549. **3 . 2 . 13** (*a*) The *Qur'án* in two vols., incomplete at end, illuminated, in a large hand of a Maghribí type. Given by Sir William Mainstone.

1550. **3 . 2 . 14** (*p*) A Persian mystical *Tarjí'-band* in good *ta'líq* hand, with the refrain:

چند پرسی ز قطره و دریا ' هر دو هستند در ظهور از ما '

1551. **3 . 2 . 15** (*a*) Arabic prayers and forms of visitation (*ziyárát*).

1552. **3 . 2 . 16** (*a*) Part of the *Qur'án* (*Súratu'n-Nisá*) in a firm, large hand, five lines to the page, illuminated.

1553. **3 . 2 . 17** (? = **4 . 2 . 1**), missing. The poems of Khusraw in Persian. **1051**

1554. **3 . 2 . 18** (*p*) *Díwán* of Ḥáfiẓ, missing since 1830 at any rate.

1555. **3 . 2 . 19** (*a*) Devotional work, apparently missing.

1556. **3 . 2 . 20** (*ch*) A Chinese book.

1557. **3 . 2 . 21** (*a*) An Arabic religious work of which the leaves are in hopeless confusion.

1558. **4 . 2 . 19** (*a*) A *Qur'án*, "picked up at Delhi after the capture of the town in 1857 by Captain Lionel Francis Wells of the Bengal Army, then serving with Hodson's Horse, by whom it was presented to the College by his brother, then a student." **925**

Besides the MSS. enumerated above, there are two without class-marks, a wooden roll inscribed with pious formulae and the names of the Twelve Imáms, derived from the same source as the last; and a palm-leaf MS. in the Tamil character.

FITZWILLIAM MUSEUM.

Amongst the two hundred and odd MSS. bequeathed to the Fitzwilliam Museum by the late Mr Frank McClean, who died at Brussels on Nov. 8, 1904, are about a dozen Arabic and Persian books. A description of these was contributed by me to Dr M. R. James's *Descriptive Catalogue of the McClean Collection of Manuscripts in the Fitzwilliam Museum* (Cambridge, 1912), pp. 358–364, to which the reader is referred for further details. In brief they are as follows :

1559. **188ª, 188ᵇ** (*a*) Two (the sixteenth and twenty-third) of the thirty parts (*ajzá*) into which the *Qur'án* is divided. **942**

1560. **189** (*a*) *Kitábu'l-Qalá'id wa'l-Fawá'id* of al-Ahwází (d. 446/1055). See Brockelmann, i, 407 ; *B.M.A.S.*, **No. 85.** **997**

1561. **190** (*a*) *Qalá'idu'l-'Iqyán wa Maḥásinu'l-A'yán* of Ibn Kháqán (d. 528/1133–4). See *B.M.A.C.*, p. 175 ; *B.M.A.S.*, **No. 664.** **996**

1562. **191** (*a*) *Mughni'l-Ḥabíb 'an Kutubi'l-a'áríb.* See *B.M.A.S.*, **Nos. 976–8.** **1219**

1563. **192** (*a*) *Al-Kawkabu'd-Darriyyu'l-mustakhraj min Kalámi'n-Nabiyyi*, containing seven fragmentary treatises on Traditions, etc. **1593**

1564. **193** (*a*) Two works on the miraculous eloquence of the *Qur'án*, the first by al-Báqilání, the second by Fakhru'd-Dín ar-Rází. **1005, 1340**

1565. **194** (*a*) The *Qur'án*, an undated but modern copy. **926**

1566. **198** (*p*) The *Mawáhib-i-Iláhí* of Mu'ín-i-Yazdí. See *B.M.P.C.*, pp. 168–9. An old and good MS. dated 778/1376–7. **1277**

1567. **199** (*p*) The *Díwán* of Amír Khusraw, dated 800/1397–8. **506**

1568. **200** (*a*) The *Qur'án*, dated 1074/1663–4. **927**

1569. **200*** (*a, p*) A scrap-book containing some pieces of Arabic and Persian writing.

1570. **201** (*a*) Another scrap-book containing four leaves of Arabic (Kufic and *naskh*) on vellum. **1520**

Most Recent Acquisitions (see p. 289).

Or. 968 (8) (*a*) *Qur'án*, inscribed as follows: "The Koran hand-written in Pushto (*sic*); taken from the ruins of Umrah Khán's fort at Mundah, 18. iv. 1895, by a Gordon Highlander, during the Chitral expedition." Presented by Mr L. B. de Beaumont, July 17, 1917. Modern, undated, leaves (unnumbered) of 21·25 × 14 c. and 12 ll.; last leaf misplaced.

Or. 971 (in envelope, inscribed "Bought from an old man who had it from Prince 'Azíz Ḥasan in payment for camel-hire. Subject: Treasure un-trove. Yours R. S[torrs].") It is entitled *Dalá'ilu maṭlabi'l-Kunúz wa'l-Khabáyá*, contains many words in a cabbalistic script, and professes to guide the reader to hidden treasure. Ff. 41 of 18 × 13 c. and 15 ll.; poor, coarse, illiterate writing, dated 1177/1763–4. It formerly belonged to Jáhín Ághá 'Abdu'lláh resident at Mecca.

Or. 972 (*a*, *p*) *Ṣaḥífa-i-Kámila*, the text in Arabic, with Persian interlinear glosses in red, in an Indian hand; copied in 1212/1797 at Ḥaydarábád. The pages, unnumbered, measure 31 × 20·5 c. and each contains 7 ll. of text. A note says: "This book is of Arabic origin with a Persian translation, and was found in an old vacated Sheik's house in Persia during the operations of 1918."

Or. 974 (*a*) Fragments of an Arabic devotional work in a Maghribí hand, in three envelopes. The leaves, measuring 11 × 10·5 c., are loose and disarranged. The second fragment (10 ff.) contains a rough sketch of the Prophet's tomb. Presented by Major R. B. Haselden.

Or. 976 (11) (*a*) *Qur'án*, dated 12 Rajab, 1051/17 Oct. 1641, copied in a fairly good hand by Darwísh Muṣṭafá b. Muḥammad Adhamí and Khálid b. Mullá Muḥammad b. Muḥammad 'Umar. Presented by S. Gaselee, July 23, 1919.

Or. 980 (*a*) Another *Qur'án*, written in coarse but legible *naskh*, punctuated in gold, between yellow borders. Some of the leaves, which measure 28 × 21·5 c. and contain 15 ll., are misplaced and bound upside down.

Or. 983 (Collectanea). (i) A number of proof-sheets from an article on Sanskrit palaeography and some derived Indian script from an article contributed by Mr James Prinsep to the *Journal of the Asiatic Society of Bengal* for 1838, vol. vii, p. 276. (ii) Correspondence with Miss Edith Barry, who painted a portrait of Mírzá Yaḥyá *Ṣubḥ-i-Azal* at Famagusta in Cyprus, including a letter and poem in Persian addressed to her by him. (iii) Typewritten Coronation Ode by V. Muthaswami Iyer, dated 11. xii. 1912. (iv) Note on a Syriac MSS. (**No. 9**) belonging to the India Office, possibly by the late Dr W. Wright. Pp. 16 of 24·25 × 19·25 c.

Or. 984 (*a*, *p*) Sixteen specimens of modern Arabic and Persian writing of no particular merit.

INDEX

Since the books described in this *Hand-List* are arranged alphabetically under their titles, according to the plan adopted by Ḥájji Khalífa and other Oriental bibliographers, only such references as occur outside the main article are given in this Index. Thus, for example, the main article *Gulistán* (گلستان) occurs on pp. 180–181, but additional incidental references will be found on pp. 32, 220, 256, 265, etc., and only the latter are included in the Index. Titles of books are in all cases printed in *italics*.

As regards names of persons, which constitute the greater part of the Index, those of authors represented in this collection are distinguished by an asterisk (*), those of copyists by a dagger (†), and those of former owners (including, of course, donors) by a double line (‖). Numbers enclosed in brackets and following a proper name indicate the year or century of the Christian era in which the person in question was born (*b.*), flourished (*fl.*) or died (*d.*). A hyphen prefixed to a name indicates that it should be preceded by the Arabic definite article *al-*. Prefixes like **Abú** and **Ibn** in Oriental, and **de, le, von** in European names are disregarded in the alphabetical arrangement. The letter **b.** between two Arabic names stands for **Ibn** ("son of —"). To avoid needless repetition, all references to any name common to several persons mentioned in the text are brought together under one heading, which in this case is printed in **Clarendon** type, as are also the first entries under each letter.

A few references of a general character, such as Alchemy, Astrology and the like, are also included in the Index.

*Manṣúr b. Muḥammad b. Aḥmad b. Yúsuf b. Ilyás (xv), 173, 250; Ibn —, 253
Manṭiqu'ṭ-Ṭayr, 257, 297
Maqámátu'l-Aqṭáb, 238
Maqámát-i-Awliyá, 238
*-Maqqarí, Shaykh Abú 'Abdu'lláh —, 70
*-Maqrízí, 204
Maqṣad-i-Aqṣá, 267
†Maqṣúd 'Alí (xvi), 90, 310
-Márdíní, Badru'd-Dín —, 108
†-Mardashtí, Báyazíd —, 179
-Marghínání (d. 1197), 223, 224
Margoliouth, Rev. Prof. D. S. —, 298
Mar Hanna, Convent of —, 318
*Mar'í b. Yúsuf b. Abí Bakr (d. 1624), 42
*-Marjání, Jamálu'd-Dín Muḥammad —, 195–6
‖Marling, C. —, 78, 287
Maronites, 144, 195, 309
Marriage, Traditions about —, 166
*Marwáríd, 19
Maṣábíḥu'l-Qulúb, 296
*Maṣḥafí, 99, 293
Abú Ma'shar-Balkhí, 304
Masíḥí (Turkish poet), 71; *—, 103
*Mas'úd-i-Sa'd-i-Salmán (d. 1121), 99
*-Mas'údí, 195, 243
Mas'úd Sháh u 'Azíz Sháh, Qiṣṣa-i- —, 293, 297
Maṭáli'u'l-Anwár, 267, 296, 303, 306
Mátam-kada, 296
Materia Medica, 17, 26, 50, 61, 107, 119, 132, 149, 152, 187, 200
Mathnawí (of Jalálu'd-Dín Rúmí), 62, 257, 297, 302, 306
Maṭla'u'l-Anwár (Amír Khusraw), 76
Maṭla'u's-Sa'dayn, 310
Maṭmaḥu'l-Anẓár, 187
Matthew, Gospel of St —, 308
*-Máturídí, Abú Manṣúr Muḥammad (d. 944), 167
Mawáhib-i-'Aliyya, 302
Mawáhib-i-Iláhí, 324
-Mawáqif, 306
*-**Maybudí**, Mír Ḥusayn —, 60; *—, Ḥusayn b. Mu'ínu'd-Dín — (d. 1485), 225
*-Maydání, 123
*Maẓhar (poet), 99, 296, 304
‖McClean, Frank — (d. 1904), 86, 324
Mecca, 14, 325
Medicine, 49, 50, 53, 62, 69, 73, 120, 132, 138, 169, 173, 179, 191, 203, 209, 213, 216, 226, 251–2
"Mehdevee Putans," 317
Mi'at 'Ámil, 254
Miftáḥ-i-Kutub-i-Ḥurúfiyán, 95
Miftáḥu'l-Mughlaqát, 201
Miftáḥu'l-Qulúb, 312
Miftáḥu'l-'Ulúm, 199
Mihrábí, Ibn 'Umar —, 67
Mihr u Máh, Qiṣṣa-i- —, 262, 293, 296, 297
Mihr u Mushtarí of Aṣṣar, 31
Mill, W. H. —, 86, 319
Miller, A. S. B. —, 246, 285
Minháju'ṭ-Ṭálibín of -Nawawí, 4
Míná Bázár, 84, 294
Mír 'Alí Shír Nawá'í, 19
Mi'ráju'l-'Ulúm, 307
*Míram Siyáh of Qazwín, 21, 299
Mirátu'l-Ḥadá'iq, 68
Mirátu'l-Muḥaqqiqín, 240
Mirátu'ṭ-Ṭálibín, 239
*Mírkhwánd (d. 1497), 75, 118, 304
*Mír Taqí, 100
†Mírzá Bábá, 23
Miṣbáḥ, 75, 299
Miṣbáḥu'l-Hudá, 242
Miṣbáḥu'l-Mubtadí, 296
Mízán, 254
Mízánu'ṭ-Ṭibb, 293
Moghul Dynasty, 41, 42, 51, 63, 115
Mongols, 44, 98, 177
Moore, Thomas —, 319
Morocco, 164
Motí Masjid, 75
Mu'addilu'ṣ-Ṣalát, 210
Mu'ammá (Acrostic), 110, 111
Mu'ammá'í, Mír Ḥusayn —, 22
*-Mubarrad, 164
Mubashshirát (Ibnu'l-'Arabí), 220
Mufarriḥu'l-Qulúb, 294, 308
Mughni'l-Labíb, 324
Muhadhdhibu'l-Akhláq, 291
Muḥallafát of Sinán Pasha, 244
Muḥammad the Prophet, 26, 40, 60, 64, 72, 81, 116, 132, 158, 161, 162, 198, 200, 242, 267; *— 'Abdu'lláh-Qayruwání, 263; — b. 'Abdu'lláh b. 'Uthmán b. Khiḍr (pseudo-Mahdí, fl. 1500), 317; *— 'Abdu'l-Karím-Dájí Ghaznawí, 48; *— b. 'Abdu'r-Raḥman-Andalusí (xii), 140; *— b. 'Abdu'r-Raḥmán-Qurashí-'Uthmání -Dimashqí (d. 1390), 105; *— 'Abdu'r-Rasúl..., 181; *— b. 'Abdu'l-Wahháb b. Dá'úd (xix), 126; — b. 'Abdu'l-Wahháb-Hamdání, 146; †— 'Ábid (fl. 1774), 139, 312; *— Afḍal, 52, see *Sar-Khush*; *— b. Aḥmad b. Sa'íd (d. 1737), see *Ibn 'Aqílá*; — b. Aḥmad, see *Nishánjí-záda*; *— Akbar, 187, 213; †— 'Akkárí (xvii), 162; — b. 'Alí-Birkawí (or Birgilí), 210; *— b. 'Alí b. Ḥusayn b. Abi'l-Ḥasan-Ḥusayní, 193; *— b.

For EU product safety concerns, contact us at Calle de José Abascal, 56–1°,
28003 Madrid, Spain or eugpsr@cambridge.org.

www.ingramcontent.com/pod-product-compliance
Ingram Content Group UK Ltd.
Pitfield, Milton Keynes, MK11 3LW, UK
UKHW040618240426
470322UK00010B/199
9781107624030